The Anthologist's Art

Brill Studies in Middle Eastern Literatures

Edited by

Suzanne Pinckney Stetkevych (*Georgetown University*)
Ross Brann (*Cornell University*)
Franklin Lewis (*University of Chicago*)

VOLUME 37

The titles published in this series are listed at *brill.com/bsme*

The Anthologist's Art

Abū Manṣūr al-Thaʿālibī and His Yatīmat al-dahr

By

Bilal Orfali

TUTA SUB AEGIDE PALLAS · 1683 ·

BRILL

LEIDEN | BOSTON

Cover illustration: Huguette Caland, Appleton ii, 2009.

The Library of Congress Cataloging-in-Publication Data is available online at http://catalog.loc.gov
LC record available at http://lccn.loc.gov/2016023091

Typeface for the Latin, Greek, and Cyrillic scripts: "Brill". See and download: brill.com/brill-typeface.

ISSN 1571-5183
ISBN 978-90-04-31629-4 (hardback)
ISBN 978-90-04-31735-2 (e-book)

This book is printed on acid-free paper and produced in a sustainable manner.

وَقُلْ رَبِّ ارْحَمْهُمَا كَمَا رَبَّيَانِي صَغِيرًا
﴿سورة الإسراء، 42﴾

إلى أمّي . . .
إلى أبي . . .

∴

Contents

Preface XI
Acknowledgments XIII
List of Illustrations XV
Abbreviations XVI
Note on Editions and Manuscripts of the *Yatīma* and *Tatimma* XVII

1 **The Art of Anthology in Premodern Arabic Literature** 1
Anthology and *Adab* 1
Approaches to the Study of Arabic Literary Anthology in Modern Scholarship 4
Motives for Anthologizing 7
A Map of Arabic Poetry Anthologies 10

2 **Life and Legacy of Thaʿālibī** 34
Abū Manṣūr al-Thaʿālibī 34
Legacy of Thaʿālibī 38
Bibliography of Thaʿālibī 40
Printed Authentic Works 44
Printed, Authenticity Doubtful 65
Printed, Authenticity Rejected 72
In Manuscript, Authentic Works 79
In Manuscript, Authenticity Uncertain 82
In Manuscript, Authenticity Rejected 89
Works Surviving in Quotations 92
Lost Works 94

3 **An Anthologist at Work: The Organization and Structure of the *Yatīma* and *Tatimma*** 97
Organization 97
Prominent Litterateurs 99
Courts, Dynasties, and Patronage 100
Cities and Sub-regions 102
Critical Awareness in the Organization of the *Yatīma* and *Tatimma* 105
Selection of Material 106
The Arrangement of Entries in a Chapter: Proximity and Resemblance 111
References and Cross-References 118
Cross-References 118

References in the Tatimma *to the* Yatīma 121
References to the Earlier Version of the Yatīma 123
References to Other Works by Thaʿālibī 125
Later Additions to the *Yatīma* 126
Authenticity and Misattribution 128
Forgotten, Lost, and Inconsistent Material 132

4 **The Sources of Thaʿālibī in *Yatīmat al-Dahr* and *Tatimmat al-Yatīma*** 139
Written Sources 140
Dīwāns 142
Books 142
Other Written Media 144
Oral/Aural Sources 146
Main Guarantors in the Yatīma 150
Main Guarantors in the Tatimma 154
Conclusion 156

5 **Material within the Entry** 158
Categorization and Arrangement of Material within Entries 158
The Biographical Summary 160
Dates 162
Deaths of Poets 164
Religious Views 164
Training and Education 166
Professions 167
Families of Litterateurs 167
Characterization of Litterateurs and Their Literary Oeuvres 168
Geographical Context 170
Social Context 171
Historical Context 172
Comparing Litterateurs 172
Knowledge of Persian 174
Relations between Contemporaries 174
Physical and Character Features 176
Patronage 178
Patron-Littérateur Relations 179
Admission to a Court 179
Meeting a Patron 182
Leaving a Court 182
Prison Incidents and Stories 184

Description of Courtly Majālis 186
Evaluating Literary Production 188

Conclusion 194

Appendix 1: Outline of *Yatīmat al-dahr* and *Tatimmat al-Yatīma* 197
Appendix 2: Sources of *Yatīmat al-dahr* 203
Appendix 3: Sources of *Tatimmat al-Yatīma* 225
Appendix 4: Comparisons between Poets 233
Bibliography 238
Index 257

Preface

Readers of premodern Arabic literature often find themselves in front of a gigantic sum of anthologies. Much of medieval Arabic literature consists of compilations of poetry, accounts, proverbs, and other quotable material. To outsiders, it can seem like litterateurs in the Arabic-Islamic civilization preferred to "select" rather than to "author" works. In this book I study the literary anthology as a general category of *adab*, encompassing a range of compilations, as well as the function and motives behind them. I show how an anthology that consists of reproduced texts can be regarded as original and possessing a structure and an agenda of its own. I focus foremost on the efforts of Abū Manṣūr al-Thaʿālibī (429/1039), a prolific anthologist and towering figure in Arabic literature who hailed from Khurāsān in the eastern part of the Muslim world.

Thaʿālibī's magnum opus, *Yatīmat al-dahr fī maḥāsin ahl al-ʿaṣr,* and its sequel, *Tatimmat al-Yatīma*, both of which are the focus of this book, offer a panorama of Arabic literature in the fourth/tenth and early fifth/eleventh centuries, and they are the first anthologies to deal exclusively with contemporary literature and to categorize that literature not chronologically or thematically, but on the basis of geographical region. In doing so, they influenced the subsequent development of the genre of literary anthology in Arabic literature. In this book, I approach these two works as original works of literature that possess a structure and an aim: to demonstrate the merit of contemporary litterateurs. Despite their remarkable fame in premodern times, the *Yatīma* and the *Tatimma* have not received due attention in modern scholarship. This book aims to remediate this neglect through a detailed examination of the sources, structure, organizational principles, goals, content, and criteria of selection for these two works.

Chapter 1 presents a map of Arabic poetry anthologies and places these within the framework of *adab*. The chapter asks a number of questions: Why did litterateurs compile anthologies? Why were they so popular in the Arabic-Islamic civilization? What agendas do these anthologies have? Which methods has modern scholarship developed in the study of these texts? Chapter 2 focuses on the life and vita of Thaʿālibī; it is based on primary sources and autobiographical information provided in his own writings. The chapter also presents an up-to-date bibliography for Thaʿālibī. While several scholars have undertaken this task, a number of works attributed to Thaʿālibī around the world remained unexamined, and this chapter adds new information.

The organization and structure of the *Yatīma* and *Tatimma* are the subject of chapter 3. How did an anthologist from Khurāsān view Arabic literature in the fourth/tenth century? The chapter outlines the internal logic and methodological considerations in the compilation of the *Yatīma* and *Tatimma.* Chapter 4 analyzes the written and oral sources of the *Yatīma* and *Tatimma,* uncovering a whole network of litterateurs who were active in the second half of the fourth/tenth century and who constituted the major guarantors for both works. Finally, chapter 5 focuses on the unit of the single entry in the *Yatīma* and *Tatimma.* Which criteria did Thaʿālibī employ in selecting "good" literature and which information did he think worthy of inclusion? The chapter pays special attention to the biographical summaries with which Thaʿālibī introduces entries, insights into patronage and courtly life in the fourth/tenth century, and Thaʿālibī's personal assessments of his selections.

Acknowledgments

Throughout its inception and evolution, this study has benefited from the support and expertise of many individuals and institutions. The project began as a PhD dissertation at Yale University under the supervision of Beatrice Gruendler. Her mentorship, encouragement, and support have been unfailing. I thank Dimitri Gutas for his guidance throughout my graduate work. Heartfelt thanks to Everett Rowson for reading my dissertation and for stimulating conversations at conferences and through many emails with the subject line "Thaʿālibīnā."

My friends at Yale University, American University of Beirut, Ohio State University, and elsewhere have provided intellectual and emotional support. I have space here to name only a few. Whether they realized it or not, Ramzi Baalbaki and Wadad Kadi have changed my life; they saw in me a reflection of their own selves and careers and supported me enthusiastically and unconditionally. Through the highs and lows of this project, I have been blessed with the love, support, and company of many friends, colleagues, and teachers. I thank Vahid Behmardi, Kevin van Bladel, Gerhard Bowering, Antoine Chamoun, Lina Choueri, Ibrahim Habli, Jeremy Kurzyniec, Nada Moumtaz, Shady Nasser, Racha Omari, Maurice Pomerantz, Intisar Rabb, Sayeed Rahman, Nada Saab, Ahed Sboul, Rana Siblini, and Homayra Ziad for delightful moments and support along the way. Nadia El Cheikh kept reminding me about this project, and without her this book would not have seen the light of day; her office in College Hall is a daily escape.

This project would not have been possible without generous financial support from the Graduate School at Yale University. The Robert M. Leylan Fellowship provided me with a dissertation-writing fellowship, and the John F. Enders Research Grant was valuable for acquiring microfilms of manuscripts. The Yale Beinecke Rare Books Library and the Princeton Rare Books and Special Collection Department provided me with scholarships and access to manuscripts essential for the research. The ʿĀrif Ḥikmat Library, Bayezid Umūmī Library, Cambridge University Library, Chester Beatty Library, Istanbul University Library, Kuwait University Library, Leiden University Library, Maʿhad al-Makhṭūṭāt al-ʿArabiyya, Princeton Library, Süleymaniye Library, and Topkapı Palace Museum Manuscript Library provided me with copies of manuscripts. Special thanks to the Huguette Caland Studio, especially Brigitte Caland, for granting me permission to use Huguette Caland's painting Appleton ii, 2009 for this book's cover.

The American University of Beirut is more than a university to me. It is a home and bedrock of scholarship that has weathered times of struggle and hardships; to its community of scholars I will always belong.

I am deeply appreciative of Suzanne Pinckney Stetkevych, Ross Brann, and Franklin Lewis for accepting this book into the series Studies in Middle Eastern Literatures, and to Katherine Faydash for smoothing the English style. The *Journal of Arabic Literature* and *Middle Eastern Literatures* granted permission to use three earlier works. This is my fifth book with Brill Publishers, and for a reason. I thank Joed Elich and his team, especially Kathy van Vliet, Teddi Dols, and Nicolette van der Hoek, for their encouragement, patience, ceaseless efforts, and hospitality throughout the years.

My nephews and nieces, Yossouf, Lynne, Mohammad, Yasmina, Maha, and Walid, always wanted to play a little bit more, and I hope one day they will forgive my absence. My father, Walid Orfali, taught me the true meaning of *murūʾa*, and my mother, Maha Itani, the meaning of giving, love, and *iḥsān*.

Bilal Orfali
Beirut, 2016

List of Illustrations

1 Yatīmat al-dahr, MS Escorial 350, 1v–2r xx

2 Yatīmat al-dahr, MS Laleli 1959, 1r xx

3 Yatīmat al-dahr, MS Majlis-i Milli 3094 3v–4r 42

4 MS Bayezid Umūmī 32071 45

5 Nasīm al-saḥar, MS Kuwayt Wizārat al-Awqāf 5500-1, 1v 56

6 Saj‘ al-manthūr, MS Yeni Cami 1188, 88v–89r 59

7 al-Ẓarā’if wa-l-laṭā’if, MS Majlis-i Millī 3512, 3r 63

8 Zād safar al-mulūk, MS Chester Beatty 5067, 40v 64

9 Makārim al-akhlāq, MS Leiden Or. 300, 1v–2r 67

10 Rawḥ al-rūḥ, MS al-Maktaba al-Aḥmadiyya 14476, 150v–151r 69

11 Ṭabaqāt al-mulūk, MS Ẓāhiriyya 14479, 10r 70

12 Tarjamat al-Kātib fī adab al-ṣāḥib, MS Hekimoglu 946, 86v–87r 71

13 MS Bayezid Umumi Veliyuddin Efendi 2631, 1r 75

14 MS ‘Ārif Ḥikmat 154, 1r 79

15 Khāṣṣ al-khāṣṣ fī l-amthāl, MS Aya Sofya 4824, 65v–66r 80

16 K. al-Amthāl, MS Feyzullah 2133/1, 1r 81

17 al-Anwār al-bahiyya, MS Bayezid Umumi 3709, 1r 82

18 Injāz al-ma‘rūf, MF Kuwayt 6028 83

19 Jawāhir al-ḥikam, MS Princeton 2234, 1r 84

20 Nuzhat al-albāb wa-‘umdat al-kuttāb, MS ‘Ārif Ḥikmat 271–Majāmī‘, 194r 86

21 al-Shajar wa-l-ṣuwar, MS. Dār al-Kutab al-Miṣriyya 440–adab, 2v 87

22 Ba‘th al-dawā‘ī wa-l-himam, MS Chester Beatty 4423/1, 1r 88

23 Sirr al-ḥaqīqa, MS Feyzullah 2133/7, 215r 89

24 MS ‘Ārif Ḥikmat 31–Majāmī‘, 1r 90

25 Yatīmat al-dahr, MS Escorial 350, 28r 101

26 Yatīmat al-dahr, MS Princeton 716, 130r 112

27 Yatīmat al-dahr, MS Laleli 1959, 453v 114

28 Yatīmat al-dahr, MS Toronto A13512y 116

29 Relationships in Yatīmat al-dahr 118

30 Yatīmat al-dahr, MS Laleli 1959, 612r 129

31 Yatīmat al-dahr, MS Toronto A13512y, 275v 136

32 Yatīmat al-dahr, MS Toronto A13512y, 434r 149

33 Yatīmat al-dahr, MS Toronto A13512y, 454v 163

34 Yatīmat al-dahr, MS Toronto A13512y, 453r 177

Abbreviations

EAL	Encyclopedia of Arabic Literature
EI1	Encyclopaedia of Islam, first edition
EI2	Encyclopaedia of Islam, second edition
EI3	Encyclopaedia of Islam, third edition
GAL	C. Brockelmann, Geschichte der arabischen Litteratur
GAL S	C. Brockelmann, Geschichte der arabischen Litteratur, supplement
GAS	F. Sezgin, Geschichte des arabischen Schrifttums
JAL	Journal of Arabic Literature
T	Thaʿālibī, Tatimmat al-Yatīma
Y	Thaʿālibī, Yatīmat al-dahr fī maḥāsin ahl al-ʿaṣr

Note on Editions and Manuscripts of the *Yatīma* and *Tatimma*

The texts of the standard published editions of the *Yatīmat al-dahr* are full of common scribal errors, such as confused names in *isnād*s and headings, as well as slips of the pen. Everett Rowson and Seeger Bonebakker have discussed the print editions of the *Yatīma*; an index volume of the *Yatīma* based on the Damascus edition, titled *Farīdat al-ʿaṣr*[1]; and sections of the *Yatīma* that have been edited separately, more or less critically.[2] Since the publication of their work in 1980, another edition of the *Yatīma* was published at Dār al-Kutub al-ʿIlmiyya (Beirut), edited by M. M. Qumayḥa in 1983.[3] This more recent edition does not indicate the manuscripts used, although the editor refers to manuscripts by letter in the first few pages of the text, but this convention becomes rare later on. This edition has numerous typos and other mistakes on almost every page.

A preferable edition of the *Yatīma* is the Egyptian one by Muḥammad Muḥyī al-Dīn ʿAbd al-Ḥamīd first published in 1956. This edition comprises four volumes of approximately equal length, though the volumes do not correspond to Thaʿālibī's division of the text. Rowson and Bonebakker note that the pagination of the 1956 edition differs from that of the 1947 edition, and there is a page reversal in the 1956 edition.[4]

There are two published editions of *Tatimmat al-Yatīma*: the Tehran edition of ʿAbbās Iqbāl and the Beirut edition of M. M. Qumayḥa. Both are full of errors, mainly because of the dearth of surviving manuscripts. A better text of the *Tatimma* constitutes the major part of a PhD dissertation by Ahmad Shawqi Radwan, which regrettably remains unpublished.[5] Radwan's text is handwritten and based on five different manuscripts.[6]

---

1 Rowson and Bonebakker point to another index of the poets of the *Yatīma* compiled by O. Rescher and based on the Damascus edition, *Alfabetischer Index zur Jetīma ed-Dahr des Ṯaʿālibī* (Constantinople, 1914); see Everett Rowson and Seeger A. Bonebakker, *A Computerized Listing of Biographical Data from the* Yatīmat al-Dahr *by al-Thaʿālibī* (Malibu: UNDENA Publications, 1980), 24.

2 See ibid., 12–13.

3 See chapter 2 for details on editions of the *Yatīma*.

4 See Rowson and Bonebakker, *Computerized Listing*, 12.

5 Ahmad Shawqi Radwan, *Thaʿālibī's "Tatimmat al-Yatīmah": A Critical Edition and a Study of the Author as Anthologist and Literary Critic*, PhD diss., University of Manchester, 1972.

6 Ibid., 85–91.

The philological problems in the text of the *Yatīma* and *Tatimma* could fill another monograph. The available *Yatīma* editions did not consult any of the preferred manuscripts of the work. Manuscripts of the *Yatīma* are numerous and scattered around the world. Many of them are partial. According to C. E. Bosworth, because the book is divided into geographical sections, scribes copied those with special local appeal, rather than the whole work.[7] Many other manuscripts, however, are complete: Brockelmann lists about twenty.[8] Pertsch cites fifteen from the older catalogs,[9] and C. E. Bosworth describes thirteen *Yatīma* manuscripts in the Süleymaniye Library in Istanbul and corrects the mistakes of Brockelmann and Pertsch.[10] Among these, two manuscripts, Laleli 1959 (completed in the last days of Muḥarram 569/early September 1173) and Kara Çelebizade 316 (completed in the last ten days of Muḥarram 589/end of January or beginning of February 1139), belong to the earliest extant specimens of the *Yatīma*.[11] T. R. Topuzoglu adds a further thirteen Istanbul manuscripts.[12]

In Bosworth's critical edition of the Qaṣīda al-Sāsāniyya, which survives in the *Yatīma*, he uses this poem to construct a stemma of available manuscripts. Bosworth analyzes nine important manuscripts, grouping them into three families.[13] He states, "Laleli 1959 has already furnished valuable correc-

7 See C. E. Bosworth "Manuscripts of Thaʿālibī's 'Yatīmat ad-dahr' in the Süleymaniye Library, Istanbul," *Journal of Semitic Studies* 16 (1971), 41–9.

8 See *GAL* I:284, *GAL S*, I:499.

9 See Wilhelm Pertsch, *Die arabischen Handschriften der herzoglicher Bibliothek zu Gotha* (Frankfurt am Main: Institute für Geschichte der Arabisch-Islamischen Wissenschaften an der Johann Wolfgang Goethe-Universität, 1987), IV:156–7.

10 Bosworth, "Manuscripts," 41–9.

11 The incomplete MS Escorial 350 of the first section of the *Yatīma* was copied in 536/1141; a copy of it is in the Iskandariyya Library. Another incomplete manuscript, Revan Köşkü 715, was copied before 546/1151–2. These two seem to be the oldest surviving manuscripts of the *Yatīma*. Bosworth heard through Iḥsān ʿAbbās that a third early manuscript exists in Manisa near Izmir and dates from 655/1257 or 665/1266–7 (Muradiye 1631); see Bosworth, "Manuscripts," 44. Bosworth examined this manuscript in editing the Qaṣīda al-Sāsāniyya and certifies its importance, as it furnishes valuable corrections to the text. Bosworth, however, presumes that the manuscript is a short collection of poems from the *Yatīmat al-dahr*; for a description of this manuscript, see Bosworth, *The Mediaeval Islamic Underworld: The Banū Sāsān in Arabic Society and Literature* (Leiden: Brill, 1976), 2:183–5.

12 T. R. Topozoglu, "Further Istanbul Manuscripts of Thaʿālibī Yatīmat al-dahr," *Islamic Quarterly* 15 (1971), 62–5.

13 The first and most important family includes Istanbul, Laleli 1959; Manisa, Muradiye 1631; and a third in C. E. Bosworth's private collection. The second family consists of Istanbul, Damad Ibrahim Paşa 982; and Cairo printed edition of 1956 (considered here a manuscript). The third family features Istanbul, Reisülküttap 947; Reisülküttap 946; and Laleli

tions to the text of the Qaṣīda al-Sāsāniyya as it appears in the very different printed editions of Thaʿālibī's work, and it should obviously form the basis of a badly needed critical text of the whole anthology."[14] In a later publication, Bosworth adds that the manuscript Manisa, Muradiye 1631 is of equal importance but seems incomplete. Another incomplete but important manuscript is in Bosworth's private collection; it comes from an English bookseller and includes the third and fourth regions. Though this manuscript was probably copied as late as the thirteenth/nineteenth century, according to Bosworth, it is based on a correct—and probably old—manuscript, as it provides a good number of improvements to the text of the Qaṣīda al-Sāsāniyya.[15]

To achieve a critical edition of the text, an editor must consult the surviving *dīwāns* and various quotations in other historical, biographical, and general *adab* works. The *Zahr al-ādāb* of al-Ḥuṣrī al-Qayrawānī (d. 413/1022), *Dumyat al-qaṣr* of Bākharzī (d. 467/1075), *Muʿjam al-udabāʾ* of Yāqūt al-Ḥamawī (d. 626/1229), and *al-Wāfī bi-l-wafayāt* of al-Ṣafadī (d. 764/1363) in particular are invaluable for correcting the names that appear in both works. Nevertheless, the ʿAbd al-Ḥamīd edition offers a preliminary basis for studying the *Yatīma*, even if some points will have to be changed according to what a critical edition might later reveal.

Hereafter, unless otherwise indicated, quotations and references use ʿAbd al-Ḥamīd's Cairo edition. For the *Tatimma*, I have used M. M. Qumayḥa's Beirut edition because of its availability, but occasionally I have corrected the names according to the editions of Iqbāl and Radwan. Unless otherwise indicated, the improvements to the *Yatīma* quotations in this monograph are mostly based on the Laleli 1959 manuscript, with reference to the corresponding folio.

1960 (a closely linked group); Istanbul, Es'at Efendi 2952/1 and Cambridge, Or. 1550. For a detailed description of these manuscripts, see Bosworth, *Mediaeval Islamic Underworld*, 2:181–90.

14 Bosworth, "Manuscripts," 43.

15 Bosworth, *Mediaeval Islamic Underworld*, 2:185–7.

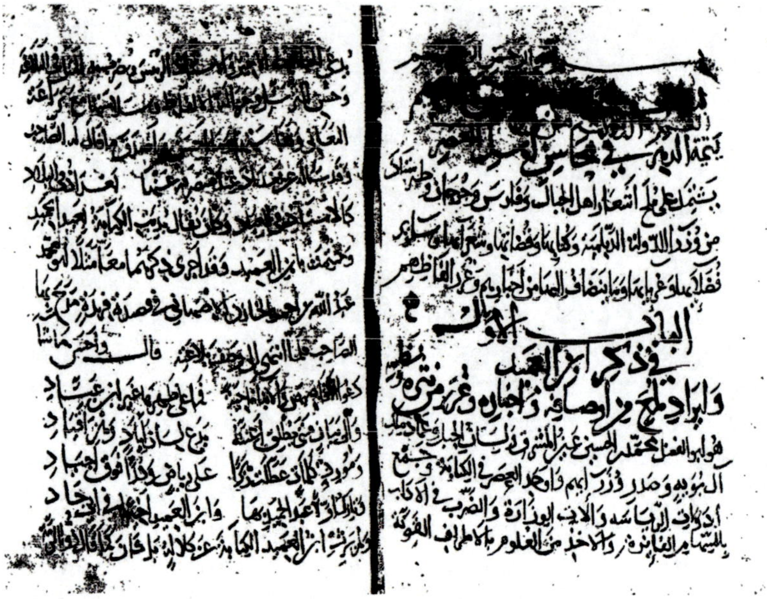

FIGURE 1 *Yatīmat al-dahr*, MS Escorial 350, 1v-2r

FIGURE 2 *Yatīmat al-dahr*, MS Laleli 1959, 1r

CHAPTER 1

The Art of Anthology in Premodern Arabic Literature

Anthology and *Adab*

Literary anthologies have enjoyed tremendous popularity throughout the history of Arabic literature, probably to a degree unmatched in other literatures of the world. Premodern Arabic scholars, however, had no special term to denote such works; rather, they described them by a variety of terms, such as *majmūʿ*, *ikhtiyār*, *dīwān*, *ḥamāsa*, and other words derived from these roots. Compiling literary anthologies was a widespread practice among *udabāʾ*, and a central activity for cultivating *adab*, a term that has resisted precise definition, despite the several attempts by modern scholars of Arabic literature. In fact, each modern attempt at definition has excluded some work that a medieval scholar would have considered *adab*.[1] Nearly all of the proposed definitions

1 Wolfhart Heinrichs notes that by the fourth/tenth century, *adab* had three meanings: good and correct behavior, the genre referred to as "*adab* literature" in modern scholarship and that usually encompassed compilations of quotable sayings, and the body of literary and linguistic knowledge presented by "*adab* disciplines," or *al-ʿulūm al-adabiyyah*. See his "The Classification of the Sciences and the Consolidation of Philology in Classical Islam," in *Centres of Learning: Learning and Location in Pre-Modern Europe and the Near East*, ed. J. W. Drijvers and A. A. MacDonald (Leiden: Brill, 1995), 119–20. Numerous studies have discussed the concept and definitions of *adab*. Gustave von Grunebaum emphasized the concept of *adab* as form and as approach or style; see his *Medieval Islam: A Study in Cultural Orientation* (Chicago: University of Chicago Press, 1953), 255. Charles Pellat stressed the functional purpose of *adab* as moral, social, and intellectual curriculum; see his "Variations sur le thème de l'adab," *Correspondance d'Orient: Études* 5–6 (1964), 19–37. Seeger A. Bonebakker has suggested a more restricted definition: *adab* is the "literary scholarship of a cultivated man presented in a systematic form"; see his "*Adab* and the Concept of Belles-Lettres," in *The Cambridge History of Arabic Literature: Abbasid Belles-Lettres*, ed. Julia Ashtiany et al. (Cambridge: Cambridge University Press, 1990), 16–30. For more comprehensive surveys of the term, see H. Fähndrich, "Der Begriff 'Adab' und sein literarischer Niederschlag," in *Orientalisches Mittelalter*, ed. Wolfhart Heinrichs (Wiesbaden: AULA-Verlag, 1990), 326–45; Hilary Kilpatrick, "Adab," in *EAL* 1:56, id., "Anthologies, Medieval," in *EAL* 94–6; id., "A Genre in Classical Arabic: The *Adab* Encyclopedia," in *Union Européenne des Arabisants et Islamisants, 10th congress, Edinburgh, September 1980, Proceedings*, ed. Robert Hillenbrand (Edinburgh: Edinburgh University Press, 1982), 34–42; J. Sadan, "Hārūn al-Rashīd and the Brewer: Preliminary Remarks on the *Adab* of the Elite versus *Ḥikāyāt*," in *Studies in Canonical*

 | DOI 10.1163/9789004317352_002

agree, however, that moral and social upbringing, intellectual education, and entertainment are the hallmarks of *adab*. This agreement prompted Hilary Kilpatrick to designate *adab* an approach to writing rather than a genre.[2]

Premodern authors did not feel bound to follow defined rules when preparing their compilations; instead, each author wrote according to his own needs and aspirations, obsessions and anxieties. *Adab* works existed in informal or semiformal literate networks that largely functioned alongside the *kuttāb* or the *madrasa*, the formal school systems; thus, they were not subject to the legitimating tendencies of these systems. Recent scholarship has shown that *adab* is a special kind of education, a moral and intellectual curriculum that reflects the interests of literate, urban Arabic-writing communities.[3] Wolfhart Heinrichs emphasizes this last aspect of *adab*, suggesting that *muḥāḍara*, or having an apposite quotation at one's fingertips, is an informing principle of *adab*. Heinrichs observes that the content of *adab* is selected according to aesthetic merit and because of its function in social discourse.[4] Jaakko Hämeen-Anttila similarly notes: "In its ethical, professional, and literary meanings, *adab*

and Popular Arabic Literature, ed. Shimon Ballas and Reuven Snir (Toronto: York Press, 1998), 1–22; Bo Holmberg, "*Adab* and Arabic Literature," in *Literary History: Towards a Global Perspective* (Berlin: W. de Gruyter, 2006), 180–205; Shawkat Toorawa, "Defining Adab by (Re) defining the Adīb," in *On Fiction and Adab in Medieval Arabic Literature*, ed. Philip F. Kennedy (Wiesbaden: Harrassowitz Verlag, 2005), 287–304; and Peter Heath, "Al-Jāḥiẓ, *Adab*, and the Art of the Essay," in *Al-Jāḥiẓ: A Muslim Humanist for Our Time*, ed. A. Heinemann et al., Beiruter Texte und Studien 119 (Würzburg: Ergon-Verlag, 2009), 133–72.

2 See Kilpatrick, "Adab," in *EAL*, 1:56.

3 See F. Gabrieli, "Adab," *EI2* I:175–6; Tarif Khalidi, *Arabic Historical Thought in the Classical Period* (Cambridge: Cambridge University Press, 1996), 89; Marshall Hodgson, *The Venture of Islam, the Classical Age of Islam* (Chicago: Chicago University Press, 1974), 451–53. For the historical, social, and literary importance of *adab*, see H. Kilpatrick, "Genre in Classical Arabic," 34–42; Franz Rosenthal, "Fiction and Reality: Sources for the Role of Sex in Medieval Muslim Society," in *Society and the Sexes in Medieval Islam*, ed. Afaf Lutfi al-Sayyid-Marsot (Malibu: UNDENA Publications, 1979), 2–22; Roberto Marín Guzmán, "La literatura árabe como fuente para la historia social: El caso del Kitab al-Bukhalaʾ de el-Jahiz," *Estudios de Asia y Africa* 28 (1993), 32–83; Abdallah Cheikh-Moussa, "L'historien et la littérature arabe médiévale," *Arabica* 43 (1996), 152–88; Nadia Maria El Cheikh, "Women's History: A Study of al-Tanūkhī," in *Writing the Feminine: Women in Arab Sources*, ed. Randi Deguilhem and Manuela Marín (London: I. B. Tauris, 2002), 129–52; id., "In Search for the Ideal Spouse," *Journal of the Economic and Social History of the Orient* 45 (2002), 179–96; Jean-Claude Vadet, "Les grands thèmes de l'adab dans le Rabīʿ d'al-Zamakhsharī," *Revue des études islamiques* 58 (1990), 189–205.

4 See W. Heinrichs, "Review of *Cambridge History of Arabic Literature: ʿAbbasid Belles-Lettres*," *al-ʿArabiyya* 26 (1993), 130.

is a term that refers not only to literature but also to an ideal of behaviour and the will and ability to put into practice the theoretical wisdom found in *adab* books. In literary *adab*, this refers to a civilised person's ability to quote the material appropriately. The social context and the appropriate use of *adab* makes [sic] a person an *adīb*."[5] Joseph Sadan has introduced two useful related notions, oral *adab* and written *adab*. Oral *adab* is the outcome of *muḥāḍarāt al-udabāʾ* (to mean literary gatherings), which is then recorded in the anthologies of written *adab*, for subsequent use in *majālis*.[6] Thus, *adab* as such keeps circulating, accumulating, and appropriating new material. Samer Ali notes that, on the one hand, *adab* denotes "a corpus of varied literary knowledge… that a young litterateur must know—akin to the Greek concept of *paideia*," and, on the other hand, it "refers to the constellation of courtly manners and tastes to be conditioned and exhibited."[7] Ali also explains how the culture of sociability (*muʾānasa*) and charm (*ẓarf*) practiced in *mujālasāt* (literary salons) influenced and shaped *adab*.[8]

Regardless of the epistemological debate over *adab* as a distinct category, form, style, or approach in Arabic literature, many *adab* works arose from an anthologist's impulse to include what, in his opinion, was good literature. Notably, *adab* makes room for works that did not typically compete for consideration as good, or even "the best," such as epistles (*rasāʾil*), orations (*khuṭab*), *séances* (*maqāmāt*), mirrors for princes (*naṣīḥat al-mulūk*), biographical dictionaries (*ṭabaqāt*), commentaries (*shurūḥ*), works of literary borrowings (*sariqāt*), and books of dictation (*amālī*), as well as many monographs that involve no selection at all, such as *al-Tarbīʿ wa-l-tadwīr* (Epistle of the Square and the Circle) of Jāḥiẓ (d. 255/868). *Adab*, therefore, is not synonymous with literary anthology; rather, literary anthology is a type of *adab*. This chapter provides an analytical framework for studying Arabic literary anthologies, mapping out these works up to the fall of Baghdad in 656/1258 by grouping titles that share characteristics of form or content, or specific goals and aspirations.

5 See Hämeen-Anttila, "*Adab*, Arabic, Early Developments," *EI3*.

6 See J. Sadan, "Hārūn al-Rashīd and the Brewer," 2–3.

7 Samer Ali, *Arabic Literary Salons in the Islamic Middle Ages* (Notre Dame: University of Notre Dame Press, 2010), 33.

8 Ibid., 35.

Approaches to the Study of Arabic Literary Anthologies in Modern Scholarship

The corpus of anthologies appears fixed, and some observers may perceive these works as lacking in originality or creativity. Modern scholars have begun to recognize, though, that the originality of a particular anthology consists precisely in the choice and arrangement of the reproduced texts,[9] which together reveal the interests and objectives of the compiler.[10] Thus, the context in which a statement or an account is placed enhances its meaning and/or changes its function.[11] The material included in an anthology, though not the original work of the compiler, substantiates a vision that is strictly his own. We can compare the composite nature of such texts to language: words are the building blocks of language, but they do not convey thought on their own. Language as a conveyor of thought is not simply a sum of words; it is the product of a special configuration of those words. Thus, a new configuration of words always conveys a new thing. In the same vein, the reconfiguration of *akhbār* or statements speaks distinctly to the anthologist's vision, to his purpose in compiling the book.[12]

Anthologies are invaluable sources for social and historical information, and moreover, they can be viewed as original works, possessing a structure and agenda in their own right. Several studies have been devoted to analyzing the structure and organization of anthologies. For example, Fedwa Malti-Douglas has shed light on the organization of subjects and the orientation of *adab*

---

9 See Abdallah Cheikh-Moussa, "L'historien et la littérature arabe médiévale," 152–88; Heidi Toelle and Katia Zakharia, "Pour une relecture des textes littéraires arabes: Éléments de réflexion," *Arabica* 46 (1999), 523–40; Stefan Leder, "Conventions of Fictional Narration in Learned Literature," in *Story-telling in the Framework of Non-fictional Arabic Literature*, ed. Stefan Leder (Wiesbaden: Harrassowitz, 1998), 34–60; id., "Authorship and Transmission in Unauthored Literature: The Akhbār of al-Haytham ibn ʿAdī," *Oriens* 31 (1988), 61–81.

10 H. Kilpatrick, "Genre in Classical Arabic Literature," 34ff.

11 Id., "Context and the Enhancement of the Meaning of *aḫbār* in The *Kitāb al-Aġānī*," *Arabica* 38 (1991), 351–68.

12 Gabriel Rosenbaum compares *adab* to a "kind of modular toy building-block kit: the same blocks can be used to create various forms, which can then be taken apart again and reused to build something different." See his "A Certain Laugh: Serious Humor and Creativity in the Adab of Ibn al-Ǧawzī," in *Israel Oriental Studies XIX: Compilation and Creation in Adab and Luġa in Memory of Naphtali Kinberg (1948–1997)*, ed. Albert Arazi, Joseph Sadan, and David J. Wasserstein (Winona Lake: Eisenbrauns, 1999), 98–9.

works, with a focus on compilations about avarice (*bukhl*).[13] Likewise, Joseph Sadan has concerned himself with the structure and organization of anthologies in his work on al-Rāghib al-Iṣfahānī's (d. 422/1031) *Muḥāḍarāt al-udabāʾ wa-muḥāwarāt al-shuʿarāʾ wa-l-bulaghāʾ* (Ready Replies of the Litterateurs and the Conversations of Poets and Prose Stylists), emphasizing Iṣfahānī's use of the dichotomy *maḥāsin-masāwiʾ* (beauties-imperfections) as an organizational device.[14] Related is Geert Jan van Gelder's research on the dichotomy *jidd-hazl* (earnestness-jest).[15] Hilary Kilpatrick has called for greater attention to techniques and methods of compilation. She examines *K. al-Aghānī* (Book of Songs) for its internal logic and coherence, investigating how entries are organized, the elements frequently encountered in them, and the anthologist's skills in compiling, arranging, and commenting on the *akhbār*.[16] Other scholars have attempted to reveal anthologists' motives by tracking the same chapter or subject matter in a variety of works. For example, in *Knowledge Triumphant*, Franz Rosenthal compares the chapter on knowledge (*ʿilm*) in several anthologies,[17] and Nadia El Cheikh has compared historical and literary reports related to marriage in two anthologies: *ʿUyūn al-akhbār* (Quintessential Accounts) of Ibn Qutayba (d. 276/889) and *al-ʿIqd al-farīd* (The Unique Necklace) of Ibn ʿAbd Rabbihi (d. 328/940).[18]

Another approach to the study of *adab* compilations is the critical assessment of their sources.[19] Shawkat Toorawa has argued that the availability of books in the third/ninth century in Baghdad made it possible for one to complete training in *adab* through self-teaching. This development, according to Toorawa, resulted in a parallel decrease in the reliance on oral and aural trans-

---

13 Fedwa Malti-Douglas, *Structures of Avarice: The Bukhalāʾ in Medieval Arabic Literature* (Leiden: Brill, 1985), 5–16.

14 Joseph Sadan, "An Admirable and Ridiculous Hero: Some Notes on the Bedouin in Medieval Arabic Belles-Lettres, on a Chapter of *Adab* by al-Rāghib al-Iṣfahānī, and on a Literary Model in Which Admiration and Mockery Coexist," *Poetics Today* 10 (1989), 471–92.

15 See Geert Jan van Gelder, "Mixtures of Jest and Earnest in Classical Arabic Literature," I: *JAL* 23 (1992), 83–108 and II: *JAL* 23, (1993): 169–90.

16 Hilary Kilpatrick, *Making the Great Book of Songs: Compilation and the Author's Craft in Abū l-Faraj al-Iṣbahānī's Kitāb al-Aghānī* (London: RoutledgeCurzon, 2003).

17 Franz Rosenthal, Knowledge Triumphant: *The Concept of Knowledge in Medieval Islam* (Leiden: Brill, 1970), 252–77.

18 El Cheikh, "In Search for the Ideal Spouse," 179–96.

19 For a theoretical treatment of source criticism applied to Arabic compilations, see Sebastian Günther, "Assessing the Sources of Classical Arabic Compilations: The Issue of Categories and Methodologies," *British Journal of Middle Eastern Studies* 32 (2005), 75–98.

mission of knowledge,[20] as well as an increase in dependence on books and written materials.[21] Walter Werkmeister has examined the sources of *al-ʿIqd al-farīd*, showing that most of the material Ibn ʿAbd Rabbihi (d. 328/940) used was obtained from *majālis* and *ḥalaqāt*, not from written sources.[22] Both Manfred Fleischhammer and Fuat Sezgin have studied the oral and written sources that Abū l-Faraj al-Iṣbahānī (d. 356/967) used in *K. al-Aghānī*.[23] Fleischhammer concludes that the compiler drew his material from a limited number of informants and indicated the main written works from which he quoted, whereas Fuat Sezgin argues that the anthologist almost always used written texts. Similarly, Sebastian Günther has reviewed the sources for another work by Abū l-Faraj al-Iṣbahānī, the *Maqātil al-ṭālibiyyīn* (Martyrdoms of the Ṭālibids), concluding that the anthologist relied on various aural and written sources, which had both collective and single *isnāds*.[24] My survey in this book of the sources of Abū Manṣūr al-Thaʿālibī (d. 429/1039) in *Yatīmat al-dahr fī maḥāsin ahl al-ʿaṣr* (The Unique Pearl Concerning the Elegant Achievements of Contemporary People) and its sequel, *Tatimmat al-Yatīma* (Completion of the *Yatīma*), reveals a strong return to oral transmission from the second half of the fourth/tenth century, albeit complemented by the use of *dīwān*s, books, and other written materials. I posit that this distribution of sources is not uniform throughout the *aqsām* of the *Yatīma* and *Tatimma* (see chapter 3).

---

20 The term *aural* is particularly useful in historical-analytical studies of the sources of medieval Arabic compilations because it entails both written material (on which most lectures, seminars and tutorials were based) and the actual way of teaching this material by reading aloud from a written text. For more information and studies on aural transmission, see Günther, "Assessing the Sources of Classical Arabic Compilations," 75–98.

21 Shawkat Toorawa, *Ibn Abī Ṭāhir Ṭayfūr and Arabic Writerly Culture: A Ninth-Century Bookman in Baghdad* (London: RoutledgeCurzon, 2005), 124. See also Gregor Schoeler, *The Genesis of Literature in Islam*, trans. and in collaboration with Shawkat M. Toorawa (Edinburgh: Edinburgh University Press, 2009), 122–5.

22 See Walter Werkmeister, *Quellenuntersuchungen zum Kitāb al-ʿiqd al-farīd des Andalusiers (240/860–328/940)* (Berlin: Klaus Schwarz Verlag, 1983).

23 Manfred Fleischhammer, *Die Quellen des Kitāb al-Aġānī* (Wiesbaden: Harrassowitz, 2004); Fuat Sezgin, "*Maṣādir kitāb al-aghānī li-Abī l-Faraj al-Iṣfahānī*," in *Vortäge zur Geschichte der Arabisch-Islamischen Wissenschaften* (Frankfurt: Maʿhad Tārīkh al-ʿUlūm al-ʿArabiyya wa-l-Islāmiyya fī iṭār Jāmiʿat Frankfūrt, 1984), 147–58.

24 See Sebastian Günther, "»… nor have I learned it from any book of theirs« Abū l-Faraj al-Iṣfahānī: a Medieval Arabic Author at Work," in *Islamstudien ohne Ende: Festschrift Für Werner Ende Zum 65. Geburtstag*, ed. R. Brunner et al. ([Heidelberg]: Deutsche Morgenländische Gesellschaft, 2000), 139–54.

Taking another approach, Stefan Leder and Hilary Kilpatrick have explored common features among *adab* anthologies,[25] in form or content, focusing on works that feature prose and thus forming subcategories that are not necessarily discrete. For example, they pointed to anthologies that obey no order, such as *al-Baṣāʾir wa-l-dhakhāʾir* (Book of Insights and Treasures) of Abū Ḥayyān al-Tawḥīdī (d. 414/1023), which includes material the anthologist considered worth recording, as well as transcriptions of dictation sessions (*amālī*). Other anthologies touch on things such as aspects of human behavior (e.g., avarice), the biographies of noteworthy people, explorations of ethical or dialectical issues (e.g., *al-maḥāsin wa-l-masāwiʾ*, *al-jidd wa-l-hazl*), and discussions of linguistic and literary topics (e.g., *majālis*).[26] Kilpatrick also has defined a subcategory of *adab* as the *adab* encyclopedia,[27] providing an analytical framework for studying and comparing the methods, goals, and structures of this class of works.

Motives for Anthologizing

Why did premodern Arab authors compile literary anthologies? What made these works so remarkably popular? One modern scholar, Ibrāhīm Najjār, has suggested that the impulse to anthologize was a necessary by-product of the vast amount of literature being produced, which required abridgments and selections in order to be passed on to subsequent generations.[28] Indeed, in his introduction to *al-ʿIqd al-farīd*, the Andalusian *adīb* Ibn ʿAbd Rabbihi (d. 328/940) declares that the litterateurs and philosophers of all nations anthologized the wisest sayings of their predecessors so enthusiastically that "the abridged became in need of further abridgment and the already selected in need of further selection" (*aktharū fī dhālika ḥattā iḥtāja l-mukhtaṣar minhā ilā ikhtiṣār wa-l-mutakhayyar ilā ikhtiyār*).

Another possible stimulus for these compilations is the role of early poetry in Arabic philology as a source of knowledge to other disciplines such as lexicography, grammar, and Qurʾānic exegesis. Early literary anthologies focused on *qaṣīda*s and were compiled for educational purposes. In the face

25 Leder and Kilpatrick use the term *compilation*.

26 S. Leder and H. Kilpatrick, "Classical Arabic Prose Literature: A Researchers' Sketch Map," *JAL* 23 (1992), 16–18.

27 See Kilpatrick, "Genre in Classical Arabic Literature," 34–42.

28 Ibrāhīm Najjār, *Shuʿarāʾ ʿabbāsiyyūn mansiyyūn* (Beirut: Dār al-Gharb al-Islāmī, 1997), 1:170–71.

of the rapid social and linguistic changes brought about by the expansion of the Islamic empire, the literary and philological importance of such poems encouraged preservation of them. Later anthologies usually followed a narrower system of organization and purpose, but only rarely did they justify the selection. *Ḥamāsa* works were considered part of a curriculum that aspiring poets needed to master. Andras Hamori has noted that the use of poetry as a badge of culture helped create an audience for anthologies.[29] Many anthologies served as manuals of themes and motifs on subjects that a prose writer, a *kātib*, or an *adīb* might have occasion to cite in his own works and epistles, or in private or official correspondence.[30] Some anthologists used quotations of aesthetic merit to illustrate a specific thesis. By the second half of the third/ninth century, artistic prose had begun to supersede poetry as the preeminent form of literary expression. Consequently, anthologies began to place prose alongside poetry, and sometimes they even presented prose in isolation.

Many anthologies were not completely devoid of critical thought and opinion; they stood out as exercises in practical criticism. Many of them reveal the knowledge, taste, and care of their compilers. "Choosing discourse is more difficult than composing it" (*ikhtiyār al-kalām aṣʿab min taʾlīfih*), affirms Ibn ʿAbd Rabbihi, who also says, "A man's selection is an indication of his mind" (*ikhtiyāru l-rajul wāfidu ʿaqlih*)[31]—a statement later quoted by many authors.[32] This reverence for anthologizing, sometimes preferred over "original" compositions, might have been an incentive for authors to compile anthologies

29 A. Hamori, "Anthologies," *EI3*.

30 Some authors spell out this goal in their openings. Abū Hilāl al-ʿAskarī (d. after 400/1010), for example, in his introduction to his voluminous manual of motifs *Dīwān al-maʿānī*, stresses the importance of citing literary masterpieces in one's writings. See the introduction of Abū Hilāl al-ʿAskarī, *Dīwān al-maʿānī*, ed. Aḥmad Salīm Ghānim (Beirut: Dār al-Gharb al-Islāmī, 2003), 101. See also the discussion later here on *al-Muntaḥal* and *Sajʿ al-manthūr* by Thaʿālibī, *al-Muntakhal* by Mīkālī, and *Rawḥ al-rūḥ* by an anonymous author.

31 Ibn ʿAbd Rabbihi, *al-ʿIqd al-farīd*, ed. Mufīd Muḥammad Qumayḥa (Beirut: Dār al-Kutub al-ʿIlmiyya, 1983), 1:4. Ibn ʿAbd Rabbihi follows this by an anonymous line of poetry sharing the same meaning—"We have known you by your selection, for man's selection shows his intelligence" (*qad ʿarafnāka bikhtiyārika idh kāna dalīlan ʿala l-labībi ikhtiyāruhu*)—and a wise saying that he attributes to Plato: "The minds of people are recorded at the tips of their pens and become evident in the beauty of their selection" (*ʿuqūl al-nās mudawwana fī aṭrāf aqlāmihim wa ẓāhira fī ḥusni ikhtiyārihim*).

32 See, for example, al-Washshāʾ, *al-Muwashshā* (Beirut: Dār Ṣādir, 1965), 10; Ibn Khallikān, *Wafayāt al-aʿyān wa-anbāʾ abnāʾ al-zamān*, ed. Iḥsān ʿAbbās (Beirut: Dār Ṣādir, 1968), 6:78; Yāqūt al-Ḥamawī, *Muʿjam al-udabāʾ: Irshād al-arīb ilā maʿrifat al-adīb*, ed. Iḥsān ʿAbbās (Beirut: Dār al-Gharb al-Islāmī, 1993), 2763.

that could demonstrate the refined literary taste of the *adīb* and his mastery of texts, and consequently his literary authority.[33] Moreover, since the act of anthologizing was an intricate task, considered worthy of verbal and material reward, patronage must have increasingly impelled litterateurs to compile works. The more works a litterateur compiled and dedicated, the more gifts and cash he received.[34]

Anthologies were not always secondary texts with selections from primary *dīwān*s and circulating books. Rather, as in the case of anthologies dedicated to contemporary literature, such as the *Yatīmat al-dahr* of Thaʿālibī and its several sequels, they became, starting from the second half of the 4th/10th century, an important vehicle for publishing original literature, especially that of amateur or novice poets who did not produce circulating *dīwān*s but were still seeking recognition and access to courts. These poets sent their literary production to Thaʿālibī on parchments and pieces of paper, in hopes that he would include it in his second edition of the *Yatīma* and in its sequel, the *Tatimma*. In cases like this, the anthologist was a gatekeeper to the realm of admired literature.[35]

In what follows, the literary anthology is understood as an *adab* work of literary building blocks that the compiler has put together for a specific purpose, following particular selection criteria. The anthology puts those building blocks into a literary context and appreciates them either for their own sake or for their function in social discourse, regardless of their wider historical, political, or social importance. As Kilpatrick has noted, a political speech in a literary anthology is read as an example of eloquence, and its meaning acquires new dimensions in books of history or statecraft.[36] Naturally, anthologists' purpose, organization, structure, and selection criteria vary, but in general, they collect the "finest" literary pieces or important statements that merit recording.

---

33 This is especially the case in later Mamlūk anthologies. See Thomas Bauer, "Literarische Anthologien der Mamlūkenzeit," in *Die Mamluken. Studien zu ihrer Geschichte und Kultur*, ed. S. Conermann and A. Pistor-Hatam (Hamburg: EB-Verlag, 2003), 94ff.; id., "Mamluk Literature: Misunderstandings and New Approaches," *Mamlūk Studies Review* 9 (2005), 122.

34 This prompted some authors to recycle the material and, in some extreme cases, to dedicate the same work with a different preface to multiple patrons. See, for example, the case of Abū Manṣūr al-Thaʿālibī in Bilal Orfali, "The Art of the *Muqaddima* in the Works of Abū Manṣūr al-Thaʿālibī (d. 429/1039)," in *The Weaving of Words: Approaches to Classical Arabic Prose*, ed. Lale Behzadi and Vahid Behmardi, Beiruter Texte und Studien 112 (Würzburg: Ergon-Verlag, 2009), 188–90; see also chapter 2.

35 See Bilal Orfali, "The Sources of al-Thaʿālibī in *Yatīmat al-Dahr* and *Tatimmat al-Yatīma*," *Middle Eastern Literatures* 16 (2013), 13; see also chapter 4.

36 See Kilpatrick, "Anthologies, Medieval," *EAL* 1:94–6.

Their collection ensures that those pieces are read, circulated, studied, quoted, taught, and passed on to later generations, in an attempt to sustain, extend, or question the literary canon.

A Map of Arabic Poetry Anthologies

The map of poetry anthologies in this chapter[37] aims to provide an analytical framework for the study of this massive group of works.[38] The discussion here is restricted to works that are mostly concerned with poetry and compiled prior to the fall of Baghdad in 656/1258.[39] Of course, *adab* anthologies often include both prose and poetry, and such a map cannot ignore these works, so there is some natural overlap with the map offered by Leder and Kilpatrick. It is also difficult to produce an accurate map of anthologized literature that encompasses all works on the subject. Many forms of *adab*, as discussed already, involve anthologizing and fall at different distances from the *adab* anthology. Moreover, many anthologies are still in manuscript form in libraries and private collections around the world, and new ones continue to be discovered.

Anthologies Concerned with Form

The collection of the seven (nine or ten) celebrated pre-Islamic *qaṣīda*s, *al-Muʿallaqāt* (lit. The Hung Odes), is considered the oldest Arabic literary anthology.[40] The reason these poems were brought together is not clear; most of the justifications offered in the sources indicate that their intent was edu-

37 For the bibliographical references of primary sources discussed or cited in this chapter, see Reinhard Weipert, *Classical Arabic Philology and Poetry: A Bibliographical Handbook of Important Editions from 1960–2000* (Boston: Brill, 2002).

38 Joseph Sadan observes that the term *adab* in classical sources excludes collections of poetry (*dīwāns*) composed solely of verse, which are strictly defined as *shiʿr*. Sadan rightly observes that classical Arabic biographies define many *udabāʾ* as *kāna shāʿiran adīban*, thus distinguishing between *adab* and *shiʿr*. See discussion in his "Hārūn al-Rashīd and the Brewer," 2–3. Nevertheless, I believe that the scope of *adab* presented here would include "nonoriginal" collections of poetry (*ikhtiyārāt*).

39 For an excellent discussion of anthologies from the Mamlūk period, see Bauer, "Literarische Anthologien der Mamlūkenzeit," 71–122. A good preliminary survey of *adab* anthologies in Arabic literature, including the post-Mongol period, is A. Hamori and T. Bauer, "Anthologies," *EI3*. My map refines and adds to this survey but excludes anthologies that are limited to prose.

40 For a detailed discussion of *al-muʿallaqāt*, their number, and authenticity, see M.J. Kister, "The Seven Odes: Some Notes on the Compilation of the *Muʿallaqāt*," *Revista degli studi*

cational and that selection was based on a poem's popularity and/or literary value.[41] A feature these poems share is the multithematic *qaṣīda* form.[42] Other anthologies of *qaṣīda*s from the early ʿAbbāsid period were similarly compiled on the basis of the importance of the poems, but without mention of what made the poems important. The selected poems of al-Mufaḍḍal al-Ḍabbī (d. ca. 164/780 or 170/786), *al-Mufaḍḍaliyyāt* (originally titled *K. al-Ikhtiyārāt*, or The Book of Selections), and the poems selected by Aṣmaʿī (d. ca. 213/828), *al-Aṣmaʿiyyāt*, exemplify this type of selection.[43] Ibn al-Nadīm mentioned that Mufaḍḍal prepared his collection for the caliph al-Mahdī (r. 159–69/775–85). Al-Qālī al-Baghdādī (d. 356/967) explains that the caliph al-Manṣūr (d. 158/775) asked Mufaḍḍal to collect choice specimens from the *muqillūn* (poets whose poetic output is minimal) for his pupil, the future caliph al-Mahdī.[44] This selection criterion explains the absence of the most famous pre-Islamic poets in the anthology. *Al-Aṣmaʿiyyāt* consists of ninety-two *qaṣīda*s by seventy-one poets (forty-four of them *jāhilī*) and has received much less attention than *al-Mufaḍḍaliyyāt*.[45]

Jamharat ashʿār al-ʿArab (Collection of the Arabs' Verses) of Abū Zayd Muḥammad b. Abī l-Khaṭṭāb al-Qurashī (d. third/ninth century) is orga-

orientali 44 (1968), 27–36; G. Lecomte, "al-Muʿallaḳāt," *EI2* VII:254–5 and sources listed there.

41 In Naḥḥās's view, Ḥammād al-Rāwiya (d. 155/771 or 158/774) collected these seven odes to draw attention to them when he saw people's loss of interest in poetry. See Naḥḥās, *Sharḥ al-qaṣāʾid al-tisʿ al-mashhūrāt*, ed. Aḥmad Khaṭṭāb (Baghdad: Wizārat al-Iʿlām, 1973), 2:681–2. See Ahlwardt's remarks on this view in *Sammlungen alter arabischer Dichter* (Berlin: Reeuther and Reichard, 1902–3), 1:xi–xii. Other reports indicate that the the caliph Muʿāwiya (d. 60/680) ordered the collection for the purpose of educating his son. See a discussion of these reports in Kister, "Seven Odes," 27–36. For a discussion of the role Ḥammād might have played in collecting the *Muʿallaqāt*, see M. B. Alwan, "Is Ḥammād the Collector of the Muʿallaqāt?" *Islamic Culture* 45 (1971), 363–4.

42 On the term *qaṣīda*, see R. Jacobi, "Qaṣīda," in *EAL* 2:630 and sources listed there. For a survey of commentaries on the *Muʿallaqāṭ*, see *GAS* 2:50–53.

43 Most sources agree that the *Mufaḍḍaliyyāt* originally included seventy or eighty poems, with other poems were added later. Whether the additions were by Mufaḍḍal himself or Aṣmaʿī is not clear; see a discussion on the authorship of the two works in Lyall, *The Mufaḍḍaliyyāt* (Oxford: Clarendon Press, 1918), 2:xiv–xvii. The editors of the Cairo edition, Aḥmad Muḥammad Shākir and ʿAbd al-Salām Hārūn, maintain that Aṣmaʿī's anthology had become mixed with *al-Mufaḍḍaliyyāt* at an early stage of transmission; see the introduction of *al-Mufaḍḍaliyyāt*, 14–19.

44 See references and details in Renate Jacobi, "al-Mufaḍḍaliyyāt," *EI2* VII:306.

45 For details, see Hamori, "Anthologies," *EI3*.

nized into seven groups, each containing seven *qaṣīdas*.[46] The work clearly involves more than one criterion for selection. The first group consists of seven poems—the *Muʿallaqāt*, the second group of seven *qaṣīdas* (*al-mujamharāt*, or "the assembled"), are poems that Qurashī held to be of the same quality as the first. Other groups were chosen according to particular principles left unspecified, but some can be inferred: for example, one group is dedicated to poems by the Aws and Khazraj tribes, another to remarkable *marāthī* (elegies), and yet another features poems "with a tincture of *kufr* and Islām."[47]

Another anthology devoted to *pre-Islamic* and *Islāmic qaṣīdas* is *al-Muntakhab fī maḥāsin ashʿār al-ʿArab* (Selection of the Finest Arab Poems), attributed to Abū Manṣūr al-Thaʿālibī, although it is the work of an anonymous author from the fourth/tenth century.[48] The anthology includes ninety-six *qaṣīdas* and four poems of *rajaz*, several of which are not found anywhere else.[49] *Mukhtārāt shuʿarāʾ al-ʿArab* (Select Poems of the Arabs) of Hibatallāh b. al-Shajarī (d. 542/1147) is a commentated anthology of pre-Islamic *qaṣīdas*. One feature all the *qaṣīdas* share is that they do not appear in their author's *dīwān*. The third section of this anthology is dedicated to the poet al-Ḥuṭayʾa and features some of his accounts and shorter poems. The enormous *Muntahā l-ṭalab min ashʿār al-ʿArab* (Ultimate Desire in the Poems of the Arabs) of Muḥammad b. al-Mubārak b. Maymūn (d. after 589/1193) comprises ten volumes, each encompassing a hundred *qaṣīdas*. The surviving manuscript of this work features the anthologist's ten volumes in six *mujalladāt*, three of which have survived. As the anthologist indicates in his introduction, the work incorporates several earlier anthologies but preserves a few *qaṣīdas* not found elsewhere.

A few anthologies are devoted to another poetic form, the *muwashshaḥ*, such as Ibn Sanāʾ al-Mulk's (d. 609/1211) *Dār al-ṭirāz* (The House of Embroidery), and ʿAlī b. al-Bishrī's *ʿUddat al-jalīs* (The Companion's Manual).[50]

---

46 For a short discussion of his identity and mention in later sources, see Nāṣir al-Dīn al-Asad, *Maṣādir al-shiʿr al-jāhilī* (Cairo: Dār al-Maʿārif, 1978), 584–8.

47 See Hamori, "Anthologies," *EI3*.

48 See Bilal Orfali, "The Works of Abū Manṣūr al-Thaʿālibī," *JAL* 40 (2009), 302; see also chapter 2.

49 The editor ʿĀdil Sulaymān Jamāl opted to leave the *urjūzas* for another edition because MS British Museum 9222 is missing a folio of this section; see *al-Muntakhab fī maḥāsin ashʿār al-ʿArab*, ed. ʿA. S. Jamāl (Cairo: Maktabat al-Khānjī, 1993–4), 1:31.

50 Also related, though from a later period, is Lisān al-Dīn al-Khaṭīb's (d. 776/1375) *Jaysh al-tawshīḥ* (The Host Muwashshaḥ).

Encyclopedic Anthologies

Hilary Kilpatrick has defined the *adab* encyclopedia as "a work designed to provide the basic knowledge in those domains with which the average cultured man may be expected to be acquainted. It is characterized by organization into chapters or books on the different subjects treated."[51] Model examples in this category include *al-ʿIqd al-farīd* of Ibn ʿAbd Rabbihi (d. 328/940) and *ʿUyūn al-akhbār* of Ibn Qutayba (d. 276/889).[52] Kilpatrick further includes Ibn ʿAbd al-Barr's (d. 463/1071) *Bahjat al-majālis wa-uns al-mujālis wa-shaḥdh al-dhāhin wa-l-hājis* (The Joy of Literary Gatherings, the Intimacy of the Companion, and the Sharpening of the Mind and Thought), al-Rāghib al-Iṣfahānī's (d. 422/1031) *Muḥāḍarāt al-udabāʾ wa-muḥāwarāt al-shuʿarāʾ wa-l-bulaghāʾ*, Zamakhsharī's (d. 538/1143) *Rabīʿ al-abrār wa-fuṣūṣ al-akhbār* (The Springtime of the Virtuous and the Gems of the Reports).[53] Kilpatrick distinguishes encyclopedias from anthologies, but she also notes the difficulty of doing so, citing as an example al-Rāghib al-Iṣfahānī's *Muḥāḍarāt al-udabāʾ*,[54] which has elements of both an encyclopedia and an anthology; the former because it attempts to cover all subjects of conversation, and the latter because it selects the best examples of those subjects' treatment in prose and poetry.[55] Most *adab* encyclopedias exhibit an anthologizing impulse, and this figures in the anthologist's

51 See Kilpatrick, "Genre in Classical Arabic Literature," 34. Accordingly, books like *al-Baṣāʾir wa-l-dhakhāʾir* by Abū Ḥayyān al-Tawḥīdī (d. 414/1023) and *Zahr al-Ādāb* (Flowers of Literature) by Ḥuṣrī (d. 413/1022) do not qualify under this category, as neither is organized consistently according to subject. Moreover, the definition excludes the *Yatīmat al-dahr* by Thaʿālibī (d. 429/1039) and *al-Aghānī* by Abū l-Faraj al-Iṣbahānī (d. 356/967), both of which are arranged biographically and provide historical and other nonliterary information only randomly.

52 See ibid., 34–5, 40. For a brief discussion of few encyclopedic works, see G. J. van Gelder, "Complete Men, Women and Books: On Medieval Arabic Encyclopaedism," in *Pre-Modern Encyclopaedic Texts*, ed. Peter Binkley (Leiden: Brill, 1997), 251–9. For the genesis of the genre, see Elias Muhanna, *Encyclopaedism in the Mamluk Period: The Composition of Shihāb al-Dīn al-Nuwayrī's (d. 1333) Nihāyat al-Arab fī Funūn al-Adab*, PhD diss., Harvard University, chap. 1.

53 Among the works compiled after the fall of Baghdād, Kilpatrick includes Nuwayrī's (733/1333) *Nihāyat al-arab fī funūn al-adab* (The Goal of Desire in Literary Arts), Qalqashandī's (d. 821/1418) *Ṣubḥ al-aʿshā fī ṣināʿat al-inshāʾ* (Morning for the Night-Blind on the Craft of Secretarial Style), and Ibshīhī's (850/1446) *al-Mustaṭraf fī kulli fann mustaẓraf* (The Ultimate on Every Refined Art).

54 For a study dedicated to this anthology, see Sadan, "Admirable and Ridiculous Hero," 471–92.

55 See Kilpatrick, "Anthologies, Medieval," 94.

introductions and titles.[56] In other words, they are anthologies that strive for comprehensiveness.

Theme and Motif Anthologies

The most notable works in the category of theme and motif anthologies are the *ḥamāsa* collections.[57] The first is arguably Abū Tammām's (d. 231/846) *K. al-Ḥamāsa*,[58] which includes ten headings: *ḥamāsa* (valor), *marāthī* (elegies), *adab* (proper conduct), *nasīb* (love), *hijā'* (invective), *al-aḍyāf wa-l-madīḥ* (hospitality and praise of the generous), *ṣifāt* (descriptive verses or epigrams), *al-sayr wa-l-nuʿās* (desert travel), *mulaḥ* (clever curiosities), and *madhammat al-nisā'* (the censure of women).[59] The first and largest section, *al-ḥamāsa* (valor), gives its name to several other anthologies of this type. The selections date back to pre-Islamic, Islamic, and early ʿAbbāsid times. Various reasons have been suggested for Abū Tammām's composition of the *Ḥamāsa*, all of them related to his personal literary tastes.[60] The work has special importance as the first anthology compiled by a poet and not a philologist, and the large number of commentaries on it suggests that it remained extremely popular

---

56 See, for example, Ibn Qutayba, *ʿUyūn al-akhbār* (Cairo: al-Mu'assasa al-Miṣriyya al-ʿĀmma li-l-Ta'līf wa-l-Tarjama, 1964), 1:10–12.

57 For a general study of the *Ḥamāsa* collections, see Adel Sulayman Gamal, "The Basis of Selection in the *Ḥamāsa* Collections," *JAL* 7 (1976), 28–44.

58 For the *Ḥamāsa* by Abū Tammām, see F. Klein-Franke, "The *Ḥamāsa* of Abū Tammām," *JAL* 2 (1971), 13–55, and *JAL* 3 (1972): 142–78; id., *Die Hamasa des Abu Tammam* (Cologne: Phil. F., Diss., 1963); M. C. Lyons, "Notes on Abū Tammām's Concept of Poetry," *JAL* 9 (1978), 57–64; G. J. H. van Gelder, "Against Women, and Other Pleasantries: The Last Chapter of Abū Tammām's *Ḥamāsa*," *JAL* 16 (1985), 61–7; Margaret Larkin, "Abu Tammam (circa 805–845)," in *Arabic Literary Culture*, ed. Michael Cooperson and Shawkat M. Toorawa, vol. 311 of *Dictionary of Literary Biography* (Detroit: Gale, 2005), 38–40. For translations of passages from the *Ḥamāsa*, a discussion of the literary *ijmāʿ* on it, and the process of "collecting" poetry up to Abū Tammām's time, see Suzanne Pinckney Stetkevych, *Abū Tammām and the Poetics of the ʿAbbāsid Age* (Leiden: Brill, 1991), 231–350.

59 Tibrīzī throws some doubt on the assumption that Abū Tammām's *Ḥamāsa* is the first of its kind, claiming that "the literary scholars of Iṣfahān concentrated on it [i.e., Abū Tammām's book] and rejected all others of its kind"; see Tibrīzī, *Sharḥ Dīwān al-Ḥamāsa*, ed. M. M. ʿAbd al-Ḥamīd (Cairo: al-Maktaba al-Tijāriyya, 1938), 1:4. However, Tibrīzī could have meant that scholars rejected the *Ḥamāsa* works that came after Abū Tammām's work or the other anthologies that circulated earlier, such as *al-Aṣmaʿiyyāt* and *al-Mufaḍḍaliyyāt*; see Gamal, "Basis of Selection in the *Ḥamāsa* Collections," 28; and Stetkevych, *Abū Tammām and the Poetics of the ʿAbbāsid Age*, 284–5.

60 See a discussion of these opinions in Gamal, "Basis of Selection in the *Ḥamāsa* Collections," 31ff.

until the modern period.[61] Abū Tammām compiled at least one more anthology: *al-Waḥshiyyāt* (Book of Stray Verse), also known as *al-Ḥamāsa al-ṣughrā* (The Lesser *Ḥamāsa*), which follows the same plan as *Dīwān al-Ḥamāsa* and contains longer poems.[62] Other *ḥamāsa* works quickly followed, though not all of them retain the method of organization. Buḥturī (d. 284/897), for example, compiled a *Ḥamāsa* divided into 174 *abwāb*. The *abwāb*, however, are arranged according to shared literary motifs rather than broader themes. They comprise short poetic epigrams, not complete poems, and thus the work resembles the *Dīwān al-maʿānī* (Register of Poetic Motifs) of Abū Hilāl al-ʿAskarī (d. after 400/1010). Later *ḥamāsa* works paid more attention to *muḥdath* poetry. For instance, in *Ḥamāsat al-ẓurafāʾ* (Poems of the Refined and Witty), al-ʿAbdalakānī al-Zawzanī (d. 431/1039) states that ancient and modern poets have equal representation in his selections and that he has included both in the hope of attracting young readers. He adds that his own work is an introduction to Abū Tammām's work.[63] Among other surviving *ḥamāsa* works is *al-Ḥamāsa al-Shajariyya* of Ibn al-Shajarī (d. 542/1148), who followed Abū Tammām's organizational method in the first part of his work, using large chapters according to the dominant themes of the poems. However, he seems to have been influenced by Buḥturī in dividing the second part of his work into shorter chapters according to motifs. Ibn al-Shajarī includes poets starting from the ʿAbbāsid period, with some chapters devoted exclusively to *muḥdath* poetry.[64] *Al-Ḥamāsa al-Maghribiyya* by Aḥmad b. ʿAbd al-Salām al-Jurāwī (d. 609/1212) includes parts of poems by poets from the west along those from the east. The work is an abridgment of the lost *K. Ṣafwat al-adab wa-nukhbat*

61 Sezgin lists thirty-six commentaries; see *GAS* 2:68–72.

62 Abū Tammām also compiled *Mukhtārāt ashʿār al-qabāʾil* (Selection from the Poetry of the Tribes), which was still known to ʿAbd al-Qādir al-Baghdādī (d. 1093/1682), who cites it in his *Khizānat al-adab* (The Repository of Culture). See *GAS* 2:42–3. This work is followed by a sequel, *Ikhtiyār al-qabāʾil al-aṣghar* (The Smaller Tribal Selection), see *GAS* 2:558. Sezgin lists a large number of tribal *dīwāns*, some of which are anthologies, but unfortunately most of them have been lost; see *GAS* 2:36–46. Sezgin adds other anthologies by Abū Tammām: On *Ikhtiyār shuʿarāʾ al-fuḥūl* or *Fuḥūl al-shuʿarāʾ* (The Champion Poets); see *GAS* 2:72, 558. This, however, is a copy of *Dīwān al-Ḥamāsa* (I thank Muhammad Kazem Rahmati for this information). On *Ikhtiyār mujarrad min ashʿār al-muḥdathīn* (Selection from the Poetry of the Moderns) and *Ikhtiyār al-muqaṭṭaʿāt* (Selection of Short Pieces), see *GAS* 2:558.

63 See al-ʿAbdalakānī al-Zawzanī, *Ḥamāsat al-ẓurafāʾ min ashʿār al-muḥdathīn wa-l-qudamāʾ*, ed. Muḥammad Jabbār al-Muʿaybid (Baghdad: Manshūrāt Wizārat al-Iʿlām, 1973), 15.

64 For a discussion of the division of this *Ḥamāsa* and Ibn al-Shajarī's contribution to the genre, see Gamal, "Basis of Selection in the *Ḥamāsa* Collections," 37–9.

dīwān al-ʿArab (The Purest in Refinement and Most Select Poems of the Arabs) by the same anthologist. It consists of nine chapters (*abwāb*) starting with *bāb al-madīḥ*; the chapters of *al-madīḥ*, *al-nasīb*, and *al-awṣāf* include various subdivisions. *Al-Ḥamāsa al-Baṣriyya* by Ṣadr al-Dīn ʿAlī b. Abī l-Faraj al-Baṣrī (d. probably 659/1249) is a work that enjoyed some fame and was frequently used by Suyūṭī, ʿAynī, and Baghdādī.[65] Baṣrī's anthology is arranged in chapters following the scheme used in Abū Tammām's *Ḥamāsa*, with an additional chapter on *al-zuhd* (asceticism). Baṣrī restricts his choice of poets to those writing before the end of the third/ninth century.[66]

65 See Hamori, "Anthologies," *EI3*.

66 According to Gamal, within the chapters' framework, five selection criteria were employed: thematic similarity, mode of expression or word choice, poets who have a particular relationship with each other, poems with problematic attribution, and poems about places. See Gamal, "Basis of Selection in the *Ḥamāsa* Collections," 40ff. From a later period, ʿUbaydī (d. eighth/fourteenth century) wrote *al-Ḥamāsa al-saʿdiyya* (known also as *al-Tadhkira al-Saʿdiyya*), in which he acknowledged three earlier *Ḥamāsa* works as his sources: those of Abū Tammām, Abū Hilāl al-ʿAskarī, and Ibn Fāris. The last two of these three works have been lost. Several *Ḥamāsa* works have not survived; among the ones we know are the *Ḥamāsa* of Ibn al-Marzubān (d. 309/921), of which we know nothing; an important *Ḥamāsa* is that of Ibn Fāris (d. 395/1004) titled *al-Ḥamāsa al-muḥdatha* (The Modern Ḥamāsa), which dealt, as the title suggests, with *muḥdath* poetry. In addition, the sources hold that Abū Hilāl al-ʿAskarī compiled a *Ḥamāsa* whose existence is fully attested to by al-ʿAynī (d. 855/1451) in his *al-Maqāṣid al-naḥwiyya* (The Grammatical Aims) and used by ʿUbaydī in *al-Ḥamāsa al-Baṣriyya* (The Ḥamāsa of al-Baṣrī). See Gamal, "Basis of Selection in the *Ḥamāsa* Collections," 28–31. Shantamarī (d. 476/1083) wrote a *Ḥamāsa* that is not to be confused with his commentary on the *Ḥamāsa* of Abū Tammām; for evidence of the existence of this work, see ibid., 30. Shāṭibī (d. 547/1152) compiled a *Ḥamāsa* mentioned in Suyūṭī, *Bughyat al-wuʿāt fī ṭabaqāt al-lughawiyyīn wa-l-nuḥāt*, ed. Abū l-Faḍl Ibrāhīm (Cairo: al-Bābī al-Ḥalabī, 1964–5), 1:261. Ibn Khallikān also mentions that the Andalusian historian, *muḥaddith*, and *rāwī* Abū al-Ḥajjāj Yūsuf b. Muḥammad b. Ibrāhīm al-Anṣārī al-Bayyāsī (d. 653/1255) compiled a *Ḥamāsa* of two volumes that Ibn Khallikān studied with him using a manuscript penned by the author. Ibn Khallikān adds that the work was completed in 646/1249 and goes on to quote its introduction. In that introduction, Bayyāsī mentions that he started collecting the material early in his life and has included *jāhilī*, *mukhaḍram*, *islāmī*, *muwallad*, and *muḥdath* poetry from the east and west. He adds that he organized the work according to the scheme of Abū Tammām's *Ḥamāsa*; see Ibn Khallikān, *Wafayāt al-aʿyān*, 7:238–9. For references and quotations from this work, see ibid., 1:232, 5:39, 7:116–17, 132, 239–43. Al-Khālidiyyān, Abū Bakr Muḥammad b. Hāshim (d. 380/990) and Abū ʿUthmān Saʿīd b. Hāshim (d. 390/999), compiled *Ḥamāsat al-muḥdathīn* (The Ḥamāsa of the Modern Poets), which is mentioned by Ibn al-Nadīm and usually confused with the surviving *al-Ashbāh wa-l-naẓāʾir*; see Ibn al-Nadīm, *al-Fihrist*, ed. Riḍā Tajaddud (Beirut:

In addition to *Ḥamāsa* works, a variety of poetry and prose anthologies are organized differently and serve numerous purposes. The collection of epigrams on descriptions (*awṣāf*) in poetic anthologies became common from the third/ninth century and reached its climax in the Mamlūk period.[67] Gustave von Grunebaum describes such *waṣf* poems as "poetical snapshot[s]: a small group of verses, usually between two and seven, purporting to capture some fleeting view, some momentary impression."[68] As Grunebaum observes, these short poems were often composed for their own sake, with no intention of making them fit into longer poetic forms such as the *qaṣīda*.[69] Beatrice Gruendler, in her study of Abū Hilāl al-ʿAskarī's (d. after 400/1010) *Dīwān al-maʿānī*, emphasizes the influence of literary sessions and courtly conversations (*majālis*) from the third/ninth and fourth/tenth centuries on both the rise of the epigrammatic collection of poetic motifs (*maʿānī*) and the principles that governed their collection.[70]

Abū Hilāl al-ʿAskarī compiled the *Dīwān al-maʿānī* (Collection of Poetic Motifs), which is devoted to selections of poetry and occasionally epistolary prose resembling *maʿānī* (formulated ideas). It is organized under thematic headings (e.g., praise, satire, description) and sometimes by subject (e.g., love, wine). Passages in this work vary in length, and sometimes it is difficult to determine whether ʿAskarī is referring to a certain motif or to a broader theme.[71] The anonymous *Majmūʿat al-maʿānī* (Collection of Poetic Motifs), probably from the fifth/eleventh century, is conceived along a similar plan

Dār al-Masīra, 1988), 195. In addition to these, Ibn al-Nadīm mentions a *Ḥamāsa* by an unknown Abū Dimāsh; see ibid., 89.

67 See Adam Talib, *Out of Many*, One: *Epigram Anthologies in Pre-Modern Arabic Literature*, PhD diss., University of Oxford, 2013. Talib notes that the anthological style of Thaʿālibī and his near contemporary al-Sarī al-Raffāʾ (d. 362/972–3) was "an influential predecessor of the epigram anthology type that developed in the 13th–14th centuries" (131).

68 Gustave von Grunebaum, "The Response to Nature in Arabic Poetry," *Journal of Near Eastern Studies* 4 (1945), 148.

69 Ibid.

70 See Beatrice Gruendler, "Motif vs. Genre: Reflections on the *Dīwān al-Maʿānī* of Abū Hilāl al-ʿAskarī," in *Ghazal as World Literature I: Transformations of a Literary Genre*, ed. Thomas Bauer and Angelika Neuwirth (Beirut: Orient-Institut; Würzburg: Ergon, 2005), 57–85.

71 For a study on Abū Hilāl al-ʿAskarī's *Dīwān al-maʿānī*, see Gruendler, "Motif vs. Genre," 57–85. George Kanazi notes that the term *maʿnā* in al-ʿAskarī's works refers to an idea, thought, or concept that is unformulated in the mind; a theme (close to *gharaḍ*); the meaning of a word, phrase, or other construction; and the quality or character of a certain object. See his *Studies in the Kitāb Aṣ-ṣināʿatayn of Abū Hilāl al-ʿAskarī* (Leiden: Brill, 1989), 84.

but focuses mainly on wisdom and advice poetry, without commentary.[72] The selections range from the pre-Islamic period to the fifth/eleventh century.

Despite the popularity of *maʿānī* books, only few have survived,[73] and those that have neither follow the same scheme nor share an understanding of the term *maʿnā*. *Maʿānī* may refer to verses that entail a certain difficulty. Examples of these surviving books are Ibn Qutayba's (d. 276/889) *Maʿānī al-shiʿr* (also known as *K. al-Maʿānī al-kabīr*) and the identically titled work (also known as *Abyāt al-maʿānī*) of Ushnāndānī (d. 288/901). A look at Ushnāndānī's commentary on the verses he chose reveals that he selected them because they render challenging or ambiguous meaning, which forms a motif that later poets either followed or reacted against. In his commentary, Ushnāndānī explained the intricate words, proverbs, and expressions, and he gave cultural context, but his intention remained clarifying the ambiguous meaning of lines themselves and/or the object of description. Ibn Qutayba's work *Maʿānī al-shiʿr* is arranged by theme, perhaps because the amount of material he included called for such a system. But here, too, the obscurity of the selected verses is the basic criterion for inclusion. This criterion makes the two books part of the broader writing genre *alghāz* (puzzles), into which books of *abyāt al-maʿānī*, especially that of Ibn Qutayba, were later categorized.[74]

---

72 A good number of poems in this work appear in *al-Tadhkira al-Ḥamdūniyya* by Ibn Ḥamdūn (495/1101–562/1166), and as the editor ʿA. M. al-Mallūḥī has noted, it is difficult to guess who the source of these poems is. See *Majmūʿat al-maʿānī*, ed. ʿAbd al-Muʿīn al-Mallūḥī (Damascus: Dār Ṭalās, 1988), 12.

73 Sezgin lists thirty-three recorded *maʿānī* and *tashbīhāt* works that have been written since the mid-second/mid-eighth century. See *GAS* 1:58–60. Wolfhart Heinrichs considers books limited to comparisons as a variation of *maʿānī* books; see "Poetik, Rhetoric, Literaturkritik, Metric und Reimlehre," in *Grundriss der arabischen Philologie II: Literaturwissenschaft*, ed. Helmut Gätje (Wiesbaden: Reichert, 1987), 177ff.

74 *Abyāt al-maʿānī* is a technical term related to the genre of *alghāz*. In a chapter on *alghāz*, Suyūṭī (d. 911/1505) defines the genre as follows: "There are kinds of puzzles that the Arabs aimed for and other puzzles that the scholars of language aim for, and also lines in which the Arabs did not aim for puzzlement, but they uttered them and they happened to be puzzling; these are of two kinds: Sometimes puzzlement occurs in them on account of their meaning, and most of *abyāt al-maʿānī* are of this type. Ibn Qutayba compiled a good volume on this, and others compiled similar works. They called this kind [of poetry] *abyāt al-maʿānī* because it requires someone to ask about its meaning and it is not comprehended on the first consideration. Some other times puzzlement occurs because of utterance, construction, or inflection (*iʿrāb*)." See Suyūṭī, *al-Muzhir fī ʿulūm al-lugha wa-anwāʿihā*, ed. Muḥammad Abū l-Faḍl Ibrāhīm et al. (Cairo: al-Bābī al-Ḥalabī, 1958), 1:578. Suyūṭī was not the first to note this obscurity in *abyāt al-maʿānī*: ʿAbd al-Qāhir al-Jurjānī (d. 392/1001) commented: "There is no line among *abyāt al-maʿānī* on this earth by any

Mubarrad (d. 285/898) compiled two multithematic anthologies, *al-Kāmil fī l-adab* (The Perfection of Education, also called *al-Kāmil fī-l-lugha wa-l-adab wa-l-naḥw wa-l-taṣrīf*) and *al-Fāḍil* (The Exquisite). Both works include significant numbers of poems, mostly embedded in anecdotes and *akhbār*. William Wright's edition of *al-Kāmil* includes sixty-one chapters that treat an extensive range of themes. The form of the book as we know it today goes back to Mubarrad's pupil Abū l-Ḥasan al-Akhfash al-Aṣghar (d. 315/927) and the arrangement of chapters is irregular, sometimes even arbitrary.[75] *Al-Fāḍil* is much shorter but better structured. It is divided into sixteen chapters (*abwāb*), with the final one consisting of seven sections (*fuṣūl*). The themes discussed include generosity, grief, youth and old age, forbearance, gratitude, envy, keeping a secret, eloquence, and beauty.[76]

Ibn Abī Ṭāhir Ṭayfūr's (d. 280/893) *al-Manẓūm wa-l-manthūr* (Book of Prose and Poetry), of which only the eleventh, twelfth, and thirteenth volumes survive, is one of the earliest anthologies to combine poetry and prose writing.[77] The extant *Balāghāt al-nisā'* (The Eloquence of Women), part of the eleventh volume, is an early attempt to draw attention to instances of women's eloquence.[78] *Al-Daʿawāt wa-l-fuṣūl* (Book of Prayers and Aphorisms) by ʿAlī b. Aḥmad al-Wāḥidī (d. 468/1075) includes both prose and poetry from all periods and representing different themes. *Ṭarā'if al-ṭuraf* (The Most Unusual Coined Sayings) of al-Ḥusayn b. Muḥammad al-Ḥārithī al-Bāriʿ al-Baghdādī (d.

poet, ancient or modern (*muḥdath*), whose meaning is not obscure and hidden. Had they not been so, then they would have been like other poetry and the compiled books would not have been devoted to them, nor would the dedicated minds have busied themselves in extracting them. We do not mean the poems whose obscurity and concealed meaning is because of the rarity of the usage (*gharābat al-lafẓ*) or the speech being rough (*tawaḥḥush al-kalām*)." See Jurjānī, *al-Wasāṭa bayna l-Mutanabbī wa khuṣūmih*, ed. Muḥammad Abū l-Faḍl Ibrāhīm and ʿAlī Muḥammad al-Bajāwī (Saida: al-Maktaba al-ʿAṣriyya, 1986), 431.

75 See R. M. Burrell, "al-Mubarrad," in *EI2*, VII:279–82.

76 Ibid.

77 For more surviving manuscripts and published parts of this work, see Toorawa, *Ibn Abī Ṭāhir Ṭayfūr and Arabic Writerly Culture*, 180.

78 Ibn Abī Ṭāhir Ṭayfūr wrote a number of other anthologies, such as *K. Ikhtiyār ashʿar al-shuʿarā'* (The Selection of the Best Poets), and several selections, seven by individual poets—Imru' al-Qays, Bakr b. Naṭṭāḥ (d. 246/860), ʿAttābī (d. after 208/823), Manṣūr al-Namarī (d. 190/805), Abū l-ʿAtāhiya (d. 211/826), Muslim b. al-Walīd (d. ca. 207/823), and Diʿbil (d. 246/860)—and one of *rajaz* meter verse. Moreover, he produced several books combining biography and anthology, with *akhbār* of poets together with their poetry; for a discussion of Ibn Abī Ṭāhir Ṭayfūr's works, see Toorawa, *Ibn Abī Ṭāhir Ṭayfūr and Arabic Writerly Culture*, 35ff., esp. 44.

524/1129) includes eleven chapters on *muḥdath* poetry, each chapter on a separate theme, and one additional multithematic chapter on prose.

Thaʿālibī and Abū l-Faḍl al-Mīkālī (d. 436/1044–5) maintain in their introductions to *al-Muntaḥal* (The Borrowing) (also known as *Kanz al-kuttāb*, or The Treasure House for Secretaries) and *al-Muntakhal* (The Sifted Poems), respectively, that their choice of verses suits private and official correspondence (*ikhwāniyyāt* and *sulṭāniyyāt*).[79] Thaʿālibī's *Muntaḥal* is an abridgment of Mīkālī's *al-Muntakhal*; both works are divided by subject—different from those of Abū Tammām—into fifteen chapters. The first chapter, for example, collects poems on the subject of writing (*fī-l-khaṭṭ wa-l-kitāba*); the tenth deals with proverbs, maxims, and proper conduct (*fī-l-amthāl wa-l-ḥikam wa-l-ādāb*); and the fifteenth is concerned with supplications (*fī-l-adʿiya*). The chronological scope of both works includes *jāhilī, islamī, muḥdath* (modern), and *muwallad* (postclassical), as well as contemporary poets (*ʿaṣriyyūn*). The material in each chapter is arranged by poet.

Another important anthology from the fifth/eleventh century is *Rawḥ al-rūḥ* (Refreshment of the Spirit) by an anonymous anthologist who seems to have been associated with Abū Manṣūr al-Thaʿālibī.[80] The anthologist was mostly concerned with poetry of the fourth/tenth to fifth/eleventh centuries, drawing heavily from the works of Thaʿālibī and stating in the introduction that his objective was to draw together the best of the best (*al-aḥāsin min al-maḥāsin, al-nutaf min al-ṭuraf*) for use in *majālis* and in written and oral correspondence.[81] The work consists of 360 chapters (*abwāb*), each describing a theme, motif, or object, and it contains 2790 selections, of which fewer than 2 percent are prose. *Al-Uns wa-l-ʿurs* (Sociability and Companionship), attributed to Abū Saʿd Manṣūr b. al-Ḥusayn al-Ābī (d. 421/1030), consists of thirty-four chapters (*abwāb*) on various topics and is mostly devoted to poetry.[82]

---

79 See Thaʿālibī, *al-Muntaḥal*, ed. Aḥmad Abū ʿAlī (Alexandria: al-Maṭbaʿa al-Tijāriyya, 1901), 5; Mīkālī, *al-Muntakhal*, ed. Yaḥyā Wahīb al-Jubūrī (Beirut: Dār al-Gharb al-Islāmī, 2000), 49.

80 For a discussion of the work's authorship, see *Rawḥ al-rūḥ*, ed. Ibrāhīm Ṣāliḥ (Abu Dhabi: Hay'at Abū Ẓabī li-l-Thaqāfa wa-l-Turāth, 2009), 1:7–9.

81 See ibid., 1:24–5.

82 MS Paris 3034 of this work is titled *Uns al-waḥīd* and attributed to Thaʿālibī on the cover. The work is printed under the title *al-Uns wa-l-ʿurs*, ed. Īflīn Farīd Yārid (Damascus: Dār al-Numayr, 1999), and attributed to the vizier and *kātib* Abū Saʿd Manṣūr b. al-Ḥusayn al-Ābī (d. 421/1030). The editor bases the attribution to Ābī on internal and external evidence. The work has been discussed in G. Vajda, "Une anthologie sur l'amitié attribuée à al-Ṭaʿālibī," *Arabica* 18 (1971), 211–13. Vajda suggests that the author is associated with the court of Ṣāḥib b. ʿAbbād.

One frequent anthologist, Thaʿālibī, seems to have been conscious of the use of artistic forms of writing, such as poetry and *sajʿ* (rhymed prose), as a model for other forms of composition. In the work *Sajʿ al-manthūr* (Rhyming Prose, also known as *Risālat Sajʿiyyāt al-Thaʿālibī*), he collects *sajʿ* and poetry (despite the name of the work) that are to be memorized by the unspecified dedicatee and used in his *mukātabāt*.[83] Thaʿālibī also compiled other anthologies concerned with prose, poetry, or both (see chapter 2). Among his multithematic anthologies is *Man ghāba ʿanhu l-muṭrib* (The Book about He Whom the Entertainer Abandons) and *Khāṣṣ al-khāṣṣ* (Outstanding Extracts from Outstanding Authors). Both works are anthologies of elegant prose and verse, and both are divided into seven thematic chapters, with emphasis on eastern poets, including Thaʿālibī's own production.[84] The work *Makārim al-akhlāq*, attributed to Thaʿālibī, includes a chapter on descriptions and similes (*awṣāf wa-tashbīhāt*). The two terms *awṣāf* and *tashbīhāt* are often related—a novel description often includes a clever simile. This chapter collects epigrams into four sections: the description of handwriting and eloquence (*fī waṣf al-khaṭṭ wa-l-balāgha*); the description of spring, its signs, the other seasons, and other "matters" (*fī waṣf al-rabīʿ wa-āthārih wa-sāʾir fuṣūl al-sana wa-ghayrih*); the description of night and day, and celestial phenomena (*fī awṣāf al-layālī wa-l-ayyām wa-l-āthār al-ʿulwiyya*; and love poetry and related matters (*fī l-ghazal wa-mā yanḥū naḥwah*).[85]

Works of *amālī* (dictation sessions) often include much poetry and on many themes, but they follow no order.[86] Muḥammad b. al-ʿAbbās al-Yazīdī's (d. 310/922) *K. al-Marāthī* (Book of Elegies), which resembles *amālī* works, is a collection of elegies and other genres, in addition to reports and philological and lexicographical discussions.

Anthologies Based on Comparisons

Anthologies based on comparisons do not collect lines or poems featuring certain motifs; instead, they are devoted to comparing how various litterateurs use

83 See introduction of *Sajʿ al-manthūr*, MS Yeni Cami 1188, fol. 82. For other surviving manuscripts, see Bilal Orfali, "The Works of Abū Manṣūr al-Thaʿālibī," 306; see also chapter 2. The work has been edited and published by Usāma al-Buḥayrī (Riyāḍ: Kitāb al-Majalla al-ʿArabiyya, 2013), but I was not able to obtain a copy of it.

84 Chapter 3 of *Khāṣṣ al-khāṣṣ* is an exception; it groups poetry and prose featuring the comparative and superlative *afʿal* form; it is titled *fī jumlat afʿal min kadhā mansūbatan ilā aṣḥābihā naẓman wa-nathran* and seems to have been intended as a separate work dedicated to an unnamed ruler.

85 See Bilal Orfali and Ramzi Baalbaki, *The Book of Noble Character* (Leiden: Brill, 2015).

86 For a list of *amālī* works, see *GAS* 2:83–5.

those motifs. *Al-Ashbāh wa-l-naẓā'ir* (Book of Similarities and Resemblances) of the Khālidī brothers, Abū Bakr Muḥammad b. Hāshim al-Khālidī (d. 380/990) and Abū ʿUthmān Saʿīd b. Hāshim (d. 390/999), is dedicated to the relative merits of the ancients and moderns and seeks to demonstrate that the ancients actually preceded the moderns in using many of the conceits and images thought to have been innovated by modern litterateurs. However, the work does not deny the moderns their merit. In *K. Muḍāhāt amthāl Kitāb Kalīla wa-Dimna bi-mā ashbahahā min ashʿār al-ʿArab* (A Comparison of the Parables of *Kalīla wa-Dimna* with Similar Ones in Arabic Poetry), Abū ʿAbdallāh al-Yamanī (d. 400/1009) assembles *jāhilī* and *islāmī* poetry that matches the proverbs and maxims of *Kalīla wa-dimna*,[87] and perhaps falls into the category of anti-*shuʿūbiyya* literature. Works of *sariqāt* (literary borrowings) border anthology and literary criticism. They assemble poetry and compare it with earlier composition, but their agenda prohibits drawing on poetic quotations simply for their aesthetic merit. Most such works are concerned with the evolution of motifs or the comparison of two poets.[88]

Monothematic Anthologies

Monothematic anthologies are devoted to a single topic or to a few related ones. Many of these themes are also found in individual chapters of multithematic anthologies. For example, among the works that discuss the theme of love is the first volume (fifty chapters) of *K. al-Zahra* (Book of the Flower) by Abū Bakr Muḥammad b. Dāwūd al-Iṣfahānī (d. 297/909). The work's second volume addresses other themes and poetry genres (e.g., *rithā'*, *ḥikma*, *madīḥ*, *hijā'*, *fakhr*). The poet and *adīb* al-Sarī al-Raffā' (d. 366/976) gathered verses for his four-volume anthology *K. al-Muḥibb wa-l-maḥbūb wa-l-mashmūm wa-l-mashrūb* (Book of Lovers, Beloveds, Fragrant Plants, and Wine). Such anthologies on the theme of love were very common; among the early ones dealing exclusively with love and containing a considerable amount of poetry are *Iʿtilāl al-qulūb* (The Malady of Hearts) by Kharā'iṭī (d. 327/938); *ʿAṭf al-alif al-ma'lūf ʿalā l-lām al-maʿṭuf* (Book of the Inclination of the Familiar Alif toward the

87 The editor Muḥammad Yūsuf Najm doubts the authenticity of some of the poems in the work; see the introduction of Yamanī, *Muḍāhāt amthāl Kitāb Kalīla wa-Dimna*, ed. Muḥammad Yūsuf Najm (Beirut: Dār al-Thaqāfa, 1961), w–ḥ.

88 On *sariqa*, see Von Grunebaum, "The Concept of Plagiarism in Arabic Theory," *Journal of Near Eastern Studies* 3 (1944), 234–53; W. Heinrichs, "An Evaluation of *Sariqa*," in *Quaderni di studi arabi* 5–6 (1987–8), 357–68; id., "Sariqa," *EI2* suppl., 707–10, 357–68; Badawī Ṭabāna, *al-Sariqāt al-adabiyya: Dirāsa fī ibtikār al-aʿmāl al-adabiyya wa-taqlīdihā* (Beirut: Dār al-Thaqāfa, 1986).

Inclined Lām) by Abū l-Ḥasan al-Daylamī (d. early fourth/tenth century), which deals with the subject of divine love; *al-Maṣūn fī sirr al-hawā l-maknūn* (Chaste Book on the Secret of the Hidden Passion) by al-Ḥuṣrī al-Qayrawānī (d. 413/1022); *Maṣāriʿ al-ʿushshāq* (Lovers' Demises) by Ibn al-Sarrāj (d. 500/1106), which collects stories and poetry on the death of lovers; *Dhamm al-hawā* (The Condemnation of Passion) by Ibn al-Jawzī (d. 597/1200); and *Rawḍat al-qulūb wa-nuzhat al-muḥibb wa-l-maḥbūb* (The Garden of Hearts and the Pastime of Lover and Beloved) by Ibn al-Faraj ʿAbd al-Raḥmān b. Naṣr al-Shayzarī (d. sixth/twelfth century).[89]

Forgiveness and apology are the subjects of *al-ʿAfw wa-l-iʿtizār* (On Forgiveness and Apology) by Abū l-Ḥasan Muḥammad b. ʿImrān al-ʿAbdī, better known as al-Raqqām al-Baṣrī (d. 321/933). The book collects the meanings of forgiveness, reprieve, and apology, and it narrates anecdotes and *akhbār*, often with poetry, on felons and how they were forgiven, and on the proper conduct of kings in such cases. On the theme of condolences and congratulations, Muḥammad b. Sahl b. al-Marzubān (d. ca. 340/951) compiled *K. al-Tahānī wa-l-taʿāzī* (Book of Felicitations and Condolences). Mubarrad (d. 285/898) is the author of *K. al-Taʿāzī* (Book of Condolences), which mixes poetry, eloquent speeches, and *rasāʾil* with edifying anecdotes on death and dying. Friendship and its etiquette are the subjects of Abū Ḥayyān al-Tawḥīdī's *al-Ṣadāqa wa-l-ṣadīq* (On Friendship and Friends) and another work attributed to Abū Manṣūr al-Thaʿālibī, *Tarjamat al-kātib fī adab al-ṣāḥib* (The Secretary's Interpretation on the Etiquette of Friendship), which most probably dates to Thaʿālibī's time, as no material later than his death appears in it. Abū Bakr Muḥammad b. Khalaf b. al-Marzubān (d. 309/921) compiled the short work *Faḍl al-kilāb ʿalā kathīr mimman labisa l-thiyāb* (Book of the Superiority of Dogs over Many of Those Who Wear Clothes), a collection of poems and anecdotes in praise of dogs.

Fuṣūl al-tamāthīl fī tabāshīr al-surūr (Passages of Poetic Similes on Joyful Tidings) of the one-day caliph Ibn al-Muʿtazz (d. 296/908) is concerned with

---

89 For more comprehensive lists of published anthologies on love, with a discussion of their content, see Lois Arita Giffen, *Theory of Profane Love among the Arabs: The Development of the Genre* (New York: University Press, 1971), 3–50. See also Stefan Leder, *Ibn al-Ǧauzī und seine Kompilation wider die Leidenschaft: Der Traditionalist in gelehrter Überlieferung und originärer Lehre* (Beirut: Orient-Institut der Deutschen Morgenländischen Gesellschaft, 1984), 54–7; and the introduction to Shayzarī, *Rawḍat al-qulūb wa-nuzhat al-muḥibb wa-l-maḥbūb*, ed. David Semah and George Kanazi (Wiesbaden: Harrassowitz, 2003), xvii–xxii. One should add to these lists Ibn al-Bakkāʾ al-Balkhī's (d. 1040/1630), *Ghawānī al-ashwāq fī maʿānī al-ʿushshāq*, ed. George Kanazi (Wiesbaden: Harrassiwitz, 2008).

wine: its preparation, characteristics, vessels, drinking etiquette, legal rulings concerning it, and its effects on the human body. The work is divided into four chapters (*fuṣūl*), each encompassing several sections (*abwāb*) on different themes and motifs. Poetry constitutes the bulk of the work, although there are some statements from the wisdom and medical literatures. *Quṭb al-surūr fī awṣāf al-khumūr* (The Pole of Pleasure on Descriptions of Liquor) by Raqīq al-Qayrawānī (d. 425/1034) is perhaps the largest anthology of *akhbār*, anecdotes, and poetry on the subject of wine. It collects selections on the etiquette of wine drinking and wine parties, wine's curative qualities, textual citations, legal arguments, and entertaining stories, and it concludes with poetry about wine arranged alphabetically by rhyme.[90]

Another monothematic anthology is from the fifth/eleventh century, by the Spaniard Abū al-Walīd al-Ḥimyarī, *al-Badīʿ fī waṣf al-rabīʿ* (Book of the New and Marvelous in the Description of Spring), which contains artistic prose and poetry focusing on Hispano-Arabic nature poems. *K. al-Anwār wa-maḥāsin al-ashʿār* (Book of Lights and the Finest Poems) by Abū l-Ḥasan ʿAlī b. Muḥammad al-ʿAdwī al-Shimshāṭī (d. ca. 376/987) focuses on the description of weapons, camels, and horses, as well as *ayyam al-ʿArab* (pre-Islamic battles). Kushājim (d. 360/971) compiled *K. al-Maṣāyid wa-l-maṭārid* (Book of Traps and Hunting Spears), in which he describes the etiquette of hunting and chasing wild animals and assembles the best examples of the genre beside the verses of its masters Abū Nuwās and Ibn al-Muʿtazz. The Khālidī brothers are also the anthologists of *K. al-Tuḥaf wa-l-hadāyā* (Book of Gifts and Bequests), in which they collect stories about the exchange of gifts. Another work on the subject of exchanging gifts, but one that is mostly devoted to prose, is the anonymous *K. al-Dhakhāʾir wa-l-tuḥaf* (Book of Gifts and Rarities) from the fifth/eleventh century. The editor proposes that the author is the *qāḍī* Ibn al-Zubayr, based on a comparison of some passages with al-Ghazūlī's (d. 818/1415) later collec-

90 Another important late work on wine is *Ḥalbat al-Kumayt* by Muḥammad b. Ḥasan al-Nawājī (d. 859/1455). The title of this work, "The Bay's Racecourse," is a pun alluding to *Kumayt*, bay colored, being a conventional descriptor for both horses and wine. The work discusses the origins of wine, its names, appearance, advantages, addiction to it, its qualities and correct behavior for a boon companion, wine parties and their preparation, drinking vessels, singing, instrumental music, candles, and flowers and gardens. The *Adab al-nadīm* (The Etiquette of the Boon Companion) by Kushājim (d. 360/970) is devoted to the qualities and etiquette of the boon companion and encompasses much original prose by Kushājim. Although it contains some poetry, its purpose centers on what makes a good boon companion and lies outside the anthology genre. For a listing on similar literature on the boon companion, see A. J. Chejne, "The Boon Companion in Early ʿAbbāsid Times," *Journal of the American Oriental Society* 85 (1965), 327–35.

tion *al-ʿAjāʾib wa-l-ṭuraf* (Marvels and Unusual Coined Sayings).[91] The translator of the work argues against this attribution and suggests that the author is a Fāṭimid official who was in Cairo between 444/1052 and 463/1070.[92]

Two extant works, both titled *K. al-Ḥanīn ilā l-waṭan* (Book of Yearning for the Homeland), collect poetry in connection with the extreme fatigue involved in the experience of leaving one's home—the first, formerly attributed to Jāḥiẓ, is by Mūsā b. ʿĪsā al-Kisrawī (d. third/ninth century), and the second by Ibn al-Marzubān (d. ca. 345/956). *Adab al-ghurabāʾ* (Book of Strangers), attributed to Abū l-Faraj al-Iṣbahānī (d. 356/967) contains poetry about being a stranger.[93] Thaʿālibī's *Zād safar al-mulūk* (Provisions for Kings' Travels) consists of fifty chapters on the advantages and disadvantages of all types of journeys, by land or sea; the etiquette of departing, bidding farewell, arriving, and receiving travelers; and the hardships encountered while traveling, such as poison, snow, frost, excessive cold, thirst, longing for home (*al-ḥanīn ilā l-awṭān*), being an outsider (*al-ghurba*), and extreme fatigue, as well as and their cures. Similarly, *al-Manāzil wa-l-diyār* (Book of Campsites and Abodes) of Usāma b. Munqidh (d. 584/1188) collects poetry on *aṭlāl*, abodes, cities, and homelands, as well as crying for family and friends.[94]

---

91 See *K. al-Dhakhāʾir wa-l-tuḥaf*, ed. Muḥammad Ḥamīdullāh (Kuwayt: Dāʾirat al-Maṭbūʿat wa-l-Nashr, 1959), 9–12.

92 See *Book of Gifts and Rarities*, trans. Ghāda al-Ḥijjāwī al-Qaddūmī (Cambridge: Harvard Center for Middle Eastern Studies, 1996), 12–13. Stories from books on gift exchange articulating social conflict are analyzed in Jocelyn Sharlet, "Tokens of Resentment: Medieval Arabic Narratives about Gift Exchange and Social Conflict," *Journal of Arabic and Islamic Studies* 11 (2011), 62–100.

93 For a detailed discussion of the attribution of this work, see H. Kilpatrick, "On the Difficulty of Knowing Mediaeval Arab Authors: The Case of Abū l-Faraj and Pseudo-Iṣfahānī," in *Islamic Reflections, Arabic Musings: Studies in Honour of Professor Alan Jones*, ed. Robert G. Hoyland and Philip F. Kennedy (Cambridge: Gibb Memorial Trust, 2004), 230–42.

94 In addition to these specialized books, the themes of *al-ḥanīn wa-l-awṭān*, travel, and being a stranger are to be found in many multithematic anthologies in Arabic literature; for a list of these anthologies, see the introduction of al-Thaʿālibī, *Zād safar al-mulūk*, ed. Ramzi Baalbaki and Bilal Orfali (Beirut: Bibliotheca Islamica 52, 2011). For secondary sources, see Wadad [Kadi], "Dislocation and Nostalgia: *al-Ḥanīn ilā l-awṭān*: Expressions of Alienation in Early Arabic Literature," and K. Müller, "*al-Ḥanīn ilā l-awṭān* in Early *Adab* Literature," in *Myths, Historical Archetypes and Symbolic Figures in Arabic Literature*, ed. Angelika Neuwirth et al. (Beirut: Franz Steiner Verlag Stuttgart, 1999), 3–31 and 33–58; A. Arazi, "*al-Ḥanīn ilā al-awṭān* entre la Ǧāhiliyya et l'Islam: Le Bédouin et le citadin réconciliés," *Zeitschrift der deutschen morgenländischen Gesellschaft* 143 (1993), 287–327; F. Rosenthal, "The Stranger in Medieval Islam," *Arabica* 44 (1997), 35–75; Thomas Bauer,

Aging and gray hair are the subjects of *al-Shihāb fī l-shayb wa-l-shabāb* (Book of the Blaze concerning Gray Hair and Youth) by al-Sharīf al-Murtaḍā (d. 466/1044), who collected poetry by Abū Tammām, Buḥturī, and Ibn al-Rūmī, as well as his own.[95] Abū Ḥātim al-Sijistānī (d. 250/864) treated the subject of old age and wisdom in his *al-Muʿammarūn* (Long-Lived Men). Al-Murtaḍā is also the anthologist of *Ṭayf al-khayāl* (The Nightly Phantom), which brings together verses about the nightly phantom, or dreams. ʿAlī b. Ẓāfir al-Azdī's (d. 613/1216 or 623/1226) *Badāʾiʿ al-badāʾih* (Book of Astonishing Improvisations) collects poetry and anecdotes that feature remarkable improvisation (*badīha*). Poetry by women is the subject of *Ashʿār al-nisāʾ* (Poetry of Women) by Abū ʿUbaydallāh Muḥammad b. ʿImrān al-Marzubānī (d. ca. 384/994). The work concentrates on the women poets' accounts and is more of a biographical dictionary than an anthology.

Numerous anthologies containing prose and poetry have been compiled on the subject of praise and blame. A model example is *al-Maḥāsin wa-l-masāwiʾ* (Book of Beauties and Imperfections) by Ibrāhīm b. Muḥammad al-Bayhaqī (d. fourth/tenth century). Thaʿālibī's *Taḥsīn al-qabīḥ wa-taqbīḥ al-ḥasan* (Beautifying the Ugly and Uglifying the Beautiful), *al-Yawāqīt fī baʿḍ al-mawāqīt* (Book of Gems on Some Fixed Times and Places), and *al-Ẓarāʾif wa-l-laṭāʾif* (Book of Amusing and Curious Stories on the Praise of Things and

---

"Fremdheit in der klassischen arabischen Kultur und Sprache," in *Fremdes in fremden Sprachen*, ed. Brigitte Jostes and Jürgen Trabant (Munich: W. Fink, 2001), 85–105; Muḥammad Ibrāhīm al-Ḥuwwar, *al-Ḥanīn ilā l-waṭan fī l-adab al-ʿarabī ḥattā nihāyat al-ʿaṣr al-umawī* (Cairo: Dār Nahḍat Miṣr, 1973); Yaḥyā al-Jubūrī, *al-Ḥanīn wa-l-ghurba fī l-shiʿr al-ʿarabī* (ʿAmmān: Majdalāwī li-l-Nashr wa-l-Tawzīʿ, 2008). Jubūrī (14–16) also lists a number of related books that did not survive: *Ḥubb al-waṭan* (Love of the Homeland) by Jāḥiẓ (d. 255/868), *al-Shawq ilā l-awṭān* (Longing for the Homeland) by Abū Ḥātim al-Sijistānī (d. 255/868), *Ḥubb al-awṭān* by Ibn Abī Ṭāhir Ṭayfūr (d. 280/893), *al-Ḥanīn ilā l-awṭān* by al-Washshāʾ (d. 325/937), *Ḥanīn al-ibil ilā l-awṭān* (The Book of the Yearning of Camels for the Homeland) by Rabīʿa al-Baṣrī (d. late fourth or early fifth century/late tenth or early eleventh centuries) *al-liqāʾ wa-l-taslīm* (The Etiquette of Meeting and Greeting) by Abū Bakr al-Ṣūlī (d. 336/946), *al-Wadāʿ wa-l-firāq* (The Etiquette of Bidding Farewell and Parting) by Abū Ḥātim al-Bustī (d. 354/965), *al-Manāhil wa-l-aʿṭān wa-l-ḥanīn ilā l-awṭān* (The Book of the Springs and Resting Places on Yearning for the Homeland) by Rāmahrumzī (d. 360/970), *K. al-Taslīm wa-l-ziyāra* (The Book of the Etiquette of Greeting and Visiting) by Abū ʿUbaydallāh al-Marzubānī (d. ca. 384/994), *al-Ḥanīn ilā l-awṭān* by Abū Ḥayyān al-Tawḥīdī (d. 418/1027), and *al-Nuzūʿ ilā l-awṭān* (Striving for the Homeland) by Abū Saʿd ʿAbd al-Karīm b. Muḥammad al-Samʿānī (d. 562/1167).

95 On the theme of youth versus old age in premodern Arabic literature, see Hasan Shuraydi, *The Raven and the Falcon* (Leiden: Brill, 2014).

Their Opposites) treats the same topic.[96] In *al-Fāḍil fī ṣifat al-adab al-kāmil* (Excellent Book on the Description of Perfect Education), Washshā᾽ (d. 325/937) compiles *khuṭab, akhbār*, proverbs, and poetry that combine eloquence, conciseness, and excellence (*al-balāgha wa-l-ījāz wa-l-barāʿa*). A similar work on the subject of conciseness is Thaʿālibī's *al-Iʿjāz wa-l-ījāz* (Brevity and Inimitability). One can also consider these compilations as multithematic rather than monothematic because they arrange their eloquent and concise statements under various headings. In *Bard al-akbād fī l-aʿdād* (The Cooling Refreshment of Hearts Concerning the Use of Numbers) Thaʿālibī furnishes five chapters of prose and poetry dealing with numerical divisions.

Finally, Sufi anthologies and treatises often contain hundreds of lines of poetry, and many have chapters dedicated to the performance of poetry in the beatific auditions (*samāʿ*) and others on the poetic verses chosen by Sufis to illustrate their mystical experiences. This poetry is often combined with prose and is usually borrowed from the Arabic tradition of courtly poetry. Such chapters can be found, for example, in *K. al-Taʿarruf li-madhhab ahl al-taṣawwuf* (Introducing the Ways of the Sufi People) by Kalabādhī (d. 380/990 or 384/994), *al-Lumaʿ* (Book of Flashes) by Sarrāj (d. 378/988), *Tahdhīb al-asrār* (Refining Secrets) by Khargūshī (d. 407/1016), the famous treatise on Sufism by Abū l-Qāsim al-Qushayrī (d. 465/1074); the recently published *Salwat al-ʿārifīn* (Comfort of the Mystics) by Abū Khalaf al-Ṭabarī (d. ca. 470/1077), and—of special importance because of its heavy use of poetry—*K. al-Bayāḍ wa-l-sawād* (Book of Black and White) by Abū l-Ḥasan al-Sīrjānī (d. ca. 470/1077). At least two anthologies were dedicated to the use of poetry as a *mathal* (example) or *shāhid* (illustration or witness) in early Sufism: *K. al-Amthāl wa-l-istishhādāt* (Book of Examples and Poetic Illustrations) by Abū ʿAbd al-Raḥmān al-Sulamī (d. 412/1021) and *Kitāb al-shawāhid wa-l-amthāl* (Book of Poetic Illustrations and Examples) by Abū Naṣr al-Qushayrī (465/1072).[97]

Geographical Anthologies

One of the earliest occurrences, if not the earliest, in Arabic literature of employing geographical categories for anthologizing is *Ṭabaqāt fuḥūl al-shuʿarā᾽*

---

96 On this genre, see Geert Jan van Gelder, "Beautifying the Ugly and Uglifying the Beautiful: The Paradox in Classical Arabic Literature," *Journal of Semitic Studies* 48.2 (2003), 321–51.

97 On *Kitāb al-shawāhid wa-l-amthāl*, see Francesco Chiabotti, "The Spiritual and Physical Progeny of ʿAbd al-Karīm al-Qushayrī: A Preliminary Study in Abū Naṣr al-Qushayrī's (d. 514/1120) *Kitāb al-Shawāhid wa-l-Amthāl*," *Journal of Sufi Studies* 2.1 (2013), 46–77; and Mojtaba Shahsavari, "Abū Naṣr al-Qushayrī and His *Kitāb al-Shawāhid wa-l-amthāl*," *Ishraq* 3 (2012), 279–300 (see the bibliography for references).

(Classes of Champion Poets) by Ibn Sallām al-Jumaḥī (d. 231–2/845–6).[98] The *Ṭabaqāt*, however, involves other classification criteria. Ibn Sallām organizes his poets in two large chronological sections, *jāhilī* and *islāmī*,[99] each of which includes ten classes arranged in order of merit.[100] Each class contains four equally talented poets.[101] Between the two larger sections intervenes a class of four *marāthī* poets and four sections on "town poets" (*shuʿarāʾ al-qurā*), including thirty names from Madīna, Mecca, Ṭāʾif, Baḥrayn, as well as Jewish poets. In each entry, Ibn Sallām evaluates the poet and appends a sample of his poetry and *akhbār*. Throughout the work, Ibn Sallām compares the poets and justifies

98 On this important early work, see C. Brockelmann, "Das Dichterbuch des Muḥammad ibn Sallām al-Ǧumaḥī," in *Orientalische Studien Theodor Nöldeke gewidmet* I (Gieszen: Alfrad Töpelmann, 1906), 109–26; Joseph Hell, *Die Klassen der Dichter des Muḥ. B. Sallām al-Ǧumaḥī* (Leiden: Brill, 1916); G. Levi della Vida, "Sulle Ṭabaqāt aš-šuʿarāʾ di Muḥammad b. Sallām," *Revista degli studi orientali* 8 (1919), 611–36; Ṭāhā Ibrāhīm, *Taʾrīkh al-naqd al-adabī ʿinda l-ʿarab min al-ʿaṣr al-jāhilī ilā l-qarn al-rābiʿ al-hijrī* (Beirut: Dār al-Ḥikma, n.d.), 101–23; A. Trabulsi, *La critique poétique des arabes* (Damas: Institut français de Damas, 1955), 63–6; Walid Arafat, "Landmarks of Literary Criticism in the 3rd Century A.H.," *Islamic Quarterly* 13 (1969), 70–78; Iḥsān ʿAbbās, *Tārīkh al-naqd al-adabī ʿinda l-ʿarab* (Beirut: Dār Ṣādir, 1971), 78–82; Hilary Kilpatrick, "Criteria of Classification in the Ṭabaqāt fuḥūl al-shuʿarāʾ of Muḥammad b. Sallām al-Jumaḥī (d. 232/846)," in *Proceedings of the Ninth Congress of the Union Européenne des Arabisants et Islamisants*, ed. Rudolph Peters (Leiden: Brill, 1981), 141–52; A. S. Gamal, "The Organizational Principles in Ibn Sallām's Ṭabaqāt Fuḥūl al-Shuʿarāʾ: A Reconsideration," in *Tradition and Modernity in Arabic Language and Literature*, ed. J. R. Smart (New York: Routledge, 1996), 186–210; W. Ouyang, *Literary Criticism in Medieval Arabic-Islamic Culture: The Making of a Tradition* (Edinburgh: Edinburgh University Press, 1997), 94–102.

99 As Trabulsi and Kilpatrick note, the terms *pre-Islamic* and *Islamic* are not adequate, since a number of the *islāmī* poets are *jāhilī* as well. See Trabulsi, *La critique poétique des arabes*, 36; Kilpatrick, "Criteria of Classification," 142–3. Trabulsi (37) explains that the first group covers pre-Islamic and *mukhaḍram* poets, whereas the second includes the first two centuries of Islam with the exception of two *jāhilī* poets, Bashāma b. al-Ghadīr and Qurād b. Ḥanash. Kilpatrick (146ff.) points out that Ibn Sallām used other criteria beyond chronology.

100 I. Hafsi suggests that Ibn Sallām was methodologically influenced by Ibn Saʿd (d. 230/845) and his work on the classes of the companions of the Prophet, *K. al-Ṭabaqāt al-kabīr*; see "Recherches sur le genre 'Ṭabaqāt' dans la littérature arabe," *Arabica* 24 (1977), 151. Gamal rejects the idea that Ibn Sallām intended to rank the poets; see Gamal, "Organizational Principles," 196ff.

101 Ibn Sallām explains his plan of the work in the introduction, which also deals with the authenticity of poetry and the origin of the Arabic language. See Ouyang, *Literary Criticism in Medieval Arabic-Islamic Culture*, 94–102.

their inclusion in each class.[102] The division between *islāmī* and *jāhilī* groups suggests an interest in chronology, but productivity, meter, style, versatility, and tribal adherence likewise matter.[103] Awareness of geographical differences manifests in the section on town poets. As for the sections on cities, Ibn Sallām neither defends the inclusion of poets in them nor points out common geographical features.[104]

Despite occasional comments on the relationship between poetry and place in *adab* works of the third/ninth century,[105] the idea does not seem to have played a role in Arabic anthologies before Abū Manṣūr al-Thaʿālibī's *Yatīmat al-dahr fī maḥāsin ahl al-ʿaṣr*.[106] The work presents a geographic survey of all major contemporary Arabic poets, divided into four *aqsām*, from west to east: Syria and the west (Mawṣil, Egypt, al-Maghrib); Iraq; western Iran (al-Jabal, Fārs, Jurjān, and Ṭabaristān); eastern Iran (Khurāsān and Transoxania). Each section is divided into ten *abwāb* based on individual literary figures, courts and dynasties, cities, and smaller regions.[107] The geographical order of the *Yatīma*

---

102 See Kilpatrick, "Criteria of Classification," 143ff.

103 On productivity, see Ibn Sallām al-Jumaḥī, *Ṭabaqāt fuḥūl al-shuʿarāʾ*, ed. Maḥmūd Muḥammad Shākir (Cairo: Maṭbaʿat al-Madanī, 1974), 137, 151, 155, 733. With respect to meter, Ibn Sallām devotes class IX to Islamic poets who composed *rajaz*. With respect to style, *Islāmī* class VI groups Ḥijāzī poets for their distinctive regional style. On versatility, Ibn Sallām preferred Kuthayyir to Jamīl because he covered more genres; see ibid., 2:540. With respect to tribal adherence, *islāmī* class VIII is dedicated to the Banū Murra clan (see ibid., 709n1) and class X to subtribes of ʿĀmir b. Ṣaʿṣaʿa (see ibid., 770n1).

104 M. Z. Sallām considers the section on town poets as not original to *Ṭabaqāt fuḥūl al-shuʿarāʾ* since it departs from the four-poet entity applied throughout the work; see his *Taʾrīkh al-naqd al-ʿarabī ilā l-qarn al-rābiʿ al-hijrī*, 106.

105 For a discussion of these, see Jādir, *al-Thaʿālibī nāqidan wa-adīban* (Beirut: Dār al-Niḍāl, 1991), 193ff.

106 Ḥuṣrī in *Zahr al-ādāb* states that Thaʿālibī modeled the *Yatīma* on a work by Hārūn b. ʿAlī al-Munajjim al-Baghdādī (d. 288/900) titled *al-Bāriʿ fī akhbār al-shuʿarāʾ al-muwalladīn* (The Elegant Book on the Accounts of Postclassical Poets). This lost work, according to Ḥuṣrī, comprises the names of 161 poets, starting with Bashshār b. Burd and ending with Muḥammad b. ʿAbd al-Malik b. Ṣāliḥ. See al-Ḥuṣrī al-Qayrawānī, *Zahr al-ādāb wa-thimār al-albāb*, ed. ʿA. M. al-Bajāwī (Cairo: al-Bābī al-Ḥalabī, 1970), 1:220. Most probably, Ḥuṣrī means that Thaʿālibī followed Hārūn b. ʿAlī al-Munajjim in his interest in *muḥdath* poetry and not in organizing an anthology based on geography. In fact, a few *akhbār* and anthologies dealing with *muḥdath* poetry before Thaʿālibī survive. For different attitudes toward *muḥdath* poetry, see Geert J. van Gelder, "Muḥdathūn," *EI2* suppl., 637–40, and sources there. See also Stetkevych, *Abū Tammām and the Poetics of the ʿAbbāsid Age*, 5–37.

107 On the content, organization of entries, and selection and arrangement of material in *Yatīmat al-dahr* and *Tatimmat al-Yatīma*, see chapters 3 and 5. See also the introduction

was a great success, and Thaʿālibī himself compiled its first sequel, *Tatimmat al-Yatīma*. Thereafter, the *Yatīma* would influence Arabic anthologizing for centuries to come, precisely because its geographical arrangement allowed for the inclusion of many poets; it was an easy reference; and it allowed for the study of literature by city, region, and court.

Among the anthologies following in Thaʿālibī's footsteps were *Dumyat al-qaṣr wa-ʿuṣrat ahl al-ʿaṣr* (Statue of the Palace and Refuge of the People of the Present Age) by Bākharzī (d. 1075/467), *Wishāḥ Dumyat al-qaṣr wa-laqāḥ rawḍat al-ʿaṣr* (The Necklace of the Statue of the Palace and the Fertilization of the Meadow of the Age) by Abū l-Ḥasan b. Zayd al-Bayhaqī (d. 565/1169),[108] and *Kharīdat al-qaṣr wa-jarīdat al-ʿaṣr* (The Virgin Pearl of the Palace and Register of the People of the Present Age) by ʿImād al-Dīn al-Kātib al-Iṣfahānī (d. 597/1201).[109]

---

to Rowson and Bonebakker, *Computerized Listing*.

108 This work survives in an incomplete manuscript, MS Hüseyin Celebi 870, with a microfilm in Maʿhad al-Makhṭūṭat in Cairo; see Fuʾād al-Sayyid, *Fihrist al-Makhṭūṭat al-Muṣawwara* (Cairo: Dār al-Riyāḍ li-l-Ṭabʿ wa-l-Nashr, 1954–63), 1:545. Yāqūt al-Ḥamawī mentioned it several times and used it as a source; see *Muʿjam al-udabāʾ*, 239, 244, 512, 571, 633, 651, 1664, 1683, 1736–7, 1763–7, 1782–3, 1836–7, 2095, 2355, 2363, 2369.

109 Similar works compiled later than the fall of Baghdād include *Rayḥānat al-alibbāʾ wa-zahrat al-ḥayāt al-dunyā* (The Basil of the Intelligent and the Flower of Life in this World) by Shihāb al-Dīn Aḥmad b. Muḥammad al-Khafājī (d. 1069/1659) and its sequels, the *Nafḥat al-rayḥāna wa-rashḥat ṭilāʾ al-ḥāna* (The Scent of Basil and the Flowing Tavern Wine) by al-Muḥibbī (d. 1111/1699), *Sulāfat al-ʿaṣr fī maḥāsin al-shuʿarāʾ bi-kulli miṣr* (Precedence of the Age and Pressings of the Wine Grapes on the Excellence of Poets from Every Place) by Ibn Maʿṣūm al-Madanī (d. 1104/1692). Another is *Tuḥfat al-dahr wa-nafḥat al-zahr* (The Present of Time and the Scent of the Flowers) by ʿUmar b. ʿAbd al-Salām al-Dāghistānī (d. 1206/1791), MS Cambridge University Lib. Add. 785 and MS Topkapi 519. Other lost works following *al-Yatīma* include (1) *Dhayl al-Yatīma* (Continuation of the *Yatīma*) by Abū ʿAlī al-Ḥasan b. al-Muẓaffar al-Nīshāpūrī (d. 442/1051), on which see Ḥamawī, *Muʿjam al-udabāʾ*, 1016–17; and Ḥājjī Khalīfa, *Kashf al-ẓunūn ʿan asāmī al-kutub wa-l-funūn* (Baghdad: Maṭbaʿat al-Muthannā, 1972), 2049; (2) *Jinān al-janān wa-riyāḍ al-adhhān* (The Paradise of Hearts and the Gardens of Minds) by the judge Aḥmad b. ʿAlī al-Zubayr al-Aswānī al-Miṣrī (d. 562/1166), on which see *Kharīdat al-qaṣr, qism shuʿarāʾ Miṣr*, ed. Aḥmad Amīn, Shawqī Ḍayf, and Iḥsān ʿAbbās (Cairo: Lajnat al-Taʾlīf wa-l-Tarjama wa-l-Nashr, 1951), 1:200; (3) *Durrat al-wishāḥ* (The Pearl of the Necklace) by Bayhaqī (d. 565/1169), the author of *Wishāḥ al-Dumya*, on which see Ḥamawī, *Muʿjam al-udabāʾ*, 1762; and al-Ṣafadī, *al-Wāfī bi-l-wafayāt*, ed. Aḥmad al-Arnāʾūṭ and Turkī Muṣṭafā (Beirut: Dār Iḥyāʾ al-Turāth al-ʿArabī, 2000), 20:84; (4) *Zīnat al-dahr fī laṭāʾif shuʿārāʾ al-ʿaṣr* (The Ornament of Time Concerning the Subtleties of the Poets of the Age) (a sequel to *Dumyat al-qaṣr*) by Abū l-Maʿālī al-Ḥaẓīrī (d. 568/1172–3), praised by Ibn Khallikān for the large number of poets included; it was a source for him and other authors, such as

Other geographical anthologies are regional in scope. Al-Andalus stands out in this respect, and the influence of the *Yatīma* is apparent in the anthologists' prefaces and sometimes their titles. In *Al-Dhakhīra fī maḥāsin ahl al-Jazīra* (The Treasure House Concerning the Elegance of the People of the [Iberian] Peninsula), Ibn Bassām al-Shantarīnī (d. 543/1147), inspired by Thaʿālibī, whom he mentions in the introduction, collects the poetry of al-Andalus.[110] Also concerned with the poetry and prose of the Muslim West are *Qalāʾid al-ʿiqyān fī maḥāsin al-aʿyān* (The Golden Necklaces Concerning the Elegance of the Eminent People) and the *Maṭmaḥ al-anfus wa masraḥ al-taʾannus* (The Aspiring-Point for Souls and the Open Field for Familiarity) by al-Fatḥ b. Khāqān (fl. sixth/twelfth century), and the anthology of Sicilian poetry *K. al-Durra al-khaṭīra min shuʿarāʾ al-Jazīra* (Book of Great Pearls from the Poets of the [Iberian] Peninsula) by Ibn al-Qaṭṭāʿ (d. 515/1121). *Al-Muṭrib min ashʿār ahl al-Maghrib* (Amusing Book of Poetry of People from the West) by Ibn Diḥya al-Kalbī deals with poetry from al-Andalus and al-Maghrib in *isnāds*. *Kanz al-kuttāb wa-muntakhab al-ādāb* (Treasure of the Secretaries and Selecting the Proper Conduct) by Abū Isḥāq Ibrāhīm al-Fihrī al-Būnisī (d. 651/1253) is devoted to Andalusian poetry and prose.[111]

Yāqūt al-Ḥamawī, Dhahabī, and Ṣafadī—on this see Ibn Khallikān, *Wafayāt al-aʿyān* 1:144, 2:183, 189, 366, 368, 384, 390, 4:393, 450, 5:149, 6:50–51, 70, 7:230; Ḥamawī, *Muʿjam al-udabāʾ*, 262, 1350; Dhahabī, *Taʾrīkh al-Islām wa-wafayāt al-mashāhīr wa-l-aʿlām*, ed. ʿUmar ʿAbd al-Salām Tadmurī (Beirut: Dār al-Kitāb al-ʿArabī, 1993), 36 (years 521–40): 362, 39:318, 42:319; Ṣafadī, *al-Wāfī bi-l-wafayāt* 2:74, 4:105, 5:163, 8:185, 15:106, 19:310, 27:117; (5) *al-Mukhtār fī l-naẓm wa-l-nathr li-afāḍil ahl al-ʿaṣr* (The Anthology of Poetry and Prose by the Best Men of the Age) by Ibn Bishrūn al-Ṣiqillī (d. after 561/1166), on which see Ḥ. Khalīfa, *Kashf al-ẓunūn* 2:1103, 1624; and (6) *Dhayl Yatīmat al-dahr* (Continuation of *Yatīmat al-Dahr*) by Usāma b. Munqidh (d. 584/1188), on which see Ḥamawī, *Muʿjam al-udabāʾ*, 579.

110 Ḥājjī Khalīfa mentions three further works that follow the (reduced) scheme of *Yatīmat al-dahr* in al-Andalus: *al-Unmūdhaj fī shuʿarāʾ al-Qayrawān* (Specimen of the Poets of al-Qayrawān) by Abū ʿAlī al-Ḥasan b. Rashīq al-Azdī al-Mahdawī (d. 463/1071), on which see Ḥ. Khalīfa, *Kashf al-ẓunūn* 1103; *al-Mulaḥ al-ʿaṣriyya* (The Contemporary Pleasantries) by Abū l-Qāsim ʿAlī b. Jaʿfar al-Ṣiqillī (d. 515/1121), on which see ibid., 2:1103; and *al-Ḥadīqa fī shuʿarāʾ al-Andalus* (The Garden Book on the Poets of al-Andalus) by al-Ḥākim Abū al-Ṣalt Umayya b. ʿAbd al-ʿAzīz (d. 529/1134), on which see ibid., 1:646. One, however, cannot tell from these brief mentions how precisely the *Yatīma* was followed.

111 In a later period, *Rāyāt al-mubarrizīn* (The Banners of the Champions) by Ibn Saʿīd (d. 685/1286) contains poetry from al-Andalus, North Africa, and Sicily from several centuries, organized first by place, then by the poets' professions, then by century. ʿIṣām al-Dīn ʿUthmān b. ʿAlī al-ʿUmarī (twelfth/eighteenth century) is author of *al-Rawḍ al-naḍir fī tarjamat udabāʾ al-ʿaṣr* (The Blossoming Garden of the Biographies of Contemporary

Music Anthologies

The voluminous *K. al-Aghānī* by Abū l-Faraj al-Iṣbahānī (d. 356/967) stands alone in this category. It is in great part a selection of poems and *akhbār* arranged in biographies that are based on an anthology of songs.[112] Each section is introduced by a song, followed by entries on the song's poet and composer, any information about its performance, as well as generally a title indicating the subject of the subsequent *akhbār*.[113]

Anthologies on Figures of Speech

K. al-Tashbīhāt (Book of Similes) by Ibn Abī ʿAwn (d. 322/933), the Andalusian *K. al-Tashbīhāt* by Ibn al-Kattānī (d. 420/1029), and *Gharāʾib al-tanbīhāt ʿalā ʿajāʾib al-tashbīhāt* (Unusual Notices Relating to Remarkable Similes) by ʿAlī b. Ẓāfir al-Azdī (d. 613/1216 or 623/1226) are concerned with *tashbīh* (simile). A similar chapter on *awṣāf* and *tashbīhāt* is found in *Makārim al-akhlāq*, attributed to Thaʿālibī.

Puns and wordplay are the subject of Thaʿālibī's *Ajnās al-tajnīs* (Types of Paronomasia) and *al-Anīs fī ghurar al-tajnīs* (Companion to the Best Paronomasia), in which he collects examples of modern and contemporary poetry and prose. Thaʿālibī also compiled the anthology *al-Kināya wa-l-taʿrīḍ* (Book of Hints and Allusion), which presents quotations from the Qurʾān, prose, verse, and *ḥadīth* that contain allusions and metonymies. *Al-Tawfīq li-l-talfīq* (Guide to Successful Word Sewing) encompasses thirty chapters on the use of *talfīq* in different themes; *talfīq* refers to sewing, fitting, and putting together, and in this context it signifies establishing a relationship between words or terms through homogeneity of expression (by maintaining the level of style, ambiguity, assonance, and so on).[114] Abū l-Maʿālī Saʿd b. ʿAlī b. al-Qāsim al-Ḥaẓīrī al-Warrāq, known as Dallāl al-Kutub (d. 568/1172–3), deals in his voluminous *K. Lumaḥ al-mulaḥ* (Flashes of Pleasantries) with *sajʿ* and *jinās*. After a theoretical chapter outlining the different categories of both arts,

---

Litterateurs), an anthology of the poets of Iraq and Rūm, which he wrote as a sequel to *Rayḥānat al-alibbāʾ*.

112 See H. Kilpatrick, "Cosmic Correspondences: Songs as a Starting Point for an Encyclopaedic Portrayal of Culture," in *Pre-Modern Encyclopaedic Texts*, ed. Peter Binkley (Leiden: Brill, 1997), 137–46.

113 There are cases when entries are on events and relationships rather than individuals. For a detailed study of the structure of *K. al-Aghānī* and its composition, see Kilpatrick, *Making the Great Book of Songs*.

114 For this technical use of the term *talfīq*, with examples, see M. Ullmann, *Wörterbuch der klassischen arabischen Sprache, Lām* (Wiesbaden: Harrassowitz, 1989), *talfīq*, 1035.

Ḥaẓīrī arranges poetry and prose featuring *jinās* and/or *sajʿ* solely based on rhyme, thus bringing together poetry of many themes into a single category.

Chronological Biographical Anthologies

Chronological biographical anthologies collect choice poetry of poets arranged in a chronological order. The third part of Thaʿālibī's *Lubāb al-ādāb* (Core of Culture) collects the best poetry from a considerable number of poets from the pre-Islamic era up to the anthologist's lifetime (the first part is lexicographical and the second prose). Shortly after the fall of Baghdad, Ibn Saʿīd al-Gharnāṭī (d. 685/1286) devoted his *ʿUnwān al-murqiṣāt wa-l-muṭribāt* (Verse Patterns That Evoke Dance and Song) to strikingly original such verses presented in chronological order.

Anthologies on One Poet

Several anthologies have been compiled from the works of single, well-known poets. For example, al-Khālidiyyān compiled individual anthologies from the poetry of Bashshār b. Burd, Muslim b. al-Walīd, Ibn al-Muʿtazz, and Buḥturī.[115] ʿUmar b. ʿAlī b. Muḥammad al-Muṭṭawwiʿī (d. ca. 440/1121) compiled ten chapters of the prose and poetry of Abū l-Faḍl al-Mīkālī under the title *Darj al-ghurar wa-durj al-durar* (Register of Beauties and the Drawer of Pearls). In *Durrat al-tāj min shiʿr Ibn al-Ḥajjāj* (The Crown Pearl of Ibn al-Ḥajjāj's Poetry), Hibatullāh Badīʿ al-Zamān al-Asṭurlābī (d. 534/1139–40) anthologized the subtleties and clever sayings found in the ribald poetry of Ibn al-Ḥajjāj (d. 391/1001), to facilitate its use by the *kuttāb* and the *udabā*ʾ, who needed poetry to express ideas and describe situations but lacked the talent to compose poetry themselves.[116] Finally, ʿAbd al-Qāhir al-Jurjānī (d. 471/1078) selected brief passages from the *dīwān*s of Mutanabbī, Abū Tammām, and Buḥturī.[117]

115 See Hamori, "Anthologies," *EI3*; see also *GAS* 2:457, 627–8.

116 See Asṭurlābī, *Durrat al-tāj min shiʿr Ibn al-Ḥajjāj*, ed. ʿAlī Jawād al-Ṭāhir (Baghdad: Manshūrāt al-Jamal, 2009), 42, 52.

117 These selections are published in ʿAbd al-ʿAzīz al-Maymunī, *al-Ṭarāʾif al-adabiyya* (Cairo: Maṭbaʿat Lajnat al-Taʾlīf wa-l-Tarjama wa-Nashr, 1937), 196–305. Aʿlam al-Shantamarī collected the poetry of six pre-Islamic poets in his *ashʿār al-shuʿarāʾ al-sitta al-jāhiliyyīn* (Poetry of Six Pre-Islamic Poets), but each section of the work constitutes a *dīwān* for one of the poets and cannot be regarded as an anthology.

CHAPTER 2

Life and Legacy of Thaʿālibī

Abū Manṣūr al-Thaʿālibī

Abū Manṣūr ʿAbd al-Malik b. Muḥammad b. Ismāʿīl al-Thaʿālibī was an *adīb*, poet, critic, lexicographer, historian of literature, prolific scholar, and a towering figure in Arabic literature in the second half of the fourth/tenth century and the first half of the fifth/eleventh century.[1] His earliest biographers list dozens of books that he compiled, and modern scholars list many more that are attributed to him. There is no doubt that much of the literature from the fourth/tenth to fifth/eleventh centuries would be lost without the efforts of Thaʿālibī, who wrote in Arabic and promoted Arabic literature in the eastern parts of the Islamic world.

His *nisba* refers to a furrier or tailor who works with fox fur, which prompted Ibn Khallikān (d. 681/1282) and other later classical and modern biographers

1 For a detailed biography of Thaʿālibī, see Bilal Orfali, *The Art of Anthology: Al-Thaʿālibī and His Yatīmat al-dahr*, PhD diss., Yale University, 2009; Everett Rowson, "al-Thaʿālibī, Abū Manṣūr ʿAbd al-Malik b. Muḥammad b. Ismāʿīl," *EI2* X:426a–427b; *GAL* I:284–6, SI:499–502; C. E. Bosworth, trans., *The Laṭāʾif al-Maʿārif of Thaʿālibī* [*The Book of Curious and Entertaining Information*] (Edinburgh: Edinburgh University Press 1968), 1–31; M. ʿA. al-Jādir, *al-Thaʿālibī nāqidan wa-adīban* (Beirut: Dār al-Niḍāl, 1991), 15–132; Zakī Mubārak, *al-Nathr al-fannī fī l-qarn al-rābiʿ* (Cairo: al-Maktaba al-Tijāriyya al-Kubrā, [1957]), 2:179–90. For primary sources, see (arranged chronologically) al-Ḥuṣrī al-Qayrawānī, *Zahr al-ādāb*, ed. ʿA. M. al-Bajāwī (Cairo: al-Bābī al-Ḥalabī, 1970), 1:127–8; Bākharzī, *Dumyat al-qaṣr wa ʿuṣrat ahl al-ʿaṣr*, ed. Muḥammad al-Ṭūnjī (Beirut: Dār al-Jīl, 1993), 2:966–7; Shantarīnī, *al-Dhakhīra fī maḥāsin ahl al-Jazīra*, ed. Iḥsān ʿAbbās (Beirut: Dār Ṣādir, 1998), 8:560–83; Ibn al-Anbārī, *Nuzhat al-alibbāʾ*, ed. Muḥammad Abū l-Faḍl Ibrāhīm (Cairo: Dār Nahḍat Miṣr, 1967), 365; Kalāʿī, *Iḥkām ṣanʿat al-kalām*, ed. Muḥammad Riḍwān al-Dāya (Beirut: ʿĀlam al-Kutub, 1985), 224–5; Ibn Khallikān, *Wafayāt al-aʿyān wa-anbāʾ abnāʾ al-zamān*, ed. Iḥsān ʿAbbās (Beirut: Dār Ṣādir, 1968), 3:178–90; Dhahabī, *al-ʿIbar fī khabar man ghabar* (Kuwayt: Dār al-Maṭbūʿāt wa-l-Nashr, 1960–86), 3:172; id., *Siyar aʿlām al-nubalāʾ*, ed. Shuʿayb al-Arnaʾūṭ (Beirut: Muʾassasat al-Risāla, 1990–92), 17:437–8; id., *Taʾrīkh al-Islām wa-wafayāt al-mashāhīr wa-l-aʿlām*, ed. ʿUmar ʿAbd al-Salām Tadmurī (Beirut: Dār al-Kitāb al-ʿArabī, 1993), 29:291–3; Ṣafadī, *al-Wāfī bi-l-wafayāt*, ed. Aḥmad al-Arnāʾūṭ and Turkī Muṣṭafā (Beirut: Dār Iḥyāʾ al-Turāth al-ʿArabī, 2000), 19:130–34; Kutubī, *ʿUyūn al-tawārīkh*, Ms. Ẓāhiriyya 45, 13:179v–181v; Yāfiʿī, *Mirʾāt al-jinān* (Beirut: Muʾassasat al-Aʿlamī, 1970), 3:53–4; Damīrī, *Ḥayāt al-ḥayawān* (Damascus: Dār Ṭalās, 1989), 1:223–4; ʿAbbāsī, *Maʿāhid al-tanṣīṣ*, ed. Muḥammad Muḥyī al-Dīn ʿAbd al-Ḥamīd (Beirut: ʿĀlam al-Kutub, 1947), 266–71.

 | DOI 10.1163/9789004317352_003

to consider this Thaʿālibī's first occupation.[2] However, no evidence in early sources or in Thaʿālibī's works supports this claim. Jādir suggests that Thaʿālibī's father held this occupation, citing a sentence from *Nathr al-naẓm* indicating that Abū Manṣūr was Ibn al-Thaʿālibī al-Nīshāpūrī (the son of al-Thaʿālibī from Nīshāpūr).[3]

Sources agree that Thaʿālibī was born in 350/961 in Nīshāpūr. The date of 429/1039 for his death seems to be firm, for it is given by Bākharzī, who lived a generation later and whose father was Thaʿālibī's neighbor. Thaʿālibī, in his poetry, mentions that he inherited from his father a property (*ḍayʿa*), which he squandered in his quest for *adab*.[4]

Thaʿālibī's life was politically unstable because of continual conflicts between the Būyid, Sāmānid, Ghaznavid, and Saljūq rulers who had created independent states that had become destinations for itinerant poets and prose writers. Hence, throughout his life, Thaʿālibī traveled extensively throughout the eastern part of the Islamic world, visiting centers of learning and meeting other prominent figures of his time. These travels allowed him to collect directly from various authors or written works the vast amount of material he deploys in his numerous, wide-ranging works, many of which are dedicated to his prominent patrons.

Thaʿālibī lived in Nīshāpūr and later traveled freely through the Sāmānid lands. From his book dedications to patrons and the reports he gives in his works, we know that he visited Bukhārā, Jurjān, Isfarāʾīn, Jurjāniyya, Ghazna, and Herat.[5] From his works we also know that he dedicated poems and books to his lifetime friend and supporter Abū l-Faḍl ʿUbaydallāh b. Aḥmad al-Mīkālī (d. 436/1044–5), the *amīr* Qābūs b. Wushmgīr (d. 403/1012), the *amīr* Sebüktegin (d. 412/1021), the governor of Khurāsān Abū Sahl al-Ḥamdūnī/ al-Ḥamdawī, the *amīr* Abū l-ʿAbbās Maʾmūn b. Maʾmūn Khwārizm (d. 407/1017), the Khwārizmian vizier Abū ʿAbdallāh Muḥammad b. Ḥāmid (d. after 402/1011), Abū l-Ḥasan Muḥammad b. ʿĪsā al-Karajī, the *amīr* of Ghazna Abū l-Qāsim Maḥmūd b. Nāṣir al-Dīn Sebüktegin (better known as Maḥmūd of Ghazna) (d. 421/1030), Sulṭān Maḥmūd's brother the *amīr* Abū l-Muẓaffar Naṣr b. Nāṣir al-Dīn Sebüktegin (d. 412/1021), his first vizier Abū l-ʿAbbās al-Faḍl b. ʿAlī al-Isfarāʾīnī, and the judge Abū Aḥmad Manṣūr b. Muḥammad al-Harawī

2 See Muḥammad Mandūr, *al-Naqd al-manhajī ʿinda l-ʿArab* (Cairo: Dār Nahḍat Miṣr, n.d.), 313; Muṣṭafā al-Shakʿa, *Manāhij al-taʾlīf, qism al-adab* (Beirut: Dār al-ʿIlm li-l-Malāyīn, 1974), 275.

3 See Jādir, *al-Thaʿālibī*, 22.

4 See *Dīwān al-Thaʿālibī*, ed. Māḥmūd al-Jādir (Beirut: ʿĀlam al-Kutub, 1988), 30.

5 For a chronology of these trips with references to primary sources, see Orfali, *Art of Anthology*, chap. 1.

al-Azdī. He also dedicated books to and praised Sulṭān Masʿūd of Ghazna (d. 432/1040) and to several people associated with him, such as his vizier Abū Naṣr Aḥmad b. Muḥammad b. Abī Zayd, Abū l-Ḥasan Musāfir b. al-Ḥasan, who was in charge of the Ghaznavid army in Khurāsān, and Abū l-Fatḥ al-Ḥasan b. Ibrāhīm al-Ṣaymarī who worked in Masʿūd's court and traveled to Khurāsān.[6]

In his works, Thaʿālibī drew liberally from written sources, as is evident from the numerous authors he cites without *isnād*.[7] Nevertheless, the fact that many of Thaʿālibī's works deal with contemporary literature presupposes a strong reliance on oral and aural sources, mainly because Thaʿālibī was the first to collect this literature, as he claims in the introduction to *Yatīmat al-dahr*.[8] Despite that he clearly signals the different types of sources from which he draws, it is difficult to say whether Thaʿālibī was in fact formally instructed by those whose texts he transmits. There is some evidence, however, that he studied under Abū Bakr al-Khwārizmī.[9]

Thaʿālibī had many friends, as is evident in *Yatīmat al-dahr*, *Tatimmat al-Yatīma*, and his other works. These were contemporary poets, scholars, sources for poetry or prose, people who hosted Thaʿālibī in his travels, or others who sponsored or attended *adab* gatherings. One friend whom Thaʿālibī met early in his life was Abū l-Faḍl ʿUbaydallāh b. Aḥmad al-Mīkālī. Thaʿālibī, no doubt, benefited much from Mīkālī's library and from the literary scholars who attended his *majlis*, as well as from Abū l-Faḍl himself and his works.[10] Another early friend in Thaʿālibī's life was the traditionalist and *adīb* of Nīshāpūr Abū

---

6 For exact references and discussion, see Orfali, *Art of Anthology*, chaps. 1 and 2.

7 See chapter 4; see also Gregor Schoeler, *Genesis of Literature in Islam*, trans. and in collaboration with Shawkat M. Toorawa (Edinburgh: Edinburgh University Press, 2009), 122–5.

8 See Thaʿālibī, *Yatīma* 1:17. All subsequent citations in this volume to Thaʿālibī's *Yatīma* are indicated by *Y*, and to the *Tatimma* by *T*.

9 Ibn al-Anbārī describes him saying *akhadha ʿan Abī Bakr al-Khwārizmī*; see his *Nuzhat al-alibbāʾ*, 365. In the first section of the *Yatīma*, he mentions that he has included material that Khwārizmī recited and dictated to him (*mā kāna akthar mā yunshidunī wa yuktibunī* [or *yukattibunī*]); see *Y* 1:26. Thaʿālibī ascertains this again in the entry on al-Sarī al-Raffāʾ (d. 366/976), stating that he transmitted some of the poetry he received from Khwārizmī both orally and in writing (*anshadanīhā wa-ansakhanīhā*); see *Y* 2:119.

10 Thaʿālibī acknowledges use of Mīkālī's library in *Y* 3:340 and *Fiqh al-lugha*, ed. Yāsīn al-Ayyūbī (Beirut: al-Maktaba al-ʿAṣriyya, 2000), 9. On the *majlis*, see, for example, *Y* 2:219, 4:394, 423, 432, 449. For Abū l-Faḍl al-Mīkālī's works, see Ibn Shākir al-Kutubī, *Fawāt al-wafayāt*, ed. Iḥsān ʿAbbās (Beirut: Dār Ṣādir, 1973), 2:52. Thaʿālibī's interest in the works of Mīkālī is proved by his writing *al-Muntaḥal* as an abridgment of Mīkālī's *al-Muntakhal*.

Naṣr Sahl b. al-Marzubān,[11] who continuously supported the anthologist with rare books and *dīwāns*, acted as a rich source of reports and *adab*, and occasionally compiled works especially for Thaʿālibī's use.[12] The two also engaged in literary debates and sent each other poetic riddles, some of which survive in Thaʿālibī's works.[13] Also dear to Thaʿālibī was the poet Abū l-Fatḥ al-Bustī (d. 400/1010), whom he first met in Nīshāpūr.[14] Their friendship took the form of literary correspondence and letter exchanging after Bustī left Nīshāpūr.[15]

Just as we cannot identify any of Thaʿālibī's teachers, we cannot identify his formal students. However, there is evidence that Thaʿālibī taught *Yatīmat al-dahr* in a formal literary gathering to students.[16] Moreover, Yāqūt al-Ḥamawī mentions having seen a copy of *Yatīmat al-dahr* with annotations by Yaʿqūb b. Aḥmad b. Muḥammad al-Nīshāpūrī (d. 474/1081),[17] which was recorded while studying the text with Thaʿālibī himself.[18] Yāqūt mentions another copy of the *Yatīma* copied by the judge and poet Muḥammad b. Isḥāq al-Baḥḥāthī.[19]

---

11 Originally from Iṣfahān, Ibn al-Marzubān lived for a while in Nīshāpūr, where he met Thaʿālibī; among his books are *Akhbār Ibn al-Rūmī, Akhbār Jaḥẓa al-Barmakī, Dhikr al-aḥwāl fī Shaʿbān wa-shahr Ramaḍān wa-Shawwāl*, and *al-Ādāb fī-l-ṭaʿām wa-l-sharāb*. He has an entry himself in *Y* 4:391ff.; see also Ḥamawī, *Muʿjam al-udabāʾ: Irshād al-arīb ilā maʿrifat al-adīb*, ed. Iḥsān ʿAbbās (Beirut: Dār al-Gharb al-Islāmī, 1993), 1408–9.

12 He composed at least *Akhbār Ibn al-Rūmī* especially for Thaʿālibī; see *Y* 4:392.

13 See, for example, Thaʿālibī, *al-Iqtibās min al-Qurʾān*, ed. I. al-Ṣaffār and M. M. Bahjat (Al-Manṣura: Dār al-Wafāʾ, 1992), 1:167; *Y* 4:394.

14 He describes him by saying, "We were brought together by the bond of *adab*, which is stronger than the bond of lineage"; *Y* 4:302.

15 See Thaʿālibī, *Aḥsan mā samiʿtu*, ed. A. ʿA. Tammām and S. ʿĀṣim (Beirut: Muʾassasat al-Kutub al-Thaqāfiyya, 1989), 34, 38; id., *Laṭāʾif al-maʿārif*, ed. I. al-Abyārī and Ḥ. K. al-Ṣayrafī (Cairo: Dār Iḥyāʾ al-Kutub al-ʿArabiyya, 1960), 206; id., *Khāṣṣ al-khāṣṣ*, ed. Ṣādiq al-Naqwī (Hyderabad: Maṭbūʿāt Majlis Dāʾirat al-Maʿārif al-ʿUthmāniyya, 1984), 157–8; *Y* 4:320.

16 For example, the tenth *bāb* ends in the Muḥyī al-Dīn ʿAbd al-Ḥamīd edition as follows: "This is an addendum supplemented by *al-amīr* Abū l-Faḍl ʿUbaydallāh b. Aḥmad al-Mīkālī, may God have mercy upon him, in his own handwriting at the end of the fourth volume (*mujallad*) of his copy on the authority of Thaʿālibī. *Al-Shaykh* Abū Manṣūr, may God have mercy upon him, said to one of his students while reading: I have approved the *amīr*'s action, and if you wish to record it in its place in the book, do so for I authorize you in that"; *Y* 4:450. It is worth mentioning that this addendum does not appear in MS Laleli 1959, which dates to the end of Muḥarram 569/early September 1173.

17 See his biography in *T* 201; Kutubī, *Fawāt al-wafayāt*, 2:646.

18 See Ḥamawī, *Muʿjam al-udabāʾ*, 701.

19 Ibid., 2428. For the biography of Muḥammad b. Isḥāq b. ʿAlī b. Dāwūd b. Ḥāmid Abū Jaʿfar al-Qāḍī al-Zawzanī al-Baḥḥāthī, one of Bākharzī's main sources in *Dumyat al-qaṣr*, see *T* 212; Bākharzī, *Dumyat al-qaṣr*, 1374; and Ḥamawī, *Muʿjam al-udabāʾ*, 2427.

Thaʿālibī mentions that he read the *Yatīma* with Abū l-Maḥāsin Saʿd b. Muḥammad b. Manṣūr.[20] Abū l-Faḍl Muḥammad b. al-Ḥusayn al-Bayhaqī (d. 470/1077), the famed Persian historian of the fifth/eleventh century, likewise mentions that he transmitted on the authority of Thaʿālibī when he was in Nīshāpūr.[21] Furthermore, the literary scholar al-Wāḥidī (d. ca. 469/1075), in a work that survives in the manuscript ʿĀrif Ḥikmat 154, published as *al-Daʿawāt wa-l-fuṣūl*, transmits from Thaʿālibī some of his poetry, introducing it with the words *wa-anshadanī Abū Manṣūr al-Thaʿālibī* (Abū Manṣūr al-Thaʿālibī recited to me).[22]

Jādir identifies in the *Badāʾiʿ al-badāʾih* of ʿAlī b. Ẓāfir al-Azdī (d. 613/1216) some reports whose *isnād*s end with Abū Muḥammad Ismāʿīl b. Muḥammad al-Nīshāpūrī,[23] on the authority of Thaʿālibī.[24] Finally, Jādir affirms *isnād*s for several of Thaʿālibī's works on the authority of Abū Muḥammad al-Ḥusayn b. Muḥammad b. Aḥmad al-Nīshāpūrī, and Abū Naṣr b. Muḥammad b. al-Faḍl b. Muḥammad al-Sarkhasī (or Sarakhsī) on the direct authority of Thaʿālibī.[25]

Legacy of Thaʿālibī

Thaʿālibī lived in an era when a good poet had also to be a prose writer, just as a scribe or a prose writer needed to practice poetry.[26] Thaʿālibī belonged to the group of literary scholars who mastered both arts. Early primary sources grant

20 See his biography in *T* 165; Bākharzī, *Dumyat al-qaṣr*, 573–5.

21 For Bayhaqī's biography, see Said Naficy, "Bayhaḳī," *EI2* I:1130b–2a and sources listed there. See also Bayhaqī, *Taʾrīkh-i Bayhaqī*, ed. Manūchihr Dānish Pazhūh (Tehran: Hirmand, 1380 [2002]), 624–6.

22 See Wāḥidī, *al-Daʿawāt wa-l-fuṣūl*, ed. ʿĀdil al-Furayjāt (Damascus: n.p., 2005), 91, 114, 121.

23 See his biography in *Y* 4:470.

24 See Jādir, *al-Thaʿālibī*, 54; Azdī, *Badāʾiʿ al-badāʾih*, ed. Muḥammad Abū l-Faḍl Ibrāhīm (Cairo: Maktabat al-Anjlū al-Miṣriyya, 1970), 130.

25 See Jādir, *al-Thaʿālibī*, 54; introduction to Thaʿālibī, *K. al-Tuḥaf wa-l-anwār min al-balāghāt wa-l-ashʿār*, ed. Yaḥyā al-Jubūrī (Ammān: Dār Majdalāwī, 2008), 23–4.

26 The title of Abū Hilāl al-ʿAskarī's work, *K. al-Ṣināʿatayn—al-khaṭāba wa-l-shiʿr*, "Book of the two arts: Poetry and prose," demonstrates equal emphasis on the two. In his *al-Maqāma al-Jāḥiẓiyya*, Hamadhānī uses the voice of his narrator, Abū l-Fatḥ al-Iskandarī, to criticize the celebrated Jāḥiẓ (d. 255/869) for failing in this respect. "Verily," Iskandarī claims, "Jāḥiẓ limps in one department of rhetoric and halts in the other." The narrator expands the point, saying that the eloquent man is the one "whose poetry does not detract from his prose and whose prose is not ashamed of his verse." See Badīʿ al-Zamān al-Hamadhānī, *The Maqāmāt*, trans. W.J. Pendergast (London: Luzac, 1915), 72; for the Arabic text, see id., *Maqāmāt Badīʿ al-Zamān al-Hamadhānī*, ed. M. ʿAbduh (Beirut: Dār al-Mashriq, 2000), 75.

him the title "Jāḥiẓ of Nīshāpūr."[27] Biographers and anthologists who worked shortly after his death included selections from both his prose and his poetry. He demonstrated his artistic skill in prose in the prefaces to his works,[28] the preparatory entries on poets from *Yatīmat al-dahr*, and his technique in *ḥall al-naẓm* (prosification, lit. untying the poetry), which can be seen in his *Nathr al-naẓm wa-ḥall al-ʿaqd, Siḥr al-balāgha*, and *al-Iqtibās min al-Qurʾān*.[29] As for his poetic talent, Thaʿālibī's surviving poetry displays almost all of the main

Hamadhānī's *maqāmāt* themselves are a good example of the juxtaposition of prose to poetry that is common in the literature of the period.

27 Bākharzī, *Dumyat al-qaṣr*, 2:966. According to Thaʿālibī, Ibn al-ʿAmīd is given the title of *al-Jāḥiẓ al-akhīr* (the last Jāḥiẓ); see *Y* 3:185. In later sources he is called *al-Jāḥiẓ al-thānī* (the second Jāḥiẓ); see Ibn Khallikān, *Wafayāt al-aʿyān*, 5:104; Dhahabī, *Siyar aʿlām al-nubalāʾ*, 16:137. Maḥmūd b. ʿAzīz al-ʿĀriḍ al-Khwārizmī was given the same title, *al-Jāḥiẓ al-thānī*, by Zamakhsharī; see Yāqūt al-Ḥamawī, *Muʿjam al-udabāʾ*, 2687. Hamadhānī, in *al-maqāma al-Jāḥiẓiyya*, says in the words of Iskandarī: *Yā qawmu li-kulli ʿamalin rijāl wa-li-kulli maqāmin maqāl wa-li-kulli dārin sukkān wa-li-kulli zamānin Jāḥiẓ* (O people, every work hath its men, every situation its saying, every house its occupants, and every age its Jāḥiẓ); see Hamadhānī, *Maqāmāt Badīʿ al-Zamān*, 75. Hamadhānī probably was referring to himself as the Jāḥiẓ of his own age after Ibn al-ʿAmīd. Nevertheless, the sobriquet *al-Jāḥiẓ* indicates a lofty rank among prose writers and does not necessarily imply the adoption of his literary patterns by those who were compared to him. For example, Abū Zayd al-Balkhī (d. 319/931) was called Jāḥiẓ Khurāsān (the Jāḥiẓ of Khurāsān) for his extensive range of knowledge; see Tawḥīdī, *al-Baṣāʾir wa-l-dhakhāʾir*, ed. Wadād al-Qāḍī (Beirut: Dār Ṣādir, 1988), 8:66; similarly, for Bākharzī, Thaʿālibī is the Jāḥiẓ of Nīshāpūr.

28 See Orfali, "The Art of the *Muqaddima* in the Works of Abū Manṣūr al-Thaʿālibī (d. 429/1039)," in *The Weaving of Words: Approaches to Classical Arabic Prose*, ed. Lale Behzadi and Vahid Behmardi, Beiruter Texte und Studien 112 (Würzburg: Ergon-Verlag, 2009), 181–202.

29 A thorough study of Thaʿālibī's prose was prepared by Jādir, based on Thaʿālibī's *muqaddimāt*, entries on poets from *Yatīmat al-dahr*, and various other works. In general, Jādir concentrates on Thaʿālibī's technique in *ḥall al-naẓm* (prosification, lit. untying the poetry) in his *Nathr al-naẓm wa-ḥall al-ʿaqd* and his use of *badīʿ* in general. See Jādir, *al-Thaʿālibī*, 301–33. Although Thaʿālibī implements an artistic style in his *muqaddimāt* and anthology writing, he seems to have used another less ornamental style in his *akhbār* and historical writing, given the different nature of the two genres. A comprehensive study of Thaʿālibī's prose, however, is still lacking. To conduct such a study, one would need first to verify the authenticity of some of his works. Most important in this regard is the history on Persian kings attributed to him: *Taʾrīkh ghurar al-siyar*. The problem of authorship extends to Thaʿālibī's authentic works, for in several of them, Thaʿālibī does not state whether he is quoting or composing original prose.

aghrāḍ (thematic intentions or genres) of his time.[30] His contributions to the fields of Arabic lexicography and philology, presented in his *Fiqh al-lugha* and *Thimār al-qulūb*, enjoyed wide circulation, as is evident from numerous surviving manuscripts and later abridgments of the two works. He was also a literary critic whose opinions are preserved in commentaries scattered throughout his books.[31]

Today, Thaʿālibī is best known as an anthologist of Arabic literature. His anthologies, whether multi- or monothematic, often follow the plan and purpose that are established in the introduction to the work. In these diverse works, Thaʿālibī includes literary material suitable for quotation in private and official correspondence, and he gives equal attention to prose and poetry, as well as their various combinations.

Thaʿālibī's most important contribution to Arabic literature is perhaps the literary historical work reflected in his two celebrated anthologies, *Yatīmat al-dahr* and its sequel, *Tatimmat al-Yatīma*. The originality of these two anthologies lies in the fact that they deal exclusively with contemporary literature and categorize this literature, not chronologically or thematically, but geographically by region. Both works shaped the subsequent development of the genre of Arabic literary anthology (see chapter 1).

Bibliography of Thaʿālibī

Thaʿālibī's bibliography presents numerous problems of false attribution and duplication. These problems are not always attributable to the complex process of transmission or ownership of manuscripts; sometimes they result from Thaʿālibī's own manner of working—mainly the reworking of his works, a literary and social issue that deserves some attention.

To justify the continuous reediting of his *Yatīma*, Thaʿālibī quotes the following wise saying in his preface:

---

30 Bilal Orfali, "An Addendum to the *Dīwān* of Abū Manṣūr al-Ṯaʿālibī," *Arabica* 56 (2009), 440–49.

31 For Thaʿālibī's literary opinions and theory, see Ḥasan I. al-Aḥmad, *Abʿād al-naṣṣ al-naqdī ʿinda al-Thaʿālibī* (Damascus: al-Hay'a al-ʿĀmma al-Sūriyya li-l-Kitāb, 2007); Shukrī Fayṣal, *Manāhij al-dirāsa al-adabiyya* (Cairo: Maṭbaʿat Dār al-Hanā', 1953), 170ff.; Muḥammad Mandūr, *al-Naqd al-manhajī ʿinda l-ʿarab*, 303ff.; Iḥsān ʿAbbās, *Taʾrīkh al-naqd al-adabī ʿinda l-ʿarab* (Beirut: Dār Ṣādir, 1971), 375ff.; Muḥammad Zaghlūl Sallām, *Taʾrīkh al-naqd al-adabī min al-qarn al-khāmis ilā-l-ʿāshir al-hijrī* (Cairo: Dār al-Maʿārif, n.d.), 41ff.; Jādir, *al-Thaʿālibī*, 139ff.

> The first weakness that appears in man is that he does not write a book and sleep over it without desiring on the following day to extend or abridge it; and this is only in one night, so what if it were several years?[32]

This quotation accurately describes Thaʿālibī's scholarly attitude. For Thaʿālibī, a book is a work in progress, and periodical publications of it are necessary to satisfy a "need" (*ḥāja*).[33] The circulation of a work, however, does not prevent the author or anthologist from reediting, rededicating, and even renaming it. In some instances, as in the *Yatīmat al-dahr*, there is a final version, and only that version is put into circulation, even though one or more previous versions had been widely circulated and copied, as Thaʿālibī states. Before reaching this officially published version, the work had passed through a long series of edits, which Thaʿālibī describes thus:

> I had set out to accomplish this in the year three hundred and eighty-four, when [my] age was still in its outset, and youth was still fresh. I opened it with the name of a vizier, following the convention of the people of *adab*, who do this to find favor with the people of prestige and rank.... And I recently found myself presented with many similar reports to those in it and plentiful additions that I obtained from the mouths of transmitters.... So, I started to build and demolish, enlarge and reduce, erase and confirm, copy then abrogate, and sometimes I start and do not finish, reach the middle and not the end, while days are blocking the way, promising without fulfilling, until I reached the age of maturity and experience... so I snatched a spark from within the darkness of age.... I continued in composing and revising this last version among the many versions after I changed its order, renewed its division into chapters, redid its arrangement and tightened its composition.[34]

The main reason for the reworking of the *Yatīma* seems to have been the availability of new literary material, which necessitated either including more entries or modifying old ones. However, the reasons for reworking a certain title in Thaʿālibī's bibliography differ from one case to another, and the "need" that Thaʿālibī mentions could very well be material or intellectual.

32 *Y* 1:5.

33 *Y* 1:5.

34 *Y* 1:5–6.

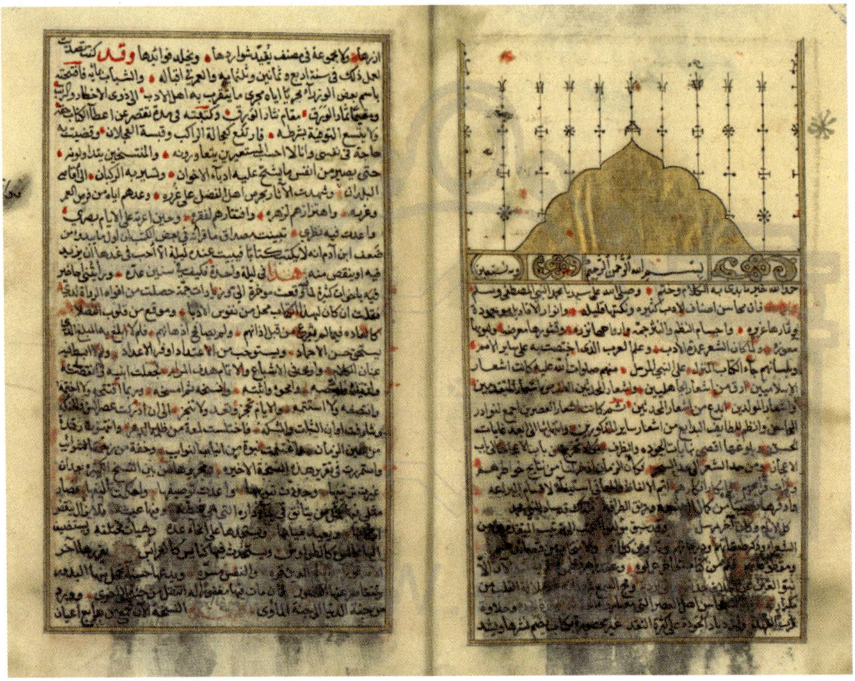

FIGURE 3 *Yatīmat al-dahr*, MS *Majlis-i Milli 3094 3v-4r*

Several of the duplicate titles of works in Thaʿālibī's bibliography result from such reworkings or rededications, as Thaʿālibī himself reveals in his prefaces.[35] In the prefaces, Thaʿālibī usually identifies the dedicatee using his titulature and/or name. These titles are helpful in identifying the dedicatee, albeit not always with accuracy, since sometimes Thaʿālibī used honorary phrases of his own invention, which are not found elsewhere in the primary sources of the period. Moreover, in several cases, Thaʿālibī is not consistent in using an honorary title, as he often bestows the same title on several patrons, or uses a different title to praise the same dedicatee in various works dedicated to him. Thaʿālibī's peripatetic travels and the diversity of his patrons and their professions complicates matters further, especially since his travel route can be reconstructed only from the dedications of his works. This difficulty has left its mark on Thaʿālibī's bibliography, since the identity of dedicatees, the chronology of the work, and sometimes its very attribution to Thaʿālibī cannot always be determined.

35 A more detailed discussion of Thaʿālibī's manner of writing, the motives behind his compilation, and the rewriting of his own works is presented in Orfali, "Art of the *Muqaddima*," 181–202.

Thaʿālibī's oeuvre is entirely in Arabic. In fact, other than the meager references to bilingual poets in the *Yatīma* and *Tatimma*, Thaʿālibī seems to have been unaffected by the rise of Persian poetry in the eastern Islamic world.[36] Many of his works survive only in manuscript and more than thirty authentic works have been published. Additionally, there are published works attributed to Thaʿālibī but lack scholarly consensus as to their authenticity.

The first detailed list of Thaʿālibī's books was given by Kalāʿī (d. sixth/twelfth century) and includes twenty-one works.[37] Ṣafadī (d. 764/1363) provides the longest list available from primary sources; his amounts to seventy works, with some duplications and false attributions.[38] Both Ibn Shākir al-Kutubī (d. 764/1363) and Ibn Qāḍī Shuhba (d. 851/1447) reproduce Ṣafadī's list.[39] Ḥājjī Khalīfa (d. 1067/1657) lists around twenty books in different entries of his *Kashf al-ẓunūn*.[40] In modern scholarship, Jurjī Zaydān mentions thirty-six works, describing the published ones and indicating the locations of those in manuscript, albeit not thoroughly.[41] The editors of *Laṭāʾif al-maʿārif* list ninety-three works,[42] while ʿAbd al-Fattāḥ al-Ḥulw counts sixty-eight, basing his list on that of al-Kutubī.[43] Brockelmann discusses fifty-one works,[44] and Sezgin gives the locations of only twelve manuscripts.[45] Ziriklī enumerates a total of thirty-

36 See Sarah Savant, *The New Muslims of Post-Conquest Iran* (Cambridge: Cambridge University Press, 2013), 122–34.

37 Kalāʿī, *Iḥkām ṣanʿat al-kalām*, 224–5.

38 See Ṣafadī, *al-Wāfī bi-l-wafayāt*, 21:194–9.

39 See Kutubī, *ʿUyūn al-tawārīkh*, Ẓāhiriyya 45, 13:179b–181b; Ibn Qāḍī Shuhba, *Ṭabaqāt al-nuḥāt wa-l-lughawiyyīn*, MS al-Ẓāhiriyya 438, 2:387–8.

40 Ḥājjī Khalīfa, *Kashf al-ẓunūn ʿan asāmī al-kutub wa-l-funūn* (Baghdad: Maṭbaʿat al-Muthannā, 1972), 14, 120, 238, 483, 523, 981, 985, 1061, 1203, 1288, 1445, 1488, 1535, 1554, 1582, 1583, 1911, 1989, 2049.

41 Jurjī Zaydān, *Taʾrīkh ādāb al-lugha al-ʿarabiyya* (Beirut: Maktabat al-Ḥayāt, 1967), 2:595.

42 See introduction to Thaʿālibī, *Laṭāʾif al-maʿārif*, ed. I. al-Abyārī and Ḥ. K. al-Ṣayrafī (Cairo: Dār Iḥyāʾ al-Kutub al-ʿArabiyya, 1960), 10–17. The editors list eighy-six works that they claim are in Ṣafadī's list, then add seven works they claim Ṣafadī missed. In fact, most of the titles they add are in Ṣafadī's list under the same or a different title. The manuscript of *al-Wāfī bi-l-wafayāt* that the editors were using must be one with additions by a later scribe or Ṣafadī himself, for most of *al-Wāfī*'s manuscripts include only seventy works. This postulate is further attested to by Kutubī's list, which copies seventy works from Ṣafadī's.

43 See introduction to Thaʿālibī, *al-Tamthīl wa-l-muḥāḍara*, ed. ʿA. al-Ḥulw (Cairo: Dār Iḥyāʾ al-Kutub al-ʿArabiyya, 1961), 14–20.

44 See *GAL* I:284–6; *GAL* SI:499–502.

45 See *GAS* VIII:231–6.

three published and unpublished works.[46] Everett Rowson describes the content of some of Thaʿālibī's authentic works.[47] A valuable tally is that of Qasim al-Samarrai, who includes thirty-eight authentic works arranged according to their dedication, as well as locations of the manuscripts.[48] Yūnus ʿAlī al-Madgharī in his introduction to *Mirʾāt al-murūʾāt* counts 128 works.[49] Hilāl Nājī collects more than one list in his introductions to editions of Thaʿālibī's works, the most extensive of which includes 109 titles.[50] The most comprehensive survey of Thaʿālibī's works, which includes a discussion of bibliographical problems and manuscript locations, has been compiled by M. ʿA. al-Jādir, in an attempt to reconstruct their chronology,[51] and including a later update with new manuscripts and editions.[52] Since then, additional manuscripts of Thaʿālibī's works have been discovered and/or published, and many published works have been reedited.

In what follows, I present an updated list of Thaʿālibī's works based on these earlier lists and newly available editions and manuscripts. For the sake of brevity, I omit manuscripts of published works; for these, one can consult Jādir's list, even if it is not comprehensive. The various titles in the headings refer to the different titles of the same work in primary sources and manuscript catalogues.[53]

Printed Authentic Works

1. *Abū l-Ṭayyib al-Mutanabbī mā lahu wa-mā ʿalayhi* = *Abū l-Ṭayyib al-Mutanabbī wa-akhbāruhu*.

This is the fifth chapter (*bāb*) of the first volume (*mujallad*) of *Yatīmat al-dahr*. Thaʿālibī, however, intended it as a separate book.[54]

46 Ziriklī, *al-Aʿlām* (Beirut: Dār al-ʿIlm li-l-Malāyīn, 1992), 4:311.

47 E. Rowson, "al-Thaʿālibī, Abū Manṣūr ʿAbd al-Malik b. Muḥammad b. Ismāʿīl," *EI2* X:426–7.

48 See Q. al-Samarrai, "Some Biographical Notes on al-Thaʿālibī," *Bibliotheca Orientalis* 32 (1975), 175–86.

49 See introduction to Thaʿālibī, *Mirʾāt al-murūʾāt*, ed. Yūnus ʿAlī al-Madgharī (Beirut: Dār Lubnān, 2003), 30–128.

50 See his introduction to Thaʿālibī, *al-Anīs fī ghurar al-tajnīs*, ed. Hilāl Nājī (Beirut: ʿĀlam al-Kutub, 1996).

51 Jādir, *al-Thaʿālibī*, 58–132.

52 See Jādir, "Dirāsa tawthīqiyya li-muʾallafāt al-Thaʿālibī," *Majallat Maʿhad al-Buḥūth wa l-Dirāsāt al-ʿArabiyya* 12 (1403/1983). This article was reprinted in *Dirāsāt tawthīqiyya wa-taḥqīqiyya fī maṣādir al-turāth* (Baghdad: Jāmiʿat Baghdād, 1990), 382–454.

53 I thank Everett Rowson for sharing his notes on Thaʿālibī's bibliography.

54 See *Y* 1:240.

FIGURE 4 *MS Bayezid Umūmī 32071*

Ed. Friedrich Dieterici: *Mutanabbi und Seifuddaula aus der Edelperle des Tsaâlibi nach Gothaer und Pariser Handschriften*, Leipzig: Fr. Chr. Wilh. Vogel, 1847; Cairo: Maṭbaʿat al-Jamāliyya, 1915; Cairo: al-Maktaba al-Tijāriyya al-Kubrā, 1925; Cairo: Maṭbaʿat Ḥijāzī, 1948; Tunis: Dār al-Maʿārif, 1997 (repr. 2000).

2. *Ādāb al-mulūk* = *Sirāj al-mulūk*[55] = *al-Mulūkī* = *al-Khwārizmiyyāt*.

This work is an example of the mirror-of-princes genre and consists of ten chapters on the following: the need for kings and the duty of obedience to them; proverbs about kings; sayings, counsel, and *tawqīʿāt* (signatory notes or apostilles) of kings; governance (*siyāsa*); the manners and customs of kings; the selection of viziers, judges, secretaries, physicians, musicians, and others; the bad manners of kings; warfare and the army; the conduct of kings; and service to kings.[56] It is dedicated in the introduction to the penultimate Maʾmūnid Khwārizmshāh, Maʾmūn b. Maʾmūn (r. 390–407/1000–1017).[57]

Ed. J. al-ʿAṭiyya, Beirut: Dār al-Gharb al-Islāmī, 1990.

3. *Aḥsan mā samiʿtu* = *Aḥsan mā samiʿtu min al-shiʿr wa-l-nathr* = *al-Laʾālī wa-l-durar*.

In this later work, Thaʿālibī extracts his particular favorites from the material he had collected, with an emphasis on modern (*muḥdath*) and eastern poets. Based on two lines in the book by Abū l-Fatḥ al-Bustī (d. 400/1010), dedicated to *al-muʾallaf lahu* (the dedicatee), Jādir suggests that Thaʿālibī dedicated the work to Abū ʿAbdallāh Muḥammad b. Ḥāmid when leaving Jurjāniyya.[58] The same two lines are attributed in the *Yatīma* to Bustī in praise of Abū ʿAbdallāh Muḥammad b. Ḥāmid.[59] Al-Samarrai points out that Thaʿālibī mentions in

55 The British Museum MS 6368 under the title *Sirāj al-mulūk*, mentioned in *GAL* SI:502, which is identical with *Ādāb al-mulūk*.

56 Such books often consist of ten chapters; see Louise Marlow, "The Way of Viziers and the Lamp of Commanders (*Minhāj al-wuzarāʾ wa-sirāj al-umarāʾ*) of Aḥmad al-Iṣfahbadhī and the Literary and Political Culture of Early Fourteenth-Century Iran," in *Writers and Rulers: Perspectives on Their Relationship from Abbasid to Safavid Times*, ed. B. Gruendler and L. Marlow (Wiesbaden: Reichert, 2004), 169–93. For the genre of mirrors for princes, see Dimitri Gutas, "Ethische Schriften im Islam," in *Orientalisches Mittelalter*, ed. W. Heinrichs (Wiesbaden: AULA-Verlag, 1990), 346–65. For the Arabic tradition, see id., *Greek Wisdom Literature in Arabic Translation: A Study of the Graeco-Arabic Gnomologia* (New Haven: American Oriental Society, 1975); id., "Classical Arabic Wisdom Literature: Nature and Scope," *Journal of the American Oriental Society* 101 (1981), 49–86 and the sources there.

57 Abū l-ʿAbbās Maʾmūn b. Maʾmūn was the penultimate Maʾmūnid. Thaʿālibī dedicated several of his books to him; see C. E. Bosworth, "Khwārazm-shāhs," *EI2* IV:1068b–1069b. See also *Ādāb al-mulūk*, ed. Jalīl ʿAṭiyya (Beirut: Dār al-Gharb al-Islāmī 1990), 29.

58 Bustī was an Arabic poet of Persian origin and a native of Bust, where he was raised and educated. He was Thaʿālibī's friend from the time of their first meeting in Nīshāpūr; see his biography in J. W. Fück, "al-Bustī, Abu' l-Fatḥ b. Muḥammad," *EI2* I:1348b and sources listed there. Ḥāmid was a vizier of Khwārizmshāh and one of the sources for the *Yatīma*; see his biography in *Y* 4:294.

59 See Jādir, *al-Thaʿālibī*, 84.

the *Yatīma* that he wrote *Aḥsan mā samiʿtu* at Bustī's request.[60] Hilāl Nājī argues, convincingly, that the work is an abridgment of the larger work *Aḥāsin al-maḥāsin*, which survives in several manuscripts. Nājī claims without offering proof that the abridgment was prepared by a later author.

Ed. M. Ṣ. ʿAnbar, Cairo: Maṭbaʿat al-Jumhūr, 1324 [1906–7] (repr. 1991); ed. and trans. O. Rescher, Leipzig: In Kommission bei O. Harrassowiz, 1916; Cairo: al-Maktaba al-Maḥmūdiyya, 1925; ed. A. ʿA. F. Tammām, Beirut: Muʾassasat al-Kutub al-Thaqāfiyya, 1989; ed. ʿA. A. ʿA. Muhannā, Beirut: Dār al-Fikr al-Lubnānī, 1990 (titled *al-Laʾālī wa-l-durar*); ed. M. I. Salīm, Cairo: Dār al-Ṭalīʿa, 1992; ed. A. ʿA. F. Tammām, Cairo: Dār al-Ṭalāʾiʿ, 1994; ed. A. Buṭrus, Tripoli: Al-Muʾassasa al-Ḥadītha li-l-Kitāb, 1999; ed. Kh. ʿI. Manṣūr, Beirut: Dār al-Kutub al-ʿIlmiyya, 2000; ed. M. Zaynahum, Cairo: al-Dār al-Thaqāfiyya, 2006.

4. *Ajnās al-tajnīs = al-Mutashābih = al-Mutashābih lafẓan wa-khaṭṭan = Tafṣīl al-siʿr fī tafḍīl al-shiʿr.*

This work is a selection of sayings illustrating paronomasia (*jinās*), with examples of modern and contemporary poetry and prose. The work is dedicated in the introduction to the Sāmānid governor and founder of the Ghaznavid dynasty, brother of Sulṭān Maḥmūd, *al-amīr al-ajall al-sayyid* Abū l-Muẓaffar Naṣr b. Nāṣir al-Dīn (Sebüktegin) (d. 412/1021).[61] Madgharī lists the section of MS Hekimoglu 946–1 titled *Tafṣīl al-siʿr as* a separate work, but in fact it is part of *Ajnās al-tajnīs*.

Ed. M. Shāfi in *Ḍamīma of Oriental College Magazine*, Lahore: May, 1950 (titled *al-Mutashābih*); ed. I. al-Sāmarrāʾī in *Majallat Kulliyyat al-Ādāb* 10 (1967), 6–33 (titled *al-Mutashābih*) (repr. Beirut: al-Dār al-ʿArabiyya, 1999; Baghdad: Maṭbaʿat al-Ḥukūma, 1967); ed. M. ʿA. al-Jādir, Beirut: ʿĀlam al-Kutub, 1997 (repr. Baghdad: Dār al-Shuʾūn al-Thaqāfiyya, 1998).

5. *al-Anīs fī ghurar al-tajnīs*. A collection of sayings on the subject of paronomasia, dedicated to *al-shaykh al-sayyid al-amīr*.[62]

---

60 See al-Samarrai, "Some Biographical Notes," 186.

61 Sulṭān Maḥmūd gave him his own place as commander of the army in the province of Khurāsān. See ʿUtbī, *Al-Yamīnī fī sharḥ akhbār al-sulṭān yamīn al-dawla wa-amīn al-milla Maḥmūd al-Ghaznawī*, ed. Iḥsān Dh. al-Thāmirī (Beirut: Dār al-Ṭalīʿa, 2004), 175; see also C. E. Bosworth, *The Ghaznavids: Their Empire in Afghanistan and Eastern Iran, 994–1040* (Edinburgh: University Press, 1963), 39–44. See also Thaʿālibī, *Ajnās al-tajnīs*, ed. M. ʿA. al-Jādir (Beirut: ʿĀlam al-Kutub, 1997), 25.

62 Thaʿālibī, *al-Anīs fī ghurar al-tajnīs*, 43.

Hilāl Najī identifies him with Mīkālī[63] based on an identical title in *Thimār al-qulūb*.[64] Thaʿālibī used this title for several rulers. Mīkālī is one of the sources for the work.

Ed. H. Nājī, *Majallat al-Majmaʿ al-ʿIlmī al-ʿIrāqī* 33 (1982), 369–80 (repr. Beirut: ʿĀlam al-Kutub, 1996).

6. *Bard al-akbād fī-l-aʿdād = al-Aʿdād.*

This is a five-chapter selection of prose and poetry dealing with lists based on numerical divisions. The dedicatee is referred to as *mawlānā* in the introduction. Jādir identifies him as the Ghaznavid official troop reviewer al-Ḥamdūnī/al-Ḥamdawī.[65] Al-Samarrai argues for Mīkālī or, possibly, Maʾmūnī.[66] Two later authors are known to have imitated the work and incorporated it in full or in part: Abū Yaḥyā Zakariyyā b. ʿAbdallāh al-Marāghī (d. sixth/twelfth century) in his *al-ʿAdad al-Maʿdūd* (MS Chester Beatty 4423) and a certain ʿAbd al-Karīm b. ʿAbd al-Munʿim al-Ṭarṭūshī in his *Bard al-akbād fī l-aʿdād* (MS Reisulkuttab 1170).[67]

In *Majmūʿat khams rasāʾil*, Istanbul: 1301/1883–4 (repr. 1325/1907; Najaf, 1970); ed. Iḥsān Dhannūn al-Thāmirī, Beirut: Dār Ibn Ḥazm, 2006.

63 Abū l-Faḍl ʿUbaydallāh al-Mīkālī belonged to one the best-known and most influential Nīshāpūr families. He is one of the main sources for and patrons of Thaʿālibī, who dedicated more than five works to him. Mīkālī was a theologian, traditionalist, poet, literary scholar, and—according to Ḥuṣrī—*raʾīs* of Nīshāpūr. See his biography in *Yatīma* 4:326; Ḥuṣrī, *Zahr al-*ādāb, 1:126; Bākharzī, *Dumyat al-qaṣr*, 2:984; Kutubī, *Fawāt al-wafayāt*, 2:52; C. E. Bosworth, "Mīkālīs," *EI2* VII:25b–26b; id., *Ghaznavids*, 176ff. For his relation with Thaʿālibī, see al-Samarrai, "Some Biographical Notes," 177–9.

64 See Thaʿālibī, *Thimār al-qulūb fī-l-muḍāf wa-l-mansūb*, ed. Muḥammad Abū l-Faḍl Ibrāhīm (Cairo: Dār Nahḍat Miṣr, 1965), 419.

65 Thaʿālibī dedicates several works to this individual. Jādir and almost all of Thaʿālibī's editors use Ḥamdūnī; al-Samarrai, however, suggests Ḥamdawī, and Bosworth uses both *nisbas*. He was an *ʿāriḍ* (troop or army reviewer) in the province of Khurāsān. According to ʿImād al-Iṣfahānī, he was *ʿamīd* of Khurāsān for Sulṭān Maḥmūd of Ghazna (d. 421/1030). After Maḥmūd's death, he was vizier to his successor Muḥammad and received further positions during Masʿūd's reign. See *T* 248; Ibn al-Athīr, *al-Kāmil fī l-Taʾrīkh*, ed. Abū l-Fidāʾ ʿAbdallāh al-Qāḍī (Beirut: Dār al-Kutub al-ʿIlmiyya, 1995), 9:379, 381, 428–9, 435–6, 446, 458; al-Samarrai, "Some Biographical Notes," 182–3; Bosworth, *Ghaznavids*, 71. See also Jādir, *al-Thaʿālibī*, 105; id., "Dirāsa," 400–401.

66 See al-Samarrai, "Some Biographical Notes," 178.

67 This scribe Yūsuf Aḥmad Jamal al-Dīn completed copying the manuscript in 19 Rabīʿ al-Awwāl 1064 (7 February 1654).

7. *Fiqh al-lugha wa-sirr al-ʿarabiyya = Sirr al-adab fī majārī kalām al-ʿArab = Shams al-adab = al-Shams = Maʿrifat al-rutab fī-mā warada min kalām al-ʿArab = al-Muntakhab min sunan al-ʿArab.*

The first half of this work is lexicographical, grouping vocabulary into thirty semantic chapters; the second half treats a variety of grammatical and lexicographical topics. Occasionally, the different titles of the work refer to constituent sections. The work enjoyed instant fame, as is evident from the number of early surviving manuscripts, and it has been versified as *Naẓm Fiqh al-lugha.*[68] The book is dedicated in its introduction to *al-amīr al-sayyid al-awḥad* Abū l-Faḍl ʿUbaydallāh b. Aḥmad al-Mīkālī (d. 436/1044).[69]

Tehran: Karakhānah-i Qulī Khan, 1855 (titled *Sirr al-adab fī majārī kalām al-ʿArab*); Cairo: Maṭbaʿat al-Ḥajar al-Nayyira al-Fākhira, 1284 [1867]; Cairo: Maṭbaʿat al-Madāris al-Malakiyya, 1880 (repr. 1900, 1994); ed. L. Cheikho, Beirut: Maṭbaʿat al-Ābāʾ al-Yasūʿiyyīn, 1885 (repr. 1903); ed. R. Daḥdāḥ, Paris: Rochaïd Dahdah, 1861; Cairo: al-Maktaba al-Adabiyya, 1899; Beirut: Dār Maktabat al-Ḥayāt, 1901 (repr. 1980); Cairo: al-Maṭbaʿa al-ʿUmūmiyya, 1901; Cairo: Maṭbaʿat al-Saʿāda, 1907; ed. M. al-Saqqā, I. al-Abyārī and ʿA. Shalabī, Cairo: Maṭbaʿat al-Ḥalabī, 1938; Cairo: al-Bābī al-Ḥalabī, 1954; Cairo: al-Maktaba al-Tijāriyya al-Kubrā, 1964; Cairo: al-Maṭbaʿa al-Ḥajariyya, 1967; Lībiyā: al-Dār al-ʿArabiyya li-l-Kitāb, 1981; ed. S. Bawwāb, Damascus: Dār al-Ḥikma, 1984; ed. F. Muḥammad and I. Yaʿqūb, Beirut: Dār al-Kitāb al-ʿArabī, 1993; Beirut: Maktabat Lubnān, 1997; ed. Kh. Fahmī and R. ʿAbd al-Tawwāb, Cairo: Maktabat al-Khānjī, 1998 (repr. 1999); ed. A. Nasīb, Beirut: Dār al-Jīl, 1998; ed. Y. Ayyūbī, Beirut: al-Maktaba al-ʿAṣriyya, 1999 (repr. 2000, 2003); commentated by Dīzīrih Saqqāl, Beirut: Dār al-Fikr al-ʿArabī 1999; ed. ʿU. al-Ṭabbāʿ, Beirut: Dār al-Arqam, 1999; ed. Ḥ. Ṭammās, Damascus: Dār al-Maʿrifa, 2004.

8. *al-Iʿjāz wa-l-ījāz = al-Ījāz wa-l-iʿjāz = K. Ghurar al-balāgha fī-l-naẓm wa-l-nathr = K. Ghurar al-balāgha wa-ṭuraf al-barāʿa.*

This work combines prose and poetry that exhibits concision. It consists of ten chapters, beginning with examples of rhetorical figures in the Qurʾān and prophetic tradition, followed by prose selections and anecdotes from a wide range of literary figures. The second half balances the prose selections with verses by influential poets from different eras. The work is dedicated to *al-qāḍī al-jalīl al-sayyid*, identified in the tenth section of the book as Manṣūr

68 Parts of this work survive in Suyūṭī, *al-Muzhir fī ʿulūm al-lugha wa-anwāʿihā*, ed. Muḥammad Abū l-Faḍl Ibrāhīm et al. (Cairo: al-Bābī al-Ḥalabī, 1958), 123, 450.

69 See Thaʿālibī, *Fiqh al-lugha*, 33.

b. Muḥammad al-Azdī al-Harawī,[70] and in one manuscript as *al-makhdūm bi-hādhā l-kitāb* (served by this book).[71] On the basis of this dedication, Jādir dates the book to 412/1021, when Thaʿālibī returned to Nīshāpūr from Ghazna.[72]

In *Khams Rasāʾil*, Istanbul: 1301 [1883–4]; ed. I. Āṣaf, Cairo: al-Maṭbaʿa al-ʿUmūmiyya, 1897; Baghdad: Maktabat Dār al-Bayān, 1972; Beirut: Dār Ṣaʿb, 1980; Beirut: Dār al-Rāʾid al-ʿArabī, 1983; Beirut: Dār al-Ghuṣūn, 1985; ed. M. al-Tunjī, Beirut: Dār al-Nafāʾis, 1992; ed. Q. R. Ṣāliḥ, Baghdad: Wizārat al-Thaqāfa—Dār al-Shuʾūn al-Thaqāfiyya, 1998 (titled *K. Ghurar al-balāgha fī-l-naẓm wa-l-nathr*); ed. M. I. Salīm, Cairo: Maktabat al-Qurʾān, 1999; ed. I. Ṣāliḥ, Damascus: Dār al-Bashāʾir, 2001 (repr. 2004); Cairo: al-Dār al-Thaqāfiyya, 2005 (repr. 2006); trans to French. O. Petit, *La beauté est le gibier des cœurs*, Paris: Sindbad, 1987.

9. *al-Iqtibās min al-Qurʾān.* Thaʿālibī's *Iqtibās* is the first book devoted exclusively to the topic of Qurʾānic quotation.

Thaʿālibī's notion of *iqtibās* (quoting the Qurʾān; lit. taking a live coal or firebrand, *qabas*, from a fire) addresses a wide range of topics that he has arranged following what appear to be several broad fields of discourse. The first part of the volume (chapters 1–5) moves from the Qurʾān as a central source of praise to God to its role in the historical foundations of the religious community. The second part of the work (chapters 6–12) considers the Qurʾānic text's place as a source of knowledge and wisdom, and as a guide to personal ethics and social comportment. The third part (chapters 13–16 and chapters 18–21) relates mainly to use of the Qurʾān in speech and writing, and prose and poetic composition. The final part (chapters 17 and 22–25) addresses the Qurʾān in dream interpretation, recitation, prayer, and magic.[73] The last two chapters may have been added by later scribes; the title of chapter 23, *fī funūn mukhtalifat al-tartīb*, is the title of the concluding chapter of several of Thaʿālibī's works. The work is dedicated to *ṣāḥib al-jaysh* Abū l-Muẓaffar Naṣr b. Nāṣir al-Dīn (Sebüktegin).[74]

70 Thaʿālibī mentions that they met while both were away from their homes and became close friends; see *T* 233.

71 Thaʿālibī, *al-Iʿjāz wa-l-ījāz*, ed. Ibrāhīm Ṣāliḥ (Damascus: Dār al-Bashāʾir, 2004), 308.

72 Jādir, *al-Thaʿālibī*, 96; id., "Dirāsa," 400.

73 For a detailed study of this work, see Bilal Orfali and Maurice Pomerantz, "'I See a Distant Fire': Al-Thaʿālibī's *Kitāb al-Iqtibās min al-Qurʾān al-Karīm*," in *Qurʾan and Adab*, ed. Omar Ali-de-Unzaga and Nuha Shaar (Oxford: Oxford University Press, forthcoming).

74 Thaʿālibī, *al-Iqtibās*, 37.

Ed. I. M. al-Ṣaffār, Baghdad: Dār al-Ḥurriyya li-l-Ṭibāʿa, 1975; ed. I. M. al-Ṣaffār and M. M. Bahjat, al-Manṣūra: Dār al-Wafāʾ, 1992 (repr. Cairo: Dār al-Wafāʾ, 1998); ed. I. M. al-Ṣaffār, ʿAmmān: Jidārā li-l-Kitāb al-ʿĀlamī, 2008.

10. *Khāṣṣ al-khāṣṣ*. This booklet epitomizes several of Thaʿālibī's earlier works.

Its seven chapters contain prose and poetry, including that of Thaʿālibī, in addition to excerpts from the Qurʾān, prophetic tradition, and proverbs. It is dedicated to *al-shaykh* Abū l-Ḥasan Musāfir b. al-Ḥasan [al-ʿĀriḍ] upon his arrival at Nīshāpūr from Ghazna with Sulṭān Masʿūd in 424/1033.[75]

Tūnis: Maṭbaʿat al-Dawla al-Tūnisiyya, 1876; Cairo: al-Khānjī, 1909; ed. M. al-Samkarī, Cairo: Maṭbaʿat al-Saʿāda, 1908; Tūnis: Maṭbaʿat al-Dawla al-Tūnisiyya, 1876; introduction by Ḥ. al-Amīn, Beirut: Dār Maktabat al-Ḥayāt, 1966 (repr. 1980, missing introduction); ed. Ṣ. al-Naqwī, Hyderabad: Maṭbūʿāt Majlis Dāʾirat al-Maʿārif al-ʿUthmāniyya, 1984; ed. M. al-Jinān, Beirut: Dār al-Kutub al-ʿIlmiyya, 1994; ed. Muḥammad Zaynahum, Cairo: al-Dār al-Thaqāfiyya li-l-Nashr, 2008.

11. *Al-Kināya wa-l-taʿrīḍ* = *al-Nihāya fī l-kināya* = *al-Nihāya fī fann al-kināya* = *al-Kunā*.

The title is a compilation of quotations from the Qurʾān, prose, verse, and prophetic tradition that contain allusions and metonymies.[76] It was originally compiled in 400/1009, then revised and rededicated in the introduction to the penultimate Khwārizmshāh Abū l-ʿAbbās Maʾmūn b. Maʾmūn in 407/1016.[77]

In *Arbaʿ rasāʾil muntakhaba min muʾallafāt al-ʿallāma al-Thaʿālibī*, Istanbul, 1301 [1883–4]; ed. M. Amīn, Makka: al-Maṭbaʿa al-Mīriyya, 1302 [1884]); ed. M. B. al-Naʿsānī al-Ḥalabī, Cairo: Maṭbaʿat al-Saʿāda, 1908 (together with Abū l-ʿAbbās al-Jurjānī: *al-Muntakhab min kināyāt al-udabāʾ wa-ishārāt al-bulaghāʾ*); in *Rasāʾil al-Thaʿālibī*, ed. ʿA. Khāqānī, Baghdad: Maktabat Dār al-Bayān, 1972; Beirut: Dār al-Kutub al-ʿIlmiyya, 1984; ed. M. F. al-Jabr, Damascus: Dār

75 He was troop reviewer of the Ghaznavid army in Khurāsān during the sultanate of Masʿūd al-Ghaznavī after the former *ʿāriḍ* Abū Sahl al-Ḥamdūnī was made civil governor of Rayy and Jibāl; see *T* 258. For the office of the *ʿāriḍ* and his duties, see Bosworth, *Ghaznavids*, 71; see also Thaʿālibī, *Khāṣṣ al-khāṣṣ*, 1.

76 On *kināya* in Arabic literature, see Erez Naaman, "Women Who Cough and Men Who Hunt: Taboo and Euphemism (*kināya*) in the Medieval Islamic World," *Journal of the American Oriental Society* 133 (2013), 467–93.

77 Thaʿālibī, *K. al-Kināya wa-l-taʿrīd aw al-Nihāya fī fann al-kināya*, ed. Faraj al-Ḥawwār (Baghdad: Manshūrāt al-Jamal, 2006), 25.

al-Ḥikma, 1994; ed. F. Hawwār, Tūnis: Dār al-Maʿārif, 1995; ed. U. al-Buḥayrī, Cairo: Maktabat al-Khānjī, 1997; ed. ʿĀ. Ḥ. Farīd, Cairo: Dār Qibāʾ, 1998; ed. M. I. Salīm, Cairo: Maktabat Ibn Sīnā, 2003; ed. F. al-Ḥawwār, Baghdad and Köln: Manshūrāt al-Jamal, 2006.

12. *Laṭāʾif al-maʿārif.*

This work assembles entertaining bits of historical lore into ten chapters. It is dedicated to a certain al-Ṣāḥib Abū l-Qāsim,[78] whom some scholars believe to be Ṣāḥib Ibn ʿAbbād (d. 385/995).[79] Jādir refutes this by proving that the book was composed after the vizier's death in 385/995. He suggests instead that it was dedicated to Abū l-Qāsim Maḥmūd b. Sebüktegin (d. 421/1030);[80] Bosworth and al-Samarrai propose the Ghaznavid vizier Abū l-Qāsim Aḥmad b. Ḥasan al-Maymandī (d. 424/1033).[81]

Ed. P. de Jong, Leiden: Brill, 1867; Cairo: al-Bābī al-Ḥalabī, 1960; ed. I. al-Abyārī and Ḥ. K. al-Ṣayrafī, Cairo: Dār Iḥyāʾ al-Kutub al-ʿArabiyya, 1960; ed. and trans. (to Uzbek) Ismatulla Abdullaev, Tashkent: 1987 (repr. Tashkent: A. Qodirii nomidagi khalq merosi nashriëti, 1995); trans. (Persian) ʿAlī Akbar Shahābī Khurāsānī (Mashhad: Muʾassasa-i Chāp wa Intishārāt-i Āstān-i Quds-i Raḍawī, 1368 [1989–90]; trans. C. E. Bosworth, *The Book of Curious and Entertaining Information*, Edinburgh: Edinburgh University Press, 1968.

13. *Laṭāʾif al-ẓurafāʾ min ṭabaqāt al-fuḍalāʾ* = *Laṭāʾif al-ṣaḥāba wa-l-tābiʿīn*= *Laṭāʾif al-luṭf.*

This twelve-chapter collection contains anecdotes about the witticisms of *ẓurafāʾ* (witty, charming, debonair persons), dedicated in the introduction to *al-shaykh al-ʿamīd* Abū Sahl al-Ḥamdūnī/al-Ḥamdawī.[82] Bosworth and al-Samarrai mention an untitled *adab* work by Thaʿālibī in MS Paris 4201/2 writ-

78 See Thaʿālibī, *Laṭāʾif al-maʿārif*, 3.

79 See, for example, E. G. Brown, *Literary History of Persia* (Cambridge: Cambridge University Press, [1928]), 2:101; introduction to Thaʿālibī, *al-Tamthīl wa-l-muḥāḍara*, 5; introduction to Thaʿālibī, *Thimār al-qulūb*, 5.

80 Abū l-Qāsim Maḥmūd served as commander of the army in Khurāsān until he became *amīr* of Ghazna after his father in 387/997; see his biography in C. E. Bosworth, "Maḥmūd b. Sebüktigin," *EI2* VI:64b; Jādir, *al-Thaʿālibī*, 87–9; id., "Dirāsa," 428–9.

81 Abū l-Qāsim Aḥmad served as Maḥmūd al-Ghaznavī's vizier from 404/1013 until 415/1020. Masʿūd brought him to power again in 421/1030, and he remained in power until his death; see Samarrai, "Some Biographical Notes," 185.

82 See Thaʿālibī, *Laṭāʾif al-ẓurafāʾ*, ed. Q. al-Samarrai (Leiden: Brill, 1978), 3.

ten for the library of Abū Sahl al-Ḥamdūnī/al-Ḥamdawī.[83] This work is actually a copy of *Laṭāʾif al-ẓurafāʾ*.

Ed. ʿU. al-Asʿad, Beirut: Dār al-Masīra, 1980 (as *Laṭāʾif al-luṭf*); ed. Q. al-Samarrai, Leiden: Brill, 1978 (facsimile); ed. ʿA. K. al-Rajab, Beirut: al-Dār al-ʿArabiyya, 1999.

14. *Lubāb al-ādāb = Sirr al-adab fī majārī kalām al-ʿArab.*

Jādir inspected a manuscript titled *Lubāb al-ādāb* (MS Jāmiʿat Baghdād 1217) and characterized it as a selection from *Siḥr al-balāgha*.[84] Qaḥṭān Rashīd Ṣāliḥ published a work of the same title based on four manuscripts, and the characteristic introduction and parallels with material found in Thaʿālibī's other works confirm his authorship.

The work consists of three parts in thirty chapters. The first part is lexicographical and draws heavily on *Fiqh al-lugha*. The second and third parts, which deal with prose and poetry, respectively, are arranged thematically. The work is dedicated to the penultimate Maʾmūnid Khwārizmshāh Maʾmūn b. Maʾmūn.

Tehran: 1272 [1855–6] (under *Sirr al-adab fī majārī kalām al-ʿarab*); ed. Ṣ. Q. Rashīd, Baghdad: Dār al-Shuʾūn al-Thaqāfiyya, 1988; ed. A. Ḥ. Basaj, Beirut: Dār al-Kutub al-ʿIlmiyya, 1997; ed. Ṣ. al-Huwwārī, Beirut: al-Maktaba al-ʿAṣriyya, 2003.

15. *al-Luṭf wa-l-laṭāʾif.* This work consists of sixteen chapters representing various professions, and it is dedicated to *mawlāna al-amīr al-sayyid al-Ṣāḥib*.

Jādir identifies him as Abū Sahl al-Ḥamdūnī/al-Ḥamdawī.[85] Al-Samarrai suggests Mīkālī or Naṣr b. Nāṣir al-Dīn Sebüktegin.[86]

Ed. M. ʿA. al-Jādir, Kuwayt: Maktabat Dār al-ʿArabiyya, 1984 (repr. Beirut: ʿĀlam al-Kutub, 1997; ed. M. ʿA. al-Jādir, Baghdad: Dār al-Shuʾūn al-Thaqāfiyya, 2002).

16. *Mā jarā bayna l-Mutanabbī wa-Sayf al-Dawla.*
Edward van Dyck states that the work was edited in Leipzig in 1835 by Gustav Flügel.[87]

---

83 Bosworth, *The Laṭāʾif al-Maʿārif*, 7; al-Samarrai, "Some Biographical Notes," 186.

84 See Jādir, "Dirāsa," 426.

85 Ibid., 429.

86 Al-Samarrai, "Some Biographical Notes," 186.

87 See Edward van Dyck, *Iktifāʾ al-qanūʿ bi-mā huwa maṭbūʿ* (Tehran: Maṭbaʿat Behman, 1988), 272. I have not been able to locate this edition.

17. *Man ghāba ʿanhu l-muṭrib = Man aʿwazahu l-muṭrib.*

Thaʿālibī wrote this book later in his life, when he was asked to extract favorites from the material he had collected on modern eastern poets. Q. al-Samarrai finds in MS. Berlin 8333 the dedicatee *al-shaykh al-ʿAmīd* and suggests that this is Ḥamdūnī or Ḥamdawī.[88] The introduction of the work is identical to that of *Aḥāsin al-maḥāsin*.

Beirut, 1831; in *al-Tuḥfa al-bahiyya*, Istanbul: 1302 [1884]; ed. M. al-Labābīdī, Beirut: al-Maṭbaʿa al-Adabiyya, 1309 [1891–2]; ed. O. Rescher, Uppsala: Almqvist and Wiksells, 1917–18; ed. N. ʿA. Shaʿlān, Cairo: Maktabat Khānjī, 1984; ed. ʿA. al-Mallūḥī, Damascus: Dār Ṭalās, 1987; ed. Y. A. al-Sāmarrāʾī, Beirut: Maktabat al-Nahḍa al-ʿArabiyya, 1987.

18. *Mirʾāt al-murūʾāt.*

This is a collection of anecdotes under the rubric of perfect virtue (*murūʾa*); it consists of fifteen chapters, each starting with the word *murūʾa*. The title of the dedicatee as given in the introduction is *al-ṣadr al-ajall al-sayyid al-Ṣāḥib akfā l-kufāt*. Jādir identifies him as Abū Sahl al-Ḥamdūnī, whereas al-Samarrai suggests Masʿūd's vizier Aḥmad b. ʿAbd al-Ṣamad.[89] The work was composed after 421/1030, the year of Sulṭān Maḥmūd of Ghazna's death; he is referred to as "the late" (*al-māḍī*).

Cairo: Maṭbaʿat al-Taraqqī, 1898; ed. Y. ʿA. al-Madgharī, Beirut: Dār Lubnān, 2003; ed. M. Kh. R. Yūsuf, Beirut: Dār Ibn Ḥazm, 2004; ed. W. b. A. al-Ḥusayn, Leeds: Majallat al-Ḥikma, 2004; ed. I. Dh. al-Thāmirī, Amman: Dār Ward, 2007.

19. *al-Mubhij.*

This collection of rhymed prose, arranged by topic and intended to inspire prose stylists, is dedicated to Qābūs b. Wushmgīr (d. 403/1012–13), the fourth ruler of the Ziyārid dynasty, who achieved great contemporary renown as a scholar and poet in both Arabic and Persian.[90] This occurred on his first visit to Jurjān, before 390/999. Thaʿālibī later reworked the book, arranging it in seventy chapters.[91] Jādir mentions a manuscript titled *al-Fawāʾid wa-l-amthāl* in MS ʿĀrif Ḥikmat 52 *qadīm*, 31 *jadīd*, Medina, which he did not examine but

88 Al-Samarrai, "Some Biographical Notes," 186.

89 He became Masʿūd's vizier after al-Maymandī in 424/1033. He died after 435/1043 while still serving Masʿūd's son, Mawdūd; see Bosworth, *Ghaznavids*, 182, 242. See also Jādir, "Dirāsa," 432, al-Samarrai, "Some Biographical Notes," 185.

90 See C. E. Bosworth, "Ḳābūs b. Wus̲h̲mgīr," *EI2* IV:357b–358b.

91 Thaʿālibī, *al-Mubhij*, ed. Ibrāhīm Ṣāliḥ (Damascus: Dār al-Bashāʾir, 1999), 23.

suggests that it is identical to *K. al-Amthāl*;[92] this manuscript is in fact a copy of *al-Mubhij*.

Cairo: Maṭbaʿat Muḥammad Maṭar, n.d.; in *Arbaʿ rasāʾil muntakhaba min muʾallafāt al-ʿallāma al-Thaʿālibī*, Istanbul, 1301 [1883–4]; Cairo: Maṭbaʿat al-Najāḥ, 1904; ed. ʿA. M. Abū Ṭālib, Ṭanṭa: Dār al-Ṣaḥāba li-l-Turāth, 1992; ed. I. Ṣāliḥ, Damascus: Dār al-Bashāʾir, 1999.

20. *al-Muntaḥal* = *Kanz al-kuttāb* = *Muntakhab al-Thaʿālibī* = *al-Muntakhab al-Mīkālī*.

This is an early collection of poetry from all periods, arranged by genre. The verses in the collection are suitable for use in both private and official correspondence (*ikhwāniyyāt* and *sulṭāniyyāt*).[93] There is confusion in the primary sources over the authorship of the book: some designate Thaʿālibī as the author, and others his friend Abū l-Faḍl al-Mīkālī.[94] Yaḥyā W. al-Jubūrī resolved the confusion by publishing the full version of al-Mīkālī's work, titled *al-Muntakhal*. A comparison of *al-Muntakhal* and *al-Muntaḥal* reveals that the latter is a selection of poems from Mīkālī's work. MS Paris 3307 of *al-Muntaḥal* preserves a more complete text than the printed one. The work is divided into fifteen chapters according to subject, and its scope includes poets from all periods, including the anthologist's own.

Ed. A. Abū ʿAlī, Alexandria: al-Maṭbaʿa al-Tijāriyya, 1321 [1901]; Cairo: Maktabat al-Thaqāfa al-Dīniyya, 1998.

21. *Nasīm al-Saḥar* = *Khaṣāʾiṣ al-lugha*.

The work is an abridgment by Thaʿālibī of his *Fiqh al-lugha* (see item 7). Jādir and al-Samarrai note that in MS Ẓāhiriyya 306, published by Khālid Fahmī, the dedicatee appears as Abū l-Fatḥ al-Ḥasan b. Ibrāhīm al-Ṣaymarī.[95] Jādir places the dedication in the year 424/1032–3 in Nīshāpūr.

Ed. M. Ḥ. Āl Yāsīn, Baghdad: *Majallat al-Kuttāb* 1 (n.d.); ed. I. M. al-Ṣaffār, Baghdad: *Majallat al-Mawrid* 1 (1971); ed. Kh. Fahmī, Cairo: Maktabat al-Khānjī, 1999 (titled *Khaṣāʾiṣ al-lugha*).

---

92 See Jādir, "Dirāsa," 424.

93 See Thaʿālibī, *al-Muntaḥal*, ed. Aḥmad Abū ʿAlī (Alexandria: al-Maṭbaʿa al-Tijāriyya, 1901), 5.

94 Ṣafadī attributes it to Thaʿālibī, and Kutubī to Mīkālī, whereas in the edition of Iḥsān ʿAbbās of Ibn Khallikān's *Wafayāt* it is attributed to Thaʿālibī once and to Mīkālī another. See Ṣafadī, *al-Wāfī bi-l-wafayāt*, 19:131; Kutubī, *ʿUyūn al-tawārīkh*, 13:181b, Ibn Khallikān, *Wafayāt al-aʿyān*, 2:361, 5:109.

95 For Ṣaymarī's biography, see Bākharzī, *Dumyat al-qaṣr*, 1:375–8. See also Jādir, *al-Thaʿālibī*, 109; id., "Dirāsa," 440; al-Samarrai, "Some Biographical Notes," 185.

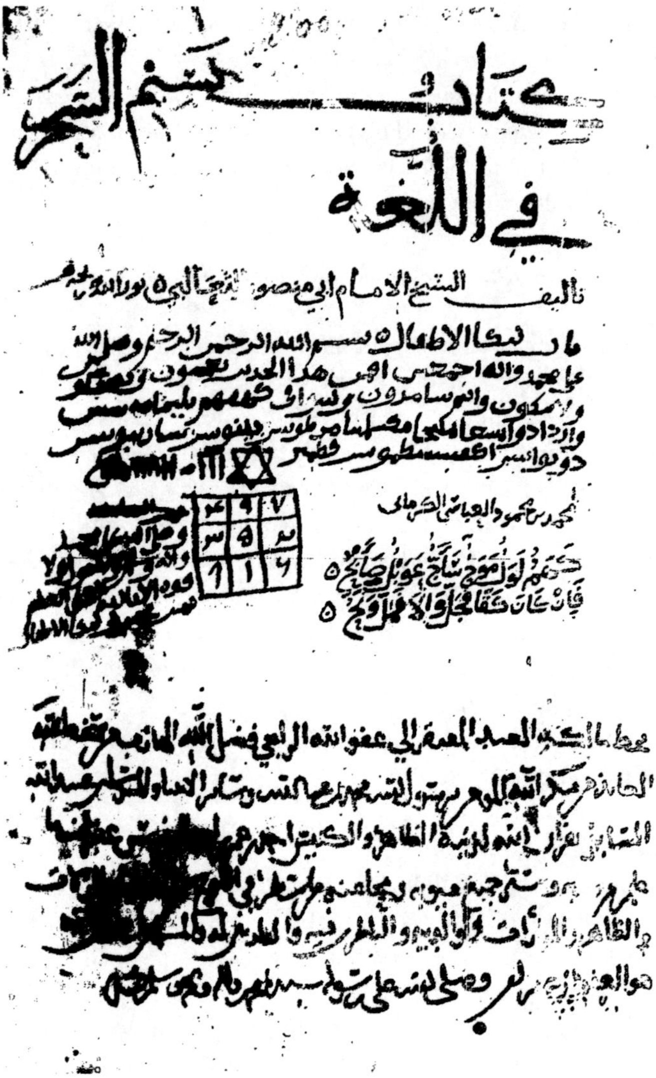

FIGURE 5 *Nasīm al-saḥar,* MS *Kuwayt Wizārat al-Awqāf 5500-1, 1v*

22. *Nathr al-naẓm wa-ḥall al-ʿaqd = Naẓm al-nathr wa-ḥall al-ʿaqd = Ḥall al-ʿaqd.*

This is a collection of rhetorical exercises recasting verses in elegant rhymed prose. The work is dedicated in the introduction to the penultimate Maʾmūnid Abū l-ʿAbbās [Maʾmūn b. Maʾmūn] Khwārizmshāh.[96]

96 See Thaʿālibī, *Nathr al-naẓm wa-ḥall al-ʿaqd*, ed. Aḥmad ʿAbd al-Fattāḥ Tammām (Beirut: Muʾassasat al-Kutub al-Thaqāfiyya, 1990), 7.

Damascus: Maṭbaʿat al-Maʿārif, 1300 [1882–3] (repr. 1301/1883–4); Cairo: al-Maṭbaʿa al-Adabiyya, 1317 [1899–1900]; in *Rasāʾil al-Thaʿālibī*, ed. ʿA. Khāqānī, Baghdad: Maktabat Dār al-Bayān, 1972; Beirut: Dār al-Rāʾid al-ʿArabī, 1983; ed. A. ʿA. Tammām, Beirut: Muʾassasat al-Kutub al-Thaqāfiyya, 1990.

23. *Sajʿ al-manthūr* = *Risālat sajʿiyyāt al-Thaʿālibī* = *Qurāḍat al-dhahab.*

This work was first mentioned by Kalāʿī, and others followed him. Jādir later mentions a manuscript of this work, MS Topkapı Ahmet III Kitāpları 2337/2; Tevfik Rüştü Topuzoğlu lists two more, MS Yeni Cami 1188 and MS Üniversite Arapça Yazmalar 741/1, and notes one more with the title *Qurāḍat al-dhahab*, MS Bayezid Umūmī 3207/1, which Jādir and Nājī list as a different work.[97] On inspection, all manuscripts include an introduction matching Thaʿālibī's style and expounding on the brevity of the work, its purpose, and his method. The work consists mostly of proverbs and poetry. Its declared purpose is for use in memorization and correspondence (*mukātabāt*). From this, it seems that Thaʿālibī views literary speech as belonging to three different registers—*nathr*, *sajʿ*, and *shiʿr*, and the *adīb* may express the same idea in more than one register, as Thaʿālibī shows here and in his *Nathr al-naẓm* (see item 22), and *Siḥr al-balāgha* (see item 24).

Ed. U. M. al-Buḥayrī, Riyāḍ: Kitāb al-Majalla al-ʿArabiyya, 2013.[98]

24. *Siḥr al-balāgha wa-sirr al-barāʿa.*

This is a collection of rhymed prose arranged in fourteen chapters and presented without attributions except for the last chapter, which credits phraseology to famous figures, such as Badīʿ al-Zamān al-Hamadhānī (d. 398/1008) and Khwārizmī (d. 383/993). The final version of the work, dedicated to ʿUbaydallāh b. Aḥmad al-Mīkālī (d. 436/1044), is the third (and possibly last) version after two previous editions "close in method and volume"; the first of these is dedicated to a certain Abū ʿImrān Mūsā b. Hārūn al-Kurdī, and the second to Abū

97 Tevfik Rüştü Topuzoğlu, "Istanbul Manuscripts of Works (Other Than *Yatīmat al-Dahr*) by Thaʿālibī," *Islamic Quarterly* 17 (1973), 68–9; Jādir, "Dirāsa," 424; introduction to Thaʿālibī, *al-Anīs fī ghurar al-tajnīs*, 40. The title given at the end of MS Bayezid Umūmī 3207/1 and on the first page of the codex is *Qurāḍāt al-dhahab*. *Qurāḍat al-dhahab fī al-naqd* is the title of a different work by Ibn Rashīq al-Qayrawānī.

98 I was not able to examine this edition, so I have based the description on available manuscripts.

Sahl al-Ḥamdūnī/al-Ḥamdawī.[99] Jādir holds that the first version of the work was completed before 403/1012, as Thaʿālibī mentions it in the *Yatīma*.[100]

In *Arbaʿ rasāʾil muntakhaba min muʾallafāt al-ʿallāma al-Thaʿālibī*, Istanbul, 1301 [1883–4]; ed. A. ʿUbayd, Damascus: al-Maktaba al-ʿArabiyya, 1931; ed. ʿA. al-Ḥūfī, Beirut: Dār al-Kutub al-ʿIlmiyya, 1984; ed. D. Juwaydī, Beirut: al-Maktaba al-ʿAṣriyya, 2006.

25. *Taḥsīn al-qabīḥ wa-taqbīḥ al-ḥasan = al-Taḥsīn wa-l-taqbīḥ.*

Here Thaʿālibī presents prose and poetry that makes the ugly seem beautiful and the beautiful, ugly.[101] The work is dedicated to the Ghaznavid courtier Abū l-Ḥasan Muḥammad b. ʿĪsā al-Karajī,[102] and Jādir places it in Ghazna between the years 407/1016 and 412/1021.[103]

Ed. Sh. ʿĀshūr, Baghdad: Wizārat al-Awqāf, 1981 (repr. Damascus: Dār al-Yanābīʿ, 2006); ed. ʿA. ʿA. Muḥammad, Cairo: Dār al-Faḍīla, 1995; ed. N. ʿA. Ḥayyāwī, Beirut: Dār al-Arqam, 2002; trans. (Persian) Muḥammad b. Abī Bakr b. ʿAlī Sāvī, ed. ʿĀrif Aḥmad al-Zughūl, Tehran: Mīrāṯ-i Maktūb 1385 [2006–7].

26. *al-Tamthīl wa-l-muḥāḍara = al-Tamaththul wa-l-muḥāḍara = Ḥilyat al-muḥāḍara = al-Maḥāsin wa-l-aḍdād = K. al-Amthāl.*[104]

This is a comprehensive collection of proverbs collected from different sources. In the introduction Thaʿālibī dedicates it to Shams al-Maʿālī Qābūs b. Wushmgīr (d. 371/981) during his second visit to Jurjān. On this basis, Jādir dates its completion between 401/1010 and 403/1012.[105] Topuzoğlu mentions nine manuscripts in Istanbul of this book.[106] In an unpublished dissertation, Zahiyya Saʿdū presents a study and critical edition of the work based on the oldest extant manuscripts, including MS Leiden Or. 454.[107]

---

99 See Thaʿālibī, *Siḥr al-balāgha wa-sirr al-barāʿa*, ed. ʿA. al-Ḥūfī (Beirut: Dār al-Kutub al-ʿIlmiyya, 1984), 4.

100 Jādir, *al-Thaʿālibī*, 68; id., "Dirāsa," 412.

101 On this genre in Arabic literature, see van Gelder, "Beautifying the Ugly and Uglifying the Beautiful," *Journal of Semitic Studies* 48.2 (2003), 321–51.

102 He was closely associated with Sulṭān Maḥmūd of Ghazna; see *T* 256–8.

103 Jādir, "Dirāsa," 402.

104 MS al-Maktaba al-Aḥmadiyya 4734, Tunis, carries the title of *al-Amthāl* and is an exact copy of *al-Tamthīl wa-l-muḥāḍara*.

105 See Jādir, *al-Thaʿālibī*, 70; id., "Dirāsa," 406.

106 Topuzoğlu, "Istanbul Manuscripts of Works," 64–74.

107 Zahiyya Saʿdū, *al-Tamaththul wa-l-muḥāḍara li-Abī Manṣūr al-Thaʿālibī: Dirāsa wa-taḥqīq*, PhD diss., Jāmiʿat al-Jazāʾir, 2005–6.

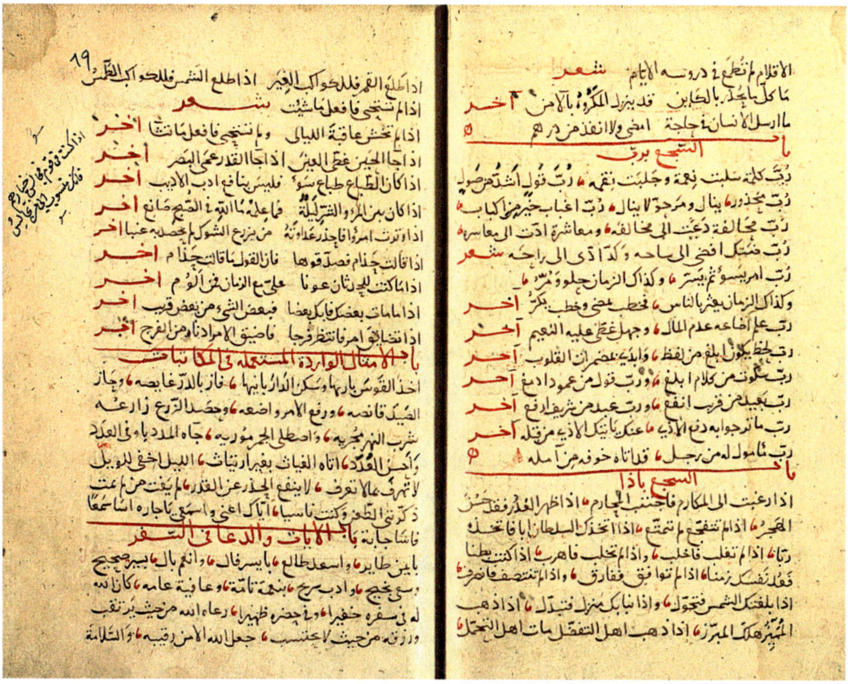

FIGURE 6 *Sajʿ al-manthūr*, MS Yeni Cami 1188, 88v–89r

In *Arbaʿ rasāʾil muntakhaba min muʾallafāt al-ʿallāma al-Thaʿālibī*, Istanbul, 1301 [1883–4]; ed. ʿA. M. al-Ḥulw, Cairo: Dār Iḥyāʾ al-Kutub al-ʿArabiyya, 1961 (repr. Cairo: al-Dār al-ʿArabiyya li-l-Kitāb, 1983); ed. Q. al-Ḥusayn, Beirut: Dār wa-Maktabat al-Hilāl, 2003.

27. *Tatimmat Yatīmat al-dahr* = *Tatimmat al-Yatīma*.

This is the supplement to *Yatīmat al-dahr* following the same principles of organization but including writers whom Thaʿālibī came to know later in his life. Like the *Yatīma*, Thaʿālibī reedited it later with several additions. Thaʿālibī states in the introduction that the first edition was dedicated to the Ghaznavid courtier *al-shaykh* Abū l-Ḥasan Muḥammad b. ʿĪsā al-Karajī. The second edition includes events that took place in year 424/1032 and thus dates to after that year. Thaʿālibī adds an epilogue that does not follow his method of geographical arrangement but includes those poets he had forgotten to include in the first four sections. The work has been critically edited in an unpublished dissertation by A. Sh. Radwan, *Thaʿalibi's Tatimmat al-Yatimah: A critical edition and a study of the author as anthologist and literary critic* (PhD diss.), University of Manchester, 1972. Radwan's edition is based on five manuscripts, the oldest of which is dated 637/1240. The text of this edition corrects numerous mistakes in Iqbāl's edition, which is based only on a single manuscript, MS arabe Paris 3308 (fols. 498–591).

ʿAbbās Iqbāl, Tehran: Maṭbaʿat Fardīn, 1934; M. M. Qumayḥa, Beirut: Dār al-Kutub al-ʿIlmiyya, 1983.

28. *al-Tawfīq li-l-talfīq*.

This work encompasses thirty chapters on the use of *talfīq* in different themes. *Talfīq* connotes sewing, fitting, and putting together, and in this context it signifies establishing a relationship between words or terms through homogeneity of expression (by maintaining the level of style, ambiguity, assonance, and so on). It is dedicated in the introduction to *al-shaykh al-sayyid*. Ibrāhīm Ṣāliḥ argues in his introduction of the edition that Thaʿālibī means Abū l-Ḥasan Musāfir b. al-Ḥasan here, on the basis of a passage from *Khāṣṣ al-khāṣṣ* (see item 10), in which Thaʿālibī addresses him by the title *al-shaykh al-sayyid*.[108] Nevertheless, this is not certain, as Thaʿālibī dedicated *Mirʾāt al-murūʾāt* to *al-shaykh al-ajall al-sayyid al-Ṣāḥib akfā l-kufāt* and *Taḥsīn al-qabīḥ* to *al-shaykh al-sayyid* Abū l-Ḥasan Muḥammad b. ʿĪsā al-Karajī.[109]

Ed. I. Ṣāliḥ, Damascus: Majmaʿ al-Lugha al-ʿArabiyya, 1983 (repr. Beirut: Dār al-Fikr al-Muʿāṣir, 1990); ed. H. Nājī and Z. Gh. Zāhid, Baghdad: Maṭbaʿat al-Majmaʿ al-ʿIlmī al-ʿIrāqī, 1985 (repr. Beirut: ʿĀlam al-Kutub, 1996).

29. *Thimār al-qulūb fī-l-muḍāf wa-l-mansūb* = *al-Muḍāf wa-l-mansūb*.

This is an alphabetically arranged lexicon of two-word phrases and clichés, dedicated in the introduction to Thaʿālibī's friend, the Nīshāpūrī notable Abū l-Faḍl al-Mīkālī. Jādir dates this after year 421/1030 because Thaʿālibī mentions the death of Sulṭān Maḥmūd al-Ghaznawī, which occurred earlier that year.[110] Jādir adds a list of later abridgments of the work.[111] Topuzoğlu mentions at least fourteen manuscripts of the book available in Istanbul under this title.[112]

Beirut: *Majallat al-Mashriq* 12 (1900) (chapter 4, with introduction); ed. M. Abū Shādī, Cairo: Maṭbaʿat al-Zāhir, 1908; ed. M. A. Ibrāhīm, Cairo: Dār Nahḍat Miṣr, 1965 (repr. Cairo: Dār al-Maʿārif, 1985); ed. I. Ṣāliḥ, Damascus: Dār al-Bashāʾir, 1994 (repr. Cairo: Maktabat al-Mutanabbī, 1998); trans. (Persian)

108 See Thaʿālibī, *Khāṣṣ al-khāṣṣ*, 239; for the full argument, see id., *al-Tawfīq li-l-talfīq*, ed. Ibrāhīm Ṣāliḥ (Beirut: Dār al-Fikr al-Muʿāṣir, 1990), 8–9.

109 For the former, see Thaʿālibī, *Mirʾāt al-murūʾāt*, 65. For the latter, see id., *Taḥsīn al-qabīḥ wa-taqbīḥ al-ḥasan*, ed. Shākir al-ʿĀshūr (Baghdad: Wizārat al-Awqāf, 1981), 27.

110 See Jādir, "Dirāsā," 407.

111 Ibid., 407–8.

112 Topuzoğlu, "Istanbul Manuscripts of Works," 62–5.

Riḍā Anzābī Nizhād, Mashhad: Intishārāt-i Dānishgāh-i Firdawsī, 1998; ed. Q. al-Ḥusayn, Beirut: Dār wa-Maktabat al-Hilāl, 2003.

30. *al-Tuḥaf wa-l-anwār.*

This is an anthology of prose and poetry ranging from before Islam to the anthologist's time. It consists of twenty-five chapters and an introduction in Thaʿālibī's style, with a dedication to an unnamed patron.

Ed. Yaḥyā al-Jubūrī, Beirut: Dār Majdalāwī, 2009.

31. *Yatīmat al-dahr fī maḥāsin ahl al-ʿaṣr.*

This is Thaʿālibī's most celebrated work. It is a four-volume anthology of poetry and prose intended as a comprehensive survey of the entire Islamic world in the second half of the fourth/tenth century. It is arranged geographically and includes a total of 470 poets and prose writers. Thaʿālibī started composing it in the year 384/994 and dedicated it to an unnamed vizier (*aḥad al-wuzarāʾ*). Jādir proposes Abū l-Ḥusayn Muḥammad b. Kathīr, who served as vizier for Abū ʿAlī b. Sīmjūrī.[113] Jādir justifies the omission of the dedication in the second edition by explaining that Thaʿālibī reworked the book during the reign of the Ghaznavids, who had succeeded Abū ʿAlī b. Sīmjūrī and opposed his vizier. Consequently, Thaʿālibī did not want to alienate the Ghaznavids by mentioning their previous enemy in the preface. Jādir, however, does not explain why Thaʿālibī did not rededicate the work to someone else.

Damascus: al-Maṭbaʿa al-Ḥanafiyya, 1885; Cairo: Maṭbaʿat al-Ṣāwī, 1934; ed. M. M. ʿAbd al-Ḥamīd, Cairo: al-Maktaba al-Tijāriyya al-Kubrā, 1946 (repr. Cairo: Maṭbaʿat al-Saʿāda, 1956; Beirut: Dār al-Fikr, 1973); ed. M. M. Qumayḥa, Beirut: Dār al-Kutub al-ʿIlmiyya, 1983 (repr. 2000, 2002).

32. *al-Yawāqīt fī baʿḍ al-mawāqīt = Yawāqīt al-mawāqīt = Madḥ al-shayʾ wa-dhammuh.*

A compilation of prose and poetry in which praise and blame of various things are paired. Thaʿālibī states in the introduction that he began the book in Nīshāpūr, worked on it in Jurjān, reached its middle in Jurjāniyya, and completed it in Ghazna, where it was dedicated to *al-amīr al-ajall*.[114] Jādir identifies this person as Abū l-Muẓaffar Naṣr b. Nāṣir al-Dīn, and on that basis dates

113 For the dedication, see ʿUtbī, *al-Yamīnī*, 125–6; Bosworth, *Ghaznavids*, 57–8. For the attribution, see Jādir, "Dirāsa," 442.

114 See Thaʿālibī, *al-Ẓarāʾif wa-l-laṭāʾif wa-l-Yawāqīt fī baʿḍ al-mawāqīt*, ed. Nāṣir Muḥammadī Muḥammad Jād (Cairo: Dār al-Kutub wa-l-Wathāʾiq, 2006), 50.

the book to 400–412/1009–21.[115] It survives together with *al-Yawāqīt fī baʿḍ al-mawāqīt* in a work compiled by Abū Naṣr al-Maqdisī and titled *al-Laṭāʾif wa-l-ẓarāʾif*. The editor of the work, Nāṣir Muḥammadī Muḥammad Jād, cites Brockelmann as listing four copies of *al-Ẓarāʾif* and more than ten copies of *al-Yawāqīt*.[116]

Cairo: 1275 [1858]; Baghdad: 1282 [1865]; Cairo: al-Maṭbaʿa al-Maymaniyya al-Wahbiyya, 1296 [1878] (repr. 1307/1889 and 1323/1906); Cairo: al-Maṭbaʿa al-ʿĀmira, 1325 [1908]; Beirut: Dār al-Manāhil, 1992; ed. ʿA. Y. al-Jamal, Cairo: Maktabat al-Ādāb, 1993; ed. N. M. M. Jād, Cairo: Dār al-Kutub wa-l-Wathāʾiq, 2006.

33. *Zād safar al-mulūk.*

Al-Samarrai lists MS Chester Beatty 5067-3, thus titled and dedicated to a certain Abū Saʿīd al-Ḥasan b. Ṣahl in Ghazna.[117] Joseph Sadan describes the work as a collection of ornate prose and poetic quotes on the subject of travel.[118] The work consists of forty-six chapters on the advantages and disadvantages of all types of journeys, by land or sea; the etiquette of departure, bidding farewell, arriving, and receiving travelers; the hardships encountered while traveling, such as food poisoning, snow, frost, excessive cold, thirst, homesickness (*al-ḥanīn ilā-l-awṭān*), being a stranger or outsider (*al-ghurba*), extreme fatigue, and their appropriate cures.[119] For cures, the book offers lengthy medical recipes. Here, Thaʿālibī demonstrates an in-depth knowledge of pharmacology and medicine, which is absent in his other works. A short chapter on *fiqh al-safar* even discusses legal issues connected with travel, such as performing ablutions, praying, and fasting while traveling. The work is not mentioned in any biographical entry on Thaʿālibī or in any of his other works. Nevertheless, internal evidence supports its attribution. Most important, in at least three separate instances, the work includes direct quotations from *al-Mubhij* of Thaʿālibī, twice introduced by the statement *wa-qultu fī Kitāb al-Mubhij* (I said in *al-Mubhij*).[120]

---

115 Jādir, "Dirāsa," 444.

116 Thaʿālibī, *al-Ẓarāʾif wa-l-laṭāʾif*, 34. For more details on the work and its textual history, see Adam Talib, "Pseudo-Ṯaʿālibī's *Book of Youths*," *Arabica* 59 (2012), 605ff.

117 Al-Samarrai, "Some Biographical Notes," 186.

118 See J. Sadan, "Vine, Women and Seas: Some Images of the Ruler in Medieval Arabic Literature," *Journal of Semitic Studies* 34 (1989), 147.

119 See the table of contents given by Thaʿālibī himself in *Zād safar al-mulūk*, ed. Ramzi Baalbaki and Bilal Orfali (Beirut: Bibliotheca Islamica 52, 2011), 2–3.

120 See the detailed argument for the attribution to Thaʿālibī in the editors' introduction of Thaʿālibī, *Zād safar al-mulūk*.

FIGURE 7 *al-Ẓarāʾif wa-l-laṭāʾif*, MS Majlis-i Millī 3512, 3r

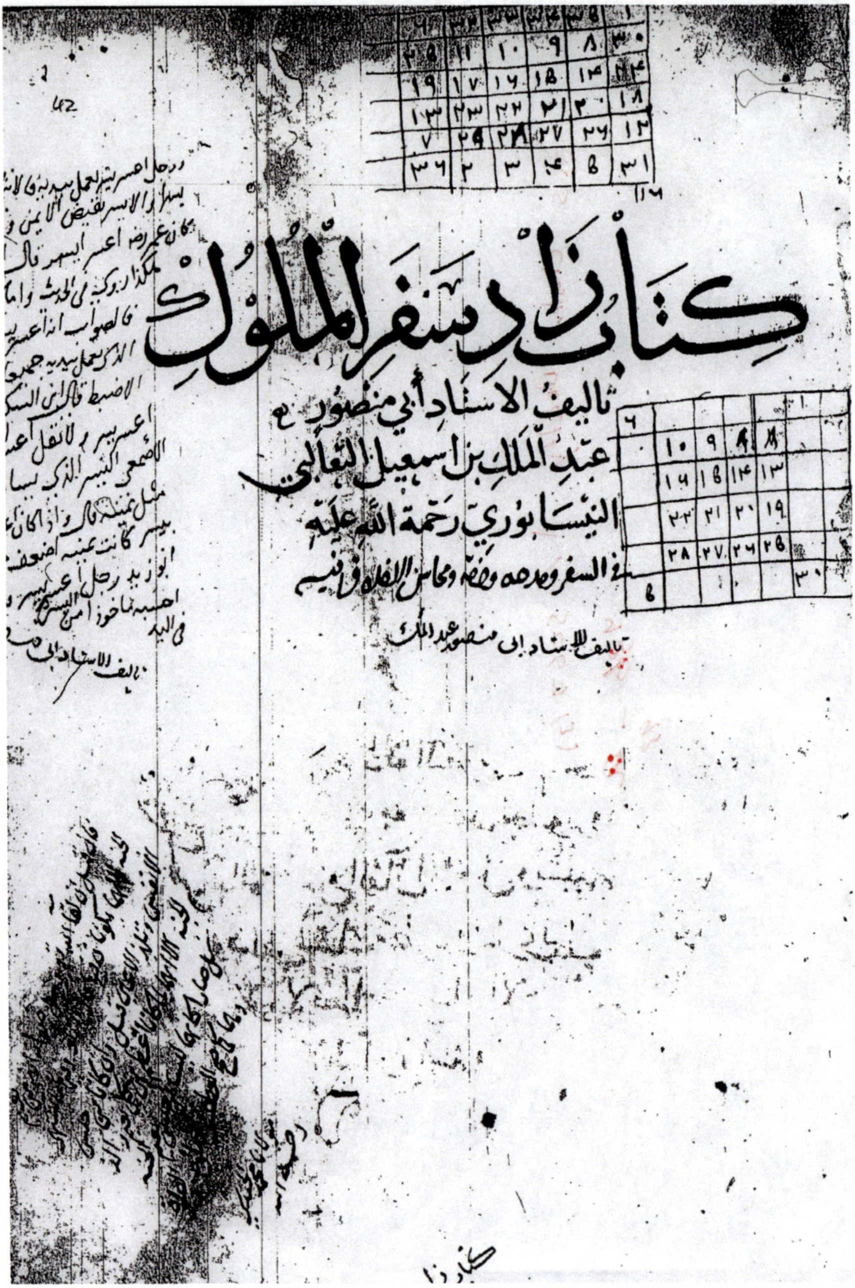

FIGURE 8 *Zād safar al-mulūk*, MS Chester Beatty 5067, 40v

Ed. Dār al-Hilāl, 2009; ed. I. Ṣāliḥ, Abu Dhabi: Dār al-Kutub al-Waṭaniyya, 2010; ed. R. Baalbaki and B. Orfali, Beirut: al-Maʿhad al-Almānī li-l-Abḥāth al-Sharqiyya, 2011.

34. *al-Ẓarāʾif wa-l-laṭāʾif* = *al-Laṭāʾif wa-l-ẓarāʾif* = *al-Ṭarāʾif wa-l-laṭāʾif* = *al-Maḥāsin wa-l-aḍdād.*

As in item 30, this compilation presents poetry and prose in pairs of praise and blame. It was published with *al-Yawāqīt fī baʿḍ al-mawāqīt* in a work compiled by Abū Naṣr al-Maqdisī and titled *al-Laṭāʾif wa-l-ẓarāʾif*. For editions, see item 32.

Printed, Authenticity Doubtful

35. *al-Ashbāh wa-l-naẓāʾir.*

In this work on homonyms in the Qurʾān, only Thaʿālibī's *nisba* is mentioned on the first page: *wāḥid dahrih wa-farīd ʿaṣrih, raʾs al-nubalāʾ wa-tāj al-fuḍalāʾ al-Thaʿālibī*. Jādir rejects the attribution of the work to Thaʿālibī without justification.[121] In support of the contrary view, Thaʿālibī did show interest in philological work in his *Fiqh al-lugha* (see item 7), *al-Tamthīl wa-l-muḥāḍara* (see item 26), and *Thimār al-qulūb* (see item 29), and in the Qurʾānic text in his *al-Iqtibās* (see item 9). The text, thus, quoting no poetry or prose later than the fourth century, could have been Thaʿālibī's. However, the anthologist calls a certain ʿAlī b. ʿUbaydallāh *shaykhunā*, and that man's name appears nowhere as a teacher or source of Thaʿālibī.

Ed. M. al-Miṣrī, Beirut: ʿĀlam al-Kutub, 1984.

36. *Makārim al-akhlāq wa-maḥāsin al-ādāb wa-badāʾiʿ al-awṣāf wa-gharāʾib al-tashbīhāt.*

Al-Samarrai was the first to mention this unattributed MS Leiden 300, which he attributes to Thaʿālibī on the basis of its content. The is an *adab* work that consists of a short introduction and three chapters (*bāb*s) each divided into several sections (*faṣl*s). The first *bāb*, which comprises twelve sections, addresses the acquisition of noble character and excellent conduct (*al-taḥalli bi-makārim al-akhlāq wa-maḥāsin al-ādāb*); the second, of eleven sections, addresses shunning away from base and ugly character traits (*al-tazakkī ʿan masāwiʾ al-akhlāq wa-maqābiḥ al-shiyam*);[122] and the third, of four sections, addresses admirable descriptions and curious similes (*badāʾiʿ al-awṣāf wa-gharāʾib al-tashbīhāt*). At

121 Jādir, *al-Thaʿālibī*, 124.

122 For a treatment of the genre of *makārim al-akhlāq*, see Bishr Fāris, *Mabāḥith ʿarabiyya* (Cairo: Maṭbaʿat al-Maʿārif, 1939), 31–2.

the end of the text is a relatively long appendix of circulating proverbs (*amthāl sāʾira*), presumably added by either the anthologist himself or a scribe. Most of the third chapter's content is taken verbatim from Thaʿālibī's *Man ghāba ʿanhu l-muṭrib* (see item 17). In fact, there is no doubt that the anthologist used *Man ghāba ʿanhu l-muṭrib*, as he selected epigrams in the same order they appear in the original. Moreover, where epigrams are not to be found in *Man ghāba ʿanhu l-muṭrib*, they can be traced to other works by Thaʿālibī, such as *al-Iʿjāz wa-l-ījāz*, *Khāṣṣ al-Khāṣṣ*, *Lubāb al-ādāb*, *Tawfīq li-l-talfīq*, and *Yatīmat al-dahr*. The appendix (*mulḥaq*) of *Makārim al-akhlāq* is devoted to proverbs (*al-amthal al-sāʾira*), specifically 410 proverbs divided into twenty-eight chapters, arranged alphabetically to begin with *alif* and end with *yāʾ*. The proverbs within each chapter, however, are not alphabetically arranged. In this respect, this collection of proverbs is similar to several collections of proverbs from the fourth/tenth and fifth/eleventh centuries that do not go beyond the first letter in arranging their material.

The published work of Louis Cheikho (*al-Machreq*, 1900) under this title is not Thaʿālibī's but instead selections from Ahwāzī's *al-Farāʾid wa-l-qalāʾid* (see item 46). Al-Samarrai's suggestion to attribute the work to Thaʿālibī is further supported by the norm of anthologists after Thaʿālibī including contemporary literary production in their works.[123] MS Leiden OR 300 contains no material that dates after Thaʿālibī's life span, circumstantial evidence that points to a fifth/eleventh century author.[124]

The Book of Noble Character: Critical Edition of Makārim al-akhlāq wa-maḥāsin al-ādāb wa-badāʾiʿ al-awṣāf wa-gharāʾib al-tashbīhāt Attributed to Abū Manṣūr al-Thaʿālibī (d. 429/1039), ed. Bilal Orfali and Ramzi Baalbaki, Leiden: Brill, 2015.

37. *al-Nuhya fī-l-ṭard wa-l-ghunya.*

Jādir mentions this title as being attributed to Thaʿālibī and printed twice in Mecca, 1301/1883–4 and Cairo, 1326/1908. It is dedicated to the Khwārizmshāh and, according to Jādir, was composed between 403/1012 and 407/1016.[125] He does not state whether he inspected a copy.[126]

---

123 See Adam Talib, *Out of Many, One: Epigram Anthologies in Pre-Modern Arabic Literature*, PhD diss., University of Oxford, 2013, 5–7.

124 For a detailed study of the work and its authenticity, see the introduction to Bilal Orfali and Ramzi Baalbaki, *The Book of Noble Character* (Leiden: Brill, 2015).

125 Jādir, "Dirāsa," 441.

126 I have not been able to find any information about this work.

FIGURE 9 *Makārim al-akhlāq*, MS Leiden Or. 300, 1v-2r

38. *Rawḥ al-rūḥ*.

Ibrāhīm Ṣāliḥ edited the work based on two manuscripts, Paris 6624 and al-Maktaba al-Aḥmadiyya 14476 (Aleppo). Hilāl Nājī draws much poetry by Thaʿālibī from a manuscript of this work but does not give its reference number or location. Thaʿālibī's name does not appear on either of the two manuscripts. The work focuses on the prose and poetry of the fourth/tenth and fifth/eleventh centuries, and the anthologist must have been very familiar with Thaʿālibī's works, as he draws heavily from them. The book deserves special attention, as it includes much poetry that has not survived in any other known source. The phrase *rawḥ al-rūḥ* does appear in Thaʿālibī's works.[127]

Ed. I. Ṣāliḥ, Abu Dhabi: Dār al-Kutub al-Waṭaniyya, 2009.

39. *Taʾrīkh ghurar al-siyar = al-Ghurar fī siyar al-mulūk wa-akhbārihim = Ghurar akhbār mulūk al-Furs wa-siyarihim = Ghurar mulūk al-Furs = Ṭabaqāt al-Mulūk = Ghurar wa-siyar.*

---

127 See, for example, Thaʿālibī, *Laṭāʾif al-ẓurafāʾ*, 4.

This work is a universal history which, according to Ḥajjī Khalīfa, extends from creation to the anthologist's own time. Initially, four manuscripts were known to exist. The first of these, dated 597/1201 or 599/1203, is preserved in the library of Dāmād Ibrāhīm Pāshā in Istanbul. The second and third manuscripts are in the Bibliothèque Nationale of Paris, Fonds arabe 1488 and Fonds arabe 5053. The fourth is MS Ẓāhiriyya 14479, dated to 1112/1700 and titled *Ṭabaqāt al-mulūk*. Only the first half of this work, up to the caliphate of Abū Bakr has survived, and thereof only the section dealing with pre-Islamic Persian history has been published. It is dedicated to Abū l-Muẓaffar Naṣr b. Sebüktegin, Sāmānid governor of Khurāsān (d. 412/1021) and, according to the editor, was probably written between 408/1017 and 412/1021. The name Brockelmann gives for the author appears to be an artificial construction. One manuscript calls the author al-Ḥusayn b. Muḥammad al-Marghanī. Another manuscript inserts the name Abū Manṣūr in several passages in which the author refers to himself. The name Abū Manṣūr al-Ḥusayn b. Muḥammad al-Marghanī al-Thaʿālibī does not appear in sources from the fourth/tenth century, which made Brockelmann reject the attribution to ʿAbd al-Malik al-Thaʿālibī.[128] On stylistic grounds, and from the appearance of certain characteristic locutions, Franz Rosenthal followed Zotenberg in identifying the author as Thaʿālibī. Both explained al-Marghanī's name, which appears in only one manuscript, as a scribal error.[129] C. E. Bosworth, in a personal communication, notes that Rosenthal later changed his opinion.[130] Jādir also attributes the work to Thaʿālibī, citing among his further evidence an *isnād* to Abū Bakr al-Khwārizmī (d. 383/993), one of Thaʿālibī's main sources.[131] Since then more evidence has been cited in favor of the attribution to Thaʿālibī.[132]

---

128 See *GAL* SI:581–2; id., "al-T͟haʿālibī Abū Manṣūr al-Ḥusayn b. Muḥammad al-Maraghānī," *EI1* VIII:732b.

129 F. Rosenthal, "From Arabic Books and Manuscripts: III. The Author of the *Ġurar as-siyar*," *JAOS* 70 [1950], 181–2. Rowson and Bonebakker note that instances of the phrase "Satan made me forget" (*ansānīhi al-shayṭān*) in the *Yatīma* should be added to those cited by Rosenthal from the *Tatimmat al-Yatīma* and *Fiqh al-lugha* as helping confirm Thaʿālibī's authorship of the *Ghurar al-siyar*, where the phrase also occurs; see Rowson and Bonebakker, *A Computerized Listing of Biographical Data from the* Yatīmat al-Dahr *by al-Thaʿālibī* (Malibu: UNDENA Publications, 1980), 23.

130 See C. E. Bosworth, "al-T͟haʿālibī, Abū Manṣūr," *EI2* X:425b.

131 See Jādir, "Dirāsa," 419.

132 See, for example, ʿAlī ʿAbdullāhi, "Ghurar al-siyar, barrasī dar bāriy-i nām-i aṣlī wa-muʾallif-i ān," *Tārīkh va-tamaddun-i islāmī* 100 (1393), 105–12; Mahmoud Omidsalar, "Thaʿālibī Nīshāpūrī yā Thaʿālibī Marghānī?" *Nama-yi Baharistan* 8–9 (1386), 131–44.

FIGURE 10 *Rawḥ al-rūḥ*, MS al-Maktaba al-Aḥmadiyya 14476, 150v-151r

Ed. H. Zotenberg, Paris: Impr. Nationale, 1900 (repr. Tehran: M. H. Asadī, 1963; Amsterdam: APA Oriental Press, 1979); trans. M. Hidāyat, Tehran: 1369/1949 (titled *Shāhnāmā-i Thaʿālibī*) (repr. Tihrān: Asāṭīr 1385 [2006]); trans. Muḥammad Faḍāʾilī [Tehran]: Nashr-i Nuqra, 1368 [1989–90].

40. *Tarjamat al-kātib fī ādāb al-ṣāḥib.*

This is a work on friendship, not mentioned in Thaʿālibī's classical biographies. Thaʿālibī's name appears in two of three manuscripts. The book foregrounds modern and contemporary poetry in twenty-one chapters; no material later than Thaʿālibī's life span appears; and a good number of the *akhbār* can be found in other works of Thaʿālibī, such as the *Yatīma*, *al-Tamthīl wa-l-muḥāḍara*, and *Man ghāba ʿanhu l-muṭrib*. It is possible that he is the anthologist.

Ed. ʿA. Dh. Zāyid, ʿAmmān: Wizārat al-Thaqāfa, 2001.

41. *Tuḥfat al-wuzarāʾ.*

This is a work on vizierate and its practices, replete with poetic quotations from famous viziers. It consists of five chapters on the origin of viziership; its virtues and benefits; its customs, claims, and necessities; and its divisions; as well as reports on the most competent viziers. After dedicating the work *al-Mulūkī* to the Khwārizmshāh, the anthologist dedicates this new work to

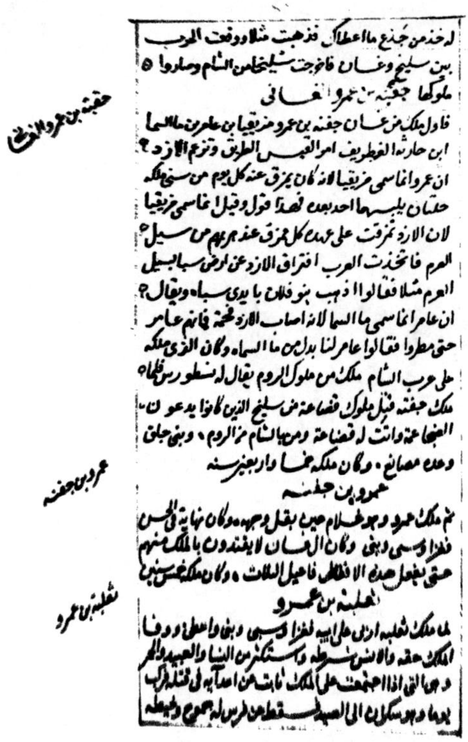

FIGURE 11 *Ṭabaqāt al-mulūk*, MS *Ẓāhiriyya 14479, 10r*

Abū ʿAbdallāh al-Ḥamdūnī. The editors of the work, Ḥabīb ʿAlī al-Rāwī and Ibtisām Marhūn al-Ṣaffār consider the work Thaʿālibī's, with some additions by a later scribe, to account for material from a much later period.[133] However, Hilāl Nājī argues that the supposed additions harmonize with the surrounding *akhbār* in the chapter, and so are original. Nājī also disputes the historicity of Ḥamdūnī (*shakhṣiyya lā wujūda lahā tarīkhiyyan*), and holds that no work titled *al-Mulūkī* by Thaʿālibī survives. Nājī states that the introduction of the work is identical with that of the sixth/twelfth century *al-Tadhkira al-ḥamdūniyya* by Ibn Ḥamdūn (d. 562/1167). Nājī, moreover, points out errors of attribution and content that he does not believe Thaʿālibī would have made. He thus considers the text an independent work from the seventh/thirteenth century.[134]

133 See Thaʿālibī, *Tuḥfat al-wuzarāʾ*, ed. Ḥ. ʿA. al-Rāwī and I. M. al-Ṣaffār (Baghdad: Wizārat al-Awqāf, 1977), 22ff.

134 See H. Nājī, "Ḥawl kitāb Tuḥfat al-wuzarāʾ al-mansūb li-l-Thaʿālibī," in *Buḥūth fī l-naqd al-turāthī* (Beirut: Dār al-Gharb al-Islāmī, 1994), 211–17.

FIGURE 12 *Tarjamat al-Kātib fī adab al-ṣāḥib*, MS Hekimoglu 946, 86v-87r

Nājī's argument fails to convince for the following reasons. First, although the introduction of *Tuḥfat al-wuzarāʾ* appears in *al-Tadhkira al-Ḥamdūniyya*, it is not the general one, but precedes the second *bāb*.[135] The author of the *Tuḥfa* may have copied *al-Tadhkira*, or vice versa. Moreover, *Tuḥfat al-wuzarāʾ* includes three chapters taken from Thaʿālibī's *Ādāb al-mulūk* (see item 2). Thus, Thaʿālibī is certainly the author of a good part of the work, and as attested earlier, he not infrequently reworked previously circulated books. In addition to these three (possibly recycled) chapters, the work includes several quotations from Thaʿālibī's other works, including his own poetry. Moreover, the dedicatee, Abū ʿAbdallāh al-Ḥamdūnī, could very well be Abū ʿAbdallāh Muḥammad b. Ḥāmid, to whom Thaʿālibī dedicated *Aḥsan mā samiʿtu* (see item 3), and who served as a vizier of the Khwārizmshāh Maʾmūn b. Maʾmūn. Finally, the introduction of *Ādāb al-mulūk* (see item 2) mentions *al-Mulūkī* as one of the variant titles Thaʿālibī had thought to give to the work, and it is indeed dedicated to the Khwārizmshāh, as he notes in the introduction of *Tuḥfat al-wuzarāʾ*.

135 See Ibn Ḥamdūn, *al-Tadhkira al-Ḥamdūniyya*, ed. Iḥsān ʿAbbās and Bakr ʿAbbās (Beirut: Dār Ṣādir, 1996), 1:237.

Evidence supports the hypothesis that the book is a reworking of Thaʿālibī's *Ādāb al-mulūk* and perhaps of another author's work on viziership.

Ed. R. Heinecke, Beirut: Dār al-Qalam, 1975; ed. Ḥ. ʿA. al-Rāwī and I. M. al-Ṣaffār, Baghdad: Wizārat al-Awqāf, 1977 (repr. Cairo: Dār al-Āfāq al-ʿArabiyya, 2000; ed. S. Abū Dayya, ʿAmmān: Dār al-Bashāʾir, 1994; ed. Ibtisām Marhūn al-Ṣaffār; ʿAmmān: Jidārā li-l-Kitāb al-ʿĀlamī 2009. Baghdad: Maṭbaʿat al-ʿĀnī, 2002; Beirut: al-Dār al-ʿArabiyya li-l-Mawsūʿāt, 2006.

Printed, Authenticity Rejected

42. *al-Ādāb.*

Jādir mentions three manuscripts of the work: MS ʿĀrif Ḥikmat 1171-H-*adab*, MS Vatican 1462, and MS Atef Efendi 2231,[136] whereas Nājī mentions only the last two.[137] The three manuscripts are attributed to Thaʿālibī. In addition, MS Leiden 478 and, in the Garrett collection, MS Princeton 205 and MS Princeton 5977 are of the same work, with the first two attributed to Ibn Shams al-Khilāfa (d. 622/1225). MS Chester Beatty 4759/2, titled *Majmūʿ fī-l-ḥikam wa-l-ādāb*, contains the same work. The title in MS Princeton 5977 was changed by one of the readers from *al-Ādāb* to *Majmūʿ fī-l-ḥikam wa-l-ādāb*. The incipit of the manuscript contains both titles; the compiler says: "*ammā baʿd fa-hādhā majmūʿun fī-l-ḥikami wa-l-ādāb… wa-ʿanwantuhu bi-kitāb al-Ādāb*." The work has been edited by M. A. al-Khānjī based on one other manuscript in the personal library of Aḥmad Effendi Āghā and attributed to Jaʿfar b. Shams al-Khilāfa.

Ed. M. A. al-Khānjī, Cairo: Maṭbaʿat al-Saʿāda, 1930 (repr. Cairo: Maṭbaʿat al-Khānjī, 1993).

43. *Aḥāsin kalim al-nabiyy wa-l-ṣaḥāba wa-l-tābiʿīn wa-mulūk al-jāhiliyya wa-mulūk al-Islām.*

This is a title in the MS Leiden Codex Orientalis 1042, of which al-Samarrai published the first section. The *Aḥāsin* occupies folios 62a–108b (see item 13). Jādir believes this is an abridgment of *al-Iʿjāz wa-l-ījāz* by Fakhr al-Dīn al-Rāzī (d. 606/1209).[138] Muḥammad Zaynahum published the work based on two manuscripts in Dār al-Kutub al-Miṣriyya and Maʿhad al-Makhṭūṭāt al-ʿArabiyya.

Ed. and trans. (Latin) J. Ph. Valeton, Leiden: 1844; ed. M. Zaynahum, Cairo: al-Dār al-Thaqāfiyya, 2006.

---

136 See Jādir, "Dirāsa," 391.

137 See introduction to Thaʿālibī, *al-Anīs fī ghurar al-tajnīs*, 26.

138 See Jādir, "Dirāsa," 393.

44. *al-Barq al-wamīḍ ʿalā al-baghīḍ al-musammā bi-l-naqīḍ.*

Madgharī mentions a work with this title printed in Qāzān in 1305/1887.[139] I was not able to locate the printed text, but MS Azhar 10032 under this title is the work of Hārūn b. Bahāʾ al-Dīn al-Marjānī.

45. *Durar al-ḥikam.*

Jādir examined MS Dār al-Kutub al-Miṣriyya 5107-*adab* under this title attributed to Thaʿālibī but rejected the authorship of Thaʿālibī based on a colophon indicating that the work was compiled by Yāqūt al-Mustaʿṣī (al-Mustaʿṣimī?) in 631/1233.[140] The work has been published based on two related manuscripts. It is a collection of maxims, mostly from the Arabic tradition, and includes poetry and *ḥadīth*. No internal evidence supports Thaʿālibī's authorship.

Ed. Y. ʿA al-Wahhāb, Ṭanṭa: Dār al-Ṣaḥāba li-l-Turāth, 1995.

46. *al-Farāʾid wa-l-qalāʾid* = *al-Amthāl* (cf. items 26, 62, 63) = *Aḥāsin al-maḥāsin* (cf. item 61) = *al-ʿIqd al-nafīs wa-nuzhat al-jalīs* = *Makārim al-akhlāq* (cf. item 36, 50).

Kalāʿī had already attributed this title to Thaʿālibī in his list. The printed text, however, is not Thaʿālibī's but by Abū l-Ḥasan Muḥammad b. al-Ḥasan b. Aḥmad al-Ahwāzī (d. 428/1036),[141] as indicated in a number of manuscripts. Moreover, as Jādir points out, Thaʿālibī himself quotes from it in his *Siḥr al-balāgha* (see item 24), attributing it to al-Ahwāzī.[142]

In *Majmūʿat khams rasāʾil*, Istanbul: 1301 [1883–4] (repr. 1325/1907; Najaf, 1970) (titled *Aḥāsin al-maḥāsin*); Cairo: al-Maṭbaʿa al-Adabiyya, 1301 [1883–4]; Cairo: Dār al-Kutub al-ʿArabiyya al-Kubrā [1909] (titled *Kitāb al-Amthāl al-musammā bi-l-Farāʾid wa-l-qalāʾid wa-yusammā ayḍan bi-l-ʿIqd al-nafīs wa-nuzhat al-jalīs*); Cairo: Maṭbaʿat al-Taqaddum al-Tijāriyya, 1327 [1910] (titled *al-Amthāl* and attributed to ʿAlī b. al-Ḥusayn al-Rukhkhajī).

47. *K. al-Ghilmān.*

MS Berlin 8334 (We[tzstein] II, 1786) includes a collection of poetry by youths from the seventeenth and eighteenth centuries, titled *K. al-Ghilmān*, attributed erroneously to Thaʿālibī. Most of the poems date from the Mamlūk period. Adam Talib has studied this manuscript in detail, and he demonstrates

139 See introduction to Thaʿālibī, *Mirʾāt al-murūʾāt*, 32.

140 See Jādir, "Dirāsa," 410–11.

141 See his biography in al-Khaṭīb al-Baghdādī, *Taʾrīkh Baghdād* (Beirut: Dār al-Kitāb al-ʿArabī, 1966), 2:218.

142 Jādir, "Dirāsa," 421.

that the collection is associated with a text by Thaʿālibī-Maqdisī's *al-Ẓarā'if wa-l-laṭā'if wa-l-Yawāqīt fī baʿḍ al-mawāqīt* and that they were copied together into a single codex at the same time. According to Talib, "The poetry collection's position in the codex suggests that it was intended to complement the far longer text, presumably as an amusing postscript."[143]

Adam Talib, "Pseudo-Ṯaʿālibī's *Book of Youths*," *Arabica* 59 (2012), 599–649.

48. *K. al-Ḥamd wa al-dhamm.*

Topuzoğlu lists MS Bayezid Umumi Veliyuddin Efendi 2631/1 under this title.[144] Thaʿālibī's name appears on the cover, but the work and the rest of the treatises in the codex are by Abū Manṣūr Muḥammad b. Sahl b. al-Marzubān (d. after 340/951) (cf. item 49).[145] The book describes the virtue of gratitude (*shukr*).

In *al-Muntahā fī l-kamāl des Muhammad Ibn Sahl Ibn al-Marzubān al-Karḫī (gest. ca. 345/956)*, ed. S. M. H. al-Hadrusi, Berlin: Klaus Schwarz Verlag, 1988.

49. *al-Jawāhir al-ḥisān fī tafsīr al-Qur'ān = Tafsīr al-Thaʿālibī.*

This is a work by ʿAbd al-Raḥmān b. Muḥammad b. Makhlūf al-Jazā'irī al-Thaʿālibī (d. 873–5/1468–70). Thaʿālibī's name is found on many manuscripts of the work because of the identical *nisba.*

al-Jazā'ir: ed. A. B. M. al-Turkī, 1905–9; Beirut: Mu'assasat al-Aʿlamī li-l-Maṭbūʿāt, n.d.; ed. ʿA. al-Ṭālibī, al-Jazā'ir: al-Mu'assasa al-Waṭaniyya li-l-Kitāb, 1985; ed. M. ʿA. Muḥammad, ʿA. M. ʿA. Aḥmad, and A. A. ʿAbd al-Fattāḥ, Beirut: Dār Iḥyā' al-Turāth, 1997; ed. M. al-Fāḍilī, Beirut: al-Maktaba al-ʿAṣriyya, 1997.

50. *Makārim al-akhlāq.*

This work published by Louis Cheikho is a selection from an unknown author from Ahwāzī's *al-Farā'id wa-l-qalā'id* (see item 46).[146] Another manuscript under this title that could be an authentic work of Thaʿālibī is discussed at item 36.

Ed. L. Cheikho, Beirut: *Majallat al-Mashriq,* 1900.

---

143 Talib, "Pseudo-Ṯaʿālibī's *Book of Youths*," 609.

144 Topuzoğlu, "Istanbul Manuscripts of Works," 73.

145 See also Ṣafadī, *al-Wāfī bi-l-wafayāt*, 3:119.

146 For a detailed discussion, see Orfali and Baalbaki, *Book of Noble Character*, 9.

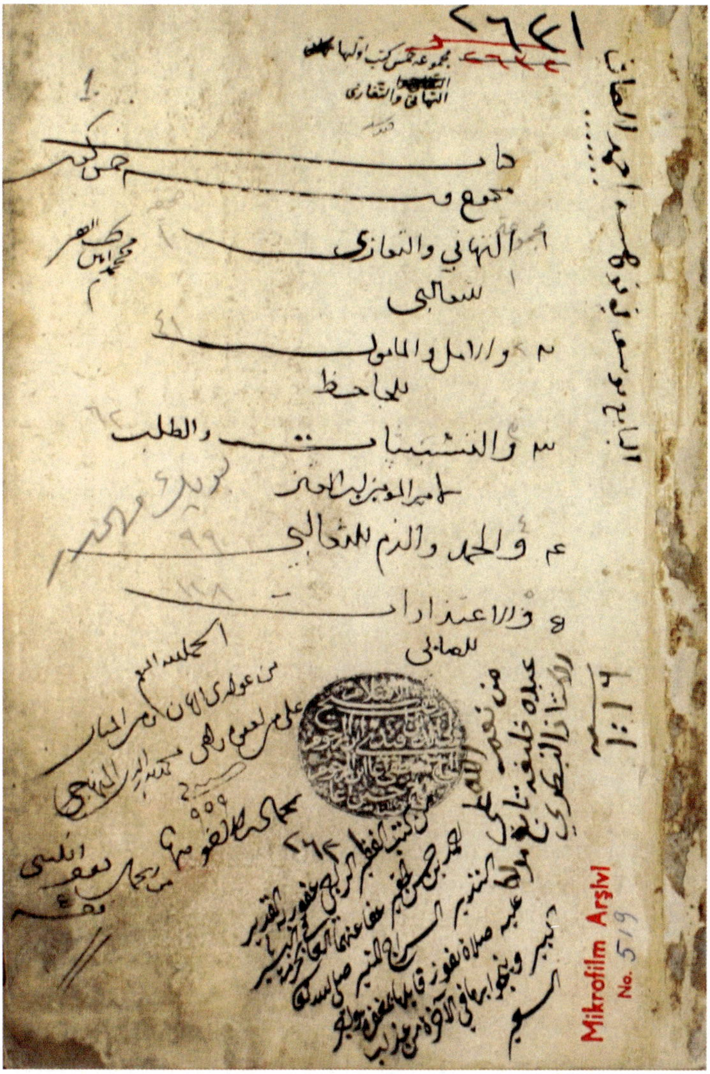

FIGURE 13 *MS Bayezid Umumi Veliyuddin Efendi 2631, 1r*

51. *Mawāsim al-ʿumr.*

Both MS Feyzullah 2133/6 (fols. 204–14)[147] and MS King ʿAbdallāh b. ʿAbd al-ʿAzīz University 6177/6 (208v–213r) carry this title. Brockelmann lists another, MS Rağıp Paşa 473/1.[148] On the basis of MS King ʿAbdallāh b. ʿAbd al-ʿAzīz

147 Dānishpažūh, *Fihrist-i Microfilmhā* (Tehran: Kitābkhāna-i-Markazī-i Dānishgāh, 1348 A.H.), 490.

148 *GAL* SI:502.

University and MS Feyzullah 2133, the work is identical to *Tanbīh al-nāʾim al-ghamr ʿalā mawāsim al-ʿumr* by Abū al-Faraj Ibn al-Jawzī (d. 597/1201). The work includes prose and poetry on the different life stages of human beings. It consists of five chapters (*mawāsim,* lit. seasons). The first covers from birth to the age of fifteen, the second to the age of thirty-five, the third to the age of fifty, the fourth to the age of seventy, and the fifth to death.

Ed. ʿA. Ḥilmī, Cairo: Dār al-Ḥadīth, 1985; ed. S. al-Ḥursh, Riyāḍ: Dār al-Miʿrāj, 1993; ed. B. A. al-Jābī. Beirut: Dār Ibn Ḥazm; Limassol: al-Jaffān wa-l-Jābī, 1997; ed. M. al-ʿAjamī, Beirut: Dār al-Bashāʾir al-Islāmiyya, 2004.

52. *Muʾnis al-waḥīd wa-nuzhat al-mustafīd.*

Jādir ascertains that this printed work has no connection with Thaʿālibī and is in fact part of *Muḥāḍarāt al-udabāʾ* by al-Rāghib al-Iṣfahānī.[149]

Trans. Gustav Flügel, *Der vertraute Gefährte des Einsamen: In schlagfertigen Gegenreden*, Vienna: Anton Edlern von Schmid, 1829.

53. *al-Muntakhab fī maḥāsin ashʿār al-ʿArab.*

This anthology is the work of an anonymous author, possibly from the fourth/tenth century. It consists of ninety-six *qaṣīda*s and four *urjūza*s, several of which are not found anywhere else.

Ed. ʿĀ. S. Jamāl, Cairo: Maktabat al-Khānjī, 1994.

54. *Natāʾij al-mudhākara.*

Jādir mentions a manuscript of this work in Medina, MS ʿĀrif Ḥikmat 31—*Majāmīʿ*, where Thaʿālibī's name appears on the front page of the codex.[150] Ibrāhīm Ṣāliḥ edited the work, attributing it to Ibn al-Ṣayrafī, Abū l-Qāsim ʿAlī b. Munjib b. Sulaymān (d. 542/1148). Ṣāliḥ bases this attribution on the text's various *isnād*s, which indicate that the author is Fāṭimid, and on a reference to a *Risālā* by Ṣayrafī.[151] Also supporting this attribution is the fact that the first work bound in the same codex is Ṣayrafī's.

Ed. I. Ṣāliḥ, Damascus: Dār al-Bashāʾir, 1999.

55. *Rawḍat al-Faṣāḥa.*

This work is incorrectly attributed to Thaʿālibī by Muḥammad Ibrāhīm Salīm. Despite the scant evidence supporting the attribution to Thaʿālibī in the

149 See ibid., 439.

150 See ibid.

151 For the complete argument, see the introduction to Ibn al-Ṣayrafī, *K. Natāʾij al-mudhākara*, ed. Ibrāhīm Ṣāliḥ (Beirut: Dār al-Bashāʾir, 1999), 9–10.

introduction of the work—mainly the excellent exordium (*barāʿat al-istihlāl*) coined with Qurʾānic quotations, and the emphasis on brevity and the worth of the book[152]—the book includes numerous quotations by later authors, including Ḥarīrī (d. 516/1122) and Zamakhsharī (d. 538/1144).

Ed. M. I. Salīm, Cairo: Maktabat al-Qurʾān, 1994.

56. *al-Shakwā wa-l-ʿitāb wa-mā li-l-khillān wa-l-aṣḥāb.*

This work, as editor Ilhām ʿAbd al-Wahhāb al-Muftī notes, is a selection of *Rabīʿ al-abrār of al-Zamakhsharī.*[153]

Ṭanṭa: Dār al-Ṣaḥāba li-l-Turāth, 1992; ed. I. ʿA. al-Muftī, Kuwayt: al-Majlis al-Waṭanī li-l-Thaqāfa, 2000; Kuwayt: Kulliyyat al-Tarbiya al-Asāsiyya, 2000.

57. *al-Tahānī wa-l-taʿāzī.*

This work, the title of which can be translated as "Congratulations and Condolences," is an etiquette manual that furnishes examples of appropriate responses to particular occasions and situations. Topuzoğlu mentions one manuscript of this work attributed to Thaʿālibī in MS Bayezid Umumi Veliyuddin Efendi 2631/3.[154] S. M. H. al-Hadrusi edited the works in this codex. Ibrāhīm b. Muḥammad al-Baṭshān edited the work using two other incomplete manuscripts and attributes it, rightly, to Abū Manṣūr Muḥammad b. Sahl b. al-Marzubān (d. after 340/951) based on several quotations found in his other works.[155] All four of the other works in the same codex are by Ibn al-Marzubān.

In *al-Muntahā fi l-kamāl des Muhammad Ibn Sahl Ibn al-Marzubān al-Karḫī (gest. ca. 345/956)*, ed. Ed. S. M. H. al-Hadrusi, Berlin: Klaus Schwarz Verlag, 1988; ed. I. al-Baṭshān, Buraydah: Nādī al-Qaṣīm al-Adabī, 2003.

152 Al-Sharīf al-Jurjānī defines the term *barāʿat al-istihlāl* as follows: "*barāʿat al-istihlāl* occurs when the author makes a statement at the beginning of his work to indicate the general subject before entering into the details"; see his *K. al-Taʿrīfāt* (Beirut: Maktabat Lubnān, 1969), 64. See also Qalqashandī, *Ṣubḥ al-aʿshā* (Cairo: Dār al-Kutub al-Miṣriyya, 1922), 11:73ff.; for the use of *barāʿat al-istihlāl* in Thaʿālibī's works, see Orfali, "Art of the *Muqaddima*," 201–2.

153 See introduction to al-Thaʿālibī [falsely attributed], *al-Shakwā wa-l-ʿitāb wa-mā waqaʿa li-l-khillān wa-l-aṣḥāb*, ed. I. ʿA al-Muftī (Kuwayt: al-Majlis al-Waṭanī li-l-Thaqāfa, 2000), 20ff.

154 Topuzoğlu, "Istanbul Manuscripts of Works," 67.

155 See also Ṣafadī, *al-Wāfī bi-l-wafayāt*, 3:119.

58. *Ṭarāʾif al-ṭuraf.*

Brockelmann mentions several manuscripts for this work.[156] Jādir finds in MS Köprülü 1326 individuals posterior to Thaʿālibī, and on this basis he rejects its attribution to Thaʿālibī.[157] Hilāl Nājī edited the work, attributing it to al-Bāriʿ al-Zawzanī on the basis of internal and external evidence. It is a work of *adab* in twelve chapters (*abwāb*).

Ed. H. Nājī, Beirut: ʿĀlam al-Kutub, 1998.

59. *Tuḥfat al-ẓurafāʾ wa-fākihat al-luṭafāʾ = al-Daʿawāt wa-l-fuṣūl.*

Jādir mentions a manuscript of this work in Medina, MS ʿĀrif Ḥikmat 154, attributed to Thaʿālibī.[158] However, this title was added on the cover by Muḥammad Saʿīd Mawlawī, a modern scholar, not by the original scribe. Many of the sayings in this work can be traced to Thaʿālibī's various works, yet he could not have written this because of the several references to his prose and poetry in the third person, introduced by *wa-anshadanī Abū Manṣūr al-Thaʿālibī.* More important, the anthologist includes his own *qaṣīda* of ten lines, six verses of which are to be found in Yāqūt al-Ḥamawī's *Muʿjam al-udabāʾ*, attributed to ʿAlī b. Aḥmad al-Wāḥidī (d. 468/1075 or 1076).[159] This caused ʿĀdil al-Furayjāt to attribute the work to al-Wāḥidī and assign it the title *al-Daʿawāt wa-l-fuṣūl*, on the basis of Wāhidī's list of works and the subject of the book.[160]

Al-Wāḥidī, ʿAlī b. Aḥmad, *al-Daʿawāt wa-l-fuṣūl*, ed. ʿĀ. al-Furayjāt, Damascus: ʿA. al-Furayjāt, 2005.

60. *al-Uns wa-l-ʿurs = Uns al-waḥīd.*

MS Paris 3034 titled *Uns al-waḥīd* (cf. item 74) and attributed to Thaʿālibī on the cover page is printed under the title *al-Uns wa-l-ʿurs* by Īflīn Farīd Yārid and attributed to the vizier and *kātib* Abū Saʿd Manṣūr b. al-Ḥusayn al-Ābī (d. 421/1030).[161] The editor bases the attribution to Ābī on internal and external evidence.[162]

Ed. Īflīn Farīd Yārid (Damascus: Dār al-Numayr, 1999).

---

156 Brockelmann, "Thaʿālibī," *EI1* VIII:731a.

157 See Jādir, "Dirāsa," 416.

158 Ibid., 403.

159 For Wāḥidī's biography, see Yāqūt al-Ḥamawī, *Muʿjam al-udabāʾ*, 1659–64.

160 See introduction to Wāḥidī, *al-Daʿawāt wa-l-fuṣūl*, 7–15.

161 The work has been discussed in G. Vajda, "Une anthologie sur l'amitié attribuée á al-Taʿālibī," 211–13. Vajda suggests that the author is associated with the court of Ṣāḥib Ibn ʿAbbād.

162 E. Rowson drew my attention to a lost work by Miskawayhi titled *Uns al-farīd*, a collection of *akhbār*, poetry, maxims, and proverbs; see Ṣafadī, *al-Wāfī bi-l-wafayāt*, 8:73.

FIGURE 14 *MS ʿĀrif Ḥikmat 154, 1r*

In Manuscript, Authentic Works

61. *Aḥāsin al-maḥāsin.*

Jurjī Zaydān mentions two manuscripts in Paris and al-Khidīwiyya (earlier name of Dār al-Kutub al-Miṣriyya), Cairo, without further reference.[163] Hilāl Nājī identifies the Paris manuscript to be MS Paris 3036. The editors of the *Laṭāʾif al-maʿārif* mention two manuscripts with this title in Dār al-Kutub al-Miṣriyya without giving specific references.[164] After examining the Paris manuscript, Nājī ascertained that the book is a fuller version of *Aḥsan mā samiʿtu* (see item 3), the latter forming only one-fourth of the original.[165] Moreover, the *Aḥāsin* includes prose along with poetry, unlike its abridgment, which contains only poetry. The longer introduction of the work is identical to the introduction of *Man ghāba ʿanhu l-muṭrib* (see item 17).

163 See Zaydān, *Taʾrīkh ādāb al-lugha al-ʿarabiyya*, 2:232.

164 See introduction to Thaʿālibī, *Laṭāʾif al-maʿārif*, 21.

165 H. Nājī, *Muḥāḍarāt fī taḥqīq al-nuṣūṣ* (Beirut: Dār al-Gharb al-Islāmī, 1994), 145ff.

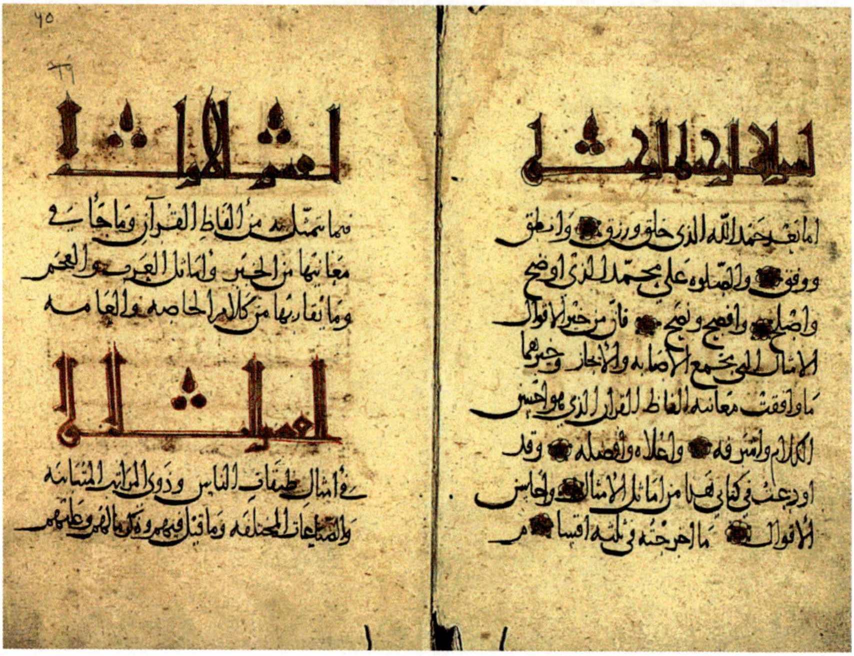

FIGURE 15 *Khāṣṣ al-Khāṣṣ fī l-Amthāl*, MS *Aya Sofya 4824, 65v-66r*

62. *Khāṣṣ al-Khāṣṣ fī l-Amthāl = al-Amthāl wa-l-istishhādāt.*

The MS Aya Sofya 4824 with this title was copied by Muḥammad b. ʿUmar b. Aḥmad in 523/1128. The work is divided into three parts: Qurʾānic proverbs and their equivalents in other cultures, proverbs related to various professions, and select proverbs following the pattern of *afʿal* and not included in the book of Abū ʿAbdallāh Ḥamza b. al-Ḥasan al-Iṣbahānī dedicated to the subject. The work quotes Thaʿālibī's *K. al-Mubhij* twice, attributing it to *muʾallif al-kitāb*.[166]

63. *al-Amthāl wa-l-tashbīhāt = al-Amthāl.*

This work is different from *al-Farāʾid wa-l-qalāʾid*, which was printed under the title *al-Amthāl* and inaccurately attributed to Thaʿālibī. Jādir lists three known manuscripts: MS al-Maktaba al-Aḥmadiyya 4734, MS Maktabat Khazna 1150, and MS Feyzullah 2133. Jādir examined these and described the work as devoting 111 chapters to different subjects, based on proverbs from the Qurʾān, *ḥadīth*, and famous Arab and non-Arab sayings. This is followed by poetry praising and blaming things (*madḥu l-ashyāʾi wa-dhammuhā*). Jādir points out the book's similarity to *al-Tamthīl wa-l-muḥāḍara*. In it Thaʿālibī mentions only

166 The book is being edited by Bilal Orfali and Ramzi Baalbaki.

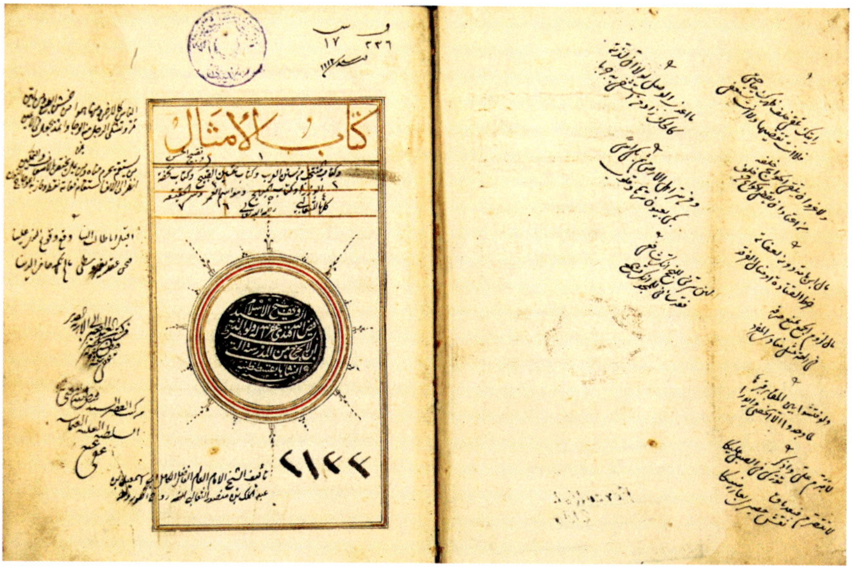

FIGURE 16 *K. al-Amthāl*, *MS Feyzullah 2133/1, 1r*

al-Mubhij among his works, which led Jādir to date the book among his earlier works.[167] The Tunis manuscript, however, carries the title of *al-Amthāl* and is an exact copy of *al-Tamthīl wa-l-muḥāḍara*. MS Feyzullah 2133/1 carries the title *al-Amthāl* and is in fact a book of *amthāl* by Abī Bakr al-Khwārizmī. The work was copied in 1028 AH in Egypt from another old manuscript that was copied in 29 Ramadan 442 AH.

64. *Asmāʾ al-aḍdād.*

This Najaf manuscript was examined by Muḥammad Ḥ. Āl Yāsīn, who identified it as part of *Fiqh al-lugha*.[168]

65. *Ghurar al-balāgha wa-durar al-faṣāḥa.*

Al-Samarrai mentions MS Beşīr Agha 150 with a colophon dedicating the work to *mawlānā l-malik al-muʾayyad al-muẓaffar walī al-niʿam*. This titulature is identical to that found in *K. Ādāb al-Mulūk*, which had been composed for and dedicated to the Khwārizmshāh Maʾmūn b. Maʾmūn. The work should not be confused with the *Ghurar al-balāgha fī-l-naẓm wa-l-nathr = al-Iʿjāz wa-l-ījāz* (see item 8).

167 See Jādir, "Dirāsa," 397.
168 See ibid., 394.

FIGURE 17 *al-Anwār al-bahiyya*, MS Bayezid Umumi 3709, 1r

In Manuscript, Authenticity Uncertain

66. *al-Anwār al-bahiyya fī taʿrīf maqāmāt fuṣaḥāʾ al-bariyya.*

Jādir lists this work mentioned by Bābānī as lost, but two manuscripts exist in MS Bayezid Umumi 3709 (completed 6 Dhū l-Ḥijja 707/27 May 1308) and Maktabat Kulliyyat al-Ādāb wa-l-Makhṭūṭāt 735 in Kuwayt (completed 11 Ṣafar 1325/18 July 1891).[169] Both manuscripts specify Thaʿālibī as compiler on the cover page. It is a work of *adab* that consists of an introduction, followed by a chapter on the merit and application of knowledge (*fī faḍīlat al-ʿilm wa-l-ʿamal bihi*), then an introduction and three other chapters (*abwāb*), one on

169 See Bābānī, *Hadiyyat al-ʿārifīn: asmāʾ al-muʾallifīn wa-āthār al-muṣannifīn* (Baghdad: Maktabat al-Muthannā, 1972), 1:625.

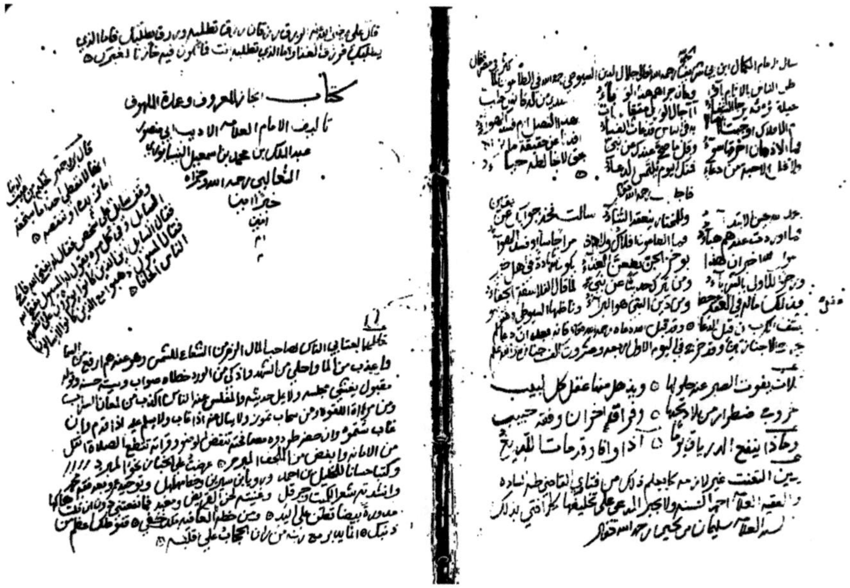

FIGURE 18 *Injāz al-maʿrūf, MF Kuwayt 6028*

the definition of knowledge and its true meaning (*al-bayān ʿan ḥadd al-ʿilm wa-ḥaqīqatihi*), another on conditions of knowledge (*al-bayān ʿan baʿḍ sharāʾiṭ al-ʿilm*), and another on the speaking occasions of scholars and sages (*al-bayān ʿan baʿḍ maqāmāt al-ʿulamāʾ wa-l-ḥukamāʾ*), which constitutes the bulk of the book. Thaʿālibī's authorship is very probable, as the introduction of the work includes several motifs and phrases that are

67. *al-Anwār fī āyāt al-nabī.*

Hilāl Nājī attributes MS Berlin 2083-Qu with this title to Thaʿālibī.[170] The work is in actually by another Thaʿālibī—Abū Zayd ʿAbd al-Raḥmān al-Thaʿālibī (d. 875/1470).

68. *Ḥilyat al-muḥāḍara wa-ʿunwān al-mudhākara wa-maydān al-musāmara.*

MS Paris 5914 carries this title.[171] The work might be identical to *al-Tamthīl wa-l-muḥāḍara* = *al-Tamaththul wa-l-muḥāḍara* = *Ḥilyat al-muḥāḍara* = *al-Maḥāsin wa-l-aḍdād* (see item 26).

170 Introduction to Thaʿālibī, *al-Anīs fī ghurar al-tajnīs*, 26.

171 See E. Blochet, *Catalogue de la collection des manuscrits orientaux, arabes, persans et turcs*, ed. Charles Shefer (Paris: Leroux, 1900), 22.

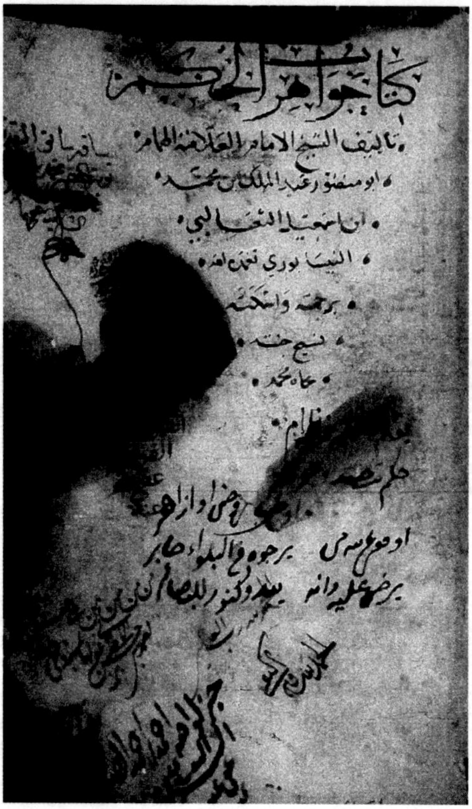

FIGURE 19 *Jawāhir al-ḥikam*, *MS Princeton 2234, 1r*

69. *al-ʿIshra al-mukhtāra.*

Hilāl Nājī, copied by Jādir, mentions a work attributed to Thaʿālibī by this title, MS Rampur 1/375-3.[172] A copy of the work is under MS Rampur 2365(1) in Maʿhad al-Makhṭūṭat al-ʿArabiyya (completed Rajab 823/July–August 1420).[173] The work consists of twelve chapters (*abwāb*), each of which starts with one or more verses from the Qurʾān, followed by a prophetic tradition, then statements by pious men. The first chapter deals with munificence to parents (*birr al-wālidayn*) and the last is on travel companionship (*bāb muʿāsharat al-rufaqāʾ fī l-safar*).

172 Introduction to Thaʿālibī, *al-Anīs fī ghurar al-tajnīs*, 44; Jādir, "Dirāsa," 417.

173 ʿIṣām Muḥammad al-Shanṭī, *Fihris al-Makhṭūṭat al-Muṣawwara* (Cairo: Maʿhad al-Makhṭūṭāt al-ʿArabiyya, 1995), *al-adab*, 1/5:36–7.

70. *Injāz al-maʿrūf wa-ʿumdat al-malhūf.*

MS Maʿhad al-Makhṭūṭāt al-ʿArabiyya 1017 in Egypt carries this title. Another manuscript (or possibly the same manuscript) is mentioned by Brockelmann as MS Khudā Bakhsh 1399.[174] Macrofilm 6028 in Kuwayt University Library (originally from Dār al-Makhṭūṭāt in Yaman) includes a work under this title. It is a work of *adab* that consists of sixteen folios in twenty-one chapters (*abwāb*) dealing with various aspects of friendship and companionship. The work has Thaʿālibī's full name on the cover page—*taʾlīf al-imām al-ʿallāma al-adīb Abī Manṣūr ʿAbd al-Malik b. Muḥammad b. Ismāʿīl al-Naysābūrī al-Thaʿālibī*—and again in the introduction.

71. *Jawāhir al-ḥikam.*

Bābānī is the only one in the sources who mentions this title.[175] Al-Jādir includes it among the lost works.[176] However, two manuscripts have survived, MS Berlin 1224 and MS Princeton 2234, although they are not identical. The title in the Berlin manuscript is *Jawāhir al-ḥikma*. The text is an anthology of ten chapters, followed by selections from *Kalīla wa-Dimna* and *al-Yawāqīt fī baʿḍ al-mawāqīt* (see item 32). Thaʿālibī's name is mentioned in the introduction and the work includes a few quotations present in Thaʿālibī's other works. Its attribution to him is possible.

The Princeton manuscript from the Yahuda section of the Garrett Collection of Arabic Manuscripts in the Princeton University Library has the title and compiler's name on the first folio. It is a collection of wise sayings in Arabic from the Greek, Byzantine, Sasanian, Hermetic, pre-Islamic, and Islamic traditions by Solomon, Socrates, Plato, Aristotle, Galen, Ptolemy, Simonides, Diogenes, Pythagoras, Khusraw, Quss b. Sāʿida, and more, without any chapter divisions. No internal evidence supports the attribution to Thaʿālibī. The work starts with a short introduction that is not characteristic of Thaʿālibī's style.

72. *al-Muhadhdhab min ikhtiyār Dīwan Abī l-Ṭayyib wa-aḥwālihi wa-sīratihi wa-mā jarā baynahu wa-bayna l-mulūk wa-l-shuʿarāʾ.*

A manuscript with this title exists in MS Dār al-Kutub al-Miṣriyya 18194-sh.[177] This work could be identical to the chapter on Mutanabbī in *Yatīmat al-dahr*.

174 See *GAL* I:340, who gives the name as *al-Injās* [?] *al-maʿrūf wa-ʿumdat al-qulūb*.

175 See Bābānī, *Hadiyyat al-ʿārifīn*, 1:625.

176 See Jādir, *al-Thaʿālibī*, 119.

177 See Jādir, "Dirāsa," 438.

FIGURE 20 *Nuzhat al-albāb wa-ʿumdat al-kuttāb*, MS *ʿĀrif Ḥikmat 271–Majāmīʿ*, 194r

73. *Nuzhat al-albāb wa-ʿumdat al-kuttāb* = *ʿUmdat al-Kuttāb.*

Jādir identifies this work with MS ʿĀrif Ḥikmat 271-*Majāmīʿ*.[178] The title on the cover page is *K. ʿUmdat al-kuttāb*, but the full title follows in the conclusion. Thaʿālibī's name appears on the cover page, and the work is dedicated to *al-amīr al-kabīr* Nāṣir al-Dawla. The style of the book closely resembles Thaʿālibī's, and some of its metaphors and phrases are common in Thaʿālibī's works. The work consists of sixty-nine short chapters (*fuṣūl*) containing mainly artistic prose and some poetry on different topics. The first covers God, the second the Qurʾān, and the last three are selections of sayings from Badīʿ al-Zamān al-Hamadhānī, Ṣāḥib Ibn ʿAbbād, and Abū Bakr al-Khwārizmī, respectively. Most of the material can be found in Thaʿālibī's *Siḥr al-balāgha* (see item 24). The work does not have a conclusion.

178 Ibid., 439.

FIGURE 21 *al-Shajar wa-l-ṣuwar*, MS. Dār al-Kutub al-Miṣriyya 440–adab, 2v

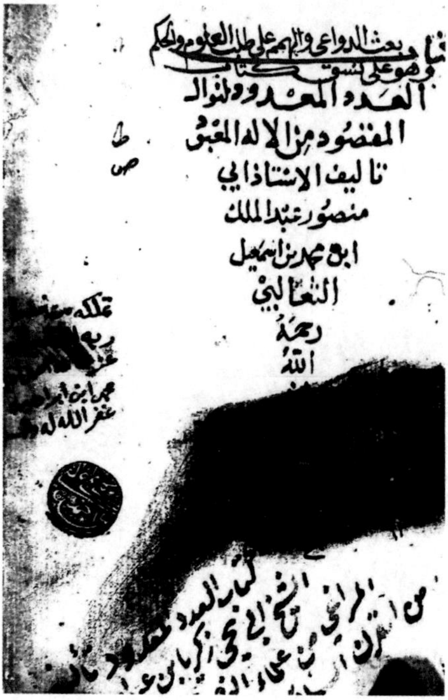

FIGURE 22 *Baʿth al-dawāʿī wa-l-himam*, MS Chester Beatty 4423¹, 1r

74. *Muʾnis al-waḥīd.*

Jādir and Nājī identify MS Cambridge 1287 as *Muʾnis al-waḥīd.*[179] The reference must be to MS Trinity College R.13.8.[180] This manuscript could be identical to MS Paris 3034, which carries the title *Uns al-waḥīd* (cf. items 44, 60). The first title is mentioned by Ibn Khallikān and in later biographical works. Al-Jādir confirms that the book published as *Muʾnis al-waḥīd wa-nuzhat al-mustafīd* is unrelated to Thaʿālibī (cf. item 52).

75. *al-Shajar wa-l-ṣuwar fī-l-ḥikam wa-l-mawʿiẓa.*

MS Dār al-Kutab al-Miṣriyya 440-*adab* (Maʿhad al-Makhṭūṭāt 1844) is a work of *adab* attributed to Thaʿālibī on its title page. The book consists of ten chapters on different aspects of religion (*shajar*): faith (*īmān*), religiosity (*diyāna*), watchfulness (*waraʿ*), renunciation (*zuhd*), trust (*tawakkul*), Sufism (*taṣawwuf*), certitude (*yaqīn*), independence (*ghinā*), pleasure (*ladhdha*), and happiness (*saʿāda*).

179 Ibid.; introduction to Thaʿālibī, *al-Anīs fī ghurar al-tajnīs*, 28.

180 I thank Michelle Barnes of Cambridge University for this information.

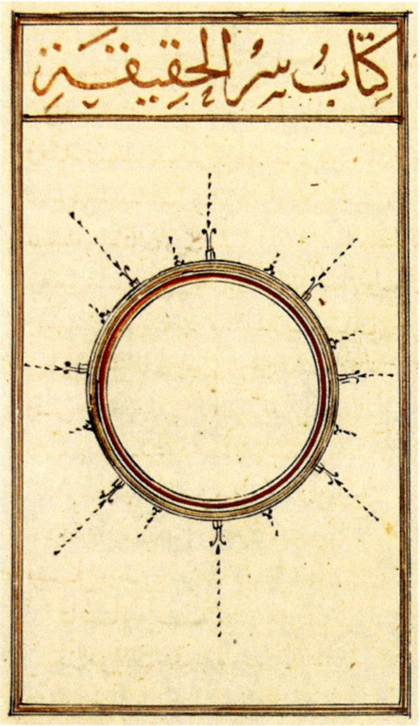

FIGURE 23 *Sirr al-ḥaqīqa, MS Feyzullah 21337, 215r*

76. *Sirr al-balāgha wa-mulaḥ al-barāʿa.*

A manuscript with this title is mentioned by Aḥmad ʿUbayd and Hilāl Nājī in MS Dār al-Kutub al-Miṣriyya 4-sh, but according to them, it is different from the printed version of *Siḥr al-balāgha* (see item 24).[181]

In Manuscript, Authenticity Rejected

77. *al-ʿAdad al-Maʿdūd li-nawāl al-maqṣūd min al-ilāh al-maʿbūd = Baʿth al-dawāʿī wa-l-himam ʿalā ṭalab al-ʿulūm wa-l-ḥikam.*

MS Chester Beatty 4423/1 is attributed to "*al-ustādh* Abī Manṣūr ʿAbd al-Malik al-Thaʿālibī" in its first folio. In another hand at the bottom of the cover page of the manuscript, it is indicated that *al-shaykh* Abū Yaḥyā Zakariyyā b. ʿAbdallāh al-Marāghī, a scholar from the second half of the sixth/twelfth century (*min ʿulamāʾ al-niṣf al-thānī min al-qarn al-sādis al-hijrī*), compiled the book. The proper title of the work as stated in the first and last folios is *Baʿth al-dawāʿī wa-l-himam ʿalā ṭalab al-ʿulūm wa-l-ḥikam*. The anthologist states

181 See introduction to Thaʿālibī, *Siḥr al-balāgha wa-sirr al-barāʿa*, ed. A. ʿUbayd (Damascus: al-Maktaba al-ʿArabiyya, 1931), 2; introduction to Thaʿālibī, *al-Anīs fī ghurar al-tajnīs*, 27.

FIGURE 24 *MS ʿĀrif Ḥikmat 31–Majāmīʿ, 1r*

in the introduction that he composed the book when he saw that a friend of his was inclined to Thaʿālibī's *Bard al-akbād* (see item 6) (*li-mayl baʿḍ aṣdiqāʾī ilā l-maʿdūd min al-kalām wa-istiṭrāfihim lamʿatan jamaʿahā al-ustādh Abū Manṣūr ʿAbd al-Malik b. Muḥammad b. Ismāʿīl al-Thaʿālibī*). The anthologist divides his work into five categories (*maqālāt*), the categories into chapters (*abwāb*), and the chapters into sections. The work follows Thaʿālibī's method in *Bard al-akbād*; it collects sayings in prose and poetry dealing with lists based on numerical divisions and incorporates much of the Thaʿālibī's content.

78. *Rusūm al-balāgha.*

Topuzoğlu mentions this title in MS Yeni Cami 1188/1.[182] It is an abridgment of *al-Tahānī wa-l-taʿāzī*, which is not by Thaʿālibī's but by Abū Manṣūr b. al-Marzubān (d. after 340/951).

79. *Sirr al-ḥaqīqa.*

Brockelmann and Hilāl Nājī point out this title in MS Feyzullah 2133/7.[183] A microfilm of the same manuscript is located in MS Maʿhad Iḥyāʾ al-Makhṭūṭāt

182 Topuzoğlu, "Istanbul Manuscripts of Works," 67.

183 Introduction to Thaʿālibī, *al-Anīs fī ghurar al-tajnīs*, 27; *GAL* SI:502.

al-ʿArabiyya 465. The book is the seventh work in a collection, which was copied in 1028/1619 from a manuscript written in 442/1050. Upon closer inspection, the title is a work of Sufism that compiles poetic verses chosen by Sufis to illustrate their mystical experiences. It is identical to Abū ʿAbd al-Raḥmān al-Sulamī's (d. 412/1021) *K. al-Amthāl wa-l-istishhādāt.*

80. *al-Tadallī fī-l-tasallī.*

Jādir mentions this title in MS ʿĀrif Ḥikmat 31-*Majāmīʿ*, which he did not examine. The manuscript mentions Thaʿālibī right after the *basmala*: "*qāla* Abū Manṣūr ʿAbd al-Malik al-Thaʿālibī." The work published with this title in *K. al-Afḍaliyyāt*, a collection of seven letters by Abū l-Qāsim ʿAlī b. Munjib b. Sulaymān Ibn al-Ṣayrafī (d. 542/1147), edited by Walīd Qaṣṣāb and ʿAbd al-ʿAzīz al-Māniʿ, is based on another manuscript, MS Fatih 5410. MS ʿĀrif Ḥikmat differs from the published one in that it includes additional pages on the subject of *rithāʾ* before the conclusion. Confusingly, these five pages include three lines attributed to the author in consolation of the Khwārizmshāh (*li-muʾallif al-kitāb fī taʿziyat Khwārizmshāh*), and the lines are by Thaʿālibī himself, as attested by his *Aḥsan mā samiʿtu* (see item 3).[184] Since Ibn Sinān al-Khafājī (d. 466/1073) and a few other later poets are quoted throughout the book, the work cannot be Thaʿālibī's. The five extra pages could have been added by a later scribe, since all the poems quoted there pertain to one subject. The poems surrounding the three quoted lines of Thaʿālibī are the same as those in *Aḥsan mā samiʿtu*. The scribe thus added material to the original work and, intentionally or mistakenly, copied a whole page of Thaʿālibī's *Aḥsan mā samiʿtu*, leaving unchanged the phrase *li-muʾallif hādha-l-kitāb*, which precedes the three lines from Thaʿālibī. The inclusion of the three lines led to the later misattribution of the whole work to Thaʿālibī.

81. *Tarājim al-Shuʿarāʾ.*

Jādir examines MS Maʿhad Iḥyāʾ al-Makhṭūṭat 2281 in Jāmiʿat al-Duwal al-ʿArabiyya and notes that it is the work of a later author because it includes people who lived beyond Thaʿālibī's lifetime. Jādir further discounts the attribution to Thaʿālibī because the work is not structured according to geographi-

---

184 The full quotation in Thaʿālibī, *Aḥsan mā samiʿtu*, 142, is as follows:

وقال مؤلّف الكتاب للأمير أبي العبّاس [خوارزمشاه] (من مخلع البسيط):

قل للمليكِ الأجلّ قدْرا لا زلتَ بدْرًا تحمل صدْرا
إنّي أعزّيكَ عنْ عزيز كان لرَيْبِ الزمانِ عُذرا
وكان طُهرًا فصار أجْرًا وكان ظُهرًا فصار ذُخْرا

cal divisions and includes pre-Islamic and Islamic poetry.[185] This, by itself, is not necessarily convincing; Thaʿālibī shows interest in non-*muḥdath* poetry in some of his works and does not always rely on a geographical division. In fact, he followed a geographical order only in the *Yatīma* and *Tatimma*.

Works Surviving in Quotations

82. *Dīwān Abī l-Ḥasan al-Laḥḥām.*

Thaʿālibī mentions this work in the *Yatīma*, where he reports searching in vain for a *dīwān* of Laḥḥām's poetry and taking it upon himself to produce one. He then states that he later chose suitable quotations for the *Yatīma*.[186]

83. *Dīwān al-Thaʿālibī.*

Bākharzī mentions that he saw a volume (*mujallada*) of Thaʿālibī's poetry and used selections from it in his anthology.[187] ʿAbd al-Fattāḥ al-Ḥulw has tried to reconstruct this lost work. Jādir then corrected misattributions in al-Ḥulw's edition and added further verses. He revised it once more and published it as *Dīwān al-Thaʿālibī*. Hilāl Nājī adds 152 lines by Thaʿālibī from four works not included by Jādir: *Aḥāsin al-maḥāsin*, *Rawḥ al-rūḥ*, *Zād safar al-mulūk*, and *al-Tawfīq li-l-talfīq*.[188] I have presented a further addendum to the *Dīwān* of Thaʿālibī.[189]

ʿA. F. al-Ḥulw, "Shiʿr al-Thaʿālibī," *Majallat al-Mawrid* 6 (1977), 139-94; M. ʿA. al-Jādir, "Shiʿr al-Thaʿālibī—dirāsa wa istidrāk," *Majallat al-Mawrid* 8 (1979); H. Nājī, "al-Mustadrak ʿalā ṣunnāʿ al-dawāwīn," *al-Mawrid* 15 (1986); ed. and collected by M. ʿA. al-Jādir, Beirut: ʿĀlam al-Kutub and al-Nahḍa al-ʿArabiyya, 1988 (as *Dīwān al-Thaʿālibī*, revision of al-Jādir 1979).

84. *K. al-Ghilmān = Alf ghulām = al-Taghazzul bi-miʾatay ghulām.*

Cited by Ibn Khallikān, Ṣafadī, Kutubī, and Ibn Qāḍī Shuhba as *K. al-Ghilmān*. Ibn Bassām, who quotes two texts thereof, calls it *Alf ghulām*.[190] Thaʿālibī himself in *Tatimmat al-Yatīma* describes a work in which he composed *ghazal* for two hundred boys (*al-taghazzul bi-miʾatay ghulām*).[191] Jurjī Zaydān mentions

---

185 Jādir, "Dirāsa," 404.

186 See *Y* 4:102.

187 See Bākharzī, *Dumyat al-qaṣr*, 967.

188 See Hilāl Nājī, "al-Mustadrak ʿalā ṣunnāʿ al-dawāwīn," *al-Mawrid* 15 (1986), 199–210.

189 Orfali, "Addendum to the *Dīwān*," 440–49.

190 Shantarīnī, *al-Dhakhīra fī maḥāsin ahl al-jazīra*, 4:72; see also Talib, "Pseudo-Ṯaʿālibī's *Book of Youths*," 602–5.

191 See *T* 277.

two manuscripts, Berlin and Escorial, without further details.[192] MS Berlin 8334 (We[tzstein] II, 1786) is not Thaʿālibī's, since most of the poems come from the Mamlūk period (see item 46). Adam Talib identifies MS Escorial árabe 461 as *K. Alf ghulām wa-ghulām* by ʿAlī b. Muḥammad b. al-Riḍā al-Ḥusaynī and notes that the author acknowledges the influence of Thaʿālibī's work.[193]

85. *Ghurar al-nawādir.*

One quotation survives in *Akhbār al-ḥamqā wa-l-mughaffalīn* by Ibn al-Jawzī.[194] This work could be identical to *al-Mulaḥ al-nawādir* (see item 110) or *ʿUyūn al-nawādir* (see item 130).

86. *Ḥashw al-lawzīnaj.*

Thaʿālibī mentions this work in *Khāṣṣ al-khāṣṣ* and, in more detail, in *Thimār al-qulūb*.[195] Other examples in *Thimār al-qulūb*, *Fiqh al-lugha*, and *Khāṣṣ al-khāṣṣ* are most probably part of this work too.[196] The book's title plays on the name of a pastry. In *Thimār al-qulūb* he describes the book as *ṣaghīr al-jirm laṭīf al-ḥajm* (short in dimension, light in size), and then cites an example. While the term *ḥashw* (insertion) usually has negative connotations, the book deals with "enhancing insertion." The poetic analogy to the *lawzīnaj*—the almond filling being tastier than the outer crust[197]—appears first in Thaʿālibī's works, although the examples in prose and verse are traceable to the pre-Islamic, Islamic, and ʿAbbāsid periods. The literary application of the term is to Ṣāḥib Ibn ʿAbbād, according to Thaʿālibī,[198] and used to describe an added, though dispensable, phrase that embellishes a sentence.

87. *al-Lumaʿ al-ghaḍḍa.*

One quotation from this work survives in *al-Tadwīn fī akhbār Qazwīn* of ʿAbd al-Karīm b. Muḥammad al-Rāfiʿī al-Qazwīnī (d. 622/1226). The quotation is a *khabar* on the authority of Abū l-Ḥasan al-Maṣṣīṣī about Abū Dulaf al-Khazrajī and Abū ʿAlī al-Hāʾim.[199]

192 Jurjī Zaydān, *Taʾrīkh ādāb al-lugha al-ʿarabiyya*, 2:332.

193 Talib, "Pseudo-Ṭaʿālibī's *Book of Youths,*" 604–5.

194 See Ibn al-Jawzī, *Akhbār al-ḥamqā wa-l-mughaffalīn*, ed. M. A. Farshūkh (Beirut: Dār al-Fikr al-ʿArabī, 1990), 41.

195 See Thaʿālibī, *Thimār al-qulūb*, 610, id., *Khāṣṣ al-Khāṣṣ*, 128.

196 See Thaʿālibī, *Thimār al-qulūb*, 610–12; id., *Khāṣṣ al-khāṣṣ*, 128; id., *Fiqh al-lugha*, 260–62.

197 See Thaʿālibī, *Thimār al-qulūb*, 611; id., *Khāṣṣ al-khāṣṣ*, 128; id., *Fiqh al-lugha*, 261.

198 See Thaʿālibī, *Fiqh al-lugha*, 262; id., *Khāṣṣ al-khāṣṣ*, 128.

199 Rāfiʿī al-Qazwīnī, *K. al-Tadwīn fī akhbār Qazwīn*, ed. ʿA. al-ʿUṭāridī (Beirut: Dār al-Kutub al-ʿIlmiyya, 1987), 1:36.

88. *al-Siyāsa.*

This work appears in Ṣafadī's list and Thaʿālibī mentions it in *Ajnās al-tajnīs*, quoting one saying from it on royal duties.[200]

Lost Works

89. *al-Adab mimmā li-l-nās fīhi arab*
90. *Afrād al-maʿānī*
91. *al-Aḥāsin min badāʾiʿ al-bulaghāʾ*
92. *Bahjat al-mushtāq* (or *al-ʿushshāq*)
93. *al-Barāʿa fī-l-takallum wa-l-ṣināʿa*[201]
94. *Faḍl man ismuhu l-Faḍl*[202]
95. *al-Farāʾid wa-l-qalāʾid*[203]
96. *al-Fuṣūl al-fārisiyya*
97. *Ghurar al-maḍāḥik*
98. *Ḥujjat al-ʿaql*
99. *al-Ihdāʾ wa-l-istihdāʾ*[204]
100. *Jawāmiʿ al-kalim*
101. *Khaṣāʾiṣ al-buldān*[205]
102. *Khaṣāʾiṣ al-faḍāʾil*
103. *al-Khwārazmiyyāt*[206]
104. *al-Laṭīf fī l-ṭīb*[207]
105. *Lubāb al-aḥāsin*

200 Thaʿālibī, *Ajnās al-tajnīs*, 51.

201 See Jādir, "Dirāsa," 400; al-Samarrai, "Some Biographical Notes," 186.

202 Thaʿālibī mentions this work in *Yatīma* 3:433 and *Thimār al-qulūb*, 393, where he states having composed it for Abū l-Faḍl al-Mīkālī.

203 Mentioned already in Kalāʿī's list and perhaps a lost work, different from that of Ahwāzī (see item 45).

204 See Thaʿālibī, *Mirʾāt al-murūʾāt*, 134.

205 The title was mentioned only by Thaʿālibī in *Thimār al-qulūb*; he stated that the work is on the characteristics of different countries and is dedicated it to *al-amīr al-sayyid* (i.e., al-Mīkālī); see Thaʿālibī, *Thimār al-qulūb*, 545. Jādir notes that Thaʿālibī's *Laṭāʾif al-maʿārif* also includes a chapter on the same subject; see Jādir, "Dirāsa," 410. H. Nājī mentions that Muḥammad Jabbār al-Muʿaybid found a section of this book in Berlin, which he is editing; see introduction to Thaʿālibī, *al-Tawfīq li-l-talfīq*, 34.

206 This could be the *Ādāb al-mulūk* (see item 2).

207 Mentioned in *al-Iʿjāz wa-l-ījāz* as dedicated to Abū Aḥmad Manṣūr b. Muḥammad al-Harawī al-Azdī in 412/1021; see Thaʿālibī, *al-Iʿjāz wa-l-ījāz*, 17.

106. *Madḥ al-shayʾ wa-dhammuh*
107. *al-Madīḥ*
108. *Man ghāba ʿanhu l-muʾnis*[208]
109. *Miftāḥ al-faṣāḥa*
110. *al-Mulaḥ al-nawādir*[209]
111. *al-Mulaḥ wa-l-ṭuraf*
112. *Munādamat al-mulūk*[210]
113. *al-Mushriq (al-mashūq?)*[211]
114. *Nasīm al-uns*
115. *al-Nawādir wa-l-bawādir*
116. *Ṣanʿat al-shiʿr wa-l-nathr*
117. *K. al-Shams*[212]
118. *Sirr al-bayān*
119. *Sirr al-ṣināʿa*[213]
120. *Sirr al-wizāra*
121. *Tafaḍḍul al-muqtadirīn wa-tanaṣṣul al-muʿtadhirīn*
122. *al-Thalj wa-l-maṭar*
123. *al-Tuffāḥa*
124. *Tuḥfat al-arwāḥ wa-mawāʾid al-surūr wa-l-afrāḥ*[214]
125. *al-Ṭuraf min shiʿr al-Bustī*
126. *al-Uṣūl fī l-fuṣūl* (or *al-Fuṣūl fī l-fuḍūl*)[215]

---

208 Perhaps identical to *Man ghāba ʿanhu l-muṭrib* (see item 17), although Ṣafadī lists a separate work titled *Man aʿwazahu l-muṭrib*.

209 Mentioned only in Thaʿālibī, *al-Ẓarāʾif wa-l-laṭāʾif*, 51.

210 This title is mentioned in Ṣafadī and could be identical to *al-Mulūkī* (see item 2) or *Taʾrīkh ghurar al-siyar* (see item 39).

211 Jādir points out that this work was composed before *al-Laṭāʾif wa-l-ẓarāʾif*, where it is mentioned; see Jādir, "Dirāsa," 432.

212 This could be *Shams al-adab = Fiqh al-lugha*.

213 Mentioned in *Mirʾāt al-murūʾāt* as a book intended on literary criticism; see Thaʿālibī, *Mirʾāt al-murūʾāt*, 14. Furthermore, Thaʿālibī mentioned in *Tatimmat al-Yatīma* that he started this work, which should contain a hundred *bāb*, and he emphasized that it included criticism of prose and poetry; see *T* 219.

214 Mentioned only as a source for Bābānī in *Hadiyyat al-ʿārifīn*, 1:625, which makes the attribution to Thaʿālibī improbable.

215 Mentioned in Ṣafadī under *al-Fuṣūl fī l-fuḍūl*, but in Kutubī and Ibn Qāḍī Shuhba's lists is mentioned as *al-Uṣūl fī l-fuṣūl*.

127. *Uns al-musāfir*
128. *ʿUnwān al-maʿārif*
129. *ʿUyūn al-ādāb*[216]
130. *ʿUyūn al-nawādir*
131. *al-Ward*

---

216 Thaʿālibī mentions this work in *al-Ẓarāʾif wa-l-laṭāʾif* without attributing it to himself, but Jādir points out that the context suggests it is his work; consequently, he considers it one of his lost works; see Jādir, "Dirāsa," 418.

CHAPTER 3

An Anthologist at Work: The Organization and Structure of the *Yatīma* and *Tatimma*

Muslim scholars based their scholarship and teaching on written materials. However, these materials were not necessarily books in the modern sense; they were more likely to be lecture scripts compiled in notebooks, or notes varying in length and content that were used as memory aids.[1] These may have been prepared by the teacher himself or by an earlier scholar.[2] Some of these "collections" gradually took on a more definite shape, acquired titles, and became "books." Both the *Yatīmat al-dahr fī maḥāsin ahl al-ʿaṣr* and its sequel, the *Tatimmat al-Yatīma*, may have started as notes, but they evolved into books during Thaʿālibī's lifetime, displaying distinctive characteristics such as a preface with a dedication and table of contents, a methodological consciousness expressed in Thaʿālibī's selections and arrangement, and a sophisticated system of internal references and cross-references to other works. This methodological consciousness involved in compiling the *Yatīma* and *Tatimma* is the subject of this chapter.

Organization

Thaʿālibī's *Yatīmat al-dahr fi maḥāsin ahl al-ʿaṣr* and its sequel, the *Tatimmat al-Yatīma*, are perhaps the oldest surviving books in Arabic that examine literature by geographical regions and contemporary production. Moreover, many of the poets mentioned in the two anthologies are known only through Thaʿālibī. Both anthologies are thus among the most important sources for literature of the second half of the fourth/tenth century.

1 See Gregor Schoeler, "W. Werkmeister: *Quellenuntersuchungen zum Kitāb al-ʿIqd al-farīd des Andalusiers Ibn ʿAbdrabbih* (246/860–328/940)," *Zeitschrift der Deutschen Morgenländischen Gesellschaft* 136 (1986), 121.

2 See S. Leder, "Riwāya," *EI2* VIII:546; id., "al-Madāʾinī's Version of Qiṣṣat al-Shūrā," in *Myths, Historical Archetypes and Symbolic Figures in Arabic Literature*, ed. Angelika Neuwirth et al. (Beirut: Franz Steiner Verlag Stuttgart, 1999), 380–84; Gregor Schoeler, "Die Frage der schriftlichen oder mündlichen Überlieferung der Wissenschaften im frühen Islam," *Der Islam* 62 (1985), 201.

 | DOI 10.1163/9789004317352_004

Despite occasional comments on the relationship between poetry and place in various *adab* works from the third/ninth century,[3] this idea of relationship does not seem to have played a role in Arabic anthologies before Thaʿālibī's *Yatīmat al-dahr*. The work presents a systematic geographic survey of all major contemporary Arabic poets, divided into four regions (*aqsām*) from west to east: Syria and the west (Mawṣil, Egypt, and al-Maghrib); Iraq; western Iran (al-Jabal, Fārs, Jurjān, and Ṭabaristān); and eastern Iran (Khurāsān and Transoxania), with special attention paid to Nīshāpūr. Thaʿālibī subsumes Syria, Egypt, and al-Maghrib under one section, justifying his decision by the fact that he collected the material secondhand from transmitters or scattered notes (*min athnāʾ al-taʿlīqāt*), not directly from the authors. Moreover, he was unable to access *dīwān*s for the poets, which would have allowed him to select a greater sampling of their poetry.[4] Evidence suggests that the selections were written in the order that they appear, at least for the last chapter, where Thaʿālibī says:

> Since the beginning of this book is dependent on its end, its first part [lit. hemistich] is contingent upon the second, and since the complete benefit could hardly be attained from its first and middle parts without the last, I appealed for God's assistance in writing this fourth quarter of it, and I fashioned it in ten chapters; God, glory to Him, is one who leads to the right guidance.[5]

Each region is subdivided into ten chapters (*abwāb*) based on individual literary figures, courts and dynasties, cities, or smaller regions. Thaʿālibī occasionally adds critical comments, a discussion of *sariqāt* (literary borrowings) and/or *muʿāraḍāt* (literary emulations), information on the historical contexts of the poems, and biographical information on the literary figures.[6]

The structure of the *Tatimma* follows the *Yatīma* in its regions, but no smaller division is attempted. The *Tatimma* has a final section that does not fit into the book's plan, since it includes litterateurs from all regions. These are either poets whose poetry Thaʿālibī became acquainted with later in life or whose poetry or prose he simply had forgotten to include in the section on the litterateur's geographic location. He notes that the litterateurs are arranged

3 See a discussion of these in Jādir, *al-Thaʿālibī nāqidan wa-adīban* (Beirut: Dār al-Niḍāl, 1991), 193ff.
4 *Y* 1:300.
5 *Y* 4:64.
6 See appendix 1 for the *aqsām* and *abwāb* of the *Yatīma* and the *Tatimma*.

neither chronologically nor by rank, and that they are to be viewed instead as dessert, served at the end of a feast.[7]

Thaʿālibī's method of categorization permits the researcher to trace the origin and development of new genres and themes in different cities, regions, and courts. It is also of great importance for the study of the court literature of the period, since Thaʿālibī gathers the poets associated with a certain court or the literature composed in that court.

At the beginning of each section, Thaʿālibī announces the plan he will follow. For example, his introduction to the section on Khurāsān in the *Tatimma* begins thus:

> I have determined in this last section of *Tatimmat al-Yatīma* to begin with the inhabitants of Nīshāpūr and its suburbs, then extend to all other regions of Khurāsān. Afterwards, I will mention the pillars of the state and the prominent people in high culture—may God protect them and keep their company—the administrative officials, those who are in its service among the residents, and others.[8]

Prominent Litterateurs

Naturally, each geographical region enjoyed its own prominent literary figures, and Thaʿālibī dedicated separate chapters to several of these. In the first region, Abū Firās al-Ḥamdānī (d. 357/967), Mutanabbī (d. 354/965), and Abū l-Faraj al-Babbaghāʾ (d. 398/1008) each occupy a chapter of their own, and Nāmī (d. 399/1009), Nāshiʾ al-Aṣghar (d. 366/976) and Zāhī (d. 352/963) are grouped together in one chapter. Khalīʿ al-Shāmī (d. after 356/967), Waʾwāʾ al-Dimashqī (d. 385/995), and Abū Ṭālib al-Raqqī (d. after 356/967) are gathered into another chapter.

In the second region, Abū Isḥāq al-Ṣābī (d. 384/994) and al-Sharīf al-Raḍī (d. 406/1015) are singled out for a chapter each, and Abū l-Qāsim ʿAbd al-ʿAzīz b. Yūsuf (d. 384/994), Abū Aḥmad ʿAbd al-Raḥmān b. al-Faḍl al-Shīrāzī (d. ca. 385/995), and Abū l-Qāsim ʿAlī b. al-Qāsim al-Qāshānī (d. ca. 385/995), all three being vizierlike secretaries (*yajrūna majrā l-wuzarāʾ*), are collected into another chapter.

The third region features Abū l-ʿAbbās Aḥmad b. Ibrāhīm al-Ḍabbī (d. 398/1008) individually, and the fourth region Badīʿ al-Zamān al-Hamadhānī (d. 398/1008) and Abū l-Faḍl al-Mīkālī (d. 436/1044–5), as well as discussions

7 *T* 283.
8 *T* 181.

of the poet al-Ma'mūnī (d. 383/993) and the *faqīh* poet al-Wāthiqī (d. before 421/1030).

The chapters dealing with prominent literary figures do not differ much in their structure or content from other entries of the *Yatīma* or the *Tatimma*. They usually exceed other entries in length, because of the poet's or *adīb*'s importance, fame, or prolific output. In fact, the chapter on Mutanabbī (d. 354/965), was originally conceived of as a book. Certain subsections of chapters in the *Yatīma*, however, can be as long and detailed as entire chapters, such as those on Abū Bakr al-Khwārizmī (d. 383/993), Ibn al-Ḥajjāj (d. 391/1001), Abū l-Fatḥ al-Bustī (d. 400/1010), Ibn Sukkara (d. ca. 385/995), and Ibn Fāris (d. ca. 398/1007).

Courts, Dynasties, and Patronage

In addition to devoting attention to prominent literary figures, Thaʿālibī organizes entries in his two anthologies according to patronage. In the first region, he devotes the second chapter to the court of Sayf al-Dawla al-Ḥamdānī (d. 356/967) and includes all other Ḥamdānid *amīr*s and their officials in the fourth chapter. The Būyid rulers (*mulūk*) are anthologized in the first chapter of the second region, and the vizier Muhallabī (d. 352/963) and his court in the second chapter, and the fourth chapter, as previously mentioned, brings together three Būyid vizierlike secretaries (*kuttāb*). The ninth chapter brings together poems of various authors in praise of the Būyid vizier Sābūr b. Ardashīr (d. 416/1025–6). The third region concentrates on individual patrons—namely al-Ṣāḥīb b. ʿAbbād (d. 385/995), Abū l-Faḍl Ibn al-ʿAmīd (d. 360/970), Abū l-Fatḥ Ibn al-ʿAmīd (d. 366/976), and Qābūs b. Wushmgīr (d. 403/1012–13). The fourth region highlights the Sāmānid court in Bukhārā.

Thaʿālibī states in his introduction that he will anthologize poetry by dignitaries, even if the poems fail to meet his standards of excellence. Of greater interest are patrons or *amīr*s with poetic talent, for these usually demonstrate their interest in literature by patronizing litterateurs. Such entries present the literary production of the patron alongside that of the literary figures at his court.

A litterateur's affiliation with a court affects Thaʿālibī's placement of his oeuvre. In entries dedicated to patrons, he examines the literary production along with the courtly life and patronage. In these sections, Thaʿālibī includes poems that eulogize, mourn, blame, or censure the patron, or poetry that the patron commissioned or composed in his court. Such is the case for Sayf al-Dawla (d. 356/967), whose accounts as a patron take up more space in the *Yatīma* than

FIGURE 25 *Yatīmat al-dahr*, MS Escorial 350, 28r

his poetry does; Thaʿālibī even includes a subsection on Sayf al-Dawla's donations and stipends to poets.[9] In contrast, the chapter dedicated to the court of Sābūr b. Ardashīr (d. 416/1025–6) says nothing about the vizier or his compositions, since he was not known to be a poet. Moreover, some of the poets included there are discussed elsewhere in the *Yatīma*, while others are not given their own entry, as Thaʿālibī himself notes at the outset.[10]

The literature in the chapters on courts is treated virtually as the patron's product rather than the product of the poet for, in including his description and attributes, it functions as a monument to or a portrait of the patron.[11] Even when this poetry does not discuss the attributes of the patron, it is still composed at his court or literary gathering and contributes to the creation of his literary image. The discussion of a certain court or patron in a chapter is meant to collate literature that was produced by the patron or about him by the literary figures that he attracted. This constitutes the literary production

9 *Y* 1:32ff.

10 *Y* 3:129.

11 For details, see Abdelfattah Kilito, *The Author and His Doubles*, trans. Michael Cooperson (Syracuse: Syracuse University Press, 2001), 24ff.

of the court and reflects its literary interests, styles, and agendas. In the chapter dedicated to Ṣāḥib b. ʿAbbād, and to some extent in the chapters on Ibn al-ʿAmīd and Muhallabī, Thaʿālibī not only presents their work and interests but also gives a detailed picture of their literary gatherings, the poets and literary scholars who frequented them, and the debates, discussions, competitions, and contests that took place there. Thaʿālibī devotes more than thirty pages to Ṣāḥib's thematic suggestions (*iqtirāḥāt*) to poets, their accounts, and the resulting poems.[12] Poems written in specific situations are labeled accordingly. In one instance, Ṣāḥib invites his companions to describe his new villa (*dār*) in Iṣbahān; the poems are labeled *al-diyārāt*. In another instance, Ṣāḥib suggests (*awʿaza*) that the poets console Abū ʿĪsā Aḥmad b. al-Munajjim upon the death of his workhorse (*birdhawn*); Thaʿālibī calls these poems *al-birdhawniyyāt*.[13] When Ṣāḥib orders (*amara*) the poets in his court to describe an elephant in the prologue of a *qaṣīda* (*fī tashbīb qaṣīda*), specifying the rhyme and meter, the poems are called *al-fīliyyāt*. Similarly, Thaʿālibī portrays Muhallabī's *majlis* on the basis of Ṣāḥib's *K. al-Rūznāmja*.[14] The chapters dedicated to these patrons are meant to draw pictures of their courts as Thaʿālibī saw or imagined them. But he distinguishes Ṣāḥib b. ʿAbbād by devoting an additional chapter to the poets who visited his court. Ṣāḥib's court is thus treated like a geographical region wherein each poet receives an article in a collective chapter.

Cities and Subregions

Not all cities enjoyed the presence of rulers and viziers who were also literary patrons, like Ṣāḥib b. ʿAbbād, ʿAḍud al-Dawla (d. 372/983), the two Ibn al-ʿAmīds, and Sayf al-Dawla al-Ḥamdānī. This did not mean, however, that such cities did not witness a literary efflorescence, or that less established *amīr*s did not sponsor literature. Many cities benefited from the presence of well-established families who patronized literature, such as the Mīkālīs of Nīshāpūr.[15] Consequently, cities and subregions are a third point of focus for Thaʿālibī in his collection of the literature of the period. Here, the entries are not centered on one figure, such as a poet or patron. There is some duplication between chapters on courts and dynasties, as well as on cities and subregions,

12 *Y* 3:207ff.

13 For information on Munajjim, see *Y* 3:393; Ṣafadī, *al-Wāfī bi-l-Wafayāt*, ed. Aḥmad al-Arnāʾūṭ and Turkī Muṣṭafā (Beirut: Dār Iḥyāʾ al-Turāth al-ʿArabī, 2000), 7:149. A literary analysis of the *birdhawniyyāt* is provided by Andras Hamori, "The Silken Horsecloths Shed Their Tears," *Arabic and Middle Eastern Literatures* 2 (1999), 43–59.

14 *Y* 2:227–31.

15 See C. E. Bosworth, "Mīkālīs," *EI2* VII:25b–26b.

since poets neither started out at courts nor stayed there, given political instability. Thaʿālibī was aware of this overlap and used cross-references to link various entries featuring poetry by one figure.

The first three regions contain very few geographical chapters. In the first region, Mawṣil is the subject of the tenth chapter. In the second region, the sixth chapter is dedicated to a group of poets from other Iraqi districts, except Baghdad, which is covered in the seventh and eighth chapters. In the third region, al-Jabal is treated in the seventh chapter, Fārs and Ahwāz in the eighth, and Jurjān and Ṭabaristān in the ninth. It is only in the fourth region that division by city and subregion takes on greater importance, presumably because of the absence of major courts in these regions. Thaʿālibī places Bukhārā in the second chapter, Khwārizm in the fourth, Bust in the sixth, and Khurāsān in the seventh. Nīshāpūr, Thaʿālibī's native city, receives special attention in the ninth and tenth chapters.

The peripatetic movement of some poets makes it difficult to associate them with a certain city or region. The *Yatīma* anthologizes local literary figures who did not move between courts and who enjoyed a stable profession, such as working as a judge (*qāḍī*), yet it also commemorates those who frequently changed location and/or spent their lives wandering from one court to another, especially if their profession required court patronage—for example, scribe or secretary (*kātib*), boon companion (*nadīm*), court poet, treasurer (*khāzin*), librarian (*khāzin kutub*), or chamberlain (*ḥājib*). In many cases, Thaʿālibī categorizes itinerant litterateurs by their city of birth. Sometimes, however, when Thaʿālibī files a poet by city of his origin, he indicates the poet's travels to another area. In the chapter dedicated to Khwārizm, for example, Thaʿālibī traces the route of Abū Bakr al-Khwārizmī (d. 383/993);[16] moreover, he includes there the secretary Muḥammad b. Ḥāmid Abū ʿAbdallāh al-Ḥāmidī (d. after 402/1011), even though he spent many years at the court of Ṣāḥib b. ʿAbbād.[17]

In a few instances, Thaʿālibī lists a poet under the city where he spent most of his life rather than the city of his birth, but he mentions the poet's birth city in the introductory section. Thaʿālibī mentions that Abū ʿAbdallāh al-Ḥusayn b. Aḥmad b. Khālawayhi (d. ca. 370/980) is from Hamadhān but settled (*istawṭana*) in Aleppo, under which his entry is included.[18] The jurist and theologian Abū Manṣūr ʿAbd al-Qādir b. Ṭāhir al-Tamīmī (d. 429/1037) hailed from

16 *Y* 4:204–9.

17 *Y* 4:248.

18 On Khālawayhi, see A. Spitaler, "Ibn Khālawayh," *EI2* III:824a–825a; see also *Y* 1:123.

Baghdad but moved to Nīshāpūr in his youth.[19] Similarly, in the *Tatimma*, Abū al-Qāsim ʿAlī b. al-Ḥusayn al-Ulaymānī is mentioned as originally from Rayy, but Thaʿālibī anthologizes him in the section on Nīshāpūr, where he lived.[20]

Thaʿālibī coins a term for those itinerant poets who composed their oeuvre in a city other than their birthplace: *al-ṭāriʾūn* (those who arrived suddenly from far away). Their visits in these cities varied from days to decades. For example, Thaʿālibī dedicates a long chapter in the *Yatīma* to *dhikr al-ṭāriʾīn ʿalā Nīshāpūr min buldān shattā* (mention of the poets who moved to Nīshāpūr from various countries), which is distinguished from the following chapter, dedicated to Nīshāpūr itself. Similarly, the eighth chapter in the second region, dedicated to the Baghdādī poets who produced little work and those who had traveled to Baghdad from afar (*wa-l-ṭāriʾīn ʿalayhā min al-āfāq*), is to be distinguished from the preceding chapter, which treats poets originally from Baghdad. In the section on al-Jabal, itinerant poets fall into two categories: "poetry of al-Jabal and those who hailed to it from Iraq" (*shiʿr al-Jabal wa-l-ṭāriʾīn ʿalayhi min al-ʿIrāq*) and "those who came to al-Jabal" (*al-ṭāriʾūn ʿala bilād al-Jabal*). Even when poets spent many years in a city, Thaʿālibī still distinguishes them from a city's natives. For example, Thaʿālibī differentiated two poets, Abū Ṭālib al-Maʾmūnī (d. 383/993) and Abū Muḥammad al-Wāthiqī (d. before 421/1030), from the natives of Bukhārā, describing them as poets "who came to Bukhārā and resided in it" (*al-ṭāriʾīn ʿalā Bukhārā wa-l-muqīmīn*). Following an organization of geographical "proximity," Thaʿālibī singles out each of those poets for a chapter of his own following a chapter on the natives of Bukhārā, "so that they may be near them on one level and distant and distinct from them on the other" (*li-yuqāribāhum min jihatin wa-yufāriqāhum wa-yubāʿidāhum min ukhrā*).[21] The group of *al-shuʿarāʾ al-ṭāriʾūn* likewise occurs in chapters on courts and dynasties. For example, Thaʿālibī distinguishes the literary figures who resided at Ṣāḥib's court from others who were mere visitors to the court (*ṭāriʾūn*).[22]

19 *Y* 4:411; see also Ḥājjī Khalīfa, *Kashf al-ẓunūn ʿan asāmī al-kutub wa-l-funūn* (Baghdad: Maṭbaʿat al-Muthannā, 1972), 1418.

20 *T* 305.

21 Another reason for singling out these two poets is their noble lineage, for they are both sons of caliphs; see *Y* 4:161.

22 *Y* 3:343ff.

Critical Awareness in the Organization of the *Yatīma* and *Tatimma*

The *Yatīma* and its sequel demonstrate that Thaʿālibī gave much thought to the organization and choice of his sections (*aqsām*) and chapters (*abwāb*). Thaʿālibī is aware of the influence of poets' environments on their literary oeuvre.[23] He was especially familiar with the influence of politics on literature, which is reflected in his use of courts and dynastic families as units of categorization in the *Yatīma* and in his emphasis on patronship as means of stimulating poets' creativity and excellence. The careful division into cities and subregions in each section/region shows Thaʿālibī's sensitivity to the particularities of each region, as in the distinction between poets who lived in a city or region and those who were only visiting one. Occasionally, Thaʿālibī commented on the influence of geography or a particular place on the literary achievement of its inhabitants. For example, he attributes the presence of numerous outstanding poets in Iṣbahān to "the positive effect of the scent of its air, the quality of its soil, and the sweetness of its water in the dispositions of its folk and the minds of its youth."[24] Moreover, Thaʿālibī's characterization of the litterateurs' oeuvres within a geographical context demonstrates many regional distinctions. One can even argue that his choice to start the work with Syria was intended to celebrate the literature of that region as surpassing that of all other regions, as is clear from the title of the *Yatīma*'s first chapter: "On the Superiority of the Poets of Syria over the Poets of the Other Lands" (*fī faḍl shuʿarāʾ al-shām ʿalā shuʿarāʾ sāʾir al-buldān*). In fact, the reasons Thaʿālibī gives to justify the superiority of the region demonstrate this:

> The Arab poets of Syria and its surroundings have been better poets than the Arab poets of Iraq and its neighboring [areas], in pre-Islam and Islam[,]... and the reason for their prominence, old and new, over others in poetry is their nearness to Arab areas, especially Ḥijāz, and their remoteness from foreign lands; together with the safety of their tongues from the depravity that afflicted the tongues of the Iraqis from being neighbors to the Persians and the Nabateans and interposing with them. When the contemporary Syrian poets combined the eloquence of the desert with the sweetness of culture and were blessed with kings and

---

23 Contrary to this, Iḥsān ʿAbbās argues that no critical awareness is behind Thaʿālibī's organizational method in the *Yatīma* and that the choice of the geographical division is merely a practical method to survey contemporary poets; see Iḥsān ʿAbbās, *Tārīkh al-naqd al-adabī* (Beirut: Dār Ṣādir, 1971), 374.

24 *Y* 3:300.

> *amīr*s from the family of Ḥamdān and Banū Warqāʾ, and they are among the remaining Arabs, enamored of *adab*, known for glory and nobility and for combining the instruments of the sword and the pen—each of them is an excellent *adīb* who likes poetry and critiques it, rewards excellent poetry generously and excessively—their talents proceeded in excellence leading the embellished discourse with the most gentle rein.[25]

Selection of Material

In his introduction to the *Yatīma* Thaʿālibī describes his criteria of selection:

> And the condition of this new edition is to include the essential core, the innermost heart, the pupil of the eye, the point of the phrase, the central [pearl] of the necklace, the engraving of the gemstone.[26]

Thaʿālibī also states in the introduction that he will include the literary production of his contemporaries and those of the preceding generation.[27] However, although the coverage of contemporary poets is quite comprehensive, non-contemporary poets in the *Yatīma* are restricted to two sections: the first comprises the ninth chapter of the first region, with entries on poets of Syria, Egypt, and al-Maghrib; and the second comprises the first chapter of the fourth region, which is dedicated to entries on Sāmānid, Bukhārī, and Khurasānī *kuttāb*-poets of an earlier time, who, presumably, had not yet been sufficiently anthologized.[28] Thaʿālibī's reason for reaching farther back in time in the first region remains unclear; it may be because these earlier poets had not been satisfactorily anthologized in the east, or because he lacked knowledge about their lives, as reflected in this section's uncharacteristic lack of dates.

Throughout the anthology, Thaʿālibī finds opportunities to remind his readers of his intention to be brief. In fact, for the sake of brevity, he even omits

---

25 *Y* 1:24–5.

26 *Y* 1:20; see also *T* 8. This sentence is also part of the modesty topos that is commonplace in the literary form of the *muqaddima*; it appears in several of Thaʿālibī's other works. See Orfali, "The Art of the *Muqaddima* in the Works of Abū Manṣūr al-Thaʿālibī (d. 429/1039)," in *The Weaving of Words: Approaches to Classical Arabic Prose*, ed. Lale Behzadi and Vahid Behmardi, Beiruter Texte und Studien 112 (Würzburg: Ergon-Verlag, 2009), 190ff.

27 See *Y* 1:19.

28 See *Y* 1:19, 4:64.

material that would otherwise meet his selection criteria. Such is the case with the poet Abū ʿAbdallāh al-Ḥusayn b. al-Ḥajjāj (d. 391/1001):

> Ibn al-Ḥajjāj's clever curiosities do not end until he ends them, and what I have included is sufficient, though this is only a trickling of the flood and a clipping from their gold, but this book does not have room for more than that, and it is God whose forgiveness I ask.[29]

He similarly describes Ṣāḥib b. ʿAbbād's writing:

> The merits of Ṣāḥib's epigrams wear out notebooks and exhaust the minds of those selecting them, and this book does not have room [for them], except for a trickling of the flood, and a drop from their running water.[30]

Thaʿālibī at times quotes entire *qaṣīda*s, especially if some of the lines do not match his criteria. The original poems often run to dozens of lines, and systematic inclusion of complete pieces would have enormously lengthened the *Yatīmat al-dahr* and defeated its purpose of including only "the elegant achievements of contemporary people" (*maḥāsin ahl al-ʿaṣr*). The incipit or a selection of good lines usually suffices; however, in some cases, in the interest of space he refrains from quoting the entire *qaṣīda*. In these cases, Thaʿālibī says, "It is a long [poem]" (*wa-hiya ṭawīla*),[31] or confirms that the whole *qaṣīda* deserves to be quoted for each line is a "jewel" (*wa-mā min abyātihā illā ghurratun aw durratun*).[32] Finally, there are times when Thaʿālibī apologizes for not being able to do justice to a certain literary figure because of limited space.[33]

Without specifying his selection criteria, Thaʿālibī offers descriptive praise while introducing the material. Noticeably, most comments in the work are positive; negative comments are very rare, which is not surprising—in a book on "the elegant achievements of contemporary people," inferior material would not have been selected. Nevertheless, Thaʿālibī keeps reminding readers

---

29 *Y* 3:31.

30 *Y* 3:256. Other examples of Thaʿālibī's brevity despite the high quality of the literary production are the cases of Abū l-Faraj al-Ṣāwī, *Y* 4:462; Abū l-Barakāt ʿAlī b. al-Ḥusayn al-ʿAlawī, *T* 182; and Abū Saʿd al-Kanjarūzī, *T* 187.

31 See, for example, *Y* 2:19; *T* 125. The phrase is common in the *Yatīma* and the *Tatimma* but is usually used to describe the length of a poem rather than qualifying it.

32 *Y* 3:336.

33 *Y* 3:192.

that the poetry he quotes has met certain criteria. In a few instances he mentions that a particular poet has abundant yet inferior poetry, so does not meet "the condition of the book."[34] In rare instances, he collaborates with friends in judging the poetry at hand:

> There was a huge volume of the Ghuwayrī's poetry in the library of the *amīr* Abū l-Faḍl ʿUbaydallāh in his own handwriting, so I borrowed it and met with Abū Naṣr Sahl b. al-Marzubān to select what matched the condition of this book of mine, and how little we attained! In fact, we did not find better lines by him than those describing a villa that I have quoted among its sister lines[35]

In the case of Khubza'aruzzī (d. ca. 327/939) Thaʿālibī seems hesitant to anthologize him, although he acknowledges that some of his literary production might be up to par:

> I was about to omit his poetry and its mention, either because of his early date, or the weakness (*safsafa*) of his poetry, but then I remembered the nearness of his period and the diligence of Ibn Lankak in collecting his *dīwān*. Thus, I thought to include in this book some gems that I remember, but to avoid thumbing through the rest of his poetry, and abandon the inquiry for his clever curiosities that befit [my work] and his mention. For I was informed from more than one source that he was illiterate, and couldn't write or spell. His profession was to make the rice bread in his shop in the Mirbad of Baṣra, where he used to make bread and recite his poems, which included only *ghazal*. People would gather around him, find amusement in listening to his poetry, and wonder about his state and matter. The young men of Baṣra competed for his affection and mention of them; they memorized his speech for its accessibility and simplicity. Ibn Lankak, despite his high status, used to haunt his shop and listen to his poetry.[36]

---

34 This is the case, for example, with Abū l-Qāsim Muḥammad b. Muḥammad b. Jubayr al-Sijzī, *Y* 4:340; and Abū l-Qāsim al-Ḥusayn b. Asad al-ʿĀmirī, *Y* 4:441. For this phrase, see *Y* 1:241, 2:216, 313, 337, 3:112, 418, 4:3, 102.

35 *Y* 3:340.

36 *Y* 2:366. Originally a camel market, Mirbad is a famous site outside Baṣra that served as a meeting place for poets and orators, both Bedouin and urban. When people began residing in Mirbad itself, it developed into the suburb of Baṣra; see G.J.H. van Gelder, "Mirbad," in *EAL* 2:527.

Thaʿālibī's hesitation to include Khubza'aruzzī is only partly because of his humble social origins and the "popular" nature of his poetry. Khubza'aruzzī's poetry is centered on *ghazal* addressed to youths (*ghilmān*), a type very frequent in the *Yatīma*, where one finds, for example, seventy-five pages of obscene poetry by Ibn al-Ḥajjāj (d. 391/1001).[37] Thaʿālibī also anthologizes two "vagabond" poets in the chapter dedicated to Ṣāḥib b. ʿAbbād: Abū l-Ḥasan ʿUqayl (or ʿAqīl) al-Aḥnaf al-ʿUkbarī (d. 385/995) and Abū Dulaf al-Khazrajī (390/1000).[38] He even dedicates long pages quoting and commenting on al-Qaṣīda al-Sāsāniyya (a poem on the activities of Banū Sāsān) of Abū Dulaf written in Arabic jargon.[39] Nevertheless, Ibn al-Ḥajjāj, ʿUkbarī, and Khazrajī were all associated with courts, and this secured them a mention in the *Yatīma*.[40] Similarly, Thaʿālibī likely ended up including Khubza'aruzzī because he attracted the attention of the poet Ibn Lankak Muḥammad b. Muḥammad al-Baṣrī (d. ca. 360/970).[41]

Thus, a poet's prestige is a criterion for inclusion by Thaʿālibī. This applies, mutatis mutandis, to prestigious authors.[42] He states in his introduction, for

---

37 See *Y* 3:31–104. Thaʿālibī justifies the inclusion of Ibn al-Ḥajjāj's poetry saying that the virtuous (*al-fuḍalā'*) amuse themselves with it, the grandees (*al-kubarā'*) find it pleasant, the *udabā'* deem it light, and the reserved (*al-muḥtashimūn*) put up with it; see *Y* 3:31. Ibn al-Ḥajjāj's poetry has been analyzed in Sinan Antoon, *The Poetics of the Obscene in Premodern Arabic Poetry: Ibn al-Ḥajjāj and* Sukhf (New York: Palgrave Macmillan, 2014). Chapter 1 is dedicated to the history and connotation of *sukhf*.

38 *Y* 3:122–4, 356–77. On the city of ʿUkbara, see G. Le Strange, *The Lands of the Eastern Caliphate: Mesopotamia, Persia, and Central Asia from the Moslem Conquest to the Time of Timur* (Cambridge: University Press, 1930), 50–51. For a detailed study of Abū Dulaf al-Khazrajī's life and his relation with his patrons, especially Ṣāḥib b. ʿAbbād, see Bosworth, *The Mediaeval Islamic Underworld: The Banū Sāsān in Arabic Society and Literature* (Leiden: Brill, 1976), 1:49ff.

39 A critical edition, study, and translation of this poem are provided in volume 2 of Bosworth, *Mediaeval Islamic Underworld*.

40 The vagabond poets, because of their travels and experience of many ranks of society, may have been of considerable political use to viziers and other officials as sources of information and intelligence, which may explain Abū Dulaf and ʿUkbarī's close association with Ṣāḥib b. ʿAbbād. On this point, see Bosworth, *Mediaeval Islamic Underworld*, 1:81.

41 See his biography in *Y* 2:348; Ch. Pellat, "Ibn Lankak," *EI2* III:854a. See also Tanūkhī, *Nishwār al-muḥāḍara*, ed. ʿAbbūd al-Shāljī (Beirut: Dār Ṣādir, 1971–3), 7:118. Jocelyn Sharlet describes how nonprofessional poets in the Arabic and Persian traditions climbed up the social ladder or changed careers to become professional litterateurs; see her *Patronage and Poetry in the Islamic World* (London: I. B. Tauris, 2011), 208ff.

42 Sharlet gives examples of dignitaries who were themselves poets and were included by anthologists and/or engaged with poets; see *Patronage and Poetry in the Islamic World*,

example, that he included some poetry by kings and other dignitaries because of the status of the authors rather than the intrinsic merit of the work:

> If one or two lines that are not lines of *qaṣīda*s, or the centerpiece stones of a necklace, appear in my writing, it is because the context depends on it, the meaning is not complete without it, or what had preceded or will follow is contingent upon it, or again because it is the poetry of a king, *amīr*, vizier, important leader (*ra'īs*), or an *imām* in *adab* and knowledge (*ʿilm*). The likes of these [lines] find merit only because of their association with the author, not because of any high worth.
> The best poetry is that of noblest
> The worst poetry is that of slaves.[43]

Consequently, we find entries on a number of rulers and *amīr*s whose poetry is of little literary importance, such as the Ḥamdānid Sayf al-Dawla (d. 356/967), the Būyid ʿAḍud al-Dawla (d. 372/983), the Fāṭimid caliphs, as well as viziers, secretaries, and religious leaders (*a'imma*).[44] Thaʿālibī distinguishes these dignitaries from the "talented" literary figures in Syria and Iraq, and thus groups them into two separate chapters: the fourth chapter of the first region and the first chapter of the second region.

In fact, the order of the sections and chapters, and to some extent the entries under the chapters reflect the prestige of the personalities. Thaʿālibī's friend ʿUmar (or ʿAmr) b. ʿAlī al-Muṭṭawwiʿī wrote in his book on Abū l-Faḍl al-Mīkālī that there are three kinds of poets: those whose poetry combines "the honor of acquisition" (*sharaf al-iktisāb*) without "honor of lineage" (*sharaf al-intisāb*), those whose poetry is honored because of their own *sharaf*, and those whose poetry combines both types of honor.[45]

In the *Yatīma*, the first region begins with the Ḥamdānid *amīr*s; the second region with the Būyids, followed by the vizier Muhallabī and the head of the register of official letters Abū Isḥāq al-Ṣābī. The third volume starts with

---

207–8.

43 *Y* 1:20. The verse Thaʿālibī quotes here is attributed to Farazdaq; see Ibn Qutayba, *al-Shiʿr wa-l-shuʿarā'* (Beirut: Dār al-Thaqāfa, 1964), 323.

44 Rowson and Bonebakker indicate that the two terms Thaʿālibī uses, *shiʿr al-kuttāb* and *shiʿr al-a'imma*, are rather pejorative; see *Y* 4:417, 419; Rowson and Bonebakker, *A Computerized Listing of Biographical Data from the* Yatīmat al-Dahr *by al-Thaʿālibī* (Malibu: UNDENA Publications, 1980), 9.

45 Muṭṭawwiʿī occupies two entries: *Y* 4:433 and *T* 191. See also al-Ḥuṣrī al-Qayrawānī, *Zahr al-ādāb wa-thimār al-albāb*, ed. ʿA. M. al-Bajāwī (Cairo: al-Bābī al-Ḥalabī, 1970), 1:133.

four viziers; the chapter on the poets of Nīshāpūr begins with two dignitaries, then an important jurist and then four ʿAlids. Similarly, the first region of the *Tatimma* starts with the Ḥamdānid *amīr* Abū l-Muṭāʿ b. Nāṣir al-Dawla (d. 428/1036),[46] and the second with the prominent ʿAlid al-Sharīf al-Murtaḍā (d. 436/1044), followed by Ashraf b. Fakhr al-Mulk. The third region opens with the *amīr* Abū l-ʿAbbās Khusraw-Fayrūz b. Rukn al-Dawla (d. after 373/983), and the fourth begins with an ʿAlid, then the *amīr* Abū Ibrāhīm al-Mīkālī.

A poet's prestige is not the only reason Thaʿālibī admits poetry that falls below his standards. It may be that he was unable to find any other poetry by a particular poet. In this case, he clarifies that the quoted poetry is not representative of the poet's output.[47] Moreover, Thaʿālibī includes inferior material if it can provide context for or explain the meaning of other indispensable material.[48] Sometimes he admits excluding inauthentic material from an entry.[49] Finally, in the case of one poet, the grammarian and philologist Abū Muḥammad Ismāʿīl b. Muḥammad al-Dahhān (d. before 429/1037),[50] Thaʿālibī refrains from including his best poetry out of respect for the poet's wish to have all love and panegyric poetry removed from his entry in order to preserve his scholarly image.[51] This case demonstrates that Thaʿālibī's anthology is an interactive work and that he sometimes allowed poets to intervene in their own entries.

The Arrangement of Entries in a Chapter: Proximity and Resemblance

Within individual chapters, the *Yatīma* follows a complex arrangement indicative of the author's planning and continuous reworking. What seems at first to be random arrangement within a chapter is in fact premeditated.

Hilary Kilpatrick first studied the function, selection, and placement of anecdotes and biographical or historical accounts in *adab* works, in particular

46 Wajīh al-Dawla Dhū l-Qarnayn b. al-Ḥasan b. ʿAbdallāh, appointed governer of Damascus three times for the Fāṭimids; on him, see Ṣafadī, *al-Wāfī bi-l-wafayāt*, 14:30.

47 See, for example, *Y* 2:69.

48 *Y* 1:20.

49 See later in this chapter for a discussion of inauthentic poetry in the *Yatīma*.

50 A grammarian and philologist who studied under Abū Naṣr Ismāʿīl b. Ḥammād al-Jawharī (d. ca. 393/1003); in addition to the *Yatīma* reference, see Yāqūt al-Ḥamawī, *Muʿjam al-udabāʾ: Irshād al-arīb ilā maʿrifat al-adīb*, ed. Iḥsān ʿAbbās (Beirut: Dār al-Gharb al-Islāmī, 1993), 2:734.

51 *Y* 1:433.

FIGURE 26 *Yatīmat al-dahr*, MS 716, 130r

the *K. al-Aghānī* by Abū l-Faraj al-Iṣbahānī (d. 356/967). Kilpatrick discusses the phenomenon of placement enhancement, showing that one account often casts into relief aspects of another account because of the relative placement of each. Kilpatrick notes that the articles of *K. al-Aghānī* form self-sufficient units, but that within a given article, interaction between accounts may add significance. According to Kilpatrick, this interaction takes the form of shared prominent features, linguistic markers, narrators' patterns, salient motifs, and parallel series of episodes.[52]

In his study of Ibn Abī Ṭāhir Ṭayfūr (d. 280/893), Shawkat Toorawa suggests "proximity" as a similar but more direct relationship between accounts. Proximity prevails when "the author/compiler chooses to record together, or in close proximity, accounts that relate to figures who are otherwise connected." In other words, "the presence of certain names in an account—whether in the chain of transmission (*isnād*) or the text itself—leads the author/compiler to include other accounts that contain other individuals who, in the author/compiler's mind, are connected." Toorawa points out that this process may lead to a sequence of entries in a biographical dictionary, and the link that is then established "gives a super-structural coherence to clusters of accounts."[53] Toorawa investigates proximity in ten *adab* and historical works that treat or quote Ibn Abī Ṭāhir Ṭayfūr.[54] He shows in each case how surrounding articles or names are associated with him, each time for a different reason. In another study of the organizational principles of Ibn al-Nadīm's *Fihrist*, Toorawa shows that proximity and resemblance are two important principles governing the order in which notices are placed and sequenced in the *Fihrist*. These two principles yield sidebars and clusters.[55]

In the *Yatīma* and *Tatimma*, this phenomenon of personal proximity in selection and arrangement can be detected in most of the chapters, whether on courts, dynastic families, individual personalities, or cities and subregions.

Because the *Yatīma*'s overall arrangement is geographical, some kind of proximity is assumed: all poets in the same region, subregion, city, or court bear some relation to one another. Proximity, furthermore, helps disclose links among the poets of a chapter. As Toorawa notes, in the absence of explicit

52 H. Kilpatrick, "Context and the Enhancement of the Meaning of *aḫbār* in The *Kitāb al-Aġānī*," *Arabica* 38 (1991), 365–6.

53 Toorawa, *Ibn Abī Ṭāhir Ṭayfūr and Arabic Writerly Culture: A Ninth-Century Bookman in Baghdad* (London: RoutledgeCurzon, 2005), 103.

54 Ibid., 104–8. These are (1) *Ṭabaqāt al-shuʿarā'* of Ibn al-Muʿtazz (d. 296/908), (2) *K. al-Waraqa* of Ibn al-Jarrāḥ (d. 296/908), (3) *Murūj al-dhahab* of al-Masʿūdī (d. 345/946), (4) *Irshād al-arīb* of Yāqūt al-Ḥamawī (d. 626/1229), (5) *al-Fihrist* of Ibn al-Nadīm (d. after 385/995), (6) *al-Tamthīl wa-l-muḥāḍara* of Thaʿālibī , (7) *al-Tatfīl wa-ḥikāyāt al-ṭufayliyyīn wa-akhbāruhum wa-nawādir kalāmihim wa-ashʿārihim* of Khaṭīb al-Baghdādī (d. 463/1071), (8) *al-Dhakhīra fī maḥāsin ahl al-Jazīra* of Ibn Bassām al-Shantarīnī (d. 542/1147), (9) *K. Nūr al-qabas* of Yaghmūrī (d. 673/1274), and (10) *Nihāyat al-arab fī funūn al-adab* of Nuwayrī (d. 732/1332).

55 Shawkat Toorawa, "Proximity, Resemblance, Sidebars and Clusters: Ibn al-Nadīm's Organizational Principles in *Fihrist 3.3*," *Oriens* 38 (2010) 217–47.

FIGURE 27 *Yatīmat al-dahr*, MS *Laleli 1959, 453v*

statements about such ties, the proximity of entries may be suggestive and consequently allow for identification of links between entries or the individuals mentioned within them. In fact, such "proximate" links are ubiquitous in the *Yatīma* and *Tatimma*, so just a few examples will suffice.

One of these links is kinship. Often in the *Yatīma* and *Tatimma*, when a father is anthologized, the son follows, or vice versa, such as with the teacher Abū Naṣr Ṭāhir b. al-Ḥusayn b. Asad al-ʿĀmirī (d. before 429/1037) and his son, the teacher and *adīb* Abū l-Qāsim al-Ḥusayn;[56] Abū l-Fatḥ (d. 366/976) and Abū l-Faḍl Ibn al-ʿAmīd (d. 360/970);[57] and Abū l-Qāsim al-Tanūkhī (d. ca. 352/963), his son, the judge Abū ʿAlī al-Muḥassin al-Tanūkhī (d. 384/994), and his grandson Abū l-Qāsim ʿAlī.[58] The poet Abū ʿAlī Muḥammad b. al-Ḥasan b. al-Muẓaffar al-Ḥātimī (d. 388/998) and his father are anthologized together in one entry.[59] Siblings also follow each other, as in the example of Abū ʿAbd

56 *Y* 4:509.

57 *Y* 3:158, 185.

58 *Y* 2:366ff.

59 *Y* 3:108. See also Ḥamawī, *Muʿjam al-udabāʾ*, 6:2505–18. Abū ʿAlī Muḥammad b. al-Ḥasan al-Ḥātimī is author of *al-Risāla al-Ḥātimiyya*, a debate between him and Mutanabbī.

al-Raḥmān Muḥammad b. ʿAbd al-ʿAzīz al-Nīlī, whose entry is followed by that of his brother, the physician and poet Abū Sahl Bakr b. ʿAbd al-ʿAzīz al-Nīlī.[60]

Isnād is another important link between entries of the *Yatīma*. Individuals follow in succession if the latter person figures in an *isnād* mentioned in the former's entry, or if Thaʿālibī received the oeuvre of the two individuals from the same written or oral source. For example, Thaʿālibī anthologizes in succession the judge Abū l-Ḥasan ʿAlī b. al-Nuʿmān b. Muḥammad al-Maghribī (d. 374/984),[61] Isḥāq b. Ahmad al-Mārdīnī, the judge Abū ʿAbdallāh Muḥammad b. al-Nuʿmān (d. after 380/990),[62] and Ṣāliḥ b. Yūnus (Mu'nis?)[63]—all from Egypt—for their poetry reached him by way of the same informant: ʿAbd al-Ṣamad b. Wahab al-Miṣrī.[64]

For more information, see Bonebakker, *Ḥātimī and His Encounter with Mutanabbī, A Biographical Sketch* (Amsterdam: North-Holland Pub. Co., 1984). Thaʿālibī clearly anthologizes two personalities in this entry, but the printed text of the *Yatīma* is confusing: محمد بن الحسين الحاتمي، حسن التصرف في الشعر، موفٍ على كثير من شعراء العصر، وأبوه أبو علي شاعر كاتب. . . The text goes on to give a selection of the poetry of the father and the son. From the context of the poetry itself (one *qaṣīda* praises the caliph al-Qādir Billāh; r. 381/991–422/1031), and in the surrounding entries it becomes clear that the main entry is for Abū ʿAlī Muḥammad b. al-Ḥasan (al-Ḥusayn?) al-Ḥātimī. Thus, the *Yatīma* text should be corrected to: وأبوه شاعر، وأبو علي كاتب.

60 *Y* 4:430ff. On him, see Bayhaqī, *Tatimmat Ṣiwān al-ḥikma*, ed. Rafīq al-ʿAjam (Beirut: Dār al-Fikr al-Lubnānī, 1994), 99–100.

61 On him, see Ibn Khallikān, *Wafayāt al-aʿyān*, ed. Iḥsān ʿAbbās (Beirut: Dār Ṣādir, 1968), 5:417; Dhahabī, *Siyar aʿlām al-nubalāʾ*, ed. Shuʿayb al-Arnaʾūṭ (Beirut: Mu'assasat al-Risāla, 1990–92), 16:367.

62 He succeeded his brother Abū l-Ḥasan ʿAlī b. al-Nuʿmān as a *qāḍī* in Egypt; see Dhahabī, *Taʾrīkh al-Islām wa-wafayāt al-mashāhīr wa-l-aʿlām*, ed. ʿUmar ʿAbd al-Salām Tadmurī (Beirut: Dār al-Kitāb al-ʿArabī, 1993), 26:560. According to Ṣafadī he was still alive in 380/990; see Ṣafadī, *al-Wāfī bi-l-wafayāt*, 21:149. Thaʿālibī does not indicate that the two are brothers and separates them by Mārdīnī.

63 The texts of all published editions of the *Yatīma* read Mu'nis but Ṣafadī in the entry on Ṣāliḥ b. Rashdīn has his name as Ṣāliḥ b. Yūnus and identifies him as a client of Banū Tamīm; see *Y* 16:143.

64 *Y* 1:400ff. For other successive articles with Ibn Wahab as common informant, see those on Abū l-Ḥasan al-Laṭīm and Sulaymān b. Ḥassān al-Naṣabī, *Y* 1:424ff.; and on Abū l-Qāsim Aḥmad b. Muḥammad b. Ismāʿīl b. Ṭabāṭabā al-Rassī and his son Abū Muḥammad al-Qāsim b. Aḥmad al-Rassī, *Y* 1:428ff. For articles grouped together by a common informant in both the *Yatīma* and the *Tatimma*, see the role played by Muḥammad b. ʿUmar al-Zāhir in *Y* 1:307 and 417ff.; the role played by Abū Yaʿlā al-Baṣrī in *T* 15–18; and the role played by Abū l-Ḥasan ʿAlī b. Ma'mūn al-Maṣṣīṣī in *Y* 1:308–10. In the last case, Thaʿālibī includes a shorter article within an article, the informant being the association.

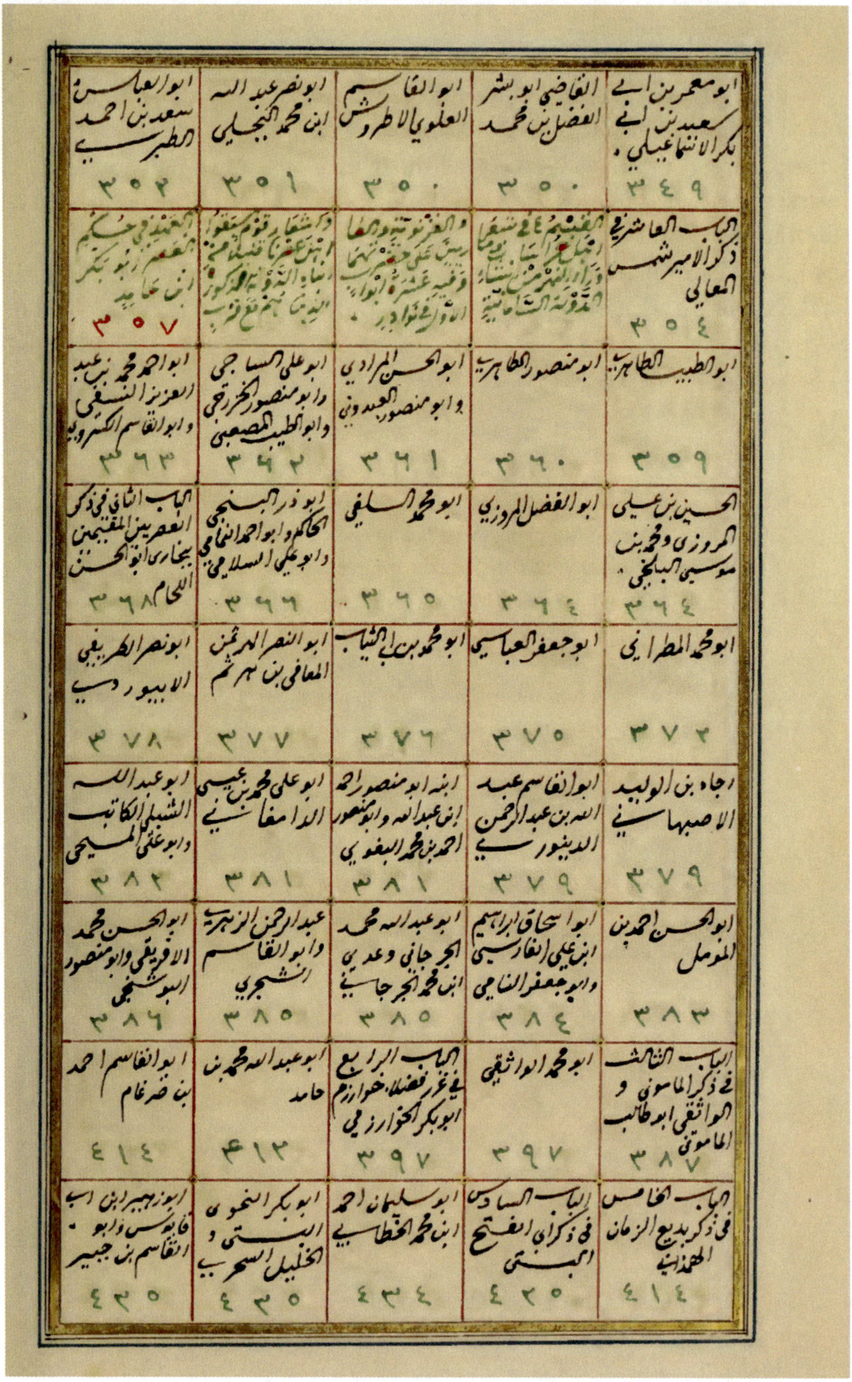

FIGURE 28 *Yatīmat al-dahr*, MS Toronto A13512y

Social relationships, between teacher and disciple, friends, acquaintances, or enemies, all influence the sequence of articles in a chapter. For example, Thaʿālibī places Abū al-ʿAbbās Aḥmad b. Ibrāhīm al-Ḍabbī (d. before 429/1037) behind Ṣāḥib b. ʿAbbād, for he was "a brand from the fire of al-Ṣāḥib Abū l-Qāsim, a river from his sea, and his deputy in his lifetime."[65] An example of such a friendship is that of the successive entries of the two Syrian poets ʿAbd al-Muḥsin b. Muḥammad al-Ṣūrī (d. 419/1028) and Aḥmad b. Sulaymān al-Fajrī (al-Fakhrī?) (d. before 429/1037).[66] Thaʿālibī does not spell out their friendship, but begins the entry on Fajrī with private correspondence (*ikhwāniyya*) addressed to Ṣūrī.[67] In the consecutive entries on the poet al-Ḥasan b. Muḥammad al-Shahwājī (d. before 429/1037) and the *kātib* Abū ʿAlī Ṣāliḥ b. Rashdīn (d. 411/1020),[68] Thaʿālibī starts the article on the former with private correspondence addressed to the latter, without noting that they were friends.[69]

An example of proximity by enmity is the relationship of the bookseller and poet al-Sarī al-Raffāʾ (d. 366/976) with the Khālidiyyān Abū Bakr Muḥammad b. Hāshim (d. 380/990) and Abū ʿUthmān Saʿīd b. Hāshim (d. 371/981), where Thaʿālibī notes Raffāʾ's accusation that they were plagiarists.[70]

Finally, proximity may explain the "disjointed" (according to Rowson and Bonebakker) structure of the ninth chapter of the first region, and what might seem initially to be a random arrangement of its 173 poets. Proximity seems to motivate the sequence of the poets within each of the chapter's components. Figure 29 specifies the relationships among the first fifty poets in this chapter, after which the poets discussed are either from Egypt or al-Maghrib and, consequently, share a geographical relation. The figure shows that the most common ties between the entries are common informants, a result that flows from the fact that Thaʿālibī collected his material from main informants for each region. Nevertheless, the sequence of the entries within each component is not entirely random but is guided by ties such as kinship, common informants, and common objects of praise. This method helped Thaʿālibī keep related literary figures together and establish the "literary clusters" of his time.

---

65 *Huwa Jadhwatun min nār al-Ṣāḥib Abī l-Qāsim, wa-nahrun min baḥrih, wa-khalīfatuh al-nāʾib manābah fī ḥayātih. Y* 3:291.

66 Aḥmad b. Sulaymān is a contemporary of Ṣūrī, his *nisba* in *Dīwān al-Ṣūrī* is al-Fakhrī; see Ṣūrī, *Dīwān al-Ṣūrī*, ed. Makkī al-Sayyid Jāsim and Shākir Hādī Shukr (Baghdad: Manshūrāt Wizārat al-Thaqāfa wa-l-Iʿlām, 1981), 1:20, 25, 202, 2:138.

67 *Y* 1:325.

68 Abū ʿAlī Ṣāliḥ b. Ibrāhīm b. Rashdīn al-Makhzūmī, according to Ṣafadī, who gives his death date, is the source of much *akhbār* from Egypt; see Ṣafadī, *al-Wāfī bi-l-wafayāt*, 16:143.

69 *Y* 1:413–17.

70 *Y* 2:117ff.

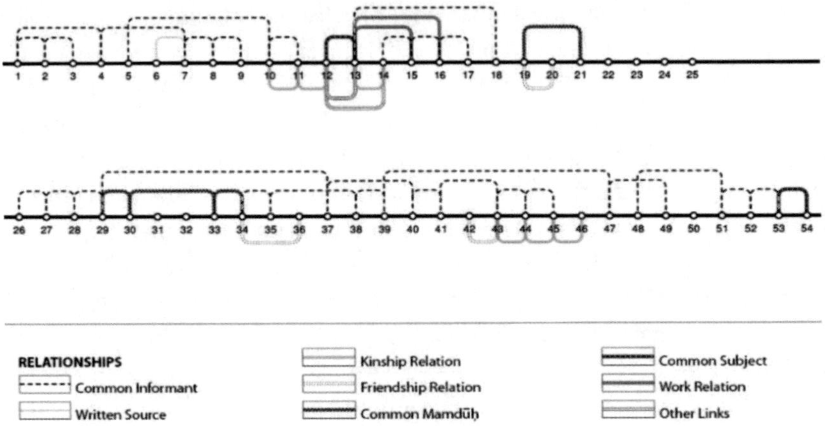

FIGURE 29 *Relationships in Yatīmat al-dahr*

References and Cross-References

Cross-References

As presented already, the personal entries of the *Yatīma* are not arranged solely by geographical region; instead, they follow a sophisticated subdivision into cities, districts, courts, and literary gatherings. With these varying foci, the work required frequent cross-references. Thaʿālibī's abundant and thorough cross-references show not only that he planned his anthology as a cohesive whole but also that he considered the people portrayed in it as a literary network.

Court Literature

While discussing a certain court, like that of the two viziers Muhallabī or Ṣāḥib b. ʿAbbād, or a famous person, such as Abū Isḥāq al-Ṣābī or Badīʿ al-Zamān al-Hamadhānī (d. 398/1008), Thaʿālibī included laudatory poetry composed for these figures that either mirrors their characteristics or serves as their epitaph.[71] The poets themselves may or may not be discussed in the same section/region, since many of them moved from one court to another. Thaʿālibī, in this case, placed the poetry with the subject of its praise, reserving a separate entry for the individual poets under their corresponding regions. That is, he links each poet and his poetry by means of a cross-reference. The chapter dedicated

71 See Kilito, *Author and His Doubles*, 24ff.; Gruendler, *Medieval Arabic Praise Poetry* (London: RoutledgeCurzon, 2003), 227ff.

to Ṣāḥib b. ʿAbbād, for example, includes numerous panegyrics and elegies. Thaʿālibī does not repeat these poems in the sections dedicated to the various authors of these poems but instead inserts a cross-reference.[72] Lampoons do not differ from panegyrics and elegies in this regard. For example, the section on Mutanābbī includes lampoon poems by Ibn Lankak, which Thaʿālibī refers to in the section devoted to the latter.[73] Alternatively, Thaʿālibī may have anthologized a poet in a certain court and so limited the entry on him in his geographical region of origin to a cross-reference. He does this, for instance, for the poet Abū ʿAlī al-Ḥasan b. ʿAlī al-Khalīʿ, who served the vizier Sābūr b. Ardashīr (d. 416/1025–6).[74] Elsewhere, he refers to a poet's poem in one place, giving the first few lines, then includes the full version in another location. Similarly, Thaʿālibī gives the incipit of an elegy by Abū Bakr al-Khwārizmī (d. 383/993) for Abū l-Fatḥ b. al-ʿAmīd (d. 366/976) in the vizier's entry and refers to its full citation in the entry on Khwārizmī.[75]

Networks

Thaʿālibī often mentions literary figures other than the main subject in a given entry, even if the former have entries of their own. He usually points to the separate entry to link the information about the individual and/or his literary cluster without repeating himself. Thus, Thaʿālibī recalls that he mentioned the secretary and poet Abū ʿAbdallāh Muḥammad b. Abū Bakr al-Jurjānī with the secretary and *adīb* Abū l-Naṣr al-Muʿāfā al-Huzaymī al-Abīwardī.[76] Similarly, in the entry on the physician and poet Abū Sahl Bakr b. ʿAbd al-ʿAzīz al-Nīlī, Thaʿālibī adds that he mentioned him elsewhere but this is the time to present his poetry (*qad taqaddama dhikruhu wa-jāʾa l-āna shiʿruhu*).[77] The entry on the poet and secretary Abū l-Qāsim ʿAlī b. Muḥammad al-Iskāfī al-Nīshāpūrī (d. ca. 350/961) references a lampoon poem of the Sāmānid *amīr* Nūḥ b. Naṣr (d. 343/954) that was included in the entry on Ibn al-ʿAmīd.[78]

Relatives

Despite the above-mentioned proximity of kinship, families are not always treated in the same chapter. A poet's entry may appear in a chapter dedicated

72 See, for example, *Y* 3:119, 149, 324.
73 See, for example, *Y* 1:137–8 and 2:354.
74 *Y* 3:126, and for his poetry, 3:133.
75 *Y* 3:192.
76 *Y* 4:132, 153. On Huzaymī, see *Y* 4:129, 133, 134.
77 *Y* 4:430.
78 *Y* 3:159, 4:97.

to a certain court or a region while his family is discussed elsewhere. In most cases, a cross-reference connects the two, which is usually a paternal, fraternal, or filial cross-reference. For example, Abū al-Qāsim ʿAlī al-Tanūkhī is mentioned in his father's entry, the judge Abū ʿAlī al-Muḥassin al-Tanūkhī (d. 384/994), where Thaʿālibī points out his role as informant for the poetry of the Ḥamdānid *amīr* Abū l-Muṭāʿ b. Nāṣir al-Dawla (d. 428/1036).[79] Thaʿālibī anthologizes the *adīb* and poet Abū l-Ḥasan ʿAlī b. Hārūn al-Munajjim (d. 352/963) in the chapter dedicated to Baghdad, but for the discussion of his family refers readers to the chapter on poets who came to Ṣāḥib b. ʿAbbād.[80]

Cited Authors

Sometimes an author is mentioned or quoted in the context of a treatise or a work cited in an entry on another individual. In this case, Thaʿālibī adds a cross-reference to the entry on the quoted person. For example, the philologist Ibn Fāris (d. 395/1004) quotes Abū ʿAbdallāh al-Mughallisī al-Marāghī in a letter arguing for the excellence of modern (*muḥdath*) poetry.[81] Thaʿālibī dedicates a separate entry to Marāghī in which he refers to his poetry in Ibn Fāris's letter.[82]

Correspondence

The *Yatīma* is rich with correspondence (*mukātabāt*) between literary figures. In each case, Thaʿālibī places the entire correspondence in the entry on one of the correspondents, and then merely refers to it in the entry on the second correspondent. Such is the case for correspondence between Abū l-Faḍl Ibn al-ʿAmīd's (d. 360/970) and the judge and traditionalist Abū Muḥammad al-Ḥasan Ibn Khallād al-Rāmahurmuzī (d. ca. 360/970) as well as the poet Abū l-ʿAlāʾ al-Sarawī (d. ca. 360).[83] Thaʿālibī includes their correspondence under the entry on Ibn al-ʿAmīd, then refers to it in the entries on the other two authors.[84]

---

79 *Y* 1:107–8, 2:347.

80 *Y* 3:119, 394. See Munajjim's biography in Ibn Khallikān, *Wafayāt al-aʿyān*, 3:375.

81 Thaʿālibī quotes Marāghī's poetry in many of his works but tells little about his life.

82 *Y* 3:404, 415.

83 On Rāmahurmuzī, see *Y* 3:423; for details about his life and travels, see Ṣafadī, *al-Wāfī bi-l-Wafayāt*, 12:42. Little is known about Sarawī other than that he was from Ṭabaristān and corresponded with Abū l-Faḍl Ibn al-ʿAmīd. Thaʿālibī quotes his poetry in many of his works, and later sources usually refer to the *Yatīma* when quoting him; see his entry in *Y* 4:50.

84 *Y* 3:423, 4:50; see the *mukātabāt* in *Y* 3:164ff, 170ff.

Mentorship

Another situation warranting cross-references is the teacher-student relationship. Thaʿālibī states, for example, that the philologist, lexicographer, and grammarian Abū Muḥammad Ismāʿīl b. Muḥammad al-Dahhān had studied with "the previously mentioned" lexicographer Abū Naṣr Ismāʿīl b. Ḥammād al-Jawharī (d. ca. 393/1003).[85]

Literary Criticism

Cross-references also mention issues of literary criticism. Following a verse by the poet Abū l-Qāsim ʿAbd al-Ṣamad b. Bābak (d. 410/1019) that likens the breath of the patron, Fakhr al-Dawla (d. 387/997), to a bouquet of wine,[86] Thaʿālibī finds the simile (*tashbīh*) befitting "a beloved," not "a venerable king." He then refers to a similar critical comment (*naqd*) in the section on Mutanabbī.[87]

Narrative

In one instance there is a narrative cross-reference. In the entry on the vizier Muhallabī, Thaʿālibī quotes the beginning of a story (*qiṣṣa*) from the *K. al-Rūznāmja* by Ṣāḥib b. ʿAbbād and refers to its continuation in the entry on the Munajjim family.[88]

References in the Tatimma *to the* Yatīma

When he found new material that meets his selection criteria, Thaʿālibī would reintroduce poets from the *Yatīma* in the *Tatimma*. However, he always mentioned the original entry and justified the second one. Some examples are the poets Abū l-Muṭāʿ b. Nāṣir al-Dawla (d. 428/1036),[89] Abū ʿAbdallāh al-Ḥusayn b. Aḥmad al-Mughallis (fl. 381/991),[90] the *amīr* Abū l-ʿAbbās Khusraw-Fayrūz b. Rukn al-Dawla (d. after 373/983),[91] the judge Abū Bakr ʿAbdallāh b. Muḥammad b. Jaʿfar al-Askī (al-Āsī?),[92] Abū Saʿd ʿAlī b. Muḥammad b. Khalaf al-Hamadhānī,[93] Abū

85 *Y* 4:432. Jawharī is mentioned in *Y* 4:406.

86 Ibn Khallikān, *Wafayāt al-aʿyān*, 3:196.

87 *Y* 3:382, and the reference is to 1:186.

88 *Y* 2:229, 3:120.

89 *T* 9; *Y* 1:107–8.

90 *T* 24; *Y* 3:415. On him, see Ṣafadī, *al-Wāfī bi-l-Wafayāt*, 12:202. The Beirut edition of the *Tatimma* reads Abū ʿAbdallāh b. al-Ḥusayn, while both the Beirut and the Tehran editions read al-Muflis—both readings are incorrect based on Ṣafadī's text and other works of Thaʿālibī.

91 *T* 111; *Y* 2:223.

92 *T* 113; *Y* 3:416. The *Tatimma* text reads al-Askī and the *Yatīma*, al-Āsī.

93 *T* 146; *Y* 3:412. He joined the circle of Abū l-Faḍl al-Mīkālī (d. 436/1044–5).

l-Faraj ʿAlī b. al-Ḥusayn b. Hindū (d. 410/1019 or 420/1029),[94] Abū l-Barakāt ʿAlī b. al-Ḥasan al-ʿAlawī,[95] Abū Ḥafṣ ʿUmar (or ʿAmr) b. al-Muṭṭawwiʿī al-Ḥākim (d. after 429/1037),[96] Abū l-Ḥasan al-ʿAbdalakānī (d. 431/1039),[97] and Abū l-Qāsim Ghānim b. Abī al-ʿAlāʾ al-Iṣbahānī (d. after 385/995).[98] With regard to the judge Abū Aḥmad Manṣūr b. Muḥammad al-Azdī al-Harawī, Thaʿālibī justified the new entry by noting that at the time of writing the *Yatīma*, he had no personal connection with Harawī (*lam yaqaʿ baynī wa-baynahu maʿrifa*), but in the interim he had become aware of his real merit.[99]

Some poets discussed anew in the *Tatimma* have no full entry of their own in the *Yatīma* but are mentioned in another or sometimes quoted. Abū l-Faraj b. Abī Ḥuṣayn al-Qāḍī al-Ḥalabī was thus mentioned in the *Yatīma* in the entry on the Ḥamdānid *amīr* poet Abū Firās al-Ḥamdānī (d. 357/967),[100] and the librarian and historian Abū ʿAlī b. Miskawayhi (d. 421/1030) in the entry on Ibn al-ʿAmīd.[101]

Moreover, references to the *Yatīma* correct misattributions of verses to poets with entries in the *Yatīma*. The *Tatimma* entry on Abū l-Ghanāʾim b. Ḥamdān al-Mawṣilī includes an eight-line poem also attributed to Abū l-Qāsim al-Zāhī in al-Sarī al-Raffāʾ's anthology *al-Muḥibb wa-l-maḥbūb wa-l-mashmūm wa-l-mashrūb*. Thaʿālibī refers to Zāhī's *Yatīma* entry to enable readers to connect the poem with Zāhī's other poetry, without passing judgment on its authenticity.[102]

References to the *Yatīma* sometimes highlight a poet's relatives, usually a father or brother, who are mentioned or anthologized; a comparison of their literary production usually follows. For example, the entry on al-Sharīf

94 *T* 155; *Y* 3:397.

95 *T* 181; *Y* 4:420.

96 *T* 191; *Y* 4:433. On him, see Bākharzī, *Dumyat al-qaṣr*, ed. Muḥammad al-Ṭūnjī (Beirut: Dār al-Jīl, 1993), 1:140, 2:1122, 1206.

97 *T* 216; *Y* 4:449. He appears in the *Yatīma* as Abū Muḥammad ʿAbdallāh b. Muḥammad al-ʿAbdalakānī and is, as Thaʿālibī mentions in the *Tatimma*, the last entry in the *Yatīma*. The correct *kunya* could be Abū l-Ḥasan, for Thaʿālibī uses it in the *Tatimma*, specifying that he is the father of Muḥammad al-ʿAbdalakānī, but later sources, such as *Dumyat al-qaṣr* and *al-Wāfī bi-l-wafayāt*, use Abū Muḥammad as his *kunya*; see Bākharzī, *Dumyat al-qaṣr*, 1:57, 105, 199, 201, 323, 326, 475, 506, 653, 654, 679, 2:835, 906, 921, 926–7, 934, 1324, 1371; Ṣafadī, *al-Wāfī bi-l-wafayāt*, 17:287.

98 *T*; *Y* 3:284, 324.

99 *T* 232; *Y* 4:350. Thaʿālibī resided with Harawī in Herat before 421/1030 and dedicated to him *al-Ījāz wa-l-iʿjāz* and *al-Laṭīf fī l-ṭīb*.

100 *T* 83; *Y* 1:67.

101 *T* 115; *Y* 3:163.

102 *T* 60; *Y* 1:249.

al-Murtaḍā (d. 436/1044) refers to that of his brother al-Sharīf al-Raḍī (d. 406/1015).[103] In the *Tatimma* entry on Muḥammad b. ʿUbaydallāh al-Baladī, Thaʿālibī also indicates the entry on his father in the *Yatīma*, adding that the son is a better poet.[104] In the entry on Abū Manṣūr al-Ṣūrī Thaʿālibī recalls the excellent lines of his brother Abū ʿUmāra al-Ṣūrī, recorded in the *Yatīma*.[105]

In his entry on the poet al-Bahdilī, Thaʿālibī mentions that after finalizing the *Yatīma*, he found in his notes (*taʿlīqāt*) a line attributed to Bahdilī without an *isnād*. Thaʿālibī might be suggesting that the poet should have received an entry there; however, he seizes the opportunity to include more of his poetry in the *Tatimma*.[106]

References to the Earlier Version of the Yatīma

Thaʿālibī began *Yatīmat al-dahr* in 384/994 and dedicated it to an unnamed vizier (*aḥad al-wuzarāʾ*).[107] Dissatisfied with its lack of comprehensiveness, he continuously reedited and reorganized the work. He described this process as follows:

> I had set out to accomplish this in the year three hundred and eighty-four, when [my] age was still in its outset, and my youth was still fresh. I opened it with the name of a vizier, following the convention of the people of *adab*, who do this to find favor with people of prestige and rank.... And I recently found myself presented with many similar reports to those in it and plentiful additions that I obtained from the mouths of transmitters.... So, I started to build and demolish, enlarge and reduce, erase and confirm, copy then abrogate, and sometimes I start and do not finish, reach the middle and not the end, while days have blocked the way, promising without fulfilling, until I reached the age of maturity and experience.... So I snatched a spark from within the darkness of age

---

103 *T* 69; *Y* 3:136.

104 *T* 66; *Y* 2:214.

105 *T* 38; *Y* 1:305.

106 See *T* 27.

107 Jādir proposes Abū l-Ḥusayn Muḥammad b. Kathīr, who served as vizier for Abū ʿAlī b. Sīmjūrī. He justifies the omission of the dedication in the second edition by explaining that Thaʿālibī reworked the book during the reign of the Ghaznavids, who succeeded Abū ʿAlī b. Sīmjūrī and opposed his vizier. Consequently, Thaʿālibī did not want to alienate the Ghaznavids by mentioning a previous enemy in the preface; see Jādir, "Dirāsa tawthīqiyya li-muʾallafāt al-Thaʿālibī," *Majallat Maʿhad al-Buḥūth wa l-Dirāsāt al-ʿArabiyya* 12 (1403/1983), reprinted in *Dirāsāt tawthīqiyya wa-taḥqīqiyya fī maṣādir al-turāth* (Baghdad: Jāmiʿat Baghdād, 1990), 442.

> [and] I continued composing and revising this last version among the many versions after I changed its order, revised its division into chapters, redid its arrangement, and tightened its composition.... This version now contains marvels by the prominent people of merit, the contemporary stars of the earth, and by those who slightly preceding them in time,... comprising witty, new coined sayings and anecdotes, more pleasurable than early-blooming basil... [and that] the first widely circulating version did not include.[108]

Thaʿālibī provides no date for the second edition of the *Yatīma*. The editor of the *Tatimma*, ʿAbbās Iqbāl, describes a manuscript of the fourth volume of the *Yatīma* with an introduction missing from the Damascus edition (it is also missing in all other editions).[109] In it Thaʿālibī reports having resumed work on the fourth region of his book upon his arrival at the court of the Khwārizmshāh Maʾmūn b. Maʾmūn, after having been interrupted by various difficulties and travels. However, Q. al-Samarrai objects that this Khwārizmshāh is not mentioned in the *Yatīma* at all, and his vizier al-Suhaylī is mentioned once in passing.[110] Rowson and Bonebakker find many references in the last region of the *Yatīma* indicating Thaʿālibī's absence from home.[111] Thaʿālibī himself notes that in 403/1012 he stayed with the *raʾīs* Abū Saʿd Muḥammad b. Manṣūr in Jurjān and completed the *Yatīma* there.[112] Abū Saʿd Muḥammad is mentioned twice in the fourth volume.[113] Rowson and Bonebakker suggest this year as a plausible date for the completion of the *Yatīma*, given that the latest date mentioned in the work is Muḥarram 402 (August 1011).[114] In support of this are Thaʿālibī's references to the Jurjān *amīr* Qābūs b. Wushmgīr and the Ghaznavid vizier Abū l-ʿAbbās al-Faḍl b. Aḥmad al-Isfarāyīnī, which show no knowledge of their depositions and deaths, which occurred in early 403/1012 and 404/1013–14, respectively.[115]

The edited text of the *Yatīma* refers only rarely to the earlier edition. In the entry on Abū al-Qāsim ʿAlī b. Jalabāt (d. after 416/1025), for example, Thaʿālibī

108 *Y* 1:5–6, MS Laleli 1959, 2v–3r.

109 A. Iqbāl, introduction to *T* 1:5. Iqbāl paraphrases the Arabic text in Persian without giving the original.

110 Q. al-Samarrai, "Some Biographical Notes on al-Thaʿālibī," *Bibliotheca Orientalis* 32 (1975), 179. Suhaylī is mentioned as the recipient of a poem.

111 See Rowson and Bonebakker, *Computerized Listing*, 8, and the sources listed there.

112 Ibid., 8.

113 *Y* 4:257, 283.

114 *Y* 4:254.

115 Rowson and Bonebakker, *Computerized Listing*, 8–9; *Y* 4:59–61, 437.

states that although he included his poetry, he doubted its authenticity after finding that it had been attributed to another poet. Acting on his doubts, Thaʿālibī replaced it with verse he considered authentic.[116]

In fact, one cannot retrace with certainty the process by which the text of the *Yatīma* reached its current state. Rowson and Bonebakker suggest that the last two sections of the second region—comprising panegyrics by sixteen poets on the Būyid vizier Sābūr b. Ardashīr (d. 416/1025–6—and the chapter on al-Sharīf al-Raḍī (d. 406/1015), as well as the final unit of the third volume (on Qābūs b. Wushmgīr; d. 403/1012), were probably completely new.[117] But Thaʿālibī did not consider even the last version of the *Yatīma* as a final text, and he left many gaps to be filled later, by himself or other scholars.

References to Other Works by Thaʿālibī

Thaʿālibī refers to some of his earlier works in the *Yatīma*. The entry dedicated to the vizier *adīb* al-Muhallabī contains a section titled "Excerpts from his [Muhallabī's] chapters that lack poetry, parts of which I included in the course of my book titled *Siḥr al-balāgha*."[118] This reference indicates the source of the material in the section. Similarly, Thaʿālibī refers to a *dīwān* he compiled from the poetry of Abū l-Ḥasan al-Laḥḥām and from which he then selected suitable quotations for his *Yatīma*.[119]

Expounding on Abū Isḥāq al-Ṣābī's (d. 384/994) religion and knowledge of Islam, Thaʿālibī mentions that he memorized the Qurʾān and used to quote and refer to it in his prose. Thaʿālibī then notes that he included examples by Ṣābī in his *al-Iqtibās min al-Qurʾān*,[120] which allows him to leave them aside and proceed directly to Ṣābī's poetry and accounts, especially since his intention was not to analyze or qualify Ṣābī's knowledge of the Qurʾān as much as to indicate that Ṣābī knew much about Islam without converting to the religion.

In *Tatimmat al-Yatīma*, Thaʿālibī refers to a saying of his own from *al-Mubhij* that was put into verse by the *adīb* and poet Abū Jaʿfar Muḥammad b. ʿAbdallāh al-Iskāfī, thus providing a source for the two lines.[121] He refers to another one of his works, *al-Taghazzul bi-miʾatay ghulām*, as having been read by the Nīshāpūrī

116 See *Y* 3:104.

117 Rowson and Bonebakker, *Computerized Listing*, 11.

118 *Y* 2:235; Thaʿālibī, *Siḥr al-balāgha wa-sirr al-barāʿa*, ed. ʿA. al-Ḥūfī (Beirut: Dār al-Kutub al-ʿIlmiyya, 1984), 188.

119 *Y* 4:102.

120 *Y* 2:242–3; Thaʿālibī, *al-Iqtibās min al-Qurʾān*, ed. I. al-Ṣaffār and M. M. Bahjat (Al-Manṣūra: Dār al-Wafāʾ, 1992), 1:150, 216, 2:79, 86, 90–102.

121 *Y* 231; Thaʿālibī, *al-Mubhij*, ed. Ibrāhīm Ṣāliḥ (Damascus: Dār al-Bashāʾir, 1999), 117.

poet Abū l-Fatḥ al-Muẓaffar b. al-Ḥasan al-Dāmghānī, either to give information about the latter's breadth of knowledge or to attest to his own popularity.[122]

Later Additions to the *Yatīma*

The suggested date of completion for the second edition of the *Yatīma*, 403/1012, presents some problems. First, Ibn Shuhayd (d. 426/1035) from al-Andalus appears in the *Yatīma*,[123] but in 403/1012 he was only twenty-one years old, which likely would have made it difficult for Thaʿālibī who was writing in the the Eastern parts of the Muslim world to assemble sixteen pages of his prose and verse.[124] Rowson and Bonebakker notice that this material, except for the last two poems, is selected from Ibn Shuhayd's *Risālat al-tawābiʿ wa-l-zawābiʿ*, whose date of composition its editor Buṭrus al-Bustānī places as later than 414/1023.[125] Even Charles Pellat's earlier dating of the *Risāla*, before 401/1011,[126] makes its citation in the *Yatīma* improbably quick. Examining the *isnād*s of this entry, Rowson and Bonebakker point out that Thaʿālibī reports the first *qaṣīda* on the authority of Abū Saʿd b. Dūst from al-Walīd b. Bakr al-Faqīh al-Andalusī, from Ibn Shuhayd. However, all the succeeding selections of verse and prose appear without an indicated source, except for the last two poems, which display the same *isnād*. This *isnād* appears elsewhere in the *Yatīma* as well.[127] Abū Saʿd b. Dūst (d. 431/1039 or 1040) was a Nīshāpūrī and a friend of Thaʿālibī;[128] Walīd b. Bakr visited Nīshāpūr and died in Dīnawar in 392/1002,[129] when Ibn Shuhayd was only ten.[130] In the Damascus edition of the *Yatīma*, this section is titled "*al-wazīr* Abū ʿAmr Aḥmad b. ʿAbd al-Malik b. Shuhayd."[131] In the Cairo and Beirut editions the *kunya* is given as Abū ʿĀmir. This may only be, as Rowson and Bonebakker indicate, a tacit emendation by

122 See *T* 277.

123 *Y* 2:36–50.

124 On Ibn Shuhayd's life, see J. Dickie, "Ibn Shuhayd: A Biographical and Critical Study," *al-Andalus*, 29 (1964), 243–310.

125 Ibn Shuhayd, *Risālat al-tawābiʿ wa-l-zawābiʿ*, ed. Buṭrus al-Bustānī (Beirut: Dār Ṣādir, 1967), 67ff. J. Monroe dates the work more precisely to 416–18/1025–7; see the introduction to the translation (Berkeley, 1971), 14–17.

126 Ch. Pellat, "Ibn Shuhayd," *EI2* III:938b–940a.

127 *Y* 1:310–12, 2:74–5.

128 See *Y* 4:425–8.

129 See al-Khaṭīb al-Baghdādī, *Taʾrīkh Baghdād* (Beirut: Dār al-Kitāb al-ʿArabī, 1966), 8:450ff.

130 Rowson and Bonebakker, *Computerized Listing*, 9.

131 *Y* (Damascus: al-Maṭbaʿa al-Ḥanafiyya, 1885), 1:382.

the editors. It seems that there was confusion between Ibn Shuhayd and his grandfather Abū ʿĀmir, a vizier and a poet.[132] Rowson and Bonebakker attribute the last two poems, which are not attested to elsewhere, to Ibn Shuhayd's grandfather, and suggest that after 414/1023, excerpts from the *Risālat al-tawābiʿ wa-l-zawābiʿ* were added to the *Yatīma* and mistakenly given the same *isnād*.[133] This addition to the *Yatīma* could have been Thaʿālibī's own. Another problem in the Andalusian section, a panegyric by Ibn Darrāj al-Qasṭallī (d. 421/1030) of the Tujībid Yaḥyā b. Mundhir of Saragossa, who was in power from 414/1023 to 420/1029,[134] is also explained by Rowson and Bonebakker as a later addition, possibly by Thaʿālibī himself.[135]

Both interpolations belong to the ninth chapter of the *Yatīma*, *mulaḥ ahl al-shām wa-miṣr wa-l-maghrib wa-ṭuraf ashʿārihim wa-nawādirihim* (the clever curiosities of the inhabitants of al-Shām, Miṣr, and al-Maghrib, and the unusual coining of their poems and rarities). One of the best surviving manuscripts of the *Yatīma*, MS Laleli 1959, is missing more than 250 pages of this chapter; the lacuna starts a few paragraphs before its opening. Because the lacuna starts in the middle of a page (and the text is coherent without it), it creates further doubt about this section of the *Yatīma*, for it is not the result of a binding error. Moreover, this uncharacteristically long chapter, around 265 pages, is not consistent with other chapters in the same region. The missing material, moreover, cannot be an addition by another author since the chains of transmission occur elsewhere in the *Yatīma* and the style and critical comments are consistent with those of Thaʿālibī's in the *Yatīma*. On the basis of Rowson and Bonebakker's discussion of the entry on Ibn Shuhayd and the text of MS Laleli, it is possible that Thaʿālibī added this material to the *Yatīma* later in his life, before writing *Tatimmat al-Yatīma*.

One certain addition to the *Yatīma* is by Abū l-Faḍl al-Mīkālī; it is present in all the printed editions of the text and in some manuscripts. It is introduced in the text as follows:

> This is an addendum supplemented by *al-amīr* Abū l-Faḍl ʿUbaydallāh b. Aḥmad al-Mīkālī, may God have mercy upon him, in his own handwriting at the end of the fourth volume (*mujallad*) of his copy on the authority of Thaʿālibī. Al-Shaykh Abū Manṣūr, may God have mercy upon him, said to one of his students while reading: I have approved the *amīr*'s

132 Ch. Pellat, "Ibn Shuhayd," *EI2* III:938b–940a.

133 Rowson and Bonebakker, *Computerized Listing*, 8.

134 *Y* 2:108ff.; C. E. Bosworth, *The Islamic Dynasties* (Edinburgh: University Press, 1967), 17.

135 Rowson and Bonebakker, *Computerized Listing*, 9.

> action, and if you wish to record it in its place in the book, go ahead, you have the authority for that.[136]

Authenticity and Misattribution

Thaʿālibī dealt with an enormous amount of material from numerous local poets whose work was not widely circulated or recorded; this naturally increased the possibility of misattribution. He mentions this problem in his long discussion of al-Sarī al-Raffāʾ's (d. 366/976) attempt to defame the two Khālidī brothers by inserting their poems into the copies he made of Kushājim's *Dīwān*, giving the impression that they were plagiarizing him. Thaʿālibī says:

> When al-Sarī became serious in his service of *adab* and changed from embroidering clothes to embroidering books, he felt the excellence of his poetry, he quarreled with the two Mawṣilī Khālidiyyān, showed them hostility, claimed that they had plagiarized his poetry and the poetry of others. He started to reproduce and copy the poetry *dīwān* of Abū l-Fatḥ Kushājim, who was at that time the perfume of the litterateurs in those lands; al-Sarī followed his way, and composed poetry in his style [lit. strikes in his cast]. And he used to smuggle into the poetry he copied the best poetry of al-Khālidiyyān, so that the size of what he copied would increase, sell faster, and its price rise, [and simultaneously] he would stir hatred for al-Khālidiyyān by means of this [smuggling], diminish their prestige, and demonstrate the truth of his accusation concerning their literary theft. On this account there appear in some copies of the *dīwān* of Kushājim additions that are not in its known originals. I have found all of these in the handwriting of one of the Khālidiyyān, Abū ʿUthmān Saʿīd b. Hāshim, under his name in a volume that the *warrāq* known as al-Ṭarsūsī has bestowed upon Abū Naṣr Sahl b. al-Marzubān, who sent it to Nīshāpūr among the rare books he had obtained. In it I found the hard-sought goal: the poetry of the aforementioned Khālidī and his brother Abū Bakr Muḥammad b. Hāshim. I saw in it verses Abū ʿUthmān had composed for himself and other [verses] he had written for his brother; and these very lines in the aforementioned volume of Abū Naṣr are in al-Sarī's handwriting [in the Kushājim *dīwān*].[137]

---

136 *Y* 4:450.

137 *Y* 2:118; and Ṣābī, *al-Mukhtār min rasāʾil Abī Isḥāq Ibrāhīm b. Hilāl b. Zahrūn al-Ṣābī*, ed. Shakīb Arslān (Beirut: Dār al-Nahḍa al-Ḥadītha, 1966), 164–5.

FIGURE 30 *Yatīmat al-dahr*, MS *Laleli 1959, 612r*

In this case, Thaʿālibī has done the necessary collation to isolate the poems of dubious attribution in a separate section under the entry dedicated to al-Khālidiyyān.[138]

On many occasions, Thaʿālibī mentions that a poem in question has already been attributed to more than one poet or that, later in life, he became aware of another attribution. The phrases he uses in this case are *wa-yurwā li-ghayrihi* (it is reported as by someone else),[139] *wa-yurwā li-*,[140] *thumma wajadtuhu* (*li-ghayrihi, li-*, or *bi-khaṭṭ*) (then I found it attributed to someone else),[141] *wa-huwa mutanāzaʿun baynahu wa-bayna* (it is contested),[142] *wa-arānī samiʿtuhu li-ghayrihi* (and I heard it reported as by someone else),[143] *thumma raʾaytu*

---

138 *Y* 2:186ff. Rowson and Bonebakker hold that Thaʿālibī is not careful in this section; see *Computerized Listing*, 11. However, most of the poems included in this section are in fact attributed to both poets in contemporary and later sources.

139 *Y* 2:325, 3:261; *T* 15, 16, 28, 34, 38, 43, 112.

140 *Y* 1:110, 116, 308, 2:365, 4:81, 93, 415; *T* 42, 43, 46, 58, 59, 60, 65, 74, 90.

141 *Y* 1:117, 4:143; *T* 38, 102.

142 *Y* 2:406; *T* 21.

143 *T* 39.

(then I found),[144] *wa-huwa mimmā yunsabu li-* (and it is among that which is attributed to).[145] Sometimes he expresses his own reservations about the authenticity of a poem by saying *wa-ashukku fīhi* (I have doubts about it),[146] *wa-anā murtābun bihi* (I am skeptical about it),[147] *zuʿima* (it is claimed),[148] or *wa-lastu adrī a-humā lahu am li-ghayrihi* (and I do not know whether it is by him or someone else).[149] At other times, he hints at his doubts by distancing himself from the poetry he quotes. Such is the case with phrases like *wa-mimmā yunsabu ilayhi* (among that which is attributed to him) when used instead of the more confident and common *wa-lahu* (and by him), *wa-anshadanī* (he recited to me), *wa-qāla* (he said), or *wa-huwa l-qāʾil* (and he is the one who said).[150] Such doubts mostly result from the attribution of the poem to another poet, in an oral or written tradition. When available, Thaʿālibī includes the name of the second poet and identifies the informant and/or written source. In other cases, he expresses uncertainty because the quoted poetry seems incompatible with his own assessment of the poet's talent. In these cases, Thaʿālibī uses phrases like *wa-anā murtābun bihi li-farṭi jūdatihi wa-irtifāʿihi ʿan ṭabaqatihi* (and I am skeptical about it because of its extreme excellence and superiority to its class).[151] A further cause for doubt is an informant's lack of authority (*thiqa*).[152] Indeed, there are cases in which double attribution comes from the same informant. For example, two lines in the entry of the poet Abū l-Qāsim al-Muḥassin b. ʿAmr b. al-Muʿallā reached Thaʿālibī by way of Abū l-Ḥasan ʿAlī b. Maʾmūn al-Maṣṣīṣī, one of his frequent informants (see chapter 4). Yet Thaʿālibī mentions that the same informant had attributed those lines to someone else on a different occasion.[153] Uncertainty about a poem's authenticity may also occur when a poet recites or writes certain lines without claiming them as his own. For example, in the case of the librarian Abū Bakr Muḥammad b. ʿUthmān al-Nīshāpūrī (d. before 429/1037), Thaʿālibī mentions that he found a poem penned by him but does not recall whether

144 *T* 45.

145 *Y* 2:187, 199, 200, 218.

146 *T* 85, 143, 241.

147 *Y* 2:347.

148 *T* 143.

149 *Y* 3:191.

150 *Y* 1:105, 2:347; *T* 21, 43, 46.

151 *Y* 2:406; see also *T* 21.

152 *Y* 2:347.

153 *T* 17. The same occurs with two lines attributed to Talʿafrī by way of Abū Bakr al-Khwārizmī; *Y* 1:300.

the lines are actually his own.[154] In the case of Abū ʿAlī Muḥammad b. ʿUmar al-Balkhī al-Zāhir (d. before 429/1037), the lines in question were given by the poet himself, but Thaʿālibī mentions that the same lines had been attributed to Abū l-Ḥasan ʿAlī b. Muḥammad al-Ghaznawī.[155] Similarly, Thaʿālibī relates that before his imprisonment, Abū l-Fatḥ Ibn al-ʿAmīd (d. 366/976) would frequently recite two lines, but then Thaʿālibī admits uncertainty as to whether the lines were truly his.[156] Finally, in the case of Abū al-Qāsim ʿAlī b. Jalabāt (d. after 416/1025), Thaʿālibī corrects his work after discovering the real author of the poems.[157]

Rowson and Bonebakker point to two identical poems in the *Yatīma* that are attributed to different authors.[158] Double attribution is also found between the *Yatīma* and other works of Thaʿālibī. Rowson and Bonebakker specify two instances of double attribution in the *Yatīma* and *Tatimma*. The first is a poem attributed by Ibn Khallikān to ʿAbd al-Muḥsin al-Ṣūrī (d. 419/1028) in the *Yatīma* but to Ibn Abū Ḥusayn in the *Tatimma*.[159] The second poem was noticed by Ibn al-Abbār (d. 658/1260); it consists of a few lines attributed to Muḥammad b. ʿAbd al-Malik b. ʿAbd al-Raḥmān al-Nāṣir.[160] One can add to the list by looking at other works of Thaʿālibī or other sources; a few other examples from Thaʿālibī's works will suffice. Two lines in the *Yatīma* entry on Abū l-Qāsim Ismāʿīl b. Aḥmad al-Shajarī appear in the *Tatimma* attributed to

154 *Y* 4:84.

155 *Y* 4:415.

156 *Y* 3:191.

157 *Y* 3:104.

158 Rowson and Bonebakker specify: *Y* 1:248 (Nāshiʾ al-Aṣghar) and 3:394 (Abū Muḥammad al-Munajjim); 3:122 (Abū Muḥammad b. al-Munajjim) and 3:214 (Abū ʿĪsā b. al-Munajjim); and 1:249 (Abū ʿĀmir Ismāʿīl b. Aḥmad al-Shāshī) and 3:389 (Abū Ibrāhīm Ismāʿīl b. Aḥmad al-Shāshī). One can certainly add to this list 1:425 (Sulaymān b. Ḥassān al-Naṣībī) and 4:127 (Abū Muḥammad b. Abī al-Thayyāb), as well as 4:349.

159 *Y* 1:316; *T* 1:68; Rowson and Bonebakker, *Computerized Listing*, 11. Rowson and Bonebakker quote Ibn Khallikān's remark on this misattribution in his biography of Ṣūrī: "Another poem of his—in which Thaʿālibī in the book he wrote as a supplement to the *Yatīmat al-dahr* attributed to Abū l-Faraj b. Abī Ḥusayn… and God knows best; but it is in the *Dīwān* of ʿAbd al-Muḥsin, and Thaʿālibī used to attribute things to the wrong people, and make mistakes in them; so perhaps this is also one of his mistakes" (11).

160 The full quotation Rowson and Bonebakker translate is as follows: "Abū Manṣūr al-Thaʿālibī reported these verses in his work *al-Yatīma* and attributed them to al-Ḥakam al-Mustanṣir Billāh; he claimed that they were from a *qaṣīda* which (the latter) wrote boastingly to the ruler of Egypt. This is one of the errors and gross delusions of Abū Manṣūr; because of his great distance (from Andalusia) he wrote things without substantiating them, and passed unconfirmed reports from people he knew nothing about." Ibid., 11.

Abū l-Ḥasan al-Aghājī (d. after 429/1037).[161] Similarly, in the *Yatīma*, two lines attributed to Manṣūr b. al-Ḥākim Abī Manṣūr al-Harawī are attributed in the *Tatimma* to Abū l-Ḥasan ʿAlī b. Muḥammad al-Ḥimyarī.[162] Other than the *Tatimma*, four *Yatīma* lines attributed to Abū Aḥmad al-Nāmī al-Būshanjī (fl. ca. 385/995) appear to have been attributed to a certain al-Tamīmī (possibly Abū l-Faḍl al-Tamīmī) in *Thimār al-Qulūb*.[163] Moreover, Thaʿālibī includes two lines in the *Yatīma* entry on the *wazīr* Abū ʿAlī Muḥammad b. ʿĪsā al-Damghānī that he says are attributed to another poet—the same lines are attributed to ʿUbaydallāh b. ʿAbdallāh b. Ṭāhir in *Man ghāba ʿanhu l-muṭrib*.[164]

Forgotten, Lost, and Inconsistent Material

Thaʿālibī drew the material for his anthology from a vast array of written and oral sources (see chapter 4). His continuous travels allowed him to collect his material directly from various authors, and the anthology reflects this in dealing solely with literary figures of his time (*ahl al-ʿaṣr*). Travel, however, has its drawbacks: Thaʿālibī had to rely primarily on his memory and notes, not only because most of this contemporary poetry was unrecorded but also because travel necessitated a constant change of library. Notes can get lost and memory can fail us, as Thaʿālibī admits throughout the *Yatīma*. He in fact mentions the circumstances and anxieties under which he was acting.

Thaʿālibī readily admits his memory lapses. For example, he forgets some lines by the *kātib* Abū Jaʿfar Muḥammad b. al-ʿAbbās b. al-Ḥasan in praise of al-Ḥusayn b. Muḥammad al-ʿAmīd (d. after 343/954),[165] father of the celebrated vizier Abū l-Faḍl b. al-ʿAmīd, having misplaced the papers on which he once recorded them.[166] In the case of Abū l-ʿAbbās Khusraw-Fayrūz (or b.

161 *Y* 2:155; *T* 314.

162 *Y* 4:349; *T* 304–5.

163 *Y* 4:93; Thaʿālibī, *Thimār al-qulūb fī-l-muḍāf wa-l-mansūb*, ed. Muḥammad Abū l-Faḍl Ibrāhīm (Cairo: Dār Nahḍat Miṣr, 1965), 692. The lines in Thaʿālibī, *Khāṣṣ al-khāṣṣ*, ed. Ṣādiq al-Naqwī (Hyderabad: Maṭbūʿāt Majlis Dāʾirat al-Maʿārif al-ʿUthmāniyya, 1984), 527, agree with the attribution in the *Yatīma*.

164 *Y* 4:143; Thaʿālibī, *Man Ghāba ʿanhu l-muṭrib*, ed. Yūnus Aḥmad al-Sāmarrāʾī (Beirut: ʿĀlam al-Kutub, 1987), 100.

165 His father was vizier of Muktafī (*r.* 289–95/902–8) and Muqtadir (r. 295–320/908–32); see *Y* 4:123ff.

166 *Y* 3:159.

Fayrūz) b. Rukn al-Dawla (d. after 373/983),[167] Thaʿālibī forgets what he had once transmitted (and probably memorized), and includes under this entry only the three lines he could recall.[168] The same occurs while he discusses the *adīb* Abū l-Ḥasan (or al-Ḥusayn?) al-Muzanī and the poet Abū ʿAlī Muḥammad b. ʿUmar al-Balkhī al-Zāhir (d. before 429/1037),[169] where Thaʿālibī points out that he was able to memorize only a few lines of their abundant poetry, probably because of a lack of any written sources.[170] The phrases Thaʿālibī uses are *lam yaʿlaq bi-ḥifẓī… ghayru* (nothing got stuck in my mind… except) and *wa-mimmā ʿaliqa bi-ḥifẓī* (and among that which got stuck in my mind).[171] In many cases Thaʿālibī uses phrases like *lam yaḥḍurnī shiʿruhu* (his poetry is not with me), *lam yaḥḍurnī minhu illā* (nothing [of his poetry] is with me except), or *wa yaḥḍurunī minhu* (with me [from his poetry] is),[172] followed by a few lines by the poet. In the context of Thaʿālibī's anthology, these phrases mean either that he had memorized the poetry but then forgotten it or lost his notes, or that he had never acquired firsthand knowledge of the poetry. In such a case, he uses a phrase such as *lam yattaṣil bī min shiʿrihi ghayru* (his poetry did not reach me except for).[173] In a few instances the lost lines had been acquired in both oral and written forms, as is the case with the jurist Abū l-Qāsim Yaḥyā b. ʿAlī al-Bukhārī and the judge Abū Bakr ʿAbdallāh b. Muḥammad al-Bustī.[174]

In cases when Thaʿālibī wrote his notes on slips of paper but then lost them, he sometimes comments on the value of the lost material and his plans to restore it at a later date. Other times he declares that what he has included

---

167 On him, see Ibn al-Athīr, *al-Kāmil fī l-tārīkh*, ed. Abū l-Fidāʾ ʿAbdallāh al-Qāḍī (Beirut: Dār al-Kutub al-ʿIlmiyya, 1995), 7:409.

168 *Y* 2:223. Thaʿālibī reanthologizes him in the *Tatimma* (111) and cites more poetry in his other works; see, for example, Thaʿālibī's *Laṭāʾif al-ẓurafāʾ*, ed. Q. al-Samarrai (Leiden: Brill, 1978), 59b; and *Khāṣṣ al-khāṣṣ*, 257.

169 Muzanī was a contemporary of Abū Bakr al-Khwārizmī (d. 383/993); on him, see *Y* 3:328, 4:165, 208, 225, 346. On Zāhir, see *Y* 4:415 and 1:116, 119.

170 *Y* 4:346, 415.

171 Such phrases sporadically occur in the *Yatīma*; see also *Y* 4:419. They become more frequent in the *Tatimma*; for example, see *T* 39, 41, 87, 226, 296, 305.

172 Such is the case with Abū l-Qāsim al-Ādamī; see *Y* 1:125; Abū ʿAlī al-Ḥātimī, *Y* 3:120; Abū ʿAbdallāh Muḥammad b. Ḥāmid, *Y* 4:248; Aḥmad b. Abī ʿAlī al-ʿAlawī, *Y* 4:419; Abū l-ʿAbbās al-Faḍl b. ʿAlī al-Isfarāʾīnī, *Y* 4:438; Abū Manṣūr Muḥammad b. ʿAlī al-Juwaynī, *Y* 4:445; and al-Ismāʿīlī al-Juwaynī, *Y* 4:514.

173 Such is the case with the poet Ibrāhīm Abū Isḥāq, son of the famous Ibn Lankak; see *Y* 2:358.

174 For Bukhārī, see *Y* 4:415. For Bustī, see *Y* 4:424.

is sufficient.[175] Sometimes, he points out that he has no access to the material because he is on the road. On the Ṭabaristānī poet Abū Saʿīd Aḥmad b. Shabīb al-Shabībī (d. 383/993), Thaʿālibī states that he composed short poems (*maqṭūʿāt*) that would perfectly fit the context of what he is quoting, but unfortunately, he did not have them with him (*ghāʾiba ʿannī*).[176] In the entry on the secretary Abū ʿAbdallāh Muḥammad b. Ḥāmid al-Ḥāmidī (d. after 402/1011), Thaʿālibī justifies the omission of the best of his poetry by noting that he is away from his house, and thus cannot access much good literature (*li-ghaybatī ʿan manzilī fa-taʾakhkhara kathīrun mimmā aḥtāju ilayhi ʿannī*).[177] In the section on poets who visited Nīshāpūr, *fī dhikr al-ṭāriʾīn ʿalā Nīshāpūr min buldān shattā*, and in the section on poets who hailed from that city, Thaʿālibī regrets not being able to cite the poetry of some of them because of his absence from his library; he promises to add the missing material upon his return, adding that if he is not able to do so, he hopes future scholars will fulfill the task.[178] Regrettably, most of these poets are not included in the *Tatimma*.

Thaʿālibī realizes that his anthology is not comprehensive. He sometimes expresses the desire to link any missing material, once he acquires it, to similar material already in his possession. When he anthologizes the *adīb*, secretary, and judge Abū ʿAlī al-Muḥassin al-Tanūkhī (d. 384/994), author of *al-Faraj baʿda l-shidda*,[179] Thaʿālibī states that Abū Naṣr Sahl b. al-Marzubān had seen a massive collection of his poetry in Baghdad but could not bring it back and later tried in vain to obtain it. Thaʿālibī adds that, had Ibn al-Marzubān acquired this *dīwān*, he would have selected more from Tanūkhī's poetry.[180] Likewise, he includes only what is available from the secretary and poet Abū Saʿd Naṣr b. Yaʿqūb al-Dīnawarī (who according to Thaʿālibī was a prolific poet)[181] and hopes to add its like (*akhawātuh*) in the future.[182] On Abū Manṣūr Aḥmad b ʿAbdallāh al-Dīnawarī, Thaʿālibī mentions that he had no access to his poetry but anticipates an appointment with him (*ʿalā mawʿidin minhu*) to select from his poems those that meet the inclusion criteria for the anthology.[183] Again, unfortunately, Thaʿālibī does not seem to have updated the anthology

175 *Y* 4:167.
176 *Y* 4:194.
177 *Y* 4:248.
178 *Y* 4:416, 450.
179 See his biography in H. Fähndrich, "al-Tanūkhī," *EI2* X:192b–193b.
180 *Y* 2:346.
181 On him, see *Y* 4:389; Ṣafadī, *al-Wāfī bi-l-wafayāt*, 27:57.
182 *Y* 4:390.
183 *Y* 4:142.

with the outcome of that meeting.[184] In a section that discusses the *fīliyyāt* (poems on elephants) at the court of Ṣāḥib, Thaʿālibī lists three poems available to him but expresses the hope of eventually adding more.[185] In another case, he refrains from adding a separate entry for Abū al-Qāsim ʿAlī, the son of Abū ʿAlī al-Muḥassin al-Tanūkhī (d. 384/994), because his poetry did not reach him; instead, he refers to a few lines from the Ḥamdānid *amīr* Abū Muṭāʿ b. Nāṣir al-Dawla Dhū l-Qarnayn (d. 428/1036) that he transmitted by way of Abū al-Ḥasan ʿAlī b. Mūsā al-Karkhī.[186] Likewise, he affirms that he will include poetry by the sons of ʿAlī b. Ḥafṣ al-ʿUmrawī—Abū ʿUmar Ḥafṣ and Abū ʿAbdallāh Muḥammad—because of their well-known merit, once he is able to retrieve it.[187]

Only once, in the entry on the Khurāsānī secretary, poet, and *adīb* Abū Manṣūr Aḥmad b. Muḥammad al-Baghawī,[188] does Thaʿālibī forget a hemistich and blame Satan (*ansānīhi al-shayṭān*); but because he does not possess any other material by the poet, and given his importance, he cites the first hemistich and composes the second himself.[189] In another rare circumstance, Thaʿālibī forgets the full name of a poet, Jurayj al-Muqill, but not his poetry.[190] In two cases, Thaʿālibī cannot remember a poet's name at all and places a poem or passage by him under a related subject. For example, the subject, meter, and rhyme of the two lines by the vizier, *adīb*, and poet Abū l-Faḍl Muḥammad b.

184 We know that the meeting took place, since Thaʿālibī quotes on the authority of Abū Manṣūr al-Dīnawarī a few lines by his father, Abū l-Qāsim al-Dīnawarī; see his *Khāṣṣ al-khāṣṣ*, 145.

185 *Y* 3:239.

186 *Y* 2:347. The lines are in 1:107–8.

187 *T* 226.

188 See the entry on him at *Y* 4:142–3 and 4:205.

189 *Y* 4:143.

190 See *T* 58. Little is known about the poet. He was a contemporary of Abū l-Faḍl b. al-ʿAmīd and joined his court; see Tawḥīdī, *Akhlāq al-wazīrayn*, ed. Muḥammad b. Tāwīt al-Ṭūnjī (Beirut: Dār Ṣādir, 1992), 326, 379, 380, 383, 435. Thaʿālibī repeats one of the three *Yatīma* couplets he ascribes to him in his *al-Tamthīl wa-l-muḥāḍara*, ed. ʿA. al-Ḥulw (Cairo: Dār Iḥyāʾ al-Kutub al-ʿArabiyya, 1961), 239, with no ascription. The three couplets occur in other sources attributed to anonymous or other poets. See, for example, Tawḥīdī, *al-Baṣāʾir wa-l-dhakhāʾir*, ed. Wadād al-Qāḍī (Beirut: Dār Ṣādir, 1988), 9:150; Tanūkhī, *Nishwār al-muḥāḍara*, ed. ʿAbbūd al-Shāljī (Beirut: Dār Ṣādir, 1971–3), 6:150; Ibn Abī Ḥajala, *Dīwān al-ṣabāba*, ed. Muḥammad Zaghlūl Sallām (Alexandria: Munshaʾāt al-Maʿārif, 1987), 241; al-Rāghib al-Iṣfahānī, *Muḥāḍarāt al-udabāʾ*, ed. Riyāḍ ʿAbd al-Ḥamīd Murād (Beirut: Dār Ṣādir, 2006), 1:562. Thaʿālibī himself mentions in the *Yatīma* that the last couplet is ascribed to another poet, Abī al-ʿAlāʾ al-Asadī (d. after 385/995); see *Y* 3:339.

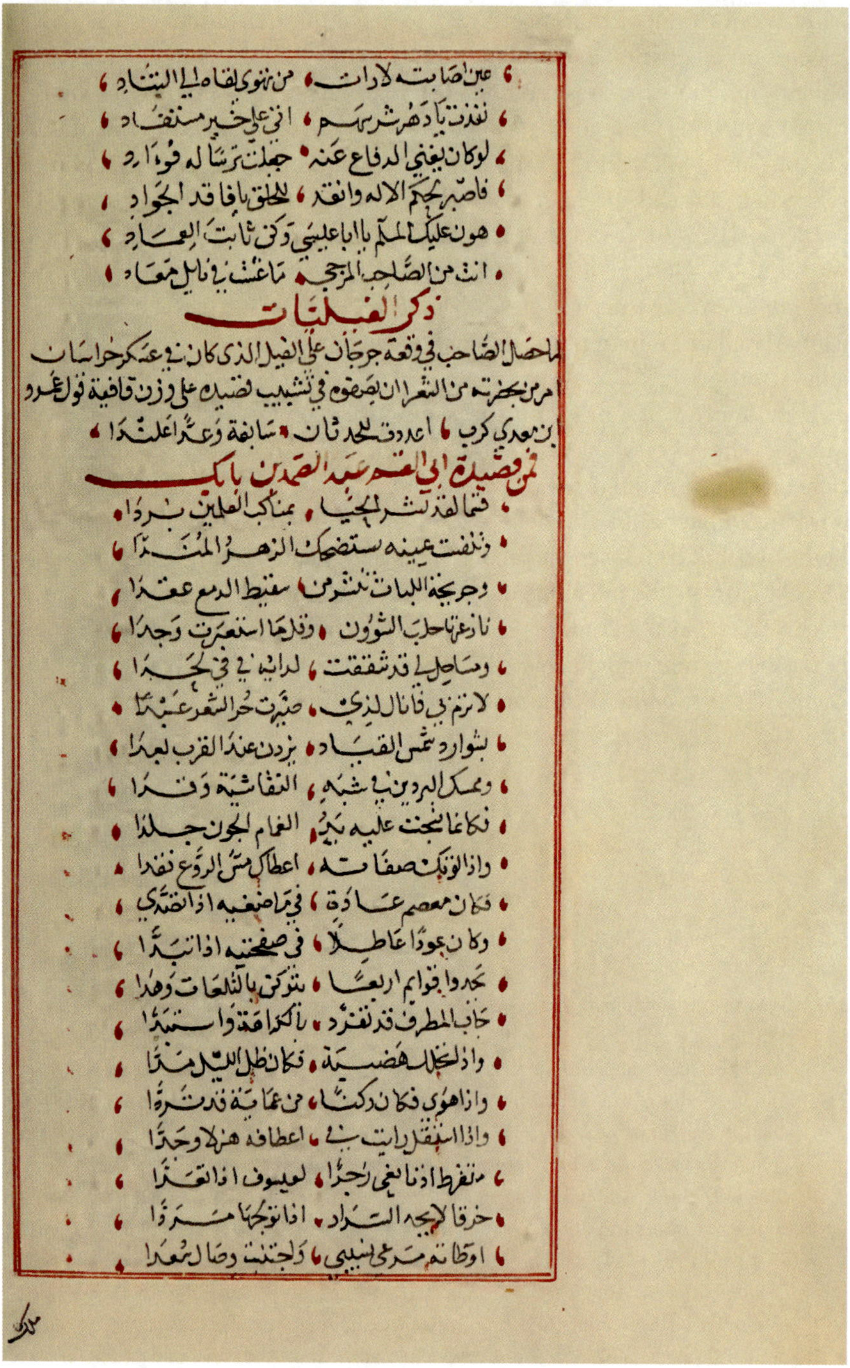

عين اصابته لا دات • من ينوي لقاه الى البناد •
نفذت يا دهر شر سهم • اني على خير مستفاد •
لو كان يغني الدفاع عنه • جعلت ترسا له فؤادي •
فاصبر لحكم الاله وانقد • للخلق يا فاقد الجواد •
هون عليك المكلم يا ابا علي • وكن ثابت العماد •
انت من الصاحب المرجى • ما عشت في نائل معاد •

ذكر الفيليات

لما حصل الصاحب في وقعة جرجان على الفيل الذي كان في عسكر خراسان امر من بحضرته من الشعراء ان يصفوه في تشبيب قصيدة على وزن قافية قول عمرو بن معدي كرب • اعددت للحدثان سابغة • وعدّا علندا •

فمن قصيدة ابي القاسم عبد الصمد بن بابك

فما لقد نشر الحيا • بمناكب العلمين بردا •
ونفست عينه ستضحك الزهر المنضدا •
وجريحة اللبات تنثر من • سقيط الدمع عقدا •
نازعتها حلب الشؤون • وقلما استعبرت وجدا •
ومساحل قد شققت • لرائيه في لجبا •
لا ترم بي فانا الذي • صيرت حر الشعر عبدا •
بشوارد تمس القياد • يزدن عند القرب بعدا •
ومشكل البردين في شبه • النقاشية وقدا •
فكانما نجت عليه يد • الغمام الجون جلدا •
واذا لوتك صفاته • اعطاك مس الروع نقدا •
فكان معصم غادة • في ما ضغيه اذا تصدى •
وكان عودا عاطلا • في صفحتيه اذا تبدى •
يحدوا قوائم اربعا • يتركن بالتلعات وهدا •
خاب المطرف قد تفرد • بالكرا قعدا واستبدا •
واذا تخلل هضبة • فكان ظل الليل مدا •
واذا هوى فكان دكا • من عماية قد تردا •
واذا استقل رايت بي • اعطافه هزلا وجدا •
متفرطا اذ نابني زجرا • لعيسوف اذا تعدا •
خرقا لايجه السراد • اذا توجهها سروا •
اوطانه مرعى سبيبي • ولجته وصال سعدا •

FIGURE 31 *Yatīmat al-dahr*, MS Toronto A13512y, 275v

ʿAbd al-Wāḥid al-Tamīmī (d. 454/1062)[191] remind Thaʿālibī of two other lines that he quotes but the name of whose author he has forgotten.[192] The second instance is an anonymous *qaṣīda* in the entry on the poet Abū l-Faḍl Aḥmad b. Muḥammad al-Sukkarī al-Marwazī (d. before 429/1037), whose poetry, based on Persian proverbs, reminds Thaʿālibī of an ode, the name of whose author escapes him.[193]

In addition to these lacunae, Rowson and Bonebakker point out several inconsistencies of which Thaʿālibī himself is unaware. In one case, Thaʿālibī mistakenly refers to a particular *rāwī* as previously mentioned (*madhkūr*).[194] In another case, he mentions someone as already introduced (*taqaddama dhikruhu*), when in fact his entry appears on the following page.[195] These inconsistencies might have resulted from constant editing and reediting. For instance, Thaʿālibī might have decided to relocate a certain entry following the relation of proximity but then neglected to change the cross-reference.

The ninth chapter of the first region of the *Yatīma*, on the poets of Syria, Egypt, and al-Maghrib, features the strongest inconsistencies. Rowson and Bonebakker include among the shortcomings of this chapter its inordinate length, the scarcity of biographical information, its extended time span, its disjointed structure, and several repetitions.[196] Rowson and Bonebakker break this chapter into the following components:

1. 7 Syrian poets (and two subarticles)[197]
2. 2 Egyptian poets (and one Iraqi)
3. 5 Andalusian poets
4. 1 Egyptian poet
5. 6 Syrian poets
6. 46 Egyptian poets
7. 106 Andalusian poets

---

191 Originally from Baghdad, he traveled in his youth to Nīshāpūr and Ghazna; later in his life he traveled to al-Qayrawān and then to al-Andalus, where he was patronized by a number of rulers until his death. For information on him, see *T* 79; Ḥumaydī, *Jadhwat al-muqtabis fī dhikr wulāt al-Andalus* (Cairo: al-Dār al-Miṣriyya li-l-Ta'līf wa-l-Tarjama, 1966), 72–3; Maqqarī, *Nafḥ al-ṭīb min ghuṣn al-Andalus al-raṭīb*, ed. Iḥsān ʿAbbās (Beirut: Dār Ṣādir, 1968), 3:121.

192 *T* 81.

193 *Y* 4:87.

194 *Y* 2:368; Rowson and Bonebakker, *Computerized Listing*, 10.

195 *Y* 4:339ff.; Rowson and Bonebakker, *Computerized Listing*, 10.

196 Rowson and Bonebakker, *Computerized Listing*, 10.

197 Material in parentheses is added to Rowson and Bonebakker.

Rowson and Bonebakker point out that section 6 concludes with poems by Tamīm b. al-Muʿizz, including one given in section 2, without a reference to the first. Likewise, the first two entries in section 7 already appeared in section 3, and the entry in section 4 reappears (with the same poem) in section 6 but under a slightly different name. Moreover, two poets are included twice in section 7.[198] Rowson and Bonebakker suggest that the sections 5–7 were added in the second edition of the *Yatīma*, without an attempt to integrate them with the earlier material in sections 1–3 (or sections 1–4).

198 Ibid., 11.

CHAPTER 4

The Sources of Thaʿālibī in *Yatīmat al-Dahr* and *Tatimmat al-Yatīma*

Premodern Muslim scholars traveled far and wide trying to earn a living while also searching for information to include in their books. These scholars were often away from their personal libraries, but they continued writing, as libraries were available in the courts that attracted them. Besides written sources, Muslim scholars relied on oral and aural sources to compile their works, recording notes on anything they could write on, and they covered far distances to access more and more material, written and oral. The nature of their sources and the scope of the information they gathered shaped their books, and the availability of new information prompted them both to author new works and to revise existing ones.

For Thaʿālibī, the main reason he reworked the *Yatīma* and *Tatimma* seems to have been the availability of new literary material that he felt necessitated either the inclusion of additional entries or the modification of old ones.[1] As mentioned in chapter 2, during the course of his life, Thaʿālibī traveled extensively through the eastern Islamic world, visiting centers of learning and meeting other prominent figures of his time. His travels allowed him to collect materials and written works directly from various authors, and he incorporated these into his two wide-ranging works.

Shawkat Toorawa has argued that the availability of books in the third/ninth century in Baghdad made it possible for individuals to complete their training in *adab* through self-teaching. This development, according to Toorawa, resulted in a parallel drop in the reliance on oral and aural transmission of knowledge and an increased dependence on books and written materials.[2] Walter Werkmeister examined the sources of *al-ʿIqd al-farīd* and showed that the majority of the material used by Ibn ʿAbd Rabbihi (d. 328/940) was obtained from *majālis* and *ḥalaqāt*, not from written sources.[3] Manfred Fleischhammer

1 *Y* 1:18.

2 Shawkat Toorawa, *Ibn Abī Ṭāhir Ṭayfūr and Arabic Writerly Culture: A Ninth-Century Bookman in Baghdad* (London: RoutledgeCurzon, 2005), 124; see also Gregor Schoeler, *Genesis of Literature in Islam*, trans. and in collaboration with Shawkat M. Toorawa (Edinburgh: Edinburgh University Press, 2009), 122–5.

3 See Werkmeister, *Quellenuntersuchungen zum Kitāb al-ʿiqd al-farīd des Andalusiers (240/860–328/940)* (Berlin: Klaus Schwarz Verlag, 1983).

 | DOI 10.1163/9789004317352_005

studied Abū l-Faraj al-Iṣbahānī's (d. 356/967) manner of working in *K. al-Aghānī* and identified the oral and written sources he used.[4] Fleischhammer's careful sifting through the *isnād*s provides two insights: first, the compiler drew his material from a limited number of informants; second, Iṣbahānī indicates the main written works from which he quoted. Fuat Sezgin also has addressed the sources of *K. al-Aghānī*. He agrees with Fleischhammer on the number of authorities from whom Abū l-Faraj draws, but he argues that the author almost always used written texts.[5] Sebastian Günther similarly reviews the sources of another work by Abū l-Faraj al-Iṣbahānī, the *Maqātil al-ṭālibiyyīn*, and concludes that the author relied on a variety of aural and written sources, with both singular and collective *isnāds*.[6]

The *Yatīma* and *Tatimma*, however, although assembled close in time to the previously mentioned compilations, are different in that they deal almost exclusively with contemporary literature—a largely unexamined corpus that had yet to be recorded in books, as Thaʿālibī notes in the introduction to the *Yatīma*. From where, then, did Thaʿālibī gather his information? This chapter provides an overview of the sources—oral, aural, and written—from which Thaʿālibī compiled *Yatīmat al-dahr* and *Tatimmat al-Yatīma*.

Written Sources

In his travels, Thaʿālibī must have had access to several libraries, but he shares few details of his experiences. He does state in the *Yatīma* that he used the library of Abū l-Faḍl ʿUbaydallāh al-Mīkālī (d. 436/1044–5).[7] In the introduction to *Fiqh al-lugha* (written only after repeated requests from the *amīr*), Thaʿālibī mentions that he stayed for four months in Mīkālī's village of Fayrūzābād, and that the patron Mīkālī ensured that Thaʿālibī would be supplied from his own library with the sources he needed.[8] Thaʿālibī also reveals the library of Abū

4 Fleischhammer, *Die Quellen des Kitāb al-Aǧānī*.

5 Sezgin, "*Maṣādir kitāb al-aghānī li-Abī l-Faraj al-Iṣfahānī*," in *Vortäge zur Geschichte der Arabisch-Islamischen Wissenschaften* (Frankfurt: Maʿhad Tārīkh al-ʿUlūm al-ʿArabiyya wa-l-Islāmiyya fī iṭār Jāmiʿat Frankfūrt, 1984), 147–58.

6 See Günther, "»... nor have I learned it from any book of theirs« Abū l-Faraj al-Iṣfahānī: A Medieval Arabic Author at Work," in *Islamstudien ohne Ende: Festschrift Für Werner Ende Zum 65. Geburtstag*, ed. R. Brunner et al. ([Heidelberg]: Deutsche Morgenländische Gesellschaft, 2000), 139–54.

7 See *Y* 3:340.

8 Thaʿālibī, *Fiqh al-lugha wa-sirr al-ʿarabiyya*, ed. Yāsīn al-Ayyūbī (Beirut: al-Maktaba al-ʿAṣriyya, 2000), 33.

Naṣr Sahl b. al-Marzubān (d. before 420/1029) to be one of the main sources for his books. The library contained rare books that Ibn al-Marzubān had obtained during two visits to Baghdad.[9] Thaʿālibī does not mention specifically that he used or saw this library, but frequently in the *Yatīma* and his other works he notes that Ibn al-Marzubān had granted him private access to a particular *dīwān* or book.

Thaʿālibī names several of his written sources, such as *dīwān*s of poets or books such as *al-Wasāṭa* by ʿAlī b. ʿAbd al-ʿAzīz al-Jurjānī (d. 392/1002), *al-Rūznāmja* by Ṣāḥib b. ʿAbbād (d. 385/995), and *al-Faraj baʿda l-shidda* by Tanūkhī (d. 384/994). His dependence on further sources can be established from either the wording of his quotations or the way he introduces them. It is, of course, impossible to trace all the sources Thaʿālibī used to make selections for the *Yatīma* and *Tatimma*, since—as was the convention of his contemporaries—he never provided a full list of his sources. A significant number of poems in the anthology are included without mention of any oral or a written source; Thaʿālibī simply introduces the poem with the words *qāla* (he said), *unshidtu* (it was recited to me), or *lahu* (to him). This is especially the case for shorter entries on minor litterateurs, and it probably served to minimize the use of *isnād*s in the work.[10] In some cases, a *dīwān* or other written record can be deduced as Thaʿālibī's source because he describes it elsewhere in the *Yatīma* or the *Tatimma*. In his entry on the poet, secretary, and scholar Abū l-Faraj al-Ḥusayn b. Muḥammad b. Hindū (d. 410/1019 or 420/1029), for instance, he includes a significant amount of poetry without indicating its source, but he later acknowledges having used the *dīwān* in his entry on Abū l-Ḥusayn ʿAlī b. Bishr al-Ramlī.[11]

---

9 See *Y* 4:391.

10 The practice of reducing *isnād*s in *adab* works is not limited to Thaʿālibī. Ibn ʿAbd Rabbihi mentions in his introduction to *al-ʿIqd al-farīd* that he will omit *isnād*s. His point is that the work is a collection of entertaining reports, maxims, and anecdotes; thus, the connection of the *isnād* to them is not necessary, and its omission will make the work lighter and shorter. He then quotes several authorities of prophetic tradition who ridicule the *isnād*, thereby arguing that if the omission of the *isnād* is permissible in prophetic tradition, then it is even more justified in the case of these entertaining reports; see Ibn ʿAbd Rabbihi, *al-ʿIqd al-farīd*, ed. Mufīd Muḥammad Qumayḥa (Beirut: Dār al-Kutub al-ʿIlmiyya, 1983), 1:4–5.

11 *T* 34. Ibn Hindū's *dīwān* is lost but Thaʿālibī and other later anthologists preserve samples of his lyric poetry, mostly *ghazal*, as well as fragments of his *al-Wasāṭa bayna al-zunāt wa-l-lāṭa* (Arbitration between the Fornicators and the Sodomites); see *GAL* SI:425–6.

In general, the written material in the *Yatīma* and *Tatimma* can be grouped as follows: *dīwans*, books, and other written materials (e.g., *rasāʾil, ruqaʿ, awrāq*).

Dīwāns

Thaʿālibī receives collections of poems (Thaʿālibī usually uses the terms *majmūʿ* or *mujallada*), which he received from the poets themselves, who were his friends: Abū ʿAbdallāh Muḥammad b. Ḥāmid al-Khwārizmī, Abū Bakr ʿAlī b. al-Ḥasan al-Quhistānī (d. after 435/1043),[12] and especially Abū Naṣr Sahl b. al-Marzubān. Other collections he compiled personally, as for the poet al-Laḥḥām (d. ca. 363/973).[13] Thaʿālibī used at least eighteen *dīwāns* to compile the *Yatīma* and at least seven for the *Tatimma*. His reliance on *dīwāns* is most apparent in the first region of the *Yatīma*, where he treats poets whom he had never met and who were not yet distinguished enough to have their *dīwāns* in circulation. Thaʿālibī often mentions how he obtained a certain *dīwān* and comments on its size, value, popularity, and copyist.[14] He also mentions *dīwāns* that he was not able to obtain.[15]

Books

Thaʿālibī often cites the books he consulted by author. Such is the case with *al-Tājī* of Ṣābī (d. 384/994), *al-Fasr* of Ibn Jinnī (d. 392/1002), *al-Wasāṭa* of Qāḍī al-Jurjānī (d. 392/1002), and *al-Rūznāmja* and *al-Kashf ʿan masāwiʾ shiʿr al-Mutanabbī* of Ṣāḥib b. ʿAbbād. Thaʿālibī does not usually mention the person who provided him with the books, and we cannot know whether they were transmitted to him in written, oral, or aural form. There is some evidence of aural transmission in the *Yatīma*.[16] Reliance on books is strongest in the first region (on Syria, Egypt, and al-Maghrib) and weakest in the fourth (on

12 Bākharzī met this person in 435/1043; see Bākharzī, *Dumyat al-qaṣr wa-ʿuṣrat ahl al-ʿaṣr*, ed. Muḥammad al-Ṭūnjī (Beirut: Dār al-Jīl, 1993), 2:778–91. For more on him, see *T* 264; Yāqūt al-Ḥamawī, *Muʿjam al-udabāʾ: Irshād al-arīb ilā maʿrifat al-adīb*, ed. Iḥsān ʿAbbās (Beirut: Dār al-Gharb al-Islāmī, 1993), 4:1677–81.

13 See appendixes 2 and 3. For more details, see B. Orfali, "The Sources of al-Thaʿālibī in *Yatīmat al-Dahr* and *Tatimmat al-Yatīma*," *Middle Eastern Literatures* 16 (2013), appendixes 2–3.

14 On how he obtained particular *dīwāns*, see *Y* 1:289, 2:117, 3:330, 379, 4:172, 439; *T* 9, 46, 106. On size, see *Y* 3:3, 4:442. On value, see *Y* 3:330, 340. On popularity, see *Y* 3:31, 330. On copyists, see *Y* 2:117, 118, 220, 3:379, 4:172; *T* 106.

15 See, for example, *Y* 2:346.

16 Thaʿālibī introduces poems by prefacing them with phrases like *aktabanī* or *kattabanī, istamlaytu minhu*, or *aqraʾanī*; see *Y* 1:26, 2:119; *T* 268, 292.

Khurāsān and Transoxania), where Thaʿālibī seems to have relied more on personal contacts. All authors quoted are contemporaries of Thaʿālibī. Their works range from history and memoirs (*al-Tājī, Tahdhīb al-taʾrīkh, al-Rūznāmja*) to poetic commentaries (*al-Fasr*), poetics (*al-Wasāṭa, al-Kashf ʿan masāwiʾ shiʿr al-Mutanabbī, al-Muwāzana*), medicine (*Risāla fī l-ṭibb*), biographical dictionaries (*K. Iṣbahān*), thematic anthologies (*Rawāʾiʿ al-tawjīhāt, al-Tuḥaf wa-l-ẓuraf, Ashʿar al-nudamāʾ, al-Faraj baʿda l-shidda*), general anthologies (*Siḥr al-balāgha*), and general collections (*Ḥāṭib layl, Safīnat al-Mīkālī*).[17]

In the *Tatimma*, books figure most prominently in the first region (four mentions) but become rare afterward (one citation in the second region and another in the third). As in the *Yatīma*, Thaʿālibī seems to have relied more on personal connections when it came to the eastern regions. The subjects of the quoted works are likewise diverse: thematic anthologies and poetics (*al-Tashbīhāt, al-Muḥibb wa-l-maḥbūb wa-l-mashmūm wa-l-mashrūb*), *rasāʾil* (*Rasāʾil al-Ṣābī*), general collections (*Safīnat al-Ḥāmidī*), and literary treatises (*al-Wasāṭa bayna l-zunāt wa-l-lāṭa*).[18] The wide range of quoted works attests to Thaʿālibī's familiarity with multiple fields and his keenness to assemble the best literary production of his day.

Thaʿālibī mentions other works that he saw but did not quote (see appendixes 2 and 3). In his entry on Abū l-Faraj al-Iṣbahānī, he says: "I have seen from his works: *K. al-Qiyān, K. al-Aghānī, Iḥsān ẓurafāʾ al-shuʿarāʾ, K. al-Diyārāt, K. Daʿwat al-Najjār, K. Mujarrad al-Aghānī, K. Akhbār Jaḥẓa al-Barmakī*, and I do not doubt he has more."[19] He sometimes mentions having read a work, then

---

17 See appendix 2. For more information, see Orfali, "Sources of al-Thaʿālibī," appendixes 2–3.

18 See appendix 2. For more information, see ibid., appendixes 2–3.

19 *Y* 3:114. Thaʿālibī mentions further the following: (1) *K. al-Asjāʿ* by Ḥasan b. ʿAbd al-Raḥīm al-Zallālī (1:307); (2) *Ikhtiṣār Kitāb al-ʿAyn, Ṭabaqāt al-naḥwiyyīn wa-l-lughawiyyīn*, and *al-Abniya fī l-naḥw* by Abū Bakr al-Zubaydī (2:71); (3) *K. al-Afʿāl* by Ibn al-Qūṭiyya (2:74); (4) *al-Maqāmāt* by Badīʿ al-Zamān al-Hamadhānī (3:358); (5) *al-Qalāʾid wa-l-farāʾid* by Abū l-Ḥusayn al-Ahwāzī (3:419); (6) *Adab al-kātib* by Ibn Qutayba (4:77); (7) *al-Bāriʿ fī akhbār wilāyat Khurāsān, Nutaf al-ẓarf* [*al-ẓuraf*?, *al-ṭuraf*?], and *al-Miṣbāḥ* by Abū ʿAlī al-Salāmī (4:95); (8) *Maḥāsin al-shiʿr* and *Aḥāsin al-maḥāsin* by Abū Naṣr al-Huzaymī (4:129); (9) *Zāmilat al-nutaf* by Abū Manṣūr Aḥmad b. Muḥammad al-Baghawī (4:142); (10) *Kitāb Fī gharīb al-ḥadīth* by Abū Sulaymān al-Khaṭṭābī (4:325); (11) *Ashʿār al-nudamāʾ* and *al-Intiṣār li-l-Mutanabbī* by Abū l-Ḥasan Muḥammad b. Aḥmad al-Ifrīqī al-Mutayyam (4:352); (12) *K. al-ʿAyn* by Khalīl b. Aḥmad al-Farāhīdī (4:352); (13) *Rawāʾiʿ al-tawjīhāt fī badāʾiʿ al-tashbīhāt, Thimār al-uns fī tashbīhāt al-furs, al-Jāmiʿ al-kabīr fī l-taʿbīr, al-Adʿiya, Ḥuqqat al-jawāhir fī l-mafākhir* by Abū Saʿd Naṣr b. Yaʿqūb (4:390); (14) *Akhbār Ibn al-Rūmī, Akhbār Jaḥẓa al-Barmakī, Dhikr al-aḥwāl fī Shaʿbān wa-shahr Ramaḍān wa-Shawwāl,*

comments on its quality or content without quoting it. For example, Thaʿālibī admits that he enjoyed reading a few volumes of Aḥmad b. Muḥammad al-Baghawī's thirty-volume work *Zāmilat al-nutaf*.[20] He then argues that *al-Ṣiḥāḥ fī l-lugha* by al-Jawharī (d. 393/1002) surpasses earlier works on the subject,[21] claims that Abū Saʿd Manṣūr b. al-Ḥusayn al-Ābī (d. 422/1031) was unprecedented in composing his *K. al-Taʾrīkh* (*lam yusbaq ilā taṣnīfi mithlihi*),[22] and praises Abū Sulaymān al-Khaṭṭābī's (d. before 429/1037) *Kitāb Fī gharīb al-ḥadīth* as the pinnacle of excellence and eloquence (*ghāya fī-l-ḥusn wa-l-balāgha*).[23]

Other Written Media

Thaʿālibī achieved a far-reaching reputation during his lifetime, especially after publication of the first edition of the *Yatīma*. His contemporary Ḥuṣrī (d. 413/1022), writing in al-Qayrawān, attests to his fame.[24] He had become best known as an anthologist of contemporary literature (especially poetry). In his introduction to the second edition of the *Yatīma*, Thaʿālibī reports on the favorable reception of his work:

> I wrote this book hastily at the time… thinking that as soon as the borrowers would lend it among themselves and the copyists would circulate it among themselves, it would become the most precious thing, avidly cherished by our literary friends and traveling the world to its farthest ends. And [indeed], reports followed in succession, testifying that people of merit were keen to sip from its sources, considering it the opportunity

al-Ādāb fī-l-ṭaʿām wa-l-sharāb by Abū Naṣr Sahl b. al-Marzubān (4:392); (15) *Laṭāʾif al-kuttāb* by Abū Naṣr Muḥammad b. ʿAbd al-Jabbār al-ʿUtbī (4:397); (16) *Man ghāba ʿanhu l-nadīm* by Abū l-Ḥusayn al-Rukhkhajī (4:397); (17) *al-Ṣiḥāḥ fī l-lugha* by Jawharī (comparing it to *al-Jamhara*, *Tahdhīb al-lugha*, and *Mujmal al-lugha*) (4:416); (18) *Darj al-ghurar wa-durj al-durar*, *Ḥamd man ismuhu Aḥmad*, and *Ajnās al-tajnīs* by Muṭṭawwiʿī (4:433); (19) *al-Iqtibās min al-Qurʾān* (2:243), *Aḥsan mā samiʿtu* (3:296), and *Faḍl man ismuhu al-Faḍl* (4:433) by Thaʿālibī himself; and *K. al-Taʾrīkh* and *Nathr al-durr* by Abū Saʿd Manṣūr b. al-Ḥusayn al-Ābī (*Tatimma*, 120).

20 See *Y* 4:142.

21 *Y* 4:416.

22 *T* 120.

23 *Y* 4:325.

24 Al-Ḥuṣrī al-Qayrawānī, *Zahr al-ādāb wa-thimār al-albāb*, ed. ʿA. M. al-Bajāwī (Cairo: al-Bābī al-Ḥalabī, 1970), 1:127–8.

> of a lifetime, keen to pick its flowers and prone to peruse its prose passages. When I lent it my sight and returned my glance to it, I confirmed what I had read in a book: The first weakness that appears in a man is that he writes no book without desiring—one night later—to add to or cut from it, and this is only in one night, so how much more so after several years!
>
> I now find that I am confronted with many things that are similar to what is [already incorporated] in the book, things that have subsequently come to my knowledge, and have fallen upon plentiful additions that I obtained from the mouths of reporters and I thought: If this book has a [high] state in the eyes of the *udabāʾ*, and a [lofty] position in the hearts of the people of merit, as happens with everything that had not struck their ears or touched their minds before, then why do I not rise to the level that is worthy of praise and abundant contemplation? And why do I not loosen the reins of speech and reach the goal of satisfaction and completion?[25]

This passage implies that the quick success of the work prompted litterateurs of the time to send their literary production to Thaʿālibī in hopes of its inclusion in his work, which would then afford them recognition as contemporary litterateurs. As is clear from the final texts of the *Yatīma* and *Tatimma*, this is the case with less notable poets, who sent Thaʿālibī their poetry on *ruqʿa*s and epistles (see appendixes 2 and 3). More eminent litterateurs, like Mīkālī (d. 436/1044–5), Bustī (d. 400/1010), Khwārizmī (d. 383/993), Abū Saʿīd b. Dūst (d. 431/1039), and Ibn al-Marzubān, sent Thaʿālibī entire works; however, this was done in private literary correspondence (*ikhwāniyyāt*) or was poetry by other poets whom they had come to appreciate and wanted to share with their renowned anthologist friend. This written material included *tawqīʿāt*, *rasāʾil*, and poems by literary figures whom Thaʿālibī had never met. Thaʿālibī's reliance on written works is common throughout the four regions of the *Yatīma*, but it takes on a special importance in the third (al-Jabal, Fārs, Jurjān, and Ṭabaristān) and fourth (Khurāsān and Transoxania) regions, which revolved around Ṣāḥib b. ʿAbbād's court. In the fourth region, devoted to Thaʿālibī's native region of Nīshāpūr, it was more common for litterateurs to send Thaʿālibī written documents, since he knew them personally. This holds true for the *Tatimma*, but more so for its first two regions, since Thaʿālibī did not use any written material

25 *Y* 1:18.

(other than edited books). In contrast, most material in the third and fourth regions was sent to Thaʿālibī by the litterateurs without solicitation. Both in the *Yatīma* and in the *Tatimma*, Thaʿālibī comments on whether any texts he had received were penned by the litterateur himself, and he often acknowledges the provenance for the quoted written source.

Oral and Aural Sources

Thaʿālibī, like many scholars in Arabic-Islamic culture, prefaces his oral and aural sources with an *isnād* (or chain of transmitters). Muslim scholars used *isnād*s to label and give credibility to accounts (*akhbār*), prophetic tradition, and other information quoted in their works. The authenticity of *isnād*s is a source of debate in modern scholarship, and some scholars go as far as denying *isnād*s any credibility at all.[26] Other scholars hold that the use of *isnād*s does not antedate the beginning of the second century after *hijra*,[27] whereas others state that the *isnād*s contain a "genuine kernel."[28] Recently, *isnād*s have found warmer reception in modern scholarship as a tool for studying early Islamic historiography and prophetic literature.[29] *Isnād*s in literary texts are slightly different; they developed in relation with the *isnād* in *ḥadīth*, but differ from this in their frequent use of incomplete chains of transmitters (*isnād munqaṭiʿ*). It is sufficient for a literary *khabar* to be considered reliable if its *isnād* ends with an authority such as the philologist al-Aṣmaʿī (d. 828/213).[30] Literary *isnād*s are viewed as a contribution to the establishment of historical truth, but they are less likely to be forged than *isnād*s in *ḥadīth* and historical

26 For example, see Patricia Crone, *Slaves on Horses: The Evolution of the Islamic Polity* (Cambridge: Cambridge University Press, 1980), 7–15.

27 For example, see Joseph Schacht, *The Origins of Muhammadan Jurisprudence* (Oxford: Clarendon, 1950), 37.

28 See Johann Fück, "Die Rolle des Traditionalismus im Islam," *Zeitschrift der Deutschen Morgenländischen Gesellschaft* 93 (1939), 1–32. See also N. J. Coulson, "European Criticism of *Ḥadīth* Literature," in *Arabic Literature to the End of the Umayyad Period* (Cambridge: Cambridge University Press, 1983), 317–21; and Th. Nöldeke, *Geschichte des Qorans* 2 (Hildesheim: Olms, 1961), 193–8.

29 See Harald Motzki, *Origins of Islamic Jurisprudence*, trans. Marion H. Katz (Leiden: Brill, 2002).

30 On narrative and rhetorical techniques of literary *akhbār*, see Stefen Leder, "The Literary Use of the *Khabar*, a Basic Form of Historical Writing," in *The Byzantine and Early Islamic Near East I: Problems in the Literary Source Material*, ed. A. Conrad and L. Conrad (Princeton: Darwin Press, 1992), 277–315; Muḥammad al-Qāḍī, *al-Khabar fī l-adab al-ʿarabī: dirāsa fī l-sardiyya al-ʿarabiyya* (Beirut: Dār al-Gharb al-Islāmī, 1998).

works, as their authors are less likely to have religious or political agendas.[31] Thaʿālibī's *isnād*s may be viewed in light of such considerations.

In his entries on major litterateurs, Thaʿālibī cites his sources meticulously; however, many poems in both the *Yatīma* and the *Tatimma* are labeled with phrases like *lahu* (by him) and *wa-qāla* (he said). It is difficult in these cases to speculate on Thaʿālibī's source, but one can assume that a good number of these poems come by way of written sources. In many other cases, Thaʿālibī uses phrases that suggest an oral or aural transmission, like *unshidtu* (it was recited to me), *anshadanī ghayru thiqatin* (an unreliable personality recited to me), and *anshadanī ghayru wāḥidin* (more than one transmitter recited to me). The most common terms Thaʿālibī employs in introducing *isnād*s are *anshadanī* (he recited to me) and *ḥaddathanī* (he told me). These phrases become less frequent in the second, third, and fourth regions, where Thaʿālibī names more of his guarantors.[32] In the introduction to the first region, Thaʿālibī acknowledges as a guarantor his learned friend Abū Bakr al-Khwārizmī (d. 383/993), who had visited Syria; thus, one can assume that some Syrian material that appears without an *isnād* or that is labeled with terms like *unshidtu* was transmitted on his authority. Two types of *isnād* can be distinguished in the *Yatīma* and *Tatimma*: direct transmission and indirect transmission (see appendixes 2 and 3 for tables of all *isnād*s that appear in the two works).

Direct transmission is rare in the first three regions of both the *Yatīma* and the *Tatimma*. The scarcity of these cases calls for special attention. The only direct transmission from the first region introduces an elegy for Mutanabbī (d. 354/965) by Abū l-Qāsim al-Muẓaffar b. ʿAlī al-Ṭabasī, a native of Nīshāpūr; thus, the *isnād* belongs to the fourth region and was moved to the first only as a literary monument to Mutanabbī. Two direct *isnād*s from the third region come by way of Abū Bakr al-Khwārizmī (d. 383/993), whom Thaʿālibī met in Nīshāpūr.

31 For a discussion of literary *isnād*s, see Nāṣir al-Dīn al-Asad, *Maṣādir al-shiʿr al-jāhilī*, (Cairo: Dār al-Maʿārif, 1978), 255–83; Hilary Kilpatrick, "The "Genuine" Ashʿab: The Relativity of Fact and Fiction in Early *Adab* Texts," in *Story-telling in the Framework of Non-fictional Arabic Literature*, ed. Stefen Leder (Wiesbaden: Harrassowitz, 1998), 95ff.; Stefen Leder, "Prosa-Dichtung in der aḫbār Überlieferung," *Der Islam* 64, 1987, 6–41.

32 A guarantor is any (preceding) person in the process of transmission on whom another (subsequent) individual relies for information; see Sebastian Günther, "Assessing the Sources of Classical Arabic Compilations," 85. The phrases are found in the *Yatīma* in the first section: 1:46, 104, 256, 306, 309, 347, 408, 409, 430, 433, 437, 438, 448, 450, 451, 2:3, 5, 10, 11, 12, 13, 14, 15, 16, 18, 20, 22, 23, 24, 25, 52, 53, 55, 56, 57, 58, 59, 60, 62, 63, 64, 65, 66, 67, 68, 69, 71, 72, 73, 100, 117; second section: 2:223, 236, 347, 377; third section: 3:201, 276, 340, 391, 383, 415; fourth section: 4:50, 91, 110, 123, 242, 337, 345; and in the *Tatimma*, 30, 45, 90, 103, 105, 216, 254, 291, 298, 300, 309.

In the *Tatimma*, Thaʿālibī obtained material from Abū l-Faḍl Muḥammad b. ʿAbd al-Wāḥid al-Tamīmī (d. 454/1062) and Abū Yaʿlā Muḥammad b. al-Ḥasan al-Baṣrī (d. after 429/1037) during their respective visits to Nīshāpūr.[33] In the third region of the *Tatimma*, Thaʿālibī informs his readers that Abū l-Qāsim ʿAbd al-Wāḥid b. al-Ḥarīsh (al-Ḥirrīsh?) (d. 424/1032) was originally from Nīshāpūr (*Nīshāpūrī al-turba*),[34] and he mentions that he met with Abū l-Fatḥ al-Dabāwandī and Abū l-Muẓaffar b. al-Qāḍī Abī Bishr al-Faḍl b. Muḥammad al-Jurjānī (d. after 429/1037) in Nīshāpūr.[35] Thus, among all the direct *isnād*s in the first three regions, in both the *Yatīma* and the *Tatimma*, Abū l-ʿAlāʾ b. al-Ḥasūl (d. 450/1058) is the only person whom Thaʿālibī does not claim to have met in Nīshāpūr.[36] These personalities who visited Nīshāpūr played an important role in conveying the poetry of their region to Thaʿālibī, as we often find them to be guarantors in the indirect *isnād*s. The fourth region, however, relies heavily on direct *isnād*s—there are thirteen such *isnād*s in the *Yatīma* and ten more in the *Tatimma*. Moreover, the three direct *isnād*s in the fifth region of the *Tatimma*, which are dedicated to litterateurs from all regions, derive from Nīshāpūrī poets. In summary, all of Thaʿālibī's direct *isnad*s are drawn from poets anthologized in the fourth region (Khurāsān and Transoxania), whom he met in Nīshāpūr or during his travels in the region, or from poets who visited Nīshāpūr.

Indirect *isnād*s are more common than direct *isnād*s in both works. They are naturally short given the novelty of the material they introduce, and they usually contain only one or two names beyond that of the source poet. Collective *isnād*s are rare.[37] In one case, Thaʿālibī states that he received the same report through three different paths of transmission (Khwārizmī, Ibn al-Marzubān, and al-Maṣṣīṣī), but later, not being able to trace each to its origin, he presents a combined narrative of the event (*fa-dakhala ḥadīthu baʿḍihim fī baʿḍin fa-zāda wa-naquṣa*).

Many guarantors lived in the cities Thaʿālibī visited, and he also met a number of them during their visits to Nīshāpūr. Most came from cities in the eastern part of the Muslim world and transmitted to Thaʿālibī the poetry of their

33 See *T* 79, 108.

34 *T* 132.

35 *T* 154, 170. His father, Abū Bishr al-Faḍl b. Muḥammad died after 391/1000; see Bākharzī, *Dumyat al-qaṣr*, 1:561.

36 Muḥammad b. ʿAlī b. Ḥasūl Ṣafī l-Ḥaḍratayn was originally from Hamadhān, raised in Rayy; see his entry in Bākharzī, *Dumyat al-qaṣr*, 1:411.

37 See *Y* 1:289, 2:224, 245, 372, 4:407; *T* 83.

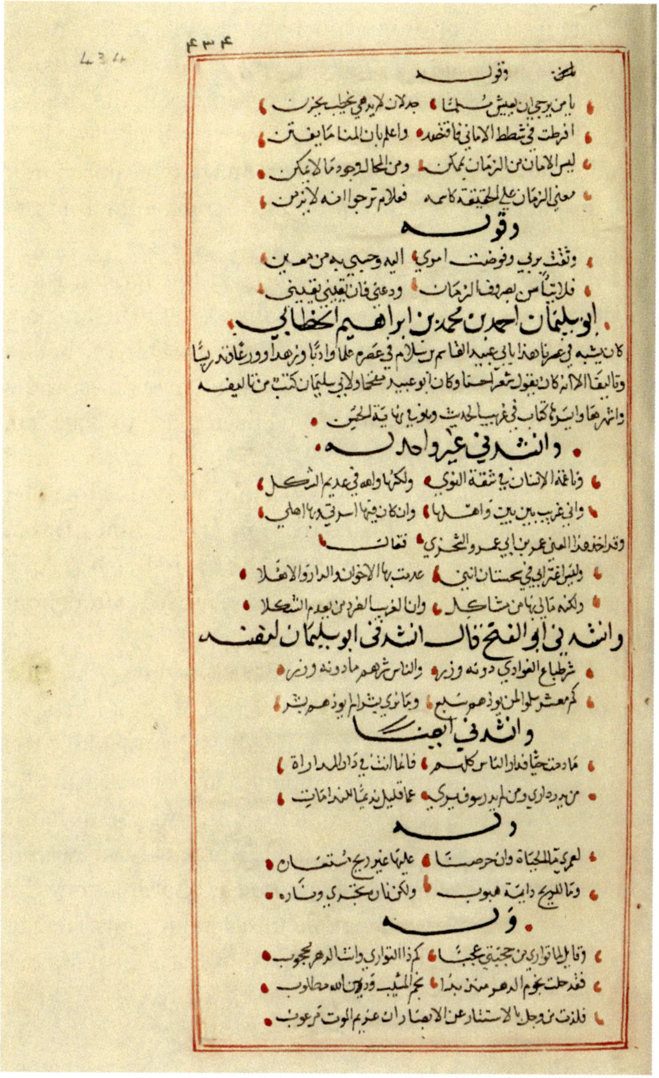

FIGURE 32 *Yatīmat al-dahr*, MS Toronto A13512y, 434r

own region as well as that of the regions they had visited. These well-traveled guarantors allowed Thaʿālibī to collect material from all regions of the Muslim world. Some guarantors, themselves litterateurs and poets, however, were originally from Iraq and had traveled east in hopes of gaining patronage at the flourishing Ghaznavid and Sāmānid courts. To reach their destinations, these poets had to pass through the cultural capital of Nīshāpūr, where they met Thaʿālibī and transmitted their poetry and that of other poets. It is important to note that these litterateurs are not professional transmitters of literary or historical accounts and/or poems. Rather, they are largely poets who shared their knowledge with Thaʿālibī, and many of them have entries in the *Yatīma*. One can presume that at least part of their cited passages trace back directly to them. Rarely did guarantors in the *Yatīma* or *Tatimma* draw their information from books or *dīwāns*; instead, they obtained most of their material from the poets themselves.

Certain guarantors were sources for specific regions in the *Yatīma*, while others transmitted poetry from any region (see appendix 2). In the first region, Khwārizmī (d. 383/993), Abū ʿAlī Muḥammad b. ʿUmar al-Zāhir (d. before 429/1037), and ʿAbd al-Ṣamad al-Miṣrī play a significant role, whereas in the second region, Abū Naṣr Sahl b. al-Marzubān, having been twice to Baghdad, assumes the central role. The chapters on Ṣāḥib b. ʿAbbād and the poets who visited his court rely on transmissions from Khwārizmī and Badīʿ al-Zamān al-Hamadhānī, both of whom attended his court. Conversely, Abū l-Ḥasan ʿAlī b. Maʾmūn al-Maṣṣīṣī (d. before 429/1037) and Abū Saʿd Naṣr b. Yaʿqūb al-Dīnawarī (d. after 400/1010) appear in the transmission process throughout the entire *Yatīma*.

Similarly, in the *Tatimma*, guarantors are from different regions. Abū Bakr al-Quhistānī (d. after 435/1043) and Abū l-Ḥasan Musāfir b. al-Ḥasan (d. after 429/1037) transmit poetry in the first region; Abū l-Faḍl Muḥammad b. ʿAbd al-Wāḥid al-Tamīmī (d. 454/1062) and Abū Yaʿlā Muḥammad b. al-Ḥasan al-Ṣūfī al-Baṣrī (d. after 429/1037) play a role in the second region. Most poems in the third region come by way of Abū l-Fatḥ Muḥammad b. Aḥmad al-Dabāwandī. The fourth region, however, features no main guarantor, as Thaʿālibī draws on the poets themselves. Other guarantors play a role in several regions, such as Abū l-Ḥasan ʿAlī b. Fāris al-Qazwīnī and Abū l-Ḥasan ʿAlī b. Maʾmūn al-Maṣṣīṣī in the first and second regions, respectively.

Main Guarantors in the Yatīma

1. ʿAbd al-Ṣamad b. Wahb al-Miṣrī. Nothing is known about the life of this major guarantor who figures in ten *isnāds* in the first region of the *Yatīma* (on Syria, Egypt, and al-Maghrib).
2. Abū ʿAlī Muḥammad b. ʿUmar al-Balkhī al-Zāhir (d. before 429/1037). A native poet of Balkh whom Thaʿālibī includes in the fourth region of the *Yatīma*, Zāhir also appears in twenty-three *isnāds*, mostly in the first region. As a youth, he left for Iraq and Syria, where he visited Naṣībīn, Aleppo, Beirut, and Mayyāfāriqīn.[38] He then moved to Khurāsān and

38 On his travels to Iraq and Syria, see *Y* 4:415. On his other travels, see *Y* 1:116, 119, 300–301.

settled in Nīshāpūr, where he met Thaʿālibī. The etymology of his name is explained in the *Yatīma* as an imitation of other poets who had taken on names following this pattern, such as al-Nājim, al-Nāshiʾ, al-Nāmī, al-Zāhī, al-Ṭāliʿ, and al-Ṭāhir.[39]

3. Abū Bakr al-Khwārizmī (d. 383/993).[40] Khwārizmī was, in his time, the most salient literary figure in the East. Over his long career, he criss-crossed the Islamic world, enjoying the patronage of *amīr*s as far west as the Ḥamdānid Sayf al-Dawla in Aleppo and as far east as the Shāh of Gharchistān; but no one favored him more generously and more consistently than Ṣāḥib b. ʿAbbād and his first master, ʿAḍud al-Dawla. He visited them over the years in their various capitals of Iṣfahān, Shīrāz, Jurjān, and Rayy, while maintaining a permanent residence in the latter part of his life in Nīshāpūr. It was there that he first met the young Thaʿālibī. He is the source of more than thirty *isnād*s in the *Yatīma* alone, in addition to having supplied much written material. He is a main source throughout the *Yatīma*, and Thaʿālibī acknowledges him especially for the material he provided in the first region.[41]

4. Abū l-Faḍl ʿUbaydallāh b. Aḥmad al-Mīkālī (d. 436/1044–5).[42] Mīkālī belonged to the most illustrious and influential family in Nīshāpūr and is one of the main patrons and friends of Thaʿālibī, who dedicated to him at least five works and compiled an entire book in praise of his *kunya* Abū l-Faḍl.[43] Mīkālī was a theologian, traditionalist, poet, *adīb*, and—according to Ḥuṣrī—*raʾīs* of Nīshāpūr. Until his death, he gave lectures in Nīshāpūr that were widely attended by scholars. His works and his *dīwān* circulated among men of letters.[44] Thaʿālibī quotes Mīkālī's verses, maxims, and compilations in almost all of his writings. Mīkālī, in turn, demonstrated his admiration of Thaʿālibī by visiting him at his house, sending *ikhwāniyyāt*, and composing verses in his praise.[45] In the *Yatīma*,

---

39 *Y* 4:415.

40 See Ch. Pellat, "al-Khʷārizmī, Abū Bakr Muḥammad b. al-ʿAbbās," *EI2* IV:1069b and sources listed there; *Y* 4:194.

41 *Y* 1:26.

42 See his biography in *Y* 4:326; Ḥuṣrī, *Zahr al-ādāb*, 1:126; Bākharzī, *Dumyat al-qaṣr*, 2:984; Kutubī, *Fawāt al-wafayāt*, ed. Iḥsān ʿAbbās (Beirut: Dār Ṣādir, 1973), 2:52; C. E. Bosworth, "Mīkālīs," *EI2* VII:25b–26b; and id., *The Ghaznavids: Their Empire in Afghanistan and Eastern Iran, 994–1040* (Edinburgh: University Press, 1963), 176ff.

43 See Orfali, "Works of Abū Manṣūr al-Thaʿālibī," *JAL* 40 (2009), 315.

44 Samʿānī, *K. al-Ansāb*, ed. ʿA. al-Bārūdī (Beirut: Dār al-Jinān li-l-Ṭibāʿa wa-l-Nashr, 1988), 5:433.

45 Ḥuṣrī, *Zahr al-ādāb*, 1:127–8, 312, 2:501–2, 955.

Abū l-Faḍl al-Mīkālī appears in eight *isnād*s in the first, third, and fourth regions. His *Mulaḥ al-khawāṭir wa-subaḥ al-jawāhir* and a few of his written notes are also cited.

5. Abū l-Ḥasan ʿAlī b. Maʾmūn al-Maṣṣīṣī (d. before 429/1037). Thaʿālibī notes in the *Tatimma*, that he met Maṣṣīṣī several times, over some thirty years (*wa-huwa man laqītuhu qadīman wa-ḥadīthan fi muddati thalāthīna sana*). He refers to him as a poet but does not give him an entry in either the *Yatīma* or the *Tatimma*.[46] He appears in eleven *isnād*s in the *Yatīma*, mostly in the first region, and to a lesser extent in the second and third regions. In the *Tatimma* he appears as an oral source in nine instances in the first and second regions. The wide reach of his network is manifest in the poetry he reports from various poets. One can assume from his *isnād*s that he was a native of Syria; the poetry he reports indicates, too, that he had visited Egypt. It is difficult to determine where Thaʿālibī met him.
6. Abū Jaʿfar Muḥammad b. Mūsā al-Mūsawī al-Ṭūsī (d. before 429/1037). Ṭūsī visited Bukhārā with his father, Abū l-Ḥasan al-Mūsawī, who must be distinguished from the famous poet Abū l-Ḥasan al-Sharīf al-Raḍī al-Mūsawī (d. 406/1015). He served as a major source for the fourth region of the *Yatīma*, where his name appears in eight *isnād*s. Additional reports from him are found throughout Thaʿālibī's other works.[47] According to a *khabar* in *al-Adhkiyāʾ* of Abū l-Faraj Ibn al-Jawzī (d. 597/1201), he attended the *majlis* of Abū Naṣr b. Abī Zayd,[48] who was, according to Thaʿālibī, the vizier of al-Raḍī (d. 387/997), and Nāṣir al-Dīn Abū Manṣūr (d. 387/997).[49]

46 *Y* 2:214.

47 For example, see Thaʿālibī, *Thimār al-qulūb fi-l-muḍāf wa-l-mansūb*, ed. Muḥammad Abū l-Faḍl Ibrāhīm (Cairo: Dār Nahḍat Miṣr, 1965), 188, 319, 498, 541, 583.

48 See Ibn al-Jawzī, *al-Adhkiyāʾ*, ed. A. ʿA. Rifāʿī (Damascus: Maktabat al-Ghazzālī, 1971), 195.

49 See Thaʿālibī, *al-Iʿjāz wa-l-ījāz*, 123; id., *Tūḥfat al-wuzarāʾ*, ed. Ḥ. ʿA. al-Rāwī and I. M. al-Ṣaffār (Baghdad: Wizārat al-Awqāf, 1977), 125. Little is known about Abū Naṣr b. Abī Zayd. Thaʿālibī mentions him several times in *Thimār al-qulūb*, *Laṭāʾif al-ẓurafāʾ*, *Tuḥfat al-wuzarāʾ*, and *Yatīmat al-dahr*. Abū Ṭālib al-Maʾmūnī (d. 383/993) composed a *qaṣīda* describing a house that Abū Naṣr built; see *Y* 4:260. I have identified al-Raḍī in Thaʿālibī's text as Abū l-Qāsim Nūḥ b. Manṣūr b. Nūḥ b. Naṣr al-Sāmānī (d. 387/997), who became ruler at the age of thirteen upon his father's death in 366/976 and was posthumously given the title al-Raḍī after his death; on him, see C. E. Bosworth, "Nūḥ b. Manṣūr b. Nūḥ," *EI2* VIII:110a. Supporting this is the fact that Abū Ṭālib al-Maʾmūnī, who praised Abū Naṣr, was in Bukhārā in 382/992 during the reign of Nūḥ b. Manṣūr; see *Y* 4:171. Naṣr al-Dīn Abū Manṣūr Sebüktigin (d. 387/997) is the father of Maḥmūd al-Ghaznawī (d. 421/1030), see C. E. Bosworth, "Sebüktigin," *EI2* IX:121a–121b. The edited text of *Tuḥfat al-wuzarāʾ*

7. Abū Naṣr Sahl b. al-Marzubān (d. before 429/1037).[50] Ibn al-Marzubān was a prolific author from Iṣbahān who lived in Nīshāpūr, where he met Thaʿālibī; his books include *Akhbār Ibn al-Rūmī*, *Akhbār Jaḥẓa al-Barmakī*, *Dhikr al-aḥwāl fī Shaʿbān wa-shahr Ramaḍān wa-Shawwāl*, and *al-Ādāb fī-l-ṭaʿām wa-l-sharāb*. Reports from him are found in almost all of Thaʿālibī's works. In the *Yatīma*, he is a guarantor for eleven reports or poems in the four *aqsām*, but his main importance lies in having provided Thaʿālibī with *dīwans* and works he acquired during his two visits to Baghdad.
8. Abū Saʿd Naṣr b. Yaʿqūb al-Dīnawarī (d. after 400/1010).[51] A native of Nīshāpūr, Dīnawarī was a scribe and secretary to Yamīn al-Dawla Maḥmūd al-Ghaznawī (d. 421/1031), and a prolific author. He is author of a number of lost *adab* works, including *Rawāʾiʿ al-tawjīhāt min badāʾiʿ al-tashbīhāt*; *Thimār al-uns fī tashbīhāt al-Furs*, *Ḥuqqat al-jawāhir fī l-mafākhir*, which is a *muzdawija* (poem written in rhyming couplets) in praise of the *amir* Khalaf b. Aḥmad al-Sijistānī (r. 352/963–399/1008); and *K. al-Adʿiya*. Bīrūnī uses a book (*maqāla*) by him in Persian on the subject of precious stones and minerals and notes that in it Dīnawarī follows and builds on Abū Yūsuf b. Isḥāq al-Kindī's (d. ca. 257/870) work *Fī l-jawāhir wa-l-ashbāh*. Thaʿālibī (d. 429/1039) dedicates an entry to him in *Yatīmat al-dahr* (4:389–91) that includes the favorable opinion of the Būyid vizier Ṣāḥib b. ʿAbbād (d. 385/995) on *Rawāʾiʿ al-tawjīhāt*, in addition to a number of his poems. Thaʿālibī also quotes poetry and reports on his authority throughout the anthology. Dīnawarī is chiefly remembered as the author of *al-Qādirī fī l-taʿbīr*, also known as *K. al-Jāmiʿ al-kabīr fī l-taʿbīr*, the oldest surviving authentic Arabic treatise on interpretation of dreams, completed in Ramaḍān 399/May 1009 and dedicated to the caliph al-Qādir Billāh (r. 381/991–422/1031).[52]
9. Abū Saʿīd (Saʿd?) ʿAbd al-Raḥmān b. Muḥammad b. Dūst al-Uṭrūsh (d. 431/1039).[53] A jurist, grammarian, and literary scholar from Nīshāpūr,

reads al-Rāḍī, instead of al-Raḍī, whom the editors identified erroneously as Abū l-ʿAbbās Aḥmad b. al-Muqtadir b. al-Muʿtaḍid (d. 329/940); see Thaʿālibī, *Tuḥfat al-wuzarāʾ*, 125.

50 *Y* 4:391; Ṣafadī, *al-Wāfī bi-l-Wafayāt*, ed. Aḥmad al-Arnāʾūṭ and Turkī Muṣṭafā (Beirut: Dār Iḥyāʾ al-Turāth al-ʿArabī, 2000), 14:16.

51 *Y* 4:389; Ṣafadī, *al-Wāfī bi-l-Wafayāt*, 27:57.

52 See Orfali, "Abū Saʿd Naṣr b. Yaʿqūb al-Dīnawarī," *EI3*.

53 *Y* 4:425; Bākharzī, *Dumyat al-qaṣr*, 2:970–72; Ṣafadī, *al-Wāfī bi-l-Wafayāt*, 18:151; ʿUtbī, *al-Yamīnī fī sharḥ akhbār al-sulṭān yamīn al-dawla wa-amīn al-milla Maḥmūd al-Ghaznawī*, ed. Iḥsān Dh. al-Thāmirī (Beirut: Dār al-Ṭalīʿa, 2004), 189.

Uṭrūsh was given the epithet of al-Uṭrūsh because he was deaf (*lā yasmaʿu shayʾan*). He studied grammar with the renowned lexicographer al-Jawharī (d. 393/1002) and taught grammar, along with literature and jurisprudence, in formal gatherings in Nīshāpūr. His close friend Thaʿālibī eulogized him after his death. In the *Yatīma*, he is the guarantor for fifteen poems and *akhbār* in all four regions, in addition to two poems by Namarī he sent to Thaʿālibī.

10. Badīʿ al-Zamān al-Hamadhānī, Abū l-Faḍl Aḥmad b. al-Ḥusayn (d. 398/1008).[54] Hamadhānī grew up in Hamadhān, where he studied with the noted grammarian and lexicographer Aḥmad b. Fāris (d. 395/1004). He began his literary career at the age of twenty-two, when he went to Rayy to seek the patronage of Ṣāḥib b. ʿAbbād. He then traveled to Jurjān and in 382/992 from there to Nīshāpūr, where he had a literary debate with Abū Bakr al-Khwārizmī. Thereafter, he undertook a number of journeys, including to Sistān, Ghazna, and Herat, where he died, barely aged forty. A collection of his poems and another of his letters have been published, but his *maqāmāt* most perpetuated his name. Thaʿālibī met him in Nīshāpūr and acquired poetry directly from him.[55] In the *Yatīma*, he appears in six *isnād*s in the second, third, and fourth regions.

Main Guarantors in the Tatimma

1. Abū Bakr al-Quhistānī (d. after 435/1054).[56] *Al-ʿAmīd* Abū Bakr ʿAlī b. al-Ḥasan al-Quhistānī from Rukhkhaj,[57] was a well-known poet and literary scholar in his day. Yāqūt al-Ḥamawī mentions his special interest in philosophy. Bākharzī notes in his entry that he met him in Khurāsān in 435/1043, transmitted a substantial number of poems through him, and mentioned in another instance that he had seen his *dīwān*.[58] In *Dumyat al-qaṣr* many individuals transmitted poetry on his authority: Abū ʿĀmir al-Jurjānī, Yaʿqūb b. Aḥmad, and Abū l-Ḥusayn al-Ṭawlaqī. Bākharzī also mentions that he headed the office of chancellery (*ṣāḥib al-dīwān*) for

54 On Badīʿ al-Zamān al-Hamadhānī, see Everett Rowson, "Religion and Politics in the Career of Badīʿ al-Zamān al-Hamadhānī," *Journal of the American Oriental Society* 107 (1987), 653–73; R. Blachere, "al-Hamadhānī," *EI2* III:106a.

55 See *Y* 4:257, 292.

56 On him, see Bākharzī, *Dumyat al-qaṣr*, 2:714ff.; *T* 264ff.; Ḥamawī, *Muʿjam al-udabāʾ*, 1677ff.

57 Rukhkhaj is the name given in medieval Islam to southeastern Afghanistan, around what became the city of Qandahār and occupying the lower basin of the Arghandāb River; see C. E. Bosworth, "al-Rukhkhadj," *EI2* VIII:595a–595b.

58 Bākharzī, *Dumyat al-qaṣr*, 2:1136.

the Ghaznavid *amīr* Muḥammad b. Maḥmūd b. Sebüktigin.[59] In the *Tatimma*, Thaʿālibī does not provide sources for the entry on him and most likely obtained his poems directly from him. He is also the source for the poetry of eight other poets in the first region.[60] It is uncertain how Quhistānī learned these poems; Yāqūt al-Ḥamawī in his entry mentions that Quhistānī traveled to Baghdad sometime after 420/1029, where he praised the caliph al-Qādir Billāh (r. 381/991–422/1031) and his secretary Abū Ṭālib b. Ayyūb, before contacting the Saljūq kings in 431/1039 in Khurāsān, Khwārizm, and al-Jabal. He most likely met Thaʿālibī in Khurāsān before the latter's death in 429/1039.

2. Abū l-Faḍl Muḥammad b. ʿAbd al-Wāḥid al-Tamīmī (d. 454/1062).[61] Tamīmī's father, Abū l-Faḍl ʿAbd al-Wāḥid al-Baghdādī al-Tamīmī, is likewise a source of the *Yatīma*. Born in 386/996 in Baghdad, Muḥammad was a poet who received an entry in the second region of the *Tatimma*. There, Thaʿālibī mentions that he traveled in his youth via Nīshāpūr to Ghazna. Later in his life he visited al-Qayrawān and then al-Andalus, where he was patronized by several rulers until his death in Toledo.[62] Thaʿālibī reports his poetry directly from him, in addition to one poem from the first region, three from the second region, and one from the fifth (a Baghdādī poet).
3. Abū l-Fatḥ Muḥammad b. Aḥmad al-Dabāwandī.[63] Dabāwandī, a poet whose entry appears in the third region of the *Tatimma*, resided in al-Rayy. He traveled to Nīshāpūr and returned to Rayy when *al-shaykh al-ʿamīd* Abū l-Ṭayyib Ṭāhir b. ʿAbdallāh called him back. In Nīshāpūr, Thaʿālibī had the chance to transmit his poetry as well as that of others. He appears in six *isnād*s, all in the third region.
4. Abū l-Ḥasan ʿAlī b. Fāris al-Qazwīnī. Thaʿālibī mentions in the *Yatīma* that he visited Nīshāpūr and became friends with Abū Bakr al-Khwārizmī,[64] but he does not contribute any information in the *Yatīma*. Strangely, no entry is dedicated to him in either the *Yatīma* or the *Tatimma*. He is the

59 Ibid., 2:1084.

60 Four of these are from the fifth section, which includes poets from all regions.

61 *T* 79.

62 Ḥumaydī, *Jadhwat al-muqtabis fī dhikr wulāt al-Andalus* (Cairo: al-Dār al-Miṣriyya li-l-Taʾlīf wa-l-Tarjama, 1966), 72–3; Maqqarī, *Nafḥ al-ṭīb min ghuṣn al-Andalus al-raṭīb*, ed. Iḥsān ʿAbbās (Beirut: Dār Ṣādir, 1968), 3:121.

63 *T* 153.

64 *Y* 4:204.

source of three poems in the first region of the *Tatimma* and two in the second.

5. Abū l-Ḥasan ʿAlī b. Maʾmūn al-Maṣṣīṣī (d. before 429/1037). *Yatīma* source no. 5.
6. Abū Yaʿlā Muḥammad b. al-Ḥasan al-Ṣūfī al-Baṣrī (d. after 429/1037).[65] Baṣrī transmitted the poetry of six poets from the first region of the *Tatimma* in addition to his own, which is included in the second region. Thaʿālibī places him among the *ṣūfī shuyūkh* who made a short visit to Nīshāpūr in 421/1030. According to Thaʿālibī, he was a rich source for the litterateurs in Nīshāpūr, as he provided access to rare information (*fa-afādanā mimmā lam najid ʿinda amthālihi*).

Conclusion

Shawkat Toorawa, Walter Werkmeister, Manfred Fleischhammer, Fuat Sezgin, and Sebastian Günther stress the importance of written and aural sources in *adab* compilations from the third/ninth and fourth/tenth centuries by examining the sources of three prominent literary scholars: Ibn Abī Ṭāhir Ṭayfūr (d. 280/893), Ibn ʿAbd Rabbihi (d. 328/940), and Abū l-Faraj al-Iṣbahānī (d. 356/967). The availability of books and paper in the Muslim world at the time made possible the use of the aural and written techniques, versus the oral transmission that had been common in the first two centuries of Islam. Thaʿālibī's *Yatīmat al-dahr* and *Tatimmat al-Yatīma* present a different case, as they feature a strong return to orality and reliance on different techniques of transmission governing each of their regions. The change in the nature of the sources of these two works is natural, as they depart from the earlier and contemporary *adab* works to deal almost exclusively with modern literature. This change in the subject matter required a corresponding change of compilation technique. This literature was by and large not yet collected, anthologized, or taught in study circles, which led to less dependence on written and aural transmission. Nonetheless, the continuous travel of litterateurs in search of patronage brought about an increase in the use of oral transmission, despite the broad geographical regions that Thaʿālibī took it upon himself to cover. The chains of *isnād*s did not usually go beyond two or three names, given the recency of the material, a fact that added to their reliability. In general, orality played a stronger role in the transmission of poetry than prose because of the dominance of the short *qiṭʿa* (short poem or epigram) over the long *qaṣīda*

---

65 *T* 108.

(multithematic ode) on the poetic tradition of the period, in addition to the presence of rhyme and meter, which helped in the transmission process.

The reliance on orality did not, however, mean the complete abandonment of written sources. The examination of Thaʿālibī's sources shows that he used several available *dīwān*s and books, but the recency of the material, the breadth of the geographical area from which it was drawn, and the competition for fame brought into play other kinds of written material as well, namely *ruqʿa*s and epistles that various litterateurs sent to Thaʿālibī, principally for inclusion in the successful anthology. This finding demonstrates that Arabic anthologies are not always secondary texts selected from primary *dīwān*s and other "written books." Rather, for Thaʿālibī and subsequent anthologists concerned with contemporary poetry, they become a primary way of publishing original literature, especially by nonprofessional poets who did not produce circulating *dīwān*s.

Interestingly, the use of the compilation techniques described here is not homogeneous across all regions. In the first region (Syria and farther west—Egypt, Maghrib, Mawṣil), there is a strong reliance on books and *dīwān*s, but this drops away gradually as Thaʿālibī moves east toward the fourth region (Khurāsān and Transoxania). Dependence on *ruqʿa*s and epistles is most apparent in the third (al-Jabal, Fārs, Jurjān, and Ṭabaristān) and fourth regions. Drawing on oral sources is common to each of the four regions, but the majority of direct *isnād*s are from the fourth region. Finally, a large amount of the *Yatīma* and *Tatimma* comes from a handful of guarantors, from Iraq and further east, whom Thaʿālibī met in Nīshāpūr or surrounding cities. These guarantors formed the backbone of an extensive network of litterateurs active in the second half of the fourth/tenth century.

CHAPTER 5

Material within the Entry

Having considered the *Yatīma* and *Tatimma* in their totality, I focus in this chapter on single entries. What types of information do readers encounter, or expect to encounter, in each entry? How does Thaʿālibī organize the material? What are his literary interests and how does he convey them? How does he evaluate the poets and their work, and which criteria underlie his choice of material?

Categorization and Arrangement of Material within Entries

The chapters of the *Yatīma* and *Tatimma* are organized only by the name of the litterateur in the biography; each name constitutes a separate entry. Beyond that, Thaʿālibī shapes each entry differently, depending on the importance of the persona, the nature of his literary production, and the amount of accessible material. Most entries begin with a summary of the litterateur's vita and information about his family and/or patrons. This is followed by other material that the anthologist considers relevant to introducing the poet's literary output. Long entries with subcategories represent more complex cases. The most common criterion in Thaʿālibī's subcategorization is genre (*gharaḍ*). Thaʿālibī devotes separate sections to genres like panegyric (*madīḥ*), blame (*ʿitāb*), elegy (*rithāʾ*), love poetry (*ghazal*), invective poetry (*hijāʾ*), obscene poetry (*mujūn*), wine poetry (*khamriyya*), proverbial poetry (*amthāl*), brotherly correspondence (*ikhwāniyyāt*), and mendicant poetry (*kudya*)[1]. Themes and motifs also play a role in the subdivision of long entries. For example, Thaʿālibī often dedicates sections to the description of a certain recurring object (e.g., instrument, dish, flower), theme (e.g., description of seasons), or motif (e.g., recalling youth). He further assembles poems written in praise or disparagement of a patron. Literary borrowing (*sariqa*) is yet another criterion of categorization by which Thaʿālibī brings together single lines or entire poems with double

1 The definitive work on *kudya* as a genre in the fourth/tenth century is C. E. Bosworth, *The Mediaeval Islamic Underworld: The Banū Sāsān in Arabic Society and Literature* (Leiden: Brill, 1976). On literary *kudya* or *al-takassub bi-l-shiʿr* (acquiring wealth through poetry), see Devin Stewart, "Professional Literary Mendicancy in the Letters and *Maqāmāt* of Badīʿ al-Zamān al-Hamadhānī," in *Writers and Rulers*, ed. Beatrice Gruendler and Louise Marlow (Wiesbaden: Reichert, 2004), 39–48.

 | DOI 10.1163/9789004317352_006

attributions. The entry on al-Sarī al-Raffāʾ (d. 366/976) illustrates the different criteria of subcategorization:[2]

- Biographical summary
- Literary borrowings (*sariqāt*)
- Recurrent ideas (*dhikru mā takarrara min maʿānīh*)
- General characterization
- Description of his poetry
- Against his plagiarists (*mā ukhrija min ghurarihi fī l-khālidiyyān wa-ghayrihimā mimman iddaʿā shiʿrahu*)
- Genres and themes
- Invective poetry (*ghurar min ahājīhi li-l-shuʿarāʾ*)
- Ghazal, elegiac love introductions, and other lyrical poetry (*ghurar min al-ghazal wa-l-nasīb wa-mā yutaghannā bihi min shiʿr al-Sarī*)
- Recalling youthful love (*tadhakkur al-ṣibā wa-mawāṭin al-hawā*)
- Elegant transitions (*ḥusn al-khurūj wa-l-takhalluṣ*)
- Panegyric (*mulaḥ min al-madḥ*)
- War poetry (*al-madḥ bi-l-baʾs wa-waṣf al-jaysh wa-l-silāḥ wa-l-ḥarb*)
- Censure and blame (*ʿitāb*)
- Descriptions of spring (*hādhā mimmā ukhrija lahu fī l-rabīʿi wa-āthārihi wa-anwārihi wa-azhārih*)
- Wine poetry (*al-sharāb wa-mā yattaṣilu bihi*)
- Petitioning for wine (*istihdāʾ al-sharāb*)
- On hosting and a description of its accessories (*hādhā mā ukhrija lahu fī-l-istizārati wa-waṣfi ālātihā*)
- Miscellaneous descriptions of various things (*awṣāf shattā*)

Ordinarily, Thaʿālibī places prose separately within an entry, and if the litterateur is famous for his prose, he subdivides the oeuvre into *rasāʾil* (letters), *amthāl* (proverbs), *khuṭab* (orations), *muqaddimāt* (prefaces), and *mukātabāt* (correspondence). Selections from a work, such as the *Rūznāmja* of Muhallabī, may constitute their own subcategory. Throughout, Thaʿālibī keeps to well-established genres and avoids novel ones. For example, he hardly mentions Hamadhānī's *maqāmāt*, although he appears familiar with the details of Hamadhānī's vita and work, and the *maqāmāt* were an instant success. Thaʿālibī focuses only on Hamadhānī's literary correspondences and poetry.[3]

2 See *Y* 2:117–82.

3 Thaʿālibī quotes from the *maqāmāt* in both his *Thimār al-qulūb* and in his *Yatīma*. He does so, however, treating the *maqāmāt* as elegant exemplum of prose stylistics. If he was aware of

Poetry that praises or eulogizes a person is included at the end of that person's entry. This poetry is considered part of the subject's portrait and anthologized there rather than in the entry on the poet. In general, invective poems do not follow this pattern. An exception to this is the entry on Abū l-Ḥasan ʿAlī b. al-Ḥasan al-Laḥḥām (d. ca. 363/973), in which Thaʿālibī includes a section of invective poems composed by Laḥḥām's enemies.[4] Like panegyrics and elegies, these types of poems are considered to add to the portrait of the poet.[5]

As mentioned earlier, some people receive entire chapters with multiple entries, such as Abū l-Faḍl b. al-ʿAmīd, his son Abū l-Fatḥ b. al-ʿAmīd, and Ṣāḥib b. ʿAbbād. The entry or chapter on Ṣāḥib b. ʿAbbād is distinguished by one long section on his accounts and others on poems he commissioned on specific themes.

The Biographical Summary

Neither the *Yatīma* nor the *Tatimma* is a biographical dictionary.[6] Rather than emphasizing biographical information about litterateurs, both works emphasize literary production, and thus fall under the category of the *adab* anthology. Nevertheless, like most *adab* anthologies, much biographical information in these anthologies is useful for scholars of Arabic-Islamic civilization. It usually occupies the first paragraphs of each entry and is rarely several pages in length.

Hilary Kilpatrick has examined Abū l-Faraj al-Iṣbahānī as a social and literary historian in his *K. al-Aghānī*. She argues that although Abū l-Faraj's own voice is traceable throughout the work, the biographical preface of each entry in *al-Aghānī* summarizes the essence of the poet's or musician's career, drawing on material Abū l-Faraj extracted from the *akhbār* he includes in the entry or

---

the *maqāma* as a distinctive literary form, he does not discuss it. Thaʿālibī, *Thimār al-qulūb fī-l-muḍāf wa-l-mansūb*, ed. Muḥammad Abū l-Faḍl Ibrāhīm (Cairo: Dār Nahḍat Miṣr, 1965), 203. For the quotations from the *Yatīma*, see Ibrāhīm Geries, "On Jaakko Hämeen-Antilla, *Maqama: A History of a Genre*," *Middle Eastern Literatures* 8 (2005), 187–95, esp. 188.

4 *Y* 4:114.

5 Sometimes the original composer of the poetry is credited with a cross-reference.

6 On biographical dictionaries, see Paul Auchterlonie, *Arabic Biographical Dictionaries: A Summary Guide and Bibliography* (Durham: Middle East Libraries Committee, 1987); Wadad Kadi, "Biographical Dictionaries: Inner Structure and Cultural Significance," in *The Book in the Islamic World*, ed. George Atiyeh (Albany, NY: State University of New York Press, 1995), 93–122; id., "Biographical Dictionaries as the Scholars' Alternative History of the Muslim Community," in *Organizing Knowledge*, ed. G. Endress (Leiden: Brill 2006), 23–75.

other excluded material.[7] The idea of a profile, as Kilpatrick notes, did not start with Abū l-Faraj; it had already been used by Ibn Sallām al-Jumaḥī in *Ṭabaqāt fuḥūl al-shuʿarāʾ*, by Ibn Qutayba in *al-Shiʿr wa-l-shuʿarāʾ*, and by al-Balādhurī in *al-Ansāb wa-l-ashrāf*. However, Kilpatrick argues convincingly that Abū l-Faraj's profile of poets often combines the literary, social, and psychological dimensions of a personality.[8] She also has identified four main categories in the prefaces of musicians and poets: a member of a society, an individual with distinctive character traits, a member of a literary community, and a writer of poems.[9]

The biographical summaries in the *Yatīma* and *Tatimma* are similar to those in *K. al-Aghānī* in terms of how they characterize the litterateur and his oeuvre. The preface is sketched in Thaʿālibī's own words and often includes quotations about the litterateur by other famous people. Unlike Abū l-Faraj, however, Thaʿālibī does not focus on the poet as a member of his society or tribe; instead, he emphasizes the subject's artistic achievements, general standing in the literary community, and relationships with fellow litterateurs and patrons. Still more important than the litterateur's social origin, family, or place of residence, however, are his political activities and associations with certain courts and patrons. In the *Yatīma* it is the court, not the tribe that is central to the biographical summary. The *Tatimma* presents a different case, as its focus is on social community, not courts; however, the community consists not of fellow tribe members, as in *K. al-Aghānī*, but of litterateurs from different professions (especially jurists and judges). These were not professional poets, scribes, or secretaries, and they did not seek patronage or a career in a court.[10] In all cases, the biographical summary specifies the litterateur's tribal or political networks, such as *khawārij* or *shīʿat ʿAlī* in *K. al-Aghānī*, courts and courtiers in the *Yatīma*, or the professional literary community in the *Tatimma*.

With respect to litterateurs as makers of literature, Thaʿālibī comments on the size of a litterateur's oeuvre, his innovations, diction and style, profession and career, specialization in certain genres, and travels. Of less importance, but included nonetheless, are the litterateur's character traits, which may have influenced his career or have been reflected in his relationships and poetry. A difference here between Thaʿālibī and Abū l-Faraj is that individual character

---

7 See H. Kilpatrick, "Abū l-Farağ's Profiles of Poets: A 4th/10th Century Essay at the History and Sociology of Arabic Literature," *Arabica* 44 (1997), 128.

8 Ibid., 98.

9 Ibid., 100.

10 See Jocelyn Sharlet's chapter "The Cosmopolitan Professional Poet," in *Patronage and Poetry in the Islamic World* (London: I. B. Tauris, 2011).

traits not only are deduced or drawn from the literature itself but also are supported by Thaʿālibī's own communication with these people.

Dates

The scarcity of dates in the *Yatīma* and *Tatimma* results from two factors. First, dates have little significance to the quality of the literary production, and Thaʿālibī may have seen no great need to include them. Second, most of the litterateurs are contemporaries of his and had not been previously anthologized or included in biographical dictionaries; consequently, Thaʿālibī had few pertinent dates at his fingertips. Most complete birth and death dates are given by Thaʿālibī to poets of renown. These include Abū l-Ḥasan al-Salāmī (336/948–393/1003), Mutanabbī (303/915–354/965), al-Sharīf al-Raḍī (359/969–406/1015), and Abū Bakr al-Khwārizmī (323/935–383/993). Death dates are slightly more common, provided for, for instance, Abū Isḥāq al-Ṣābī (d. 384/994), Abū Ṭālib al-Ma'mūnī (d. 383/993), Badīʿ al-Zamān al-Hamadhānī (d. 398/1008), Abū l-Fatḥ al-Bustī (d. 400/1010), and Abū ʿAbd al-Qāsim b. al-Ḥarīsh (al-Ḥirrīsh?) al-Iṣbahānī (d. 424/1032). For the first three of those, Thaʿālibī provides the death date with the age of the litterateur, leaving it up to the reader to calculate his birth date.[11] The less prominent litterateurs on the list were personally known to Thaʿālibī, which explains how he knew their date of death. In a few cases, Thaʿālibī was uncertain whether an individual is still alive, as with Abū l-Faraj al-Babbaghā' (d. 398/1008).[12]

Thaʿālibī sometimes cites the year in which a certain litterateur acceded to a position, as in the case of al-Sharīf al-Raḍī, who succeeded his father as marshal of the Ṭālibids (*naqīb al-Ṭālibiyyīn*).[13] Years in which renowned personalities, or Thaʿālibī himself, visited a certain city are commonly mentioned, as when poets traveled to Nīshāpūr.[14] Finally, Thaʿālibī sometimes indicates the year in which a poem or a literary correspondence was composed.[15]

11 *Y* 4:171, 258.

12 *Y* 1:252.

13 *Y* 3:136.

14 Thaʿālibī mentions that Abū l-Faraj al-Babbaghā' was in Baghdad in 390/1000; see *Y* 1:252; Abū l-Ḥasan al-Jawharī passed by Nīshāpūr in 377/987, *Y* 4:27; Badīʿ al-Zamān al-Hamadhānī left the city of Hadm in 380/990 and visited Nīshāpūr in 382/992, *Y* 4:257; Abū Yaʿlā al-Baṣrī and Abū l-Maḥāsin Saʿd b. Muḥammad b. Manṣūr traveled to Nīshāpūr in 421/1030 and 424/1033, respectively, *T* 108, 166; and he himself saw al-Ma'mūnī in Bukhārā in 382/992, *Y* 4:171, and in 403/1012 was in Jurjān, where he stayed with Abū Saʿd Muḥammad b. Manṣūr, *T* 165.

15 For example, Abū Isḥāq al-Ṣābī praised al-Sharīf al-Raḍī by correspondence in 384/994, *Y* 2:300; and Abū l-Faraj al-Babbaghā' wrote to Abū Taghlib b. Nāṣir al-Dawla asking to join

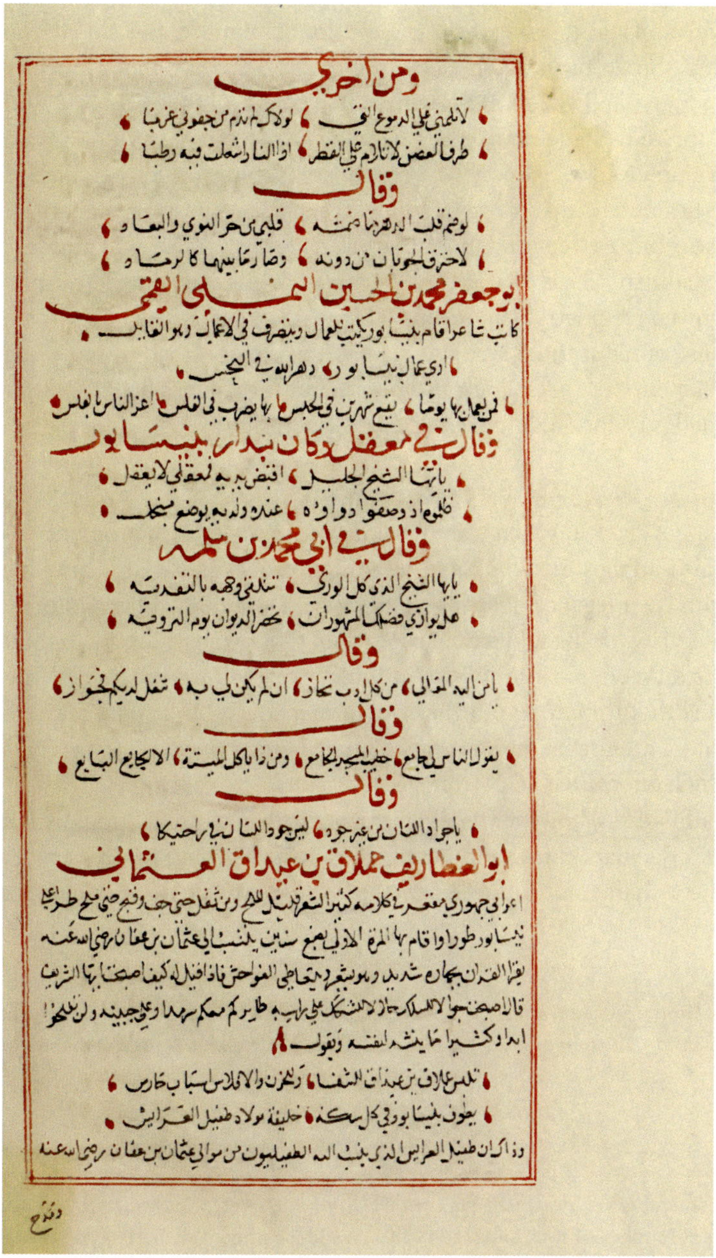

FIGURE 33 *Yatīmat al-dahr,* MS Toronto A13512y, 454v

---

his court in 358/968, *Y*1:265.

Deaths of Poets

Unnatural and unusual deaths warrant attention. Unique is the suicide by poison of Abū Aḥmad b. Abī Bakr, secretary of the Sāmānid *amīr* Ismāʿīl b. Aḥmad (d. 295/907) and vizier of *al-amīr* Aḥmad b. Ismāʿīl (d. 301/914).[16] Abū l-Ḥusayn al-Murādī recited poetry when he saw his own burial shroud, passed out for an hour, revived long enough to recite two last lines, and then passed away.[17] Some litterateurs died of severe illness, such as Abū l-Qāsim al-Iskāfī, who oversaw the office of correspondence (*dīwān al-rasāʾil*).[18] Several murders are recorded: Laḥḥām (d. ca. 363/973) was attacked while traveling because of his vitriol in invective poetry,[19] and Abū Saʿīd al-Ifyarī died at the hand of his brother because of his antireligious stance.[20] When the deceased was a young man, Thaʿālibī mentions this.[21] Poetry composed during a poet's final illness or on his deathbed is of special importance as his last words.[22]

Religious Views

Thaʿālibī does not mention sectarian divisions in the regions that he anthologizes. This also applies to the people he visited or stayed with, despite his familiarity with their legal or doctrinal affiliations. Thaʿālibī had little interest in the religious views of his subjects, except when those were essential to their literature. It is difficult, for example, to anthologize Ṣāḥib b. ʿAbbād and Abū Isḥāq al-Ṣābī without pointing out that the former was a Muʿtazilite and the latter a Ṣābiʾite. Litterateurs and patrons often openly showed their religious identities, which often affected patronage.[23]

Religious affiliations, however, rarely influenced literary production, which was mostly of a secular nature, and hence Thaʿālibī's disregard for this aspect of a litterateur's character. He asserts in the *Yatīma* that poetical talent has

---

16 *Y* 4:68–9. On the Sāmānid Ismāʿīl b. Aḥmad and Aḥmad b. Ismāʿīl, see C. E. Bosworth, *The Ghaznavids: Their Empire in Afghanistan and Eastern Iran, 994–1040* (Edinburgh: University Press, 1963), 28, 35, 99, 141.

17 *Y* 4:74–5.

18 *Y* 4:95.

19 *Y* 4:102.

20 *T* 36. Other murder victims are the vizier Abū l-Ṭayyib al-Muṣʿabī, *Y* 4:79; the prince-poet Abū Firās al-Ḥamdānī, *Y* 1:112; Mutanabbī, *Y* 1:240; and the prince Abū l-ʿAbbās Khusraw-Fayrūz b. Rukn al-Dawla, *T* 111.

21 Such is the case, for example, of ʿAlī b. Abī ʿAlī al-ʿAlawī and Abū Naṣr al-Zawzanī, *Y* 4:419, 446.

22 For example, see *Y* 1:103, 2:304, 4:68–9, 74–5.

23 See Sharlet, *Patronage and Poetry in the Islamic World*, 216ff.

nothing to do with religiosity.[24] Yet literature might reflect the religious doctrine of a litterateur; for example, the poetry of Abū Ḥafṣ ʿAmr b. al-Muṭṭawwiʿī indicates his Shāfiʿī affiliation.[25] Likewise, Thaʿālibī comments on whether a poem violates the norms of Islam. For example, he counts weak belief and bad religion (*ḍaʿf al-ʿaqīda wa-riqqat al-dīn*) among Mutanabbī's faults.[26] In the entry on Khabbāz al-Baladī (d. 380/990), Thaʿālibī introduces a line describing the patron as the provider of subsistence—*wa-huwa mimmā yustaghfaru minhu* (such a thing calls for asking forgiveness)—because of Muslims' common belief of God as provider.[27]

Thaʿālibī usually notes when a certain litterateur is a jurist or follows a particular Islamic legal school, though, not only because this presumes abstention from ribald and obscene poetry but also because he depended on such professions for his livelihood and his social and literary network. The specification of theological or legal school serves the same purpose of identifying the litterateur with his professional network. For example, Thaʿālibī qualifies ʿAbd al-Qādir b. Ṭāhir al-Tamīmī as Shāfiʿite and Ashʿarite,[28] and Abū Muḥammad ʿAbdallāh al-Khwārizmī as a famous teacher of Shāfiʿī's books in Baghdad.[29] Khalīl b. Aḥmad al-Sijzī is described as *imām* in Ḥanafī law.[30] Thaʿālibī specifies the legal school of a litterateur only if uncommon in his region, as with Abū Muḥammad ʿAbdallah al-Wāthiqī, a Mālikī in Bukhārā.

Ascetic poetry (*zuhd*) figures prominently in both the *Yatīma* and the *Tatimma*. Yet a poet did not have to be an ascetic to write ascetic poetry. In a few cases, mostly from his own region, Thaʿālibī indicates that a litterateur was famous for his asceticism, such as the judge Abū ʿAlī ʿAbd al-Wahhāb b. Muḥammad, Abū Sulaymān Ḥamad b. Muḥammad b. Ibrāhīm al-Khaṭṭābī (d. before 429/1037), Abū l-Qāsim Yaḥyā b. ʿAlī al-Bukhārī (d. before 429/1037), Abū l-Ḥasan Muḥammad b. Ẓafar al-ʿAlawī (d. before 429/1037), Abū l-Qāsim ʿAlī b. Aḥmad al-Zawzanī (d. after 429/1037),[31] and Abū Muḥammad al-Ḥasan

---

24 *Y* 1:184.

25 *T* 191.

26 *Y* 1:184–6.

27 *Y* 2:213.

28 *Y* 4:192.

29 *Y* 3:127.

30 *Y* 4:338.

31 His son Asʿad b. ʿAlī b. Aḥmad al-Zawzanī died, according to Yāqūt al-Ḥamawī, in 492/1099; see *Muʿjam al-udabāʾ: Irshād al-arīb ilā maʿrifat al-adīb*, ed. Iḥsān ʿAbbās (Beirut: Dār al-Gharb al-Islāmī, 1993), 630; see also Bākharzī, *Dumyat al-qaṣr wa-ʿuṣrat ahl al-ʿaṣr*, ed. Muḥammad al-Ṭūnjī (Beirut: Dār al-Jīl, 1993), 2:1403.

b. al-Mu'ammil al-Ḥarbī.[32] Other poets were *ṣūfīs* and their poetry reflects this. In addition to Abū l-Ḥasan al-ʿAlawī and al-Zawzanī, Thaʿālibī lists Abū Suwayd al-Ṣūfī, Abū Bakr al-ʿAnbarī (d. after 429/1037), and Abū Yaʿlā Muḥammad b. al-Ḥasan al-Baṣrī (d. after 429/1037).[33]

Training and Education

In the biographical summary, Thaʿālibī includes information about the litterateur's training or education, considering it an important aspect of his scholarship. He often gives the name of the teacher, the discipline, and the location of the litterateur's scholarly *majlis*,[34] and occasionally he describes the teacher or his relationship to the litterateur. If the teacher himself is the focus of the entry, his field, specialty, location, importance, and major students may be mentioned.[35] Most of the teachers Thaʿālibī anthologizes hail from his own region of Khurāsān. These are not professionals but rather minor poets he came to know while living in and around Nīshāpūr. Other poets resorted to the more traditional learning method, of acquiring the Arabic language directly from Bedouins, as Thaʿālibī recounts in the entry on Abū Naṣr al-Muhallabī.[36]

Some litterateurs memorized thousands of verses, which they then used as direct or indirect quotations, or in prosification.[37] The absence of one's education also calls for a special note. In the entry on al-Khabbāz al-Baladī (d. 380/990), Thaʿālibī expresses surprise that the poet is illiterate.[38] Such a comment emphasizes the ingenuity of the poet.

32 *Y* 4:334, 415, 422, 448; *T* 204, 302.

33 *T* 34, 77, 108. On Abū Bakr al-ʿAnbarī and Abū Yaʿlā al-Baṣrī, see Bākharzī, *Dumyat al-qaṣr*, 1:321 and 351, respectively.

34 See, for example, *Y* 3:291, 4:95–6, 134, 151, 257, 384, 432, 446.

35 See *Y* 3:4, 127, 4:150, 334, 407, 438, 447; *T* 205, 300.

36 *T* 308. Ibn Jinnī (d. 392/1002) in *al-Khaṣā'iṣ* relates accounts about the Bedouin (*aʿrābī*) Muḥammad b. ʿAssāf al-Shajarī al-ʿUqaylī and how he still spoke correctly in the second half of the fourth/tenth century; see Ibn Jinnī, *al-Khaṣā'iṣ*, ed. Muḥammad ʿAlī al-Najjār (Cairo: Maṭbaʿat Dār al-Kutub al-Miṣriyya, 1952–6), 1:76, 78, 240, 250, 338, 371, 2:9, 26. For a discussion of these accounts, see Abdelkader Mehiri, *Les théories grammaticales d'Ibn Ginnī* (Tunis: Université de Tunis, 1973), 125ff.

37 According to Thaʿālibī, Abū Muḥammad ʿAbdallāh b. Ismāʿīl al-Mīkālī memorized a hundred thousand lines, *Y* 4:417; Abū Muḥammad ʿAbdallāh b. Muḥammad al-Dūghābādī memorized all of *Yatīmat al-dahr*, *T* 274.

38 *Y* 2:208.

Professions

The litterateur's profession is usually mentioned in the initial summary. The most common professions listed are jurist (*faqīh*) and judge (*qāḍī*) especially in Khurāsān; in this region, Thaʿālibī was more familiar with those local poets who earned a livelihood other than by composing poetry. The list of professions in the *Yatīma* and *Tatimma* demonstrates the wide range of poets anthologized and their different geographical and social environments, and it covers the entire panorama of elite occupations. Other official positions include *amīr*s, governors (*wālī*), viziers (*wazīr*) or secretaries (*kātib*), treasurers (*khāzin māl*), and stewards (*mutaṣarrif bi-aʿmāl*). Others may have headed offices like the bureau of tort redress (*dīwān al-maẓālim*), the office of correspondence (*dīwān al-rasāʾil*), the post and surveillance office (*al-barīd*), the bureau of taxation (*dīwān al-kharāj*), or religious endowments (*yatawallā awqāf*). Some were mere entertainers who worked as boon companions (*nadīm*) at courtly gatherings. Others sought occupations and livelihoods outside of patronal benevolence and economy. In both the *Yatīma* and the *Tatimma*, there are several librarians (*khāzin kutub*), copyists (*nāsikh*), teachers (*muʾaddib, mudarris*), physicians (*ṭabīb*), compilers of books (*ṣāḥib kutub*), philologists and lexicographers (*lughawī*), grammarians (*naḥwī*), philosophers (*faylasūf*), architects (*muhandis*), and religious leaders (*imām*). A few individuals had less notable professions, such as al-Khubzaʾaruzzī, a baker and seller of rice bread,[39] and al-Khabbāz al-Baladī (d. 380/990), an illiterate baker.[40]

Thaʿālibī anthologized all of these litterateurs because, alongside their professional pursuits, they composed prose or poetry that circulated in written or oral form. Still, though, a good number of the poets in his anthology were professionals whose sole vocation was to compose poetry at the request of their patrons or to dedicate what they had already written to them.

Families of Litterateurs

Not infrequently, Thaʿālibī provides information about a litterateur's family, especially if prominent in the literary or political spheres. For example, he mentions that Ibn Muqla descended from a family of viziers, Abū l-Ḥusayn ʿAlī b. Hārūn al-Munajjim from a family of refined elegants (*ẓurafāʾ*), and both Ibn al-ʿAmīd and Abū Bakr Muḥammad b. ʿAlī b. Aḥmad al-ʿAbdānī inherited the scribal art and *adab* from their fathers.[41] Abū Muḥammad ʿAbdallāh al-Wāthiqī

39 *Y* 2:366.

40 *Y* 2:208–9.

41 On Ibn Muqla, see *Y* 3:118. On Munajjim, see *Y* 3:119. On Ibn al-ʿAmīd and ʿAbdānī, see *Y* 3:159. For other cases, see *T* 270, 301.

was descended from the caliph al-Wāthiq bi-Allāh (d. 232/847), and the judge Abū l-Faḍl Aḥmad b. Muḥammad al-Rashīdī was one of the children of Hārūn al-Rashīd (r. 170/789–193/809).[42] Finally, Abū l-Ḥasan al-Salāmī's (d. 393/1003) mother was also a poet.[43] Thaʿālibī describes Abū Maʿmar al-Ismāʿīlī as combining noble *adab* and *nasab* (lineage),[44] and Abū Aḥmad b. Abī Bakr al-Kātib as "the one who was reared in luxury, nourished by the state, and born by leadership" (*rabīb al-niʿma wa-ghadhiyyu l-dawla wa-salīlu l-riʾāsa*).[45] Blood relations with important *amīr*s or viziers are emphasized throughout the *Yatīma* and *Tatimma*. Thaʿālibī identifies, for example, Abū Firās al-Ḥamdānī as a cousin of both Sayf al-Dawla and Nāṣir al-Dawla.[46]

A detailed lineage is usually provided to certify a litterateur's Arab origin (and often to indicate his mastery of Arabic).[47] Like most anthologies and biographical dictionaries, the *Yatīma* and *Tatimma* rarely say anything about a subject's childhood. To the anthologist, an author was born when he started producing literature. Thaʿālibī gives information about a person's childhood only when relevant to his career. For example, he notes that Abū l-Ḥasan Muḥammad b. ʿAbdallāh al-Salāmī (d. 393/1003) composed poetry at the age of ten.[48]

Characterization of Litterateurs and Their Literary Oeuvres

Thaʿālibī often characterizes poets' oeuvres to give his reader a general impression before he goes into greater detail. Among his criteria is how prolific the poet is.[49] He often comments on the size, value, circulation, or price of a *dīwān*. For example, he specifies that Ibn Sukkara's *dīwān* includes more than fifty thousand lines.[50] Some *dīwān*s circulated faster than proverbs (*asyar min al-amthāl*), like that of Ibn al-Ḥajjāj,[51] and sold for more than fifty *dīnār*s.[52] Others could be found only in certain cities or regions, such as the *dīwān*

---

42 On Wāthiqī, see *Y* 4:192. On Rashīdī, see *T* 269.

43 *Y* 2:396.

44 *Y* 4:43.

45 *Y* 4:64.

46 *Y* 1:48.

47 Thaʿālibī determines that Abū l-Ḥasan al-Salāmī is from Banū Makhzūm b. Yaqẓa b. Murra b. Kaʿb b. Luʾayy b. Ghālib, *Y* 2:396; and that Abū l-Qāsim al-Dīnawarī is a descendant of ʿAbdallāh b. al-ʿAbbās b. ʿAbd al-Muṭṭalib, *Y* 4:136.

48 *Y* 2:467.

49 For example, see *Y* 1:298, 2:376, 3:112.

50 *Y* 3:3.

51 *Y* 3:31.

52 *Y* 3:35.

of Abū ʿAlī al-Muḥassin al-Tanūkhī (d. 384/994) and that of al-Sarī al-Raffāʾ (d. 366/976).[53]

Thaʿālibī describes poets themselves as naturally talented (*maṭbūʿ*), refined and elegant (*ẓarīf*), or licentious (*mājin*). When a poet excels in invective poetry, Thaʿālibī usually describes him as opprobrious (*khabīth al-lisān*). Other litterateurs are presented as more reserved. Ibn Fāris (395/1004), for example, "combines the excellence of scholars with the refinement of poets" (*yajmaʿ itqān al-ʿulamaʾ wa-ẓarf al-kuttāb wa-l-shuʿarāʾ*).[54] Abū Bakr al-Zubaydī was "most learned among his contemporaries in desinential syntax, jurisprudence, paradigm [of speech], and [other] rarities" (*aḥfaẓ ahl zamānihi li-l-iʿrāb wa-l-fiqh wa-l-maʿānī wa-l-nawādir*).

If not in a single epithet, Thaʿālibī describes a poet in a few pithy words. For example, Ibn Sukkara (d. 385/995) is described as "possessing breadth in the varieties of tropes" (*muttasiʿ al-bāʿ fī anwāʿ al-ibdāʿ*).[55] Ibn al-Ḥajjāj (d. 391/1001) "possesses a costly dowry of words" (*ghālī mahr al-kalām*).[56] Khalīʿ al-Shāmī (d. ca. 356/966) and Abū l-Fayyāḍ al-Ṭabarī (d. ca. 385/995) are each described as "a skillful poet", or *shāʿir mufliq* (lit. one who splits). Abū l-Faḍl and Abū l-Fatḥ b. al-ʿAmīd are "excellent in epistolography" (*ḥasan al-tarassul*).[57] Abū Saʿīd al-Rustamī (d. after 385/995) "exhausted the full share of beauty and genius" (*mustawfī aqsām al-ḥusn wa-l-barāʿa*) and "perfect[ed] the eloquence of Bedouins along with the ease of urbanity" (*mustakmil faṣāḥat al-badāwa wa-ḥalāwat al-ḥaḍāra*).[58] Nāmī (d. 399/1009), Ibn Darrāj al-Qasṭallī al-Andalusī (d. 421/1030), and Ibn Nubāta al-Saʿdī (d. 405/1014) are among "the champion poets" (*fuḥūl al-shuʿarāʾ*).[59] Abū l-Ḥasan al-Laḥḥām (d. ca. 363/973) possesses a "pleasant conviviality" (*ḥasan al-muḥāḍara*),[60] and many others showed "good disposition" (*ḥusn al-taṣarruf*).

Thaʿālibī often characterizes literary production rather than the litterateur himself. The expressions he uses show much perception and nuance. For instance, Thaʿālibī describes the poetry of Abū Manṣūr al-ʿAbdūnī (d. before 430/1038) as "sweet to taste, easy to swallow, and highly light spirited" (*ʿadhb al-madhāq, ḥulw al-masāgh fī nihāyat khiffat al-rūḥ*); that of Abū l-Ṭayyib

53 *Y* 2:140, 405.
54 *Y* 3:400.
55 *Y* 3:3.
56 *Y* 3:32.
57 *Y* 2:148, 3:185.
58 *Y* 3:304–5.
59 *Y* 1:241, 2:104.
60 *Y* 4:102.

al-Muṣʿabī (d. ca. 331/942) as "the offspring of excellence and the fruit of reason" (*nitāj al-faḍl wa-thimār al-ʿaql*); and that of al-Ḥasan b. ʿAlī al-Muṭrānī (d. ca 363/973) as "a record crammed with curiosities" (*mudawwan kathīr al-laṭāʾif*).[61] Similarly, Muḥammad b. Mūsā al-Ḥaddādī's (d. before 429/1037) poetry is "a record full of proverbs and beauties" (*mudawwan kathīr al-amthāl wa-l-ghurar*).[62] The poetry of Abū l-Ḥusayn Aḥmad b. Muḥammad al-Baghdādī (d. before 429/1037) and Abū Naṣr Sahl b. al-Marzubān (d. before 429/1037) is "of abundant wit" (*kathīr al-nukat*).[63] Abū Saʿd Aḥmad b. Muḥammad al-Harawī's (d. before 429/1037) poetry "combines pithiness, ease, firmness, and sweetness" (*yajmaʿ al-jazāla wa-l-suhūla wa-l-matāna wa-l-ʿudhūba*).[64] That of Abū Muḥammad al-Ḥasan al-Barūjirdī (d. 429/1037) is "scribal with many beauties and harmonious composition" (*kitābī kathīr al-maḥāsin mustamirr al-niẓām*).[65] Most of the poetry of Abū l-Fatḥ al-Baktamarī (Ibn al-Kātib al-Shāmī) (d. ca. 384/994) is "sung for its beauty and eloquence" (*yutaghannā bi-aktharihi malāḥatan wa-faṣāḥatan*).[66]

The dearth of sources makes it difficult to assess whether Thaʿālibī intended to differentiate between an author and his work (or the persona adapted within it). Thaʿālibī sometimes describes the litterateurs and at other times focuses on their oeuvre; but often he treats both together. In these instances, the description of the litterateur in the biographical summary dwells on character, and the discussion of his oeuvre follows where he describes the litterateur's poetry or prose. Furthermore, Thaʿālibī places his subjects in their geographical, social-historical contexts; although unstinting in his praise, he carefully chooses the titles and attributes he bestows upon them.

Geographical Context

Thaʿālibī repeatedly portrays authors as unsurpassed in their tribe, city, or region. For example, al-Sharīf al-Raḍī (d. 406/1015) is "the most distinguished among the Prophet's descendants in Iraq" (*anjab sādat al-ʿIrāq*), Abū l-Qāsim ʿAlī b. Muḥammad al-Iskāfī al-Nīshāpūrī (d. ca. 350/961) is "the tongue of Khurāsān"

---

61 For ʿAbdūnī, see *Y* 4:77. For Muṣʿabī, see *Y* 4:79. For Ḥaddādī, see *Y* 4:115.

62 *Y* 4:86.

63 *Y* 4:158, 392.

64 *Y* 4:347.

65 *Y* 4:394.

66 *Y* 1:120. This is the only location in the *Yatīma* and the *Tatimma* where Thaʿālibī uses music to characterize a poet's oeuvre, but there are several instances when he mentions that certain lines are used as melodies; see *Y* 1:292–3, 296, 318, 401, 429, 454, 4:61; *T* 38, 69, 70, 76, 77, 85.

(*lisān Khurāsān*), and Ibn Lankak (360/970) is "the matchless [one] in Baṣra" (*fard al-Baṣra*).[67] Similarly, Abū l-Ḥasan al-Salāmī (d. 393/1003) is "absolutely among the best poets of Iraq" (*min ash'ar ahl al-'Irāq qawlan bi-l-iṭlāq*).[68] The judge Abū l-Ḥasan 'Alī b. 'Abd al-'Azīz al-Jurjānī (d. 392/1002) is "the ornament of Jurjān" (*min ḥasanāt Jurjān*).[69] And Abū l-Ḥasan 'Alī b. Aḥmad al-Jawharī (d. 377/987) is "the star of Jurjān" (*najm Jurjān*).[70] Abū l-Ḥusayn Muḥammad b. Muḥammad al-Murādī (d. ca. 331/942) is the poet (*shā'ir*) of Bukhāra. Similarly, Abū l-Faḍl al-Sukkarī al-Marwazī (d. before 420/1037) is the poet of Marw, Abū Aḥmad al-Būshanjī *shā'ir Būshanj*, al-Ḥasan b. 'Alī b. Muṭrān (d. ca. 363/973) of al-Shāsh, and so on.[71] In these cases, only one poet in a region is awarded the rank of "poet of the region"; other poets are granted different laudatory titles. Some litterateurs distinguished themselves in certain genres. For example, Tha'ālibī considers Abū Isḥāq al-Ṣābī (d. 384/994) "unique in Iraq in rhetoric" (*awḥad al-'Irāq fī l-balāgha*).[72]

Social Context

Tha'ālibī accounts for the social context of a poet by judging him on the basis of local expectations. For example, he considers Aḥnaf al-'Ukbarī (d. 385/995) "the refined poet of the mendicants good in the general and the particular" (*shā'ir al-mukaddīn wa ẓarīfuhum wa-malīḥ al-jumla wa-l-tafṣīl minhum*).[73] Al-Sharīf al-Raḍī is "the best Ṭālibid poet" (*ash'ar al-Ṭālibiyyīn*), Abū l-Qāsim 'Umar b. Ibrāhīm al-Za'farānī (d. ca. 385/995) "the central stone in the necklace of the courtiers of al-Ṣāḥib" (*wāsiṭat 'iqd nudamā' al-Ṣāḥib*), and Abū l-Qāsim 'Abdallāh b. 'Abd al-Raḥmān al-Dīnawarī (d. before 429/1037) "among the chief litterateurs and head secretaries" (*min ru'asā' al-udabā' wa-ru'ūs al-kuttāb*).[74] Similarly, Abū l-Qāsim Yaḥyā b. 'Alī al-Bukhārī (d. before 429/1037) is "among the best most educated and most knowledgeable jurists in the requirement of elegant conversations" (*min ādab al-fuqahā' wa-aḥfaẓihim li-mā yaṣluḥu li-l-muḥāḍara*).[75] Abū l-'Abbās al-Ma'mūnī (d. before 429/1037) is "among the most knowledgeable and elite teachers" (*min 'ulamā' al-mu'addibīn*

---

67 On Raḍī, see *Y* 3:136. On Nīshāpūrī, see *Y*: 4:95. On Ibn Lankak, see *Y* 2:248.

68 *Y* 2:396.

69 *Y* 4:3.

70 *Y* 4:27.

71 *Y* 4:74, 87, 93, 115.

72 *Y* 2:242.

73 *Y* 3:122.

74 On Raḍī, see *Y* 3:136. On Za'farānī, see *Y* 3:346. On Dīnawarī, see *Y* 4:136.

75 *Y* 4:415.

wa-khawāṣṣihim).[76] Abū l-Faḍl Ismāʿīl al-Karābīsī (d. after 429/1037) is "among the best poets among jurists and the best jurists among poets" (*min ashʿar al-fuqahāʾ wa-afqah al-shuʿarāʾ*).[77] Ḥusayn b. ʿAlī al-Marwarrūzī (d. ca. 329/940) is "one of the best litterateurs among the army commanders in Khurāsān" (*min ādab aṣḥab al-juyūsh* bi-Khurāsān).[78] Abū Jaʿfar Aḥmad b. al-Ḥasan al-Bākharzī (d. after 429/1037) is "the judge of the refined" (*qāḍī al-ẓurrāf*).[79]

Historical Context

Thaʿālibī situates each litterateur's achievements within his historical context by comparing him to his peers. Thus, Ibn al-Ḥajjāj (d. 391/1001) is ranked as "among the bewitching poets and the wonders of the age" (*min saḥarati l-shiʿr wa-ʿajāʾibi l-ʿaṣr*) and "unique in his time for the art he made famous" (*fardu zamānihi fī fannihi l-ladhī ishtuhira bihi*).[80] Thaʿālibī hesitates to declare Ibn al-Ḥajjāj the best poet of his time, and so restricts his superiority to a specific genre—*mujūn* (licentious or bawdy poetry). Similarly, he states that Abū Aḥmad b. Abī Bakr al-Kātib (d. before 429/1037) was "among the first to have culture, elegance, brilliance, and poetry in Transoxania" (*min awwal man taʾaddaba wa-taẓarrafa wa-baraʿa wa-shaʿara bi-mā warāʾ l-nahr*).[81] In his entry on Abū l-Faḍl Ibn al-ʿAmīd, Thaʿālibī singles him out without reservation as "unique in his time in epistolography and scribal art" (*awḥad al-ʿaṣr fī l-kitāba*).[82]

Comparing Litterateurs

Thaʿālibī sometimes compares a litterateur to a predecessor,[83] a successor,[84] a contemporary litterateur from another region,[85] or someone in a different

76 *Y* 4:447.

77 *T* 197.

78 *Y* 4:85.

79 *T* 224.

80 *Y* 3:31.

81 *Y* 4:64.

82 *Y* 2:157.

83 Thaʿālibī states, for example, that the poetry of Abū ʿAlī al-Salāmī is similar to Ṣūlī's, since both poets use the style of book authors (*ashʿār maʾallifī l-kutub*); see *Y* 4:95.

84 Abū ʿĀmir Ismāʿīl b. Aḥmad (al-Shajarī) replaced al-Ḥasan b. ʿAlī b. Muṭrān in Transoxania; see *Y* 4:132.

85 Thaʿālibī, for example, considers Ibn Darrāj al-Qasṭallī in al-Andalus the equal of Mutanabbī, *Y* 2:119; see also B. Gruendler, "Originality in Imitation: Two *Muʿāraḍa*s by Ibn Darrāj al-Qasṭallī," in *al-Qantara* 29.2 (2008), 437–65. Abū al-Ḥusayn Aḥmad b. Fāris is compared to Ibn Lankak in Iraq, Ibn Khālawayhi in Syria, Ibn al-ʿAllāf in Fārs, and Abū

field.[86] These case-based comparisons best demonstrate Thaʿālibī's critical sense for the literature anthologized, his awareness of distinct personal styles, and his ambition to identify the "best" classical models. These comparisons can be in Thaʿālibī's own words or borrowed from others. Occasionally, Thaʿālibī rejects a given analogy or comparison. [87] These comparisons characterize the litterateur and his oeuvre and help the reader situate him in relation to the large number of personalities anthologized (see appendix 4).

Thaʿālibī mentions the special themes, motifs, and genres in which a poet excelled. For example, he called Aḥnaf al-ʿUkbarī (d. 385/995) the mendicants' poet (*shāʿir al-mukaddīn*). Ibn al-Ḥajjāj and Ibn Sukkara excelled in licentious and ribald poetry (*mujūn*) and obscenity (*sukhf*), while al-Sharīf al-Raḍī shone in elegies (*marāthī*).[88] Ibn Lankak's poetry consisted mostly of witticisms (*mulaḥ*) and bons mots (*ẓuraf*).[89] Abū Saʿd Aḥmad b. Muḥammad al-Harawī (d. before 429/1037) and the secretary Abū Naṣr Manṣūr b. Mushkān (d. after 429/1037) penned much good prose but little poetry.[90] And ʿAlī b. al-Ḥasan al-Laḥḥām al-Ḥarrānī (d. ca. 363/973) and Abū l-Qāsim al-Wāsānī (d. before 429/1037) composed little else aside from invective poetry (*hijāʾ*).[91]

Thaʿālibī also points out weaknesses in certain genres. Abū l-ʿAlāʾ al-Asadī (d. ca. 385/995), for example, was "poor" in panegyric compositions, and Abū l-Qāsim ʿAlī b. Muḥammad al-Iskāfī (d. ca 350/961) did not do well when writing brotherly private correspondence (*ikhwāniyyāt*) but excelled in official correspondence (*sulṭāniyyāt*).[92] Abū Muḥammad al-Mīkālī wrote good prose, but his poetry was unimpressive.[93]

Bakr al-Khwārizmī in Khurāsān, for combining the precision of scholars and the elegance of prose writers (*kuttāb*) and poets; see *Y* 3:400.

86 Thaʿālibī cites in the entry of Muḥammad b. Mūsā al-Ḥaddādī al-Balkhī a statement that claims that the city of Balkh contributed only four distinguished personalities: Abū l-Qāsim al-Kaʿbī in speculative theology (*ʿilm al-kalām*), Abū Zayd al-Balkhī in rhetoric and *adab* compilations (*al-balāgha wa-l-taʾlīf*), Sahl b. al-Ḥasan in Persian poetry, and Muḥammad b. Mūsā himself in Arabic poetry. See *Y* 4:97.

87 For example, see *Y* 3:343

88 On the former, see *Y* 3:3, 31. On the latter, see *Y* 3:136.

89 *Y* 1:352.

90 *Y* 4:346; *T* 250.

91 *Y* 2:348, 4:102.

92 On the former, see *Y* 3:339. On the latter, see *Y* 4:95.

93 His father, Abū ʿAbbās al-Mīkālī, became the first Mīkālī *raʾīs* in Nīshāpūr and was the elder brother of Abū l-Qāsim ʿAlī al-Mīkālī (d. 376/986–7), the grandfather of Abū l-Faḍl al-Mīkālī (d. 436/1044–5); see Bosworth, *Ghaznavids*, 179ff. On his unimpressive poetry, see *Y* 4:417.

Knowledge of Persian

Although Thaʿālibī seems indifferent to the newly rising Persian poetry in the eastern Islamic world, he does indicate in the *Yatīma* and the *Tatimma* whether a litterateur composed prose or poetry in Persian. Nevertheless, Arabic poetry invariably secures a subject a place in the anthology. The expressions Thaʿālibī uses here are "poet in two languages" (*shāʿir bi-l-lisānayn*) or "he composed poetry in Persian" (*wa-lahu shiʿrun bi-l-fārisiyya*). These poets are Abū l-Ṭayyib al-Muṣʿabī (d. ca. 331/942), Abū ʿAbdallāh al-Ghawwāṣ (d. before 429/1037), Abū Ibrāhīm Naṣr b. Aḥmad al-Mīkālī (d. after 429/1037), Abū Manṣūr Qāsim b. Ibrāhim al-Qāʾinī (d. after 429/1037), and Abū l-Ḥasan al-Aghājī (d. after 429/103).[94] In addition to these names, Thaʿālibī often comments that a certain litterateur knew Persian and translated select verses, proverbs, or motifs into elegant Arabic.[95] In his entry on the secretary and poet Abū Ibrāhīm b. Abī ʿAlī, he gives the Persian original.[96] The lines are usually introduced by expressions like "it is translated from Persian" and "he said in a proverb (or line) translated from Persian," or "translated from Persian." Thaʿālibī includes one line by the poet al-Maʿrūfī (fl. ca. 345/956) in Persian while commenting on the motif history of two lines by the poet al-Badīhī.[97] Finally, Thaʿālibī sometimes supplies the Persian translation of an Arabic word that appears in poetry of a Persian origin.[98] Curiously, knowledge of Persian, except in the case of Badīʿ al-Zamān al-Hamadhānī, is not used to characterize the litterateur at the beginning of the entry.[99]

Relations between Contemporaries

The *Yatīma* and *Tatimma* offer a wealth of information on the litterateurs' social relations and networks. Apparently, most litterateurs within a region were

94 See Bosworth, *Ghaznavids*, 181. See also *Y* 4:79, 442; and *T* 184, 231, 314, respectively. For more information on al-Aghājī, see A. V. Williams Jackson. *Early Persian Poetry: From the Beginnings Down to the Time of Firdausi* (New York: Macmillan, 1920), 119; On Abū Manṣūr Qāsim b. Ibrāhim al-Qāʾinī (known as Buzurjmihr), see ʿArūḍī Niẓāmī, *The Chahār Maqāla (The Four Discourses)*, trans. E. G. Browne (Hertford: S. Austin and Sons, 1899), 46; R. Q. Kh. Hidāyat, *Majmaʿ al-Fuṣaḥāʾ* (Tehran: Karkhānah-i Āghā Mīr Muḥammad Bāqir, 1295 [1878]), 1:66.

95 See, for example, *Y* 4:88–9, 90–91, 155, 257; *T* 142, 144, 207, 238, 313.

96 See *T* 207.

97 See *Y* 3:245.

98 See *Y* 3:296, 4:68.

99 On Thaʿālibī's lack of interest in Persian, see Bosworth's translation of *Laṭāʾif al-maʿārif*, 11ff. For the use of Persian in Ṣāḥib b. ʿAbbād's court, see Erez Naaman, *Literature and Literary People at the Court of al-Ṣāḥib Ibn ʿAbbād*, PhD diss., Harvard University, 2009, 8.

acquainted with one another, had the same teachers, attended the same literary gatherings (*majālis*) and study circles (*ḥalaqāt*), and worked in the same markets or courts. Thaʿālibī shows an awareness of the connection among a litterateur's environment, personality, and poetry. In addition to the teacher-pupil relationship, Thaʿālibī notes friendships and rivalries between poets.

The *Yatīma* and *Tatimma* include significant amounts of private correspondence (*ikhwāniyyāt*), both in prose and in poetry, that demonstrates friendships between litterateurs of the time.[100] Many of the elegies in both works also illustrate friendships. As reflected in the *Yatīma*, friends formed literary clusters or networks; they commented on one another's literary production, recommended one another for positions, hosted one another, and exchanged advice, poems, and letters.

Also, though, the animosity between some litterateurs was legendary. The *Yatīma* recounts the fallout of the bookseller and poet al-Sarī al-Raffāʾ's (d. 366/976) accusations that the Khālidiyyān brothers, Abū Bakr Muḥammad b. Hāshim (d. 380/990) and Abū ʿUthmān Saʿīd b. Hāshim (d. 371/981), were plagiarists.[101] Another anecdote is that of Abū Ṭālib al-Maʾmūnī (d. 383/993), who traveled to Rayy and succeeded in gaining Ṣāḥib b. ʿAbbād's appreciation. However, envious poets at the court slandered him as an extreme Sunnite (*ghuluww fī l-naṣb*) who considered the Shīʿa and Muʿtazila to be disbelievers (Ṣāḥib being both a Shīʿite and Muʿtazilite), and as a supporter of the ʿAbbāsids. They attributed to him forged poems that disparaged Ṣāḥib and swore that the praise poetry of Abū Ṭālib for Ṣāḥib was forged (a betrayal to any patron).[102] In turn, Abū Aḥmad b. Abī Bakr al-Kātib, whose father served as secretary to the Sāmānid *amīr* Ismāʿīl b. Aḥmad (d. 295/907) and vizier for *al-amīr* Aḥmad b. Ismāʿīl (d. 301/914), declared himself, because of his lineage and literary skills, more deserving of the vizierate than his colleagues Jabahānī and Balʿamī (d. 329/940).[103] Therefore, he defamed them in his poems until

---

100 *Ikhwāniyya* (brotherly or private correspondence) is a genre of Arabic literature. In epistolography (and sometimes in poetry), it expresses affection, compassion, protestation, congratulation, condolences, declarations of solidarity, gratitude, nostalgia, and the like. For the most part, it is a personal letter or poem, unlike *sulṭāniyyāt* or *dīwāniyyāt*, which deal with official matters. *Ikhwāniyyāt* and *sulṭāniyyāt* merge in brotherly correspondences commissioned on behalf of the patron to his friends. For a short discussion of the two, see A. Arazi, "Risāla," *EI2* VII:532–44, especially the parts on *risāla ikhwāniyya* and *risāla dīwāniyya*.

101 *Y* 2:117.

102 *Y* 4:161.

103 Abū ʿAbdallāh al-Jabahānī al-Kabīr was vizier of *al-amīr* Aḥmad b. Ismāʿīl (d. 301/914) after Abū Aḥmad b. Abī Bakr al-Kātib's father. Most probably Abū l-Faḍl al-Balʿāmī is meant

they threatened his life and forced him to take temporary refuge in Baghdad.[104] The invective poems scattered throughout the *Yatīma* and *Tatimma* reflect the numerous rivalries among litterateurs of the period. However, invective poetry was also composed for mere entertainment; Abū Aḥmad b. Manṣūr asked the poet al-Laḥḥām (d. ca. 363/973), known for criticizing prominent figures in his *hijā'* poems, to write an invective poem about him but without resorting to insult (*dhamm*).

Physical and Character Features

Thaʿālibī rarely describes a poet's appearance unless relevant to his career. Thus, he notes whether a poet is blind, or remarkably handsome, as was Abū l-Ḥasan ʿAlī b. Aḥmad al-Jawharī, whose beauty "filled the eyes" (*yamla'u l-ʿuyūna jamālan*).[105] His handsomeness, along with the similitude of his spirit and nature, his amiability (*khiffa*), and his elegance (*ẓarf*) prompted Ṣāḥib to send him on missions to various provinces.[106] Unattractive poets were ridiculed by their contemporaries, as was the diminutive Abū ʿAlī al-Zawzanī.[107]

Thaʿālibī describes Badīʿ al-Zamān al-Hamadhānī as "easygoing" (*khafīf al-rūḥ*), "pleasant in company" (*ḥasan al-ʿishra*), of "pure grace" (*nāṣiʿ al-ẓarf*), "grand character" (*ʿaẓīm al-khulq*), "noble soul" (*sharīf al-nafs*), "kind manners" (*karīm al-ʿahd*), "sincere affection" (*khāliṣ al-wudd*), "sweet friendship" (*ḥulw al-ṣadāqa*), and "bitter enmity" (*murr al-ʿadāwa*).[108] In contrast, Thaʿālibī

---

here rather than Abū ʿAlī Muḥammad al-Balʿamī (d. 386/996), who appears elsewhere in *Y* 4:108, 116, 134, 204, and in ʿUtbī, *al-Yamīnī fī sharḥ akhbār al-sulṭān yamīn al-dawla*, ed. Iḥsān Dh. al-Thāmirī (Beirut: Dār al-Ṭalīʿa, 2004), 99. This opinion is supported by the fact that Thaʿālibī cites two lines by Abū Aḥmad b. Abī Bakr al-Kātib in praise of Abū l-Faḍl al-Balʿāmī in Thaʿālibī, *Thimār al-qulūb*, 676, and id., *Nathr al-Naẓm*, 39. Abū Aḥmad b. Abī Bakr al-Kātib is among the poets whom Thaʿālibī anthologized in the section dedicated to the poets who slightly preceded his time. On Abū l-Faḍl al-Balʿamī, see Subkī, *Ṭabaqāt al-shāfiʿiyya*, ed. ʿAbd al-Fattāḥ al-Ḥulw and Maḥmūd Muḥammad al-Ṭanāḥī (Cairo: Dār Iḥyā' al-Kutub al-ʿArabiyya, 1992), 3:188; al-Kirmānī, *Nasā'im al-asḥār*, ed. Jalāl al-Dīn Ḥusaynī Urmavī (Tehran: Dānishgāh-i Tehrān, 1959), 35; Samʿānī, *al-Ansāb*, 1:391; Ghiyāth al-Dīn Khāndamīr, *Dustūr al-wuzarā'*, trans. Amīn Sulaymān (Cairo: al-Hay'a al-Miṣriyya al-ʿĀmma li-l-Kitāb, 1980), 212.

104 *Y* 4:64.

105 See *Y* 3:385.

106 *Y* 4:27. Other cases are those of Badīʿ al-Zamān al-Hamadhānī and Abū Naṣr al-Zawzanī; see *Y* 4:257, 446.

107 *Y* 4:144.

108 *Y* 4:257.

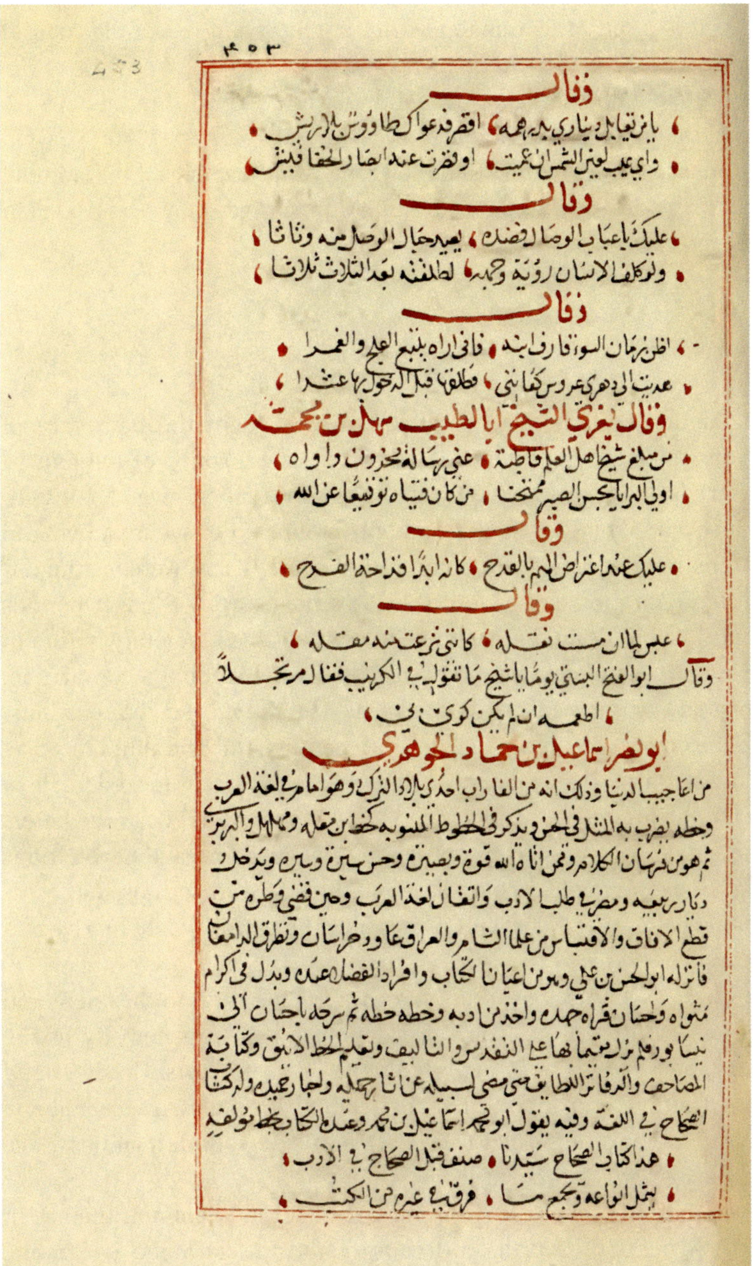

FIGURE 34 *Yatīmat al-dahr*, MS Toronto A13512y, 453r

describes Abū l-Ḥasan Muḥammad al-Ifrīqī al-Mutayyam as "an old man of shabby appearance" (*shaykh rathth al-hay'a*).[109]

He also remarks on the beautiful handwriting of Abū l-Faraj al-Sāwī (d. ca. 388/998), the judge ʿAlī b. ʿAbd al-ʿAzīz al-Jurjānī (392/1002), Abū l-Ṭayyib al-Muṣʿabī (d. ca. 331/942), Abū ʿAlī al-Zawzanī, Abū Naṣr Ismāʿīl b. Ḥammād al-Jawharī (d. before 429/1037), and Abū Muḥammad Yaḥyā b. ʿAbdallāh al-Arzanī (415/1024).[110]

Patronage

Many litterateurs, both poets and prose writers, sought the patronage of *amīr*s, viziers, rulers, or important local families. These courts of the fourth/tenth century Islamic world were located in various cities, given the establishment of rivalry dynasties, and litterateurs competed to secure a living in them. Patrons were selective and competition fierce. There were visiting litterateurs (*al-ṭāriʾūn*) and those who resided in the courts for longer periods (*al-muqīmūn*). Some desired a position in court, such as secretary, scribe in the office of correspondence (*dīwān al-rasāʾil*), librarian, or boon companion. Others pursued a patron's gifts and allowances. The *Yatīma* and *Tatimma* illustrate both the courtly life in the fourth/tenth century and Thaʿālibī's role as a historian of literature. Thaʿālibī often tells us what the patrons looked for; how they selected the litterateurs who applied to their courts; and what the letters of recommendations, entrance exams, job interviews, offers, and negotiations looked like. Books were often composed and dedicated to patrons, and occasionally named after them. Thaʿālibī relates how the patron would receive and remunerate such a work.

Most of these accounts are success stories, and thus attest to the talent and excellence of the litterateurs. They also demonstrate the generosity of the patrons and their care in selecting litterateurs to their courts. On one hand they are entertaining, and on the other, they contain examples of excellent sayings, signatory notes or apostilles (*tawqīʿāt*), and letters. Both qualities make them suitable for *adab* anthologies.

Moreover, patronage and the quest for patronage are common themes in literary anthologies of the fourth/tenth century, and one can argue that among Thaʿālibī's goals for his anthology was to find jobs for his contemporaries.

---

109 *Y* 4:157.

110 *Y* 3:396, 4:3, 79, 145, 406; and *T* 300, respectively. See Yāqūt al-Ḥamawī, who mentions Arzanī's name as Abū Muḥammad Yaḥyā b. Muḥammad: *Muʿjam al-udabāʾ*, 2830.

Anthologies were not always secondary texts selected from primary *dīwāns* and circulating "books." Rather, as mentioned earlier, anthologies of contemporary literature, such as the *Yatīma* and its several sequels, became important vehicles for publishing original literature, that of nonprofessional poets who did not produce circulating *dīwāns* and were still seeking recognition and access to courts. Thaʿālibī thus was acting as a gatekeeper to the realm of admired literature. Through these accounts Thaʿālibī guides the litterateurs of his age, especially his fellow Khurāsānīs, on how they can secure and keep a position at court, and what to do should they lose it.

Patron-Littérateur Relations

A poet was wise to conceal his true feelings about a patron he disliked. Abū l-Ṭayyib al-Ṭāhirī (d. ca. 321/933), for example, served the Sāmānids in public but disparaged them in private (*kāna yakhdim Āl Sāman jahran wa-yahjūhum sirran*). His hatred extended to their viziers, officials, and even their capital, Bukhāra.[111] Some poets remained loyal to one patron, spending most of their lives at his court or residence. Thaʿālibī mentions, for example, that Abū l-Faraj al-Iṣfahānī (d. 356/967) remained at the court of Muhallabī.[112] The judge Abū l-Ḥasan ʿAlī b. ʿAbd al-ʿAzīz al-Jurjānī (d. ca. 403/1012) settled at the court of Ṣāḥib after many journeys.[113] Abū l-Ḥasan ʿAlī b. Aḥmad al-Jawharī (d. 377/987) was one of Ṣāḥib's favorites.[114] Abū l-ʿAbbās al-Nāmī (d. 399/1009) adhered to Sayf al-Dawla's court and was second only to Mutanabbī.[115] Abū Manṣūr Yaḥyā b. Yaḥyā al-Kātib was close to the *amīr* Abū l-Faḍl al-Mīkālī.[116] Thaʿālibī labels such close relations with phrases such as "exclusively dedicated to" (*shadīd al-ikhtiṣāṣ bi-*), "dedicated to" (*ikhtaṣṣa bi-*), and "made him his protégé" (*iṣṭanaʿahu li-nafsihi*).

Admission to a Court

The courts of the era were few and located in major cities. Litterateurs competed to secure a living in any of them. Renowned litterateurs wandered almost freely from one court to another. Abū Bakr al-Khwārizmī, for example, moved among six courts without an invitation letter; however, he needed Ṣāḥib b. ʿAbbād's intercession to visit ʿAḍud al-Dawla. Interestingly, there was an alle-

111 *Y* 4:96.
112 *Y* 3:114.
113 *Y* 4:3.
114 *Y* 4:27.
115 *Y* 1:241.
116 *T* 194.

gation in Tawḥīdī's *Akhlāq al-wazīrayn* that Khwārizmī was spying for Ṣāḥib, which justifies the reluctance of ʿAḍud al-Dawla to admit him to his court.[117]

A patron might invite a luminary to his court and encourage the visit with gifts, as happened with Ṣāḥib b. ʿAbbād and Abū Isḥāq al-Ṣābī.[118] A litterateur's refusal could incur the wrath of his host. Both Ṣāḥib b. ʿAbbād and Muhallabī instigated the litterateurs at their court to write against Mutanabbī after he declined their respective invitations.[119] In some cases an offer had to be politely declined for practical reasons. The Sāmānid *amīr* Nūḥ b. Manṣūr extended an invitation to Ṣāḥib b. ʿAbbād to serve as his vizier. Ṣāḥib, however, declined and justified this by not being able to move with a load of four hundred camels' worth of books.[120]

Seeking or meeting a patron is a frequent topic in *akhbār* since the third/ninth century.[121] For a poet to be received at a court, the patron needed to know his work. Ideally, the candidate's reputation should have preceded him, but he might have had to establish (or reestablish) ties with a patron by sending a writing sample (a letter, poem, or book) that demonstrated his talent. The litterateur might explicitly declare his wish to visit the court. If returning to a court, it was opportune to justify one's absence and apologize for it.[122] In other cases, news of a litterateur's intended visit reached the court and the patron issued an invitation.[123]

A litterateur might have requested someone else's intercession. When he was young, Hamadhānī's father brought him to Ṣāḥib's court.[124] The fre-

---

117 Tawḥīdī, *Akhlāq al-wazīrayn*, ed. Muḥammad b. Tāwīt al-Ṭūnjī (Beirut: Dār Ṣādir, 1992), 108. For details, see Erez Naaman, *Literature and Literary People at the Court of al-Ṣāḥib Ibn ʿAbbād*, 61.

118 *Y* 2:246.

119 *Y* 1:136, 138.

120 *Y* 3:196–7.

121 For a study of this type of accounts and its consequences, see B. Gruendler, "Meeting the Patron: An *Akhbār* Type and Its Implication for *Muḥdath* Poetry," in *Ideas, Images, and Methods of Portrayal*, ed. Sebastian Günther (Leiden: Brill, 2005), 59–88.

122 See, for example, Abū Taghlib with ʿAḍud al-Dawlā, *Y* 2:117; and Abū l-Qāsim al-Zaʿfarānī with Ṣāḥib b. ʿAbbād, *Y* 3:354.

123 See, for example, the case of Ṣāḥib b. ʿAbbād and the judge Abū Bishr al-Faḍl b. Muḥammad al-Jurmānī, *Y* 3:254.

124 *Y* 3:197, 4:257. Thaʿālibī does not specify the location of Ṣāḥib's court, but in 380/990 it was at Rayy; see ʿUtbī, *Al-Yamīnī*, 116. E. Rowson notes that if we can trust an anecdote in Hamadhānī's *dīwān*, then he had already been introduced to Ṣāḥib as a boy of twelve; see Rowson, "Religion and Politics in the Career of Badīʿ al-Zamān al-Hamadhānī," *Journal of the American Oriental Society* 107 (1987), 654.

quent accounts of intercessions gave rise, according to Beatrice Gruendler, to a new subgenre of praise poetry that lauded the intercessor and the patron who responded to the intercession.[125] Abū Ṭālib al-Maʾmūnī was advised by Khwārizmī to praise *al-shaykh* Abū Manṣūr Kuthayyir b. Aḥmad to have him intercede on his behalf to join the literary circle of the army commander Abū l-Ḥasan b. Sīmjūr.[126] The intercession sometimes took the form of a written recommendation. Thaʿālibī, for example, includes three letters by Ṣāḥib b. ʿAbbād recommending Abū Ḥasan al-Salāmī (d. 393/1003), who wished to join the court of ʿAḍud al-Dawla; Abū l-Ḥasan al-Jawharī, who wished to be patronized by Abū l-ʿAbbās al-Ḍabbī; and Abū l-Ḥasan al-Sijzī al-Nūqātī, who specifically requested such a letter before returning to his homeland, Sijistān.[127] In Salāmī's case, the letter was addressed directly not to the new patron, ʿAḍud al-Dawla, but to his secretary and vizier ʿAbd al-ʿAzīz b. Yūsuf (d. 388/998).[128] Thaʿālibī also describes the reception of Ṣāḥib's letter:

> Salāmī stayed at Ṣāḥib's court in great favor, noble rank, and bright pleasures until he preferred to visit the court of ʿAḍud al-Dawla at Shīrāz. Then Ṣāḥib prepared him and gave him a letter in his handwriting to Abū l-Qāsim ʿAbd al-ʿAzīz b. Yūsuf. The text is:
> My master, may God prolong his life, knows that the merchants of poetry are numerous like hair, while those one trusts to present jewels fashioned of their talent, and to offer ornaments woven with their minds, are fewer. Among those I have tested and then praised, and urged by examination then chosen, is Abū l-Ḥasan Muḥammad ʿAbdallāh al-Makhzūmī al-Salāmī, may God support him. He has a quick wit that surpasses deliberation and a way in excellence that piques the ear's attention, just as the gaze pleases by its pasture. He has ridden [the back of] hope and was advised [to aim for] the glorious court, to attain [the rank of] his peers and disclose among them the brightness of his condition. I have prepared the *amīr* of poetry for his parade and adorned the horse of eloquence with him as a rider. This letter of mine is his scout for raindrops, rather his

---

125 See Gruendler, *Medieval Arabic Praise Poetry* (London: RoutledgeCurzon, 2003), 9.

126 *Y* 4:163–4. On Abū l-Ḥasan al-Sīmjūrī, see Bosworth, *Ghaznavids*, 58; ʿUtbī, *al-Yamīnī*, 143.

127 *Y* 4:342. Interestingly, Ṣāḥib concludes the letter by stating that its authenticity is established by his distinctive handwriting and articulation. For a translation and discussion of this letter, see Naaman, *Literature and Literary People at the Court of al-Ṣāḥib Ibn ʿAbbād*, 69–70. Thaʿālibī mentions also that Abū Dulaf al-Khazrajī carried with him letters of recommendation written by Ṣāḥib that opened doors of patronage for him. See *Y* 3:357.

128 On him, see *Y* 2:313ff.

road to the sea. If my lord heeds my words about him and takes it among the reasons to accept him, may he do it, if God, exalted is He, wishes.
When he arrived, Abū l-Qāsim helped him, was gracious to him and brought him to ʿAḍud al-Dawla so he recited his *qaṣīda*:...
Then the wing of welcome enveloped him and offered him the key of hope.[129]

Meeting a Patron

A first meeting with a patron required special performance on the part of the litterateur, for introductory words set the tone for the relationship.[130] Among the many such stories Thaʿālibī recounts of Abū l-Ḥasan al-ʿAlawī al-Waṣī al-Hamadhānī (d. after 388/998) is that he thought long and hard about his first meeting with Ṣāḥib, and finally chose to use a Qurʾānic reference to Yūsuf: "This is but a noble man" (*mā hādhā illā basharun karīm*).[131] Ṣāḥib cleverly retorted with a verse from the same *sūra*: "Surely, I perceive the scent of Yūsuf, unless you think I am senile" (*innī la-ajidu rīḥa Yūsufa lawlā an tufannidūn*).[132]

Leaving a Court

Litterateurs anthologized in the *Yatīma* and *Tatimma* often roamed from one court to another in search of patronage, easily changing loyalties. Patronage is a contract, and the violation of its terms by either party would terminate the relationship. The poet Abū l-Ḥasan al-Nawqātī succinctly explains the terms of this relation:

If you are stingy with beneficence to me
And I do not attain a gift from you

129 *Y* 2:401–2.

130 Examining the meeting of a patron as a standard element at the beginning of entries on an individual in the third/ninth century, Beatrice Gruendler identifies some recurrent props and personages in this plot type; see Gruendler, "Meeting the Patron." As in the third/ninth century, this type of *akhbār* in the *Yatīma* portrays the poets met with success together with the poets who failed and remained obscure.

131 He served after Ṣāḥib in the court of *al-amīr* Maḥmūd al-Ghaznawī (d. 421/1030); see ʿUtbī, *al-Yamīnī*, 163. *Mā hādhā basharan in hādhā illā malakun karīm*, *Q*. 12:31 (all Qurʾānic translations are based on Arberry's *The Koran Interpreted* (New York: Macmillan, 1955), with few changes).

132 *Y* 3:204; *Q*. 12:94.

> You are a slave like me
> And why should I serve a slave?[133]

In many cases, an incident that enraged the patron or humiliated the litterateur would compel the latter to leave. Several such incidents are listed in the entry on Ṣaḥib b. ʿAbbād, such as an unfortunate bout of flatulence, which occurred twice in Ṣāḥib's court:

> Hamadhānī related to me saying: A jurist known as Ibn al-Khuḍayrī attended the debate circle (*majlis al-naẓar*) that Ṣāḥib held nightly. One day he dozed off (*ghalabathu ʿaynāhu*) and a loud fart escaped from him. He was ashamed and avoided the *majlis*. So Ṣāḥib said: Relay to him:
> "O Ibn al-Khuḍayrī do not go in shame
> Because of an accident from you that was as the flute (*nāy*) or the lute (*ʿūd*)
> You cannot imprison the wind (*rīḥ*)
> Since you are not Solmon son of David"
> A similar affair was said to have happened to Ḥamadhānī in the *majlis* of Ṣāḥib, and he was ashamed and said: [it was] the squeaking of the sofa (*takht*). Al-Ṣāḥib said: I am afraid it was the squeaking from underneath (*taḥt*). One says that this embarrassment was the reason for his departure from the court for Khurāsān.[134]

The two incidents are combined because of their similarity and because both occurred in Ṣāḥib's court. This allows Thaʿālibī to dispense with the first part of the second story and concentrate on the different outcome: Ibn al-Khuḍayrī showed remorse and was forgiven; Hamadhānī did not admit his mistake and had to leave. In some cases, a litterateur has to flee without even waiting for a caravan, as happened with one of the false poets (*mutashāʿirūn*) who plagiarized Ṣāḥib.[135] The patron, however, might tolerate the bad manners of a talented litterateur, as was the case with Ibn Lankak al-Baṣrī and Muhallabī; Thaʿālibī says:

> One day the vizier Muhallabī invited him [Ibn Lankak] to a meal and while he was eating with him [the poet] suddenly blew his nose into a

---

133 *Y* 4:343. The translation is from Naaman, *Literature and Literary People at the Court of al-Ṣāḥib Ibn ʿAbbād*, 59.

134 *Y* 3:202.

135 *Y* 3:200.

> large handkerchief and spit into it. Then he took an olive from a bowl and bit it so violently that its pit sprang out and hit the eye of the *wazīr*. [The *wazīr*] was amazed at his ill-mannered gluttony but he bore with him because of his strength in *adab*.[136]

In some cases, a litterateur and a patron patched up their relationship. The poet and librarian Abū Muḥammad al-Khāzin (d. ca. 383/998), for example, contacted Ṣāḥib b. ʿAbbād after a decade of estrangement and apologized for having "voluntarily" left his court. He described the misfortunes that had afflicted him in the intervening years, said that he was coming back "out of necessity," and stressed that the exile had taught him a lesson.[137]

Departure from a court was not necessarily because of ill feelings between patron and client. Ibn al-Ḥajjāj left the court of Ibn al-ʿAmīd still praising him and without specifying his destination or reason for departure.[138] In other cases, the poet asked the patron's permission to leave. This is the case of Abū Ṭālib al-Maʾmūnī (d. 383/993), after his enemies poisoned his relation with Ṣāḥib (he was said to have cursed the Muʿtazila).[139] Maʾmūnī stresses in his departure poem that he will spread the word of Ṣāḥib's generosity. Some poets enjoyed their time at the court but desired to return home. This occurred with Abū l-Ḥusayn Muḥammad b. al-Ḥusayn al-Fārisī and Abū l-Ḥasan al-Sijzī al-Nūqātī, who obtained written permission from Ṣāḥib to depart. In these documents, Ṣāḥib praises them, comments on their literary ability and character, and confirms his wish to have kept them at court.[140] The poet Salāmī obtained an introduction to the court of ʿAḍud al-Dawla from his former patron Ṣāḥib b. ʿAbbād.[141]

Prison Incidents and Stories

If a poet had spent time in prison, Thaʿālibī mentioned this in the biographical introduction to an entry. Perhaps the most elaborate account of imprisonment in the *Yatīma* is that of Abū l-Qāsim ʿAlī b. Muḥammad al-Iskāfī al-Nīshāpūrī. In the biographical introduction, Thaʿālibī says of Iskāfī:

---

136 *Y* 2:352.

137 *Y* 3:325; for stories of this type, see *Y* 3:203. On Khāzin's escape from Ṣāḥib's court, see Naaman, *Literature and Literary People at the Court of al-Ṣāḥib Ibn ʿAbbād*, 58.

138 *Y* 3:94.

139 *Y* 4:161–2. This story has been analyzed by Naaman, *Literature and Literary People at the Court of al-Ṣāḥib Ibn ʿAbbād*, 47ff.

140 *Y* 4:342–3, 385.

141 *Y* 2:401.

> In the bloom of his life and the peak of his strength he came to Abū ʿAlī al-Ṣāghānī, who chose him, and his reception was good, and he singled him out exclusively for his service and appointed him to the office of correspondence (*dīwān al-rasāʾil*). The news about him was good, his renown (*athar*) reached far (*sāfara*), and his writings (*kutub*) used to reach the court in extreme beauty and freshness; [others] competed for him and Abū ʿAlī was asked to yield him to the court. Then Abū ʿAlī would offer excuses and evasion, and did not let him go until Abū ʿAlī disclosed the mask of rebellion, lost the battle of Kharjīk and [retreated] to al-Ṣaghāniyyān.[142] He [Iskāfī] was among the companions of Abū ʿAlī and was kept in the prison of al-Qamandar, and shackled despite the good opinion about him and the strong inclination toward him.
> The glorious *amīr* Nūḥ b. Naṣr wanted to probe his heart and find out what was hidden in his breast. So he ordered that a note be written in the name of a *sheikh* saying to him: "Abū l-ʿAbbās al-Ṣāghānī has written to the court to request you from the *sulṭān* and invite you to Shāsh to undertake the writing of official correspondence (*al-kutub al-sulṭāniyya*). What do you think of that?
> He wrote at the bottom of the note (*waqqaʿa*): "My Lord, the prison is dearer to me than that which they call me to" [Q. 12:33]. When the reply (*tawqīʿ*) was shown to al-Ḥamīd he thought well of him, admired him, ordered his release, gave him a robe of honor (*khalaʿa ʿalayhi*) and set him over all the office of correspondence as deputy to Abū ʿAbdallāh. The title was his, but the [actual] work was Abū l-Qāsim's.[143]

The *khabar* demonstrates in detail how Iskāfī started his career, achieving a connection with Nūḥ b. Naṣr, and ascending to the office of correspondence (*dīwān al-rasāʾil*). Moreover, it exemplifies Iskāfī's signatory notes or apostilles (*tawqīʿāt*), demonstrating his ingenuity. Both factors make this account an ideal opening for Iskāfī's entry. The same can be said about most prison stories in the *Yatīma* and *Tatimma*. Thaʿālibī usually explains the reason for a litterateur's imprisonment and its effect on his career. More important, he quotes the literary production (usually poetry) composed in captivity.

142 Saghāniyyān—spelled according to *Muʿjam al-buldān*, but Ṣighāniyān is common in secondary sources—is in Transoxania near Tirmidh and Gubádhiyan; see Yāqūt al-Ḥamawī, *Muʿjām al-Buldān*, 2:144, 346, 3:408–9.

143 *Y* 4:96. For more historical background and an elaborate version of this account, see ʿArūḍī Niẓāmī, *The Chahār Maqāla*, 26.

Prison stories are also cited in the entry of the patron who ordered the confinement, to illustrate his taste in literature. For example, to demonstrate Ṣāḥib's appreciation of Qur'ānic quotations (*iqtibāsāt*), Thaʿālibī relates the imprisonment of the singer Makkī (*al-munshid*):

> The grammarian Abū l-Ḥusayn related to me saying: Makkī, the singer, frequented Ṣāḥib at Jurjān, being an old servant, and corrected him many times, so Ṣāḥib ordered him to be imprisoned. He was held in the mint (*dār al-ḍarb*) near his residence in Jurjān. Ṣāḥib once went up to the roof of his house for an urge he felt and looked down at the mint below. When Makkī saw him he cried out at the top of his voice: "Then he looked and saw him in the midst of Hell." [Q. 37:55]. Laughing, Ṣāḥib replied: "Rot in it and do not speak to me" [Q. 23:108]. Then he gave word to release him.[144]

This literary production gains more importance in the case of the princely poet Abū Firās al-Ḥamdānī, whose prison experience largely shaped his career; Thaʿālibī devotes a separate section to these prison poems.[145] Thaʿālibī assigns special importance in these accounts to the ode, poem, or saying responsible for a capture or release. In the account quoted earlier, the *tawqīʿ*, which cleverly employs a famous Qur'ānic quotation, seems to play an integral part in the discharge, which holds true in many of the prison accounts. Qur'ān is the primary source of divine law, and its use in such a context adds a divine aspect to the patron's nonnegotiable decision; moreover, it helps make the ruler's verdict concise, a basic characteristic of *tawqīʿ*.[146]

Description of Courtly Majālis[147]

Thaʿālibī's time witnessed the cultural efflorescence of the Būyid, Sāmānid, Ghaznavid, and Saljūq dynasties. The rulers of these independent states, along

144 *Y* 3:201.

145 *Y* 1:75.

146 On the history, procedure, composition, linguistic economy, and performance of *tawqīʿ*. see B. Gruendler, "*Tawqīʿ*," in *The Weaving of Words: Approaches to Classical Arabic Prose*, ed. Lale Behzadi and Vahid Behmardi (Beirut: Orient Institut, 2009), 101–29.

147 The semantic field of *majlis* is wide; among its meanings are "meeting place," "meeting assembly," "reception hall of a caliph, high dignitary, or other personage," and "a session held there." For a discussion of the role of *majālis* and their description in Arabo-Islamic civilization, see W. Madelung, "Madjlis," *EI2* V:1031ff.; Joel L. Kraemer, *Humanism in the Renaissance of Islam* (Leiden: Brill, 1986), 54ff., 268; A. Shalaby, *History of Muslim Education* (Beirut: Dār al-Kashshāf, 1954), 32–42; M. Ahmad, *Muslim Education and the Scholars' Social Status up to the 5th Century Muslim Era in the Light of Ta'rīkh Baghdād*

with their viziers, competed for fame and honor by attracting the most famous and able litterateurs and scholars of their time. Culture and power became an ornament and expression of power manifested in the *amīr* or the vizier's *majlis*. The litterateurs, on their part, had to compromise their literary taste and dignity to satisfy their patrons. The *Yatīma* also reflects rivalry among the courts of Shīrāz, Rayy, Iṣbahān, Baghdad, Hamadhān, Bukhārā, and Ḥalab through the description of their literary *majālis*, their etiquette, and the litterateurs who attended them. Under the judge Abū l-Qāsim ʿAlī b. Dāwūd al-Tanūkhī (d. ca. 352/963), Thaʿālibī recounts that Muhallabī's circle met twice a week in his palaces and gardens, and its members included Ibn Qurayʿa (d. 367/977), Ibn Maʿrūf (d. 363/973), and al-Qāḍī al-Tanūkhī himself.[148] Thaʿālibī divulges how these venerable sheikhs and judges indulged in revelry and drinking, only to return the next day to the dignity of their office.

Other courtly *majālis* involved discussions, competitions, and contests. It was common for a patron to request occasional poetry on specific themes—be it a dish, instrument, plant, fruit, animal, house, or literary motif—sometimes even indicating the rhyme and meter.[149] These accounts are listed in the entries dedicated to patrons to illustrate their generosity or to validate their own literary talent, especially when the patron participated in the literary discussion or gave the incipit for the poets to follow. However, these types of accounts also occur in the entry on the litterateur, especially if he succeeded in meeting the patron's expectations or outdid his colleagues. Finally, in the context of *majālis*, Thaʿālibī indicates lines or *qaṣīda*s that won prizes such as gifts or money.[150] These panegyrics were necessary to reaffirm the loyalty of the litterateur in speech acts since a formal written contract did not exist.

(Zürich: Verlag "Der Islam," 1968), 59–72; *The Majlis: Interreligious Encounters in Medieval Islam*, ed. H. Lazarus-Yafeh et al. (Wiesbaden: Harrassowitz, 1999); M. ʿA. Maghribī, *Majālis al-adab wa-l-ghināʾ fī l-ʿaṣr al-umawī* (Cairo: Dār al-Hudā li-l-Ṭibāʿa, 1985); Ibrāhīm Najjār, *Shuʿarāʾ ʿabbāsiyyūn mansiyyūn* (Beirut: Dār al-Gharb al-Islāmī, 1997), 1:160ff.

148 *Y* 2:336–7. Ibn Qurayʿa was a prominent judge; see H. Busse, *Chalif und Grosskönig; die Buyiden im Iraq (945–1055)* (Beirut: In Kommission bei F. Steiner, Wiesbaden, 1969), 204, 503. ʿUbaydallāh b. Aḥmad b. Maʿrūf was chief judge in Baghdad from 360/971 to 363/973; see Busse, *Chalif und Grosskönig*, 275–6. Abū l-Qāsim al-Tanūkhī is the father of Abū ʿAlī al-Muḥassin al-Tanūkhī, author of *Nishwār al-muḥāḍara* and *al-Faraj baʿda l-shidda*; see *Y* 2:366ff.

149 For these, see *Y* 1:33, 248, 2:217, 397–9, 413, 3:179–82, 207, 4:396.

150 See *Y* 1:32–5, 132, 238, 2:359, 3:186, 4:75, 83.

Evaluating Literary Production

In most cases, Thaʿālibī's own appreciation of poetry or prose prompts him to quote it. Throughout the anthology, he reminds readers of his intention to be brief and to quote examples that meet his criteria. But which are these? He does not provide much of a theoretical framework in the *Yatīma* or *Tatimma*, and no work of his on theoretical poetics has survived to elucidate the aesthetic underpinnings of his anthologies.[151] The entries of the *Yatīma* and *Tatimma*, however, give some evidence of Thaʿālibī's taste, for he offers descriptive praise when introducing the material.

Much of the poetry in the *Yatīma* and *Tatimma* is not commented on; Thaʿālibī simply introduces lines with "he said" (*qāla*, *aḥsana*, *ajāda*, *wa-lahu*), and leaves it to the reader to judge. Many lines are circumscribed rather vaguely as possessing pithiness (*jazāla*), purity or eloquence (*faṣāḥa*), eloquence (*balāgha*), gracefulness (*rashāqa*), beauty (*malāḥa*), sweetness (*ḥalāwa*), fluency (*salāsa*), delicacy (*riqqa*), sweetness (*ʿudhūba*), lightness (*khiffa*), or good disposition (*ḥusn taṣarruf*).[152] Other terms consistently seem to note specific meanings, such as "poetry of the scribes" (*shiʿr kitābī*), "poetry of the jurists" (*shiʿr fuqahāʾ*), "good transition from the introduction to the main theme of a

---

151 One may attempt to reconstruct the basic features of Thaʿālibī's theoretical approach by examining scattered comments in the *Yatīma* and the *Tatimma*, and in his other minor anthologies. Of special importance is the chapter on Mutanabbī in the *Yatīma*. Thaʿālibī discusses *badīʿ* in books, such as *Ajnās al-tajnīs* (also known as *al-Mutashābih*) (Types of Paronomasia), *al-Kināya wa-l-taʿrīḍ* (Book of Hints and Allusion), and *Sajʿ al-manthur* (Rhyming Prose). Thaʿālibī further comments on the dichotomy of *lafẓ* and *maʿnā*, the relation between poetry and philosophy and between poetry and religion, the superiority of poetry over prose, and the debate between ancient (*qadīm*) and modern (*muḥdath*) poetry. One may also classify and identify the different levels of *sariqa* he observed. Moreover, Thaʿālibī's awareness of the impact of social, historical, political, and intellectual surroundings on a writer deserves note. The comparisons among the poets discussed here, the biographical introductions, and the occasional comments on poetry and prose, in the *Yatīma* and the *Tatimma*, feature recurring terms worthy of study. These terms need to be traced in other works of Thaʿālibī and in earlier and contemporary theoretical and practical books of criticism in order to evaluate and credit Thaʿālibī's contributions.

152 Later critics are more specific in using these terms; Khafājī (d. 466/1073) restricts *faṣāḥa* to verbal expression but considers *balāgha* as referring to both verbal expression and meaning; see Khafājī, *Sirr al-faṣāḥa*, ed. ʿAbd al-Mutaʿāl al-Ṣaʿīdī (Cairo: Maktabat Ṣubayḥ, 1953), 20. Most of these terms are defined in Ibn al-Athīr's (d. 637/1239) *al-Mathal al-sāʾir fī adab al-kātib wa-l-shāʿir*. For a preliminary study of Thaʿālibī's literary views, see Ḥāmid Ibrāhim al-Khaṭīb, *al-Thaʿālibī nāqidan fī Yatīmat al-dahr* (Cairo: Maṭbaʿat al-Amāna, 1988); and Jādir, *al-Thaʿālibī nāqidan wa-adīban* (Beirut: Dār al-Niḍāl, 1991).

qaṣīda" (*ḥusn takhalluṣ*), "good division between sections of a *qaṣīda*" (*ḥusn al-maqṭaʿ*), "employing a far-fetched metaphor" (*ibʿād al-istiʿāra*), "excellent formulation" (*iḥsān al-sabk*), "excellent hinting" (*ḥusn al-taʿrīḍ*), "ugly incipit" (*qubḥ al-maṭlaʿ*), "difficult wording" (*taʿwīṣ al-lafẓ*), and "complicated meaning" (*taʿqīd al-maʿnā*).

Most comments in the work are flattering; criticism is rare, as the book assembles "the elegant achievements of contemporary people" (*maḥāsin ahl al-ʿaṣr*), and inferior material would have thus been excluded. However, negative judgments occasionally accompany a litterateur's production. For example, describing Muḥammad b. Mūsā b. ʿImrān, Thaʿālibī says, "He has poetry as abundant as hair but paronomasia dominates it until its splendor almost vanishes and its water clouds, for every excess is nature's enemy."[153] Thaʿālibī usually reserves negative criticism for specific lines. He also dedicates a whole section to the faults of Mutanabbī, grouping together lines containing the same mistake under the same heading.[154] Among the frequent errors in poetry that Thaʿālibī points out is the use of an inappropriate word, phrase, figure of speech, motif, or description.[155]

In the introduction to the *Yatīma*, Thaʿālibī states that the book will touch on "similar, excellent and borrowed ideas" (*al-naẓāʾir wa-l-aḥāsin wa-l-sariqāt*). Indeed, a good part of the work is dedicated to the discussion of motifs or poetic ideas (*maʿānī*), literary borrowings or theft (*sariqāt*), and related concepts such as emulation (*muʿāraḍa*), allusion (*talmīḥ*), and literary or Qurʾānic quotations (*iqtibās*).[156] Almost every long entry in the work includes a section on the poet's literary borrowings or recurrent motifs in his poetry. But how does this interest in *sariqāt* become such a concern in a work whose declared focus is "the elegant achievements of contemporary people"?

Kamal Abu Deeb argues that the fourth/tenth century was distinguished by a strong movement of practical criticism, as most of the major theoretical

153 The original reads: *lahu shiʿrun ka-ʿadadi l-shaʿr ghalaba ʿalayhi l-tajnīsu ḥattā kāda yadhhabu bahāʾuhu wa-yakduru māʾuhu wa-kullu kathīrin ʿaduwwu l-ṭabīʿa*. *Y* 4:151. For similar judgments on prolific poets with little good poetry, see *Y* 3:340, 4:340, 382, 411, 441.

154 See *Y* 1:161.

155 For example, see *Y* 1:233, 237, 291, 3:163–4, 382; 4:130, 221–2, 384; *T* 64, 88.

156 On *muʿāraḍa*, see A. Schippers, "Muʿāraḍa," *EI2* VII:261; M. Peled, "On the Concept of Literary Influence in Classical Arabic Criticism," *Israel Oriental Studies* 11 (1991): 37–46; Gruendler, "Originality in Imitation: Two *Muʿāraḍas* by Ibn Darrāj al-Qasṭallī," in *al-Qantara* 29.2 (2008), 437–65. On *taḍmīn*, see Amidu Sanni, "On *Taḍmīn* (Enjambent) and Structural Coherence in Classical Arabic Poetry," *Bulletin of the School of Oriental and African Studies* 52 (1989), 463–6.

issues of literary criticism had been defined early in that century.[157] This practiced impulse, according to Abu Deeb, found its scope in the (*muḥdath-qadīm*) debate: in the difference between the traditional literary model and "modern" poetry. ʿAbbāsid poetry was steeped in the classical tradition and valued emulation and continuity; things did not change much in the subsequent century when Thaʿālibī was writing.[158] Abu Deeb argues that this practical critical approach attempted to bring into equilibrium Arabic poetry and critical theory, and it is in this light that he understands the preoccupation with *sariqāt*. According to him, *sariqāt* literature helped reveal traces of the classical model in the new poetry. Therefore, poets whose *sariqāt* are most often pointed out represented the *muḥdath* style, as opposed to those poets who continued to write within established tradition.[159]

Sariqa was not generally frowned upon. Wolfhart Heinrichs explains that for the Arab critics "there is a stable and limited pool of motifs or poetical themes (*maʿānī*) that is worthy to be expressed in poetry"; thus, *sariqa* became "a way of life for later poets."[160] Therefore, judgment on a particular *sariqa* depends on how elegantly a poet employed the borrowed meaning and whether the poet introduced a change or improvement in structure (*lafẓ*), content (*maʿnā*), or context (e.g., use in a different genre). Heinrichs defines the common denominator of a "good *sariqa*": "It endows one's poem with a quality of intertextuality which for the connoisseur enriches it beyond what its mere words say."[161] Therefore, *sariqāt* discussions, which sometimes fill complete works, reveal the genealogical origin of motifs and demonstrate their development toward greater sophistication.

From the preceding discussion, it appears that Thaʿālibī's preoccupation with *sariqāt* aimed to credit contemporary poets (*ahl al-ʿaṣr*) with the development and superb articulation of earlier poetic ideas.[162] The fact that most

157 Kamal Abu Deeb, "Literary Criticism," in *ʿAbbasid Belles-Lettres*, ed. Julia Ashtiany et al. (Cambridge: Cambridge University Press, 1990), 350.

158 This dependence on tradition and the tension between the classical model and its ulterior variations prompted Heinrichs and Sperl to describe ʿAbbāsid poetry as mannerist; see W. Heinrichs, "'Manierismus' in der arabischen Literatur," in *Islamwissenschaftliche Abhandlungen Fritz Meier zum sechzigsten Geburtstag*, ed. R. Gramlich (Wiesbaden: Franz Steiner, 1974), 127–8; S. Sperl, *Mannerism in Arabic Poetry* (Cambridge: Cambridge University Press, 1989), 158–64.

159 Abu Deeb, "Literary Criticism," 351.

160 W. Heinrichs, "An Evaluation of *Sariqa*," in *Quaderni di studi arabi* 5–6 (1987–8), 358.

161 Ibid., 360.

162 The same holds true for related concepts such as *iqtibās*, *taḍmīn*, and *muʿāraḍa*. For originality in the practice of *muʿāraḍa*, see Gruendler, "Originality in Imitation."

of the *sariqāt* in the *Yatīma* and *Tatimma* are compared to motifs from earlier periods supports this idea. Thaʿālibī's quest for *sariqāt* utilizes the works of major pre-Islamic, Islamic, and earlier ʿAbbāsid poets, such as Aws b. Ḥajar (d. 2/620), Labīd (d. 41/661), Abū Dihbil al-Jumaḥī (d. 63/682), Kuthayyir ʿAzza (d. 105/723), Abū Nuwās (d. 198/813), Abū Tammām (d. 231/845), Dīk al-Jinn al-Ḥimṣī (d. 235/849), Diʿbil al-Khuzāʿī (d. 246/860), Ibn al-Rūmī (d. 282/896), Buḥturī (d. 284/897), Ibn al-Muʿtazz (d. 296/908), and many lesser-known poets. Thaʿālibī comments on the amendments made, whether in form or in meaning, and he reveals, in most cases, the brilliance of his contemporaries. Noticeably, most comparisons are made to poets of the early ʿAbbāsid era, including Abū Tammām and Buḥturī. As is evident in the *Yatīma*, the poetry of this "class" eventually came to be accepted. By allowing the poetry of the second half of the fourth/tenth century to challenge the best production of the earlier periods,[163] the superiority of the contemporary poets could be established. In other words, by challenging the literary canon, Thaʿālibī expanded it to include the poets of his time. Often, both the *sāriq* and the *masrūq minhu* are contemporaries, but these cases were generally less tolerated.[164] Interestingly, *sariqāt* do not play an important role in the *Tatimma*, perhaps because Thaʿālibī had already made his point by the *Yatīma*'s success and wide circulation.

Another contemporary critic who shared Thaʿālibī's opinion on the poets of the fourth/tenth century is Ibn Fāris (d. 395/1004), who in a letter to Muḥammad b. Saʿīd al-Kātib that is preserved in the Yatīma, attacks conser-

163 Thaʿālibī in the introduction of the *Yatīma* divides the history of Arabic poetry into five periods: *jāhiliyyūn, islāmiyyūn, muḥdathūn, muwalladūn,* and *ʿaṣriyyūn*; see *Y* 1:16. This division into "classes" occurs elsewhere in his works. In *al-Tamthīl wa-l-muḥāḍara, al-Muntaḥal,* and *Lubāb al-ādāb,* he adds *mukhaḍramūn* to the list; see Thaʿālibī, *al-Tamthīl wa-l-muḥāḍara,* ed. ʿA. al-Ḥulw (Cairo: Dār Iḥyāʾ al-Kutub al-ʿArabiyya, 1961), 35–129; id., *al-Muntaḥal,* ed. Aḥmad Abū ʿAlī (Alexandria: al-Maṭbaʿa al-Tijāriyya, 1901), 5; id., *Lubāb al-ādāb,* ed. Ṣ. Q. Rashīd (Baghdad: Dār al-Shuʾūn al-Thaqāfiyya, 1988), 2:7. Among the examples he gives of *muḥdathūn* are Abū Tammām (d. 230/845) and Buḥturī (d. 284/897), while Kushājim (d. 360/970) and Ṣanawbarī (d. 334/945) are considered *muwallad.* In *al-Muntaḥal,* he specifies the *muwalladūn* to be the generation of Ibn al-Muʿtazz (d. 296/908). In the *Yatīma,* Thaʿālibī refers to the poet ʿAbdān al-Iṣbahānī as being "at the tail end of the *muwalladūn* and the beginning of the *ʿaṣriyyūn*"; see *Y* 3:300. ʿAbdān al-Iṣbahānī and Abū l-ʿAlāʾ al-Asadī (d. ca. 385/995) exchanged invective poems that are scattered in Thaʿālibī's works; see, for example, *Y* 3:302.

164 In addition to the poetry translated from Persian to Arabic and discussed earlier, Thaʿālibī includes one case of a shared motif between an Arabic line by Abū l-Ḥasan ʿAlī b. Muḥammad al-Badīhī and a Persian line by the poet al-Maʿrūfī; Thaʿālibī hesitates to label this *sariqa,* however, as in all cases of *sariqāt* and shared motifs in the *Yatīma* and the *Tatimma,* he cites both lines; see *Y* 3:344–5.

vative critics who rejected any innovation in the traditional literature of the Arabs, claiming that what the predecessors had introduced was so flawless that no new elements should be added. Ibn Fāris refutes this assertion and argues that there will always be room for inventing and producing new literary material. Thaʿālibī quotes Ibn Fāris:

> Is life not periods, and does not every period have its men? And are the sciences, after the preserved roots nothing but conceptions from illusions and products of the mind? And who confined literature to a certain period and restricted it to a delimited time? And why [should not] a later [author] observe as the earlier observed, so that he composes what [the earlier one] composed, compile what [the earlier] compiled, and hold in all this the same opinion? What do you say to the experts of our time when a rare judgment that did not occur to those who preceded them comes to them?… Why was it permissible after Abū Tammām to say poetry similar to his and it was not permissible to compile the like of his compilation? Why did you limit the wide [field], prohibit the permissible, forbid the admissible, and block a well-traveled path? [165]

This passage, and the rest of the letter, suggests that when Ibn Fāris was writing these words, Abū Tammām's poetry had already been credited, and imitating it was deemed permissible; however, the issue was the permissibility of compiling a book like *al-Ḥamāsa*. After this introduction, asserting that the poetry of the *muwalladūn* (in this context, the poets of the fourth/tenth century) can be, in many respects, more profound than that of their predecessors, Ibn Fāris cites examples from minor poets and compares them to earlier poetry, showing the excellence of the new. Ibn Fāris further composed a work that has been lost, *al-Ḥamāsa al-muḥdatha*, which, from its title, seems to have been an anthology of modern poetry.[166]

Thaʿālibī also collects recurrent motifs within the oeuvre of the same poet. The phrases he uses to indicate a *sariqa* or shared motif are *akhadhahu min, saraqahu min, aghāra ʿalayhi, wa-huwa min qawl, wa-fī maʿnāh*—all of which seem to carry the same meaning of "taking over" a line. Unsuccessful *sariqāt* are generally pointed out with a phrase such as: "he did not add to its meaning" (*lam yazid ʿalā maʿnāh*) or by indicating a better line.[167] Thaʿālibī also expresses the matter in harsher terms with phrases like "this is a plagiarism and not a

165 *Y* 3:400ff.

166 See Ibn al-Nadīm, *al-Fihrist*, ed. Riḍā Tajaddud (Beirut: Dār al-Masīra, 1988), 80.

167 *Y* 3:265.

literary borrowing" (*wa-hādhihi muṣālata lā sariqa*).[168] In contrast, successful *sariqāt* or excellent uses of specific motifs are introduced by "I have found nothing better in its meaning" (*wa-lam ajid aḥsana minhu fī maʿnāh*), "the best line in this meaning" (*wa-huwa aḥsan* [or *amlāḥ*] *mā qīla fī maʿnāh*), and "the best I heard" (*wa-huwa aḥsanu mā samiʿtu*).[169] Original motifs are singled out and celebrated with phrases like "unprecedented" (*lam yusbaq ilayhi*) and "unique" (*tafarrada bihi*).[170] Similar to *sariqāt* and original and unsuccessful motifs, Thaʿālibī identifies outstanding literary quotations (*iqtibās*).[171]

Compliments are not restricted to brilliant *sariqāt* or motifs but accompany any line, sentence, paragraph, or *qaṣīda* that would support Thaʿālibī's purpose of unveiling the achievements of contemporary poets. For instance, a number of stanzas are praised for deftly combining different thematic intentions or goals (*aghrāḍ*), such as entreaty and praise (*istiʿṭāf wa-madḥ*) or self-praise and praise (*iftikhār wa-madḥ*).[172] New figures of speech are identified,[173] along with successful familiar ones, which Thaʿālibī acknowledges throughout the work, commenting on the reasons for their success. In the process, Thaʿālibī sometimes clarifies a difficult metaphor, simile, or formulated idea by quoting a similar line.[174]

---

168 *Y* 1:145.

169 These are very common in the *Yatīma* and the *Tatimma*; see, for example, *Y* 1:43, 55, 64, 105, 108, 126, 150, 198, 206, 230, 271, 276, 278, 383, 2:268, 372, 376, 383, 395, 422, 3:138, 179, 210, 300, 4:74; *T* 29, 30, 34, 36, 40, 60, 102.

170 For examples, see *Y* 2:144, 346, 3:138, 165, 241, 347, 4:32, 347, 380; *T* 30, 217.

171 For example, see *Y* 1:40, 4:105, 212.

172 See *Y* 2:144, 161.

173 For example, Thaʿālibī praises Abū l-Fatḥ al-Bustī's new method of *tajnīs* called *al-mutashābih*; see *Y* 4:302.

174 For instance, see *Y* 1:73, 242.

Conclusion

The preceding chapters discussed the life and works of Abū Manṣūr al-Thaʿālibī and his contribution to the premodern literary anthology—a widely used, but relatively understudied, form of writing in Arabic literature. The study has focused on two of his works, the *Yatīmat al-dahr fī maḥāsin ahl al-ʿaṣr* (The Unique Pearl of the Elegant Achievements of Contemporary People) and its sequel, *Tatimmat al-Yatīma* (Completion of the *Yatīma*). Many of the poets find in these works their only mention. Consequently, both works rank among the most important sources for Arabic literature of the second half of the fourth/tenth century. Nevertheless, Thaʿālibī's contribution to literature transcends mere preservation: his original and innovative organization of the anthology by geographical region later became standard. Moreover, Thaʿālibī counts among the earliest literary critics who looked favorably upon contemporary authors and gave them due credit for the form and content (*lafẓ wa-maʿnā*) of their words.

I have traced the sources and compilatory process of the *Yatīma* and *Tatimma* and have situated them within the wider context of *adab* and literary anthology. This, I hope, provides scholars of anthology literature with a companion to the *Yatīma* and *Tatimma* and their author, in order to better understand and appreciate these two anthologies, and their scope, purpose, and legacy, as well as to judiciously use the information conveyed in them.

The provided sketch map of Arabic poetry anthologies reveals that although anthologies were compiled for different purposes in Arabic literature, some general observations can be made without violating the particular context, agenda, or goal of each work. First, the vast amount of literature composed in Arabic called for abridgments and selections to facilitate study, teaching, quoting, and passing it down to subsequent generations. Second, early anthologies focused on the *qaṣīda* form were compiled for philological and/or literary importance and served an educational purpose. Third, the use of poetry and artistic prose as a mark of culture in official and private correspondences in the fourth/tenth century helped create a wider audience for both mono- and multithematic anthologies. Finally, Arabic anthologies were not always secondary texts selected from written works. Rather, with Thaʿālibī and other subsequent anthologists concerned with contemporary poetry, they became a primary way to publish original literature, especially that of nonprofessional poets who did not produce circulating *dīwāns*.

 | DOI 10.1163/9789004317352_007

The study also opens a direct window on to the workshop of an anthologist from the second half of the fourth/tenth century; how Thaʿālibī selected from the oeuvres of his contemporaries; which sources he used; how he sought, recorded, memorized, misplaced, and sometimes lost or forgot his selections; how he scrutinized the authenticity of the material, accepting, questioning, or rejecting its attribution; and the errors and inconsistencies that resulted from the process. Thaʿālibī was aware of his methodology in the *Yatīma* and *Tatimma*, and he gave special attention to their organization. Under each geographical region, Thaʿālibī defines the chapters by three criteria: individual literary figures, patrons and dynastic families, and cities or smaller geographical regions. The material in each chapter is arranged biographically and follows a relation of "proximity," by which the entries on related personalities are placed close to each other. I argued that this organization was not arbitrarily chosen by Thaʿālibī or favored merely for its practicality; rather, it was the result of a critical awareness of the influence of a poet's social, political, and intellectual environment on his literary oeuvre. The anthologies' internal cohesion is enhanced by a sophisticated system of cross-references and references to earlier editions and to other works of Thaʿālibī.

With respect to the arrangement and content of the single entry in the *Yatīma* and *Tatimma*, much of the biographical information in both works appears in the preface of each entry, where the litterateur and his oeuvre are placed into geographical, social, and historical context. The *Yatīma* documents courtly life in the fourth/tenth century through accounts on admission to and departure from courts, and the litterateurs' relations with one another and with their patrons. Finally, Thaʿālibī is shown to boast the excellence of his contemporaries through his comments on the selected material. He compares the contemporary literary production to that of earlier periods, illustrating in most cases the superiority of the former.

Despite the foregoing chapters, much work remains to be done to give both Thaʿālibī and his work their due. The need for a critical edition of the *Yatīma* and other works by Thaʿālibī cannot be overstated. While focusing on the sources, compilation, and organization of the *Yatīma* and *Tatimma*, Thaʿālibī's activity as a "practical critic" needs to be investigated in his other works. Furthermore, the *Yatīma* and *Tatimma* present a panorama of Arabic literature in Thaʿālibī's time, and their content is an apt sample for studying the trends and movements of Arabic poetry and prose in the second half of the fourth/tenth century and the beginning of the fifth/eleventh century. A comparative study between the *Yatīma* and the *Tatimma* and later geographical anthologies could help determine the value, nature, and scope of Thaʿālibī's impact on the field of Arabic anthology literature. Finally, no more fitting words could conclude this book than echoing those of Thaʿālibī's own apology for not giving the first edition of the *Yatīma* its due: "It was achieved in a manner similar to the speed of the traveler and the firebrand of the hasty, but, it satisfied a need of mine."[1]

1 Y 1:17–18.

APPENDIX 1

Outline of *Yatīmat al-dahr* and *Tatimmat al-Yatīma*

Yatīmat al-dahr

Preface by Thaʿālibī		خطبة الثعالبي
The First Region: The beautiful poetry of the Ḥamdānids and their poets, and others from the people of Syria and the neighboring [lands] of Egypt, and Mawṣil, and highlights from their accounts	I	القسم الأوّل: في محاسن أشعار آل حمدان وشعرائهم وغيرهم من أهل الشام وما يجاورها من مصر والموصل ولمع من أخبارهم
On [the] preference for Syrian poets over the poets of all regions	1	في فضل شعراء الشام على سائر البلدان
Mention of Sayf al-Dawla Abū l-Ḥasan ʿAlī b. Ḥamdān —and the telling of part of his accounts, and clever curiosities from his poetry	2	في ذكر سيف الدولة أبي الحسن عليّ بن حمدان وسياقة قطعة من أخباره وملح أشعاره
Mention of Abū Firās al-Ḥārith b. Saʿīd—the best of his accounts and poems	3	في ذكر أبي فراس الحارث بن سعيد وغرر أخباره وأشعاره
The clever curiosities of the Ḥamdānids, the amīrs of Syria, their judges and secretaries	4	في ملح آل حمدان أمراء الشام وقضاتها وكتّابها
Mention of Abū l-Ṭayyib al-Mutanabbī, his pros and cons [of his poetry]	5	في ذكر أبي الطيّب المتنبّي وما له وما عليه
Mention of al-Nāmī, al-Nāshiʾ, and al-Zāhī, and excerpts from their best poems	6	في ذكر النامي والناشئ والزاهي وإخراج غرر أشعارهم
Abū l-Faraj al-Babbaghāʾ—his best prose and poetry	7	أبو الفرج الببّغاء وغرر نثره ونظمه
Mention of Khalīʿ al-Shāmī, Wắwāʾ al-Dimashqī, and Abū Ṭālib al-Raqqī	8	في ذكر الخليع الشامي والوأواء الدمشقي وأبي طالب الرقّي
The clever curiosities of the inhabitants of Syria, Egypt, and al-Maghrib, and their unusual poems and admirable anecdotes	9	ملح أهل الشام ومصر والمغرب وطرف أشعارهم ونوادرهم
Mention of the poets of Mawṣil and the best of their poems	10	في ذكر شعراء الموصل وغرر أشعارهم

 | DOI 10.1163/9789004317352_008

The Second Region: On the Būyid kings and their poets	القسم الثاني: في ملوك آل بويه وشعرائهم	II
Mention [of the Būyid kings] and extracts from the clever curiosities of their poetry	في ذكرهم وما أُخرج من ملح أشعارهم	1
Mention of Muhallabī, the vizier—the clever curiosities of his accounts and the gemstones of his passages and poems	في ذكر المهلّبي الوزير وملح أخباره وفصوص فصوله وأشعاره	2
Mention of Abū Isḥāq al-Ṣābī and the beauties of his discourse	في ذكر أبي إسحاق الصابي ومحاسن كلامه	3
Mention of three Būyid vizierlike scribes: Abū l-Qāsim ʿAbd al-ʿAzīz b. Yūsuf, Abū Aḥmad ʿAbd al-Raḥmān b. al-Faḍl al-Shīrāzī, and Abū l-Qāsim ʿAlī b. al-Qāsim al-Qāshānī	في ذكر ثلاثة من كتّاب آل بويه يجرون مجرى الوزراء: أبو القاسم عبد العزيز بن يوسف وأبو أحمد عبد الرحمن بن الفضل الشيرازي وأبو القاسم عليّ بن القاسم القاشاني	4
The poets of Baṣra and their beautiful discourse	في شعراء البصرة ومحاسن كلامهم	5
A few poets of Iraq and its districts, save for Baghdad, and the telling of their clever curiosities	في نفر من شعراء العراق ونواحيه سوى بغداد وسياقة ملحهم	6
Mention of some poets from Baghdad and their beautiful poetry	في ذكر قوم من شعراء بغداد ومحاسن أشعارهم	7
On scatterings and highlights from the clever curiosities of minor poets of the inhabitants of Baghdad and its suburbs, those who immigrated to it from faraway places, and those who have resided there	في تفاريق ولمع من ملح المقلّين من أهل بغداد ونواحيها والطارئين عليها من الآفاق والمقيمين بها	8
Extracts from the collection of poems of the Iraqis and others in praise of the vizier Sābūr b. Ardashīr	فيما أُخرج من مجموع أشعار أهل العراق وغيرهم في الوزير أبي نصر سابور بن أردشير	9
Mention of al-Sharīf Abū l-Ḥasan al-Raḍī al-Mūsawī and the best of his poetry	في ذكر الشريف أبي الحسن الرضي الموسوي وغرر من شعره	10
The Third Region: On the clever curiosities of the inhabitants of Jibāl, Fārs, Jurjān, and Ṭabaristān by the viziers, secretaries, judges, and poets of the Daylamī dynasty, in addition to the rest of the nobles and foreigners, as well as their accounts and best discourses	القسم الثالث: يشتمل على ملح أشعار أهل الجبال وفارس وجرجان وطبرستان من وزراء الدولة الديلمية وكتّابها وقضاتها وشعرائها وسائر فضلائها وغربائها وما ينضاف إليها من أخبارهم وغرر ألفاظهم	III
Ibn al-ʿAmīd and the presentation of highlights of his descriptions and accounts, and his best prose and poetry	في ذكر ابن العميد وإيراد لمع من أوصافه وأخباره وغرر من نثره ونظمه	1

Mention of his son, Abū al-Fatḥ Dhū l-Kifāyatayn, and the choice of part of his unusual accounts and the clever curiosities among his thoughts	في ذكر ابنه أبي الفتح ذي الكفايتين والأخذ بطَرَف من طُرف أخباره ومُلح بنات أفكاره	2
Mention of Ṣāḥib Abū l-Qāsim Ismāʿīl b. ʿAbbād, the presentation of highlights of his accounts, and his best poetry and prose	في ذكر الصاحب أبي القاسم إسماعيل بن عبّاد وإيراد لمع من أخباره وغرر من نظمه ونثره	3
Mention of Abū l-ʿAbbās Aḥmad b. Ibrāhīm al-Ḍabbī and the clever curiosities of his poetry and prose	في ذكر أبي العبّاس أحمد بن إبراهيم الضبّي وملح من نظمه ونثره	4
On the beautiful poems of contemporaries from Iṣbahān	في محاسن أشعار أهل العصر من أهل إصبهان	5
Mention of the poets who came to Ṣāḥib b. ʿAbbād from faraway lands, except those mentioned among the inhabitants of Jurjān and Ṭabaristān (for they are assigned a separate chapter in the third section) and Abū Ṭālib al-Ma'mūnī, Abū Bakr al-Khwārizmī, and Badīʿ al-Zamān al-Hamadhānī (for each of them is mentioned in his place in the fourth section)	في ذكر الشعراء الطارئين على حضرة الصاحب من الآفاق سوى من يقع ذكره منهم في أهل خراسان وطبرستان فإنّ لهم بابًا مفردًا في هذا الربع الثالث، وسوى أبي طالب المأموني وأبي بكر الخوارزمي وبديع الزمان أبي الفضل الهمذاني فإنّ لذكر كلّ منهم مكانًا في الربع الرابع	6
Mention of all the poets of al-Jabal and those who went there from Iraq and other places, and the clever curiosities of their accounts and poems	في ذكر سائر شعراء الجبل والطارئين عليها من العراق وغيرها وملح أخبارهم وأشعارهم	7
Mention of those who meet the condition of this book among the people of Fārs and Ahwāz, with the exception of those already mentioned among the residents of Iraq (like ʿAbd al-ʿAzīz b. Yūsuf and Abū Ahmad al-Shīrāzī) and the exception of those who will be mentioned in the section on those who went to Khurāsān	في ذكر من هم شرط الكتّاب من أهل فارس والأهواز سوى من تقدّم منهم ذكرهم في ساكني العراق كعبد العزيز بن يوسف وأبي أحمد الشيرازي وسوى من يتأخر ذكرهم في الطارئين على خراسان	8
Mention of those who meet the condition of the book among the inhabitants of Jurjān and Ṭabaristān	ذكر من هم شرط الكتّاب من أهل جرجان وطبرستان	9
Mention of al-amīr al-sayyid Shams al-Maʿālī Qābūs b. Wushmgīr and the presentation of extracts revealing the natural disposition of his glory and casting the sea of his knowledge to the tongue of his merit	في ذكر الأمير السيّد شمس المعالي قابوس بن وشمكير وإيراد نُبذ ممّا أسفر عنه طبع مجده وألقاه بحر علمه على لسان فضله	10

The Fourth Region: On the beautiful poetry of the inhabitants of Khurāsān and Transoxania among chancellery writing of the Sāmānid and Ghaznavid dynasties, and those who came to Bukhārā from far away, and its regional officials and their elegant accounts	IV	القسم الرابع: في محاسن أشعار أهل خراسان وما وراء النهر من إنشاء الدولة السامانيّة والغزنيّة والطارئين على الحضرة ببخارى من الآفاق والمتصرّفين على أعمالها وما يستظرف من أخبارهم
The presentation of beauties and novelties among the accounts and poems of people who slightly preceded our contemporaries among the subjects of the Sāmānid dynasty and the chancellery writing of the court of Bukhāra and all the Khurāsānī poets who could be treated as contemporaries because of their recency	1	في إيراد محاسن وطرف من أخبار وأشعار قوم سبقوا أهل عصرنا هذا قليلاً وتقدّموهم يسيرًا من أبناء الدولة السامانيّة وإنشاء الحضرة البخاريّة وسائر شعراء خراسان الذين هم، مع قرب العهد، في حكم أهل العصر
Mention of the contemporaries who are residents, visitors, and regional officials in the court of Bukhāra, and the fulfillment of the conditions of this work with clever curiosities from their poems and the unusual coined sayings in their accounts	2	في ذكر العصريّين المقيمين بالحضرة البخاريّة والطارئين عليها والمتصرّفين في أعمالها وتوفية الكتاب شرطه من مُلح أشعارهم وطُرف أخبارهم
Ma'mūnī and Wāthiqī and their beautiful poetry and accounts	3	في ذكر المأموني والواثقي ومحاسن أشعارهما وأخبارهما
The best [outcome] of the nobles of Khwārizm	4	في غرر فضلاء خوارزم
Mention of Abū l-Faḍl al-Hamadhānī, his condition and attributes, and his beautiful prose and poetry	5	في ذكر أبي الفضل الهمذاني وحاله ووصفه ومحاسن نثره ونظمه
Mention of Abū l-Fatḥ al-Bustī and the rest of the inhabitants of Bust and Sijistān, and the presentation of their best [literary production]	6	في ذكر أبي الفتح البستي وسائر أهل بست وسجستان وإيراد غررهم
Scattered pieces from the clever curiosities of the inhabitants of Khurāsān, except for Nīshāpūr	7	في تفاريق من ملح أهل بلاد خراسان سوى نيسابور
Mention of al-amīr Abū l-Faḍl ʿUbayd Allāh b. Aḥmad al-Mīkālī and the presentation of his beautiful prose and poetry	8	في ذكر الأمير أبي الفضل عبيد الله بن أحمد الميكالي وإيراد محاسن من نثره ونظمه

Mention of those who came to Nīshāpūr from various lands, according to their different ranking—those who left it again and others who settled—and the telling of the clever curiosities from their speech, except those mentioned in the other bābs

9 في ذكر الطارئين على نيسابور من بلدان شتّى على اختلاف مراتبهم فمنهم من فارقها ومنهم من استوطنها، وسياقة الملح من كلامهم سوى ما تقدّم ذكره منهم في سائر الأبواب

The Nīshāpūrīs whose elegant sayings belong to this bāb and the writers of their subtleties and novelties

10 في ذكر النيسابوريّين الذين تقع محاسن أقوالهم في هذا الباب وكتبة لطائفهم وظرائفهم

Tatimmat Yatīmat al-dahr

Completion of the first section on the beauties of the inhabitants of Syria and al-Jazīra	تتمّة القسم الأوّل: في محاسن أهل الشام والجزيرة	I
Completion of the second region on the beauties of the Iraqīs—rather, their best achievements and clever related curiosities	تتمّة القسم الثاني: في محاسن أشعار أهل العراق بل أحاسنها وما يتّصل بها من ملح أخبارهم	II
Completion of the third region on the beauties of the inhabitants of Rayy, Hamadhān, Iṣbahān, the rest of the Jabal lands, and neighboring lands in Jurjān and Ṭabaristān	تتمّة القسم الثالث: في محاسن أهل الريّ وهمذان وإصبهان وسائر بلاد الجبل وما يجاورها من جرجان وطبرستان	III
Completion of the fourth region on the beauties of Khurāsānīs and the rest of the lands connected to it	تتمّة القسم الرابع: في محاسن أهل خراسان وما يتّصل بها من سائر البلدان	IV
Mention of the inhabitants of Nīshāpūr	ذكر أهل نيسابور	
Mention of the rest of the inhabitants of the suburbs of Nīshāpūr	ذكر سائر أهل نواحي نيسابور	
The rest of the inhabitants of Khurāsān	سائر أهل بلاد خراسان	
Mention of the pillars of the dynasty and the prominent figures of the court [in Bukhāra], the administrative officials in and from it, those who served it, and the choice of the best flowers of their poetry and fruit of their prose	ذكر أركان الدولة وأعيان الحضرة والمتصرّفين بها ومنها والمنتسبين إلى خدمتها واختيار غرر من أنوار نظمهم وثمار نثرهم	
Conclusion of the work: This includes from all four regions the mention of uncategorized people, of different dates, who have not been given their due in the proper order	خاتمة الكتاب: يشتمل على ذكر أقوامٍ مختلفي الترتيب متفاوتي التاريخ غير معطين حقوقهم من التقديم والتأخير وهم من كلّ الأقسام الأربعة	V

APPENDIX 2

Sources of *Yatīmat al-dahr*

Written Sources

TABLE 2.1 *Dīwāns*

Poet	Region	Reference.
Abū l-ʿAbbās Aḥmad b. Muḥammad al-Nāmī (d. 399/1009)	I	1:241
Abū l-Faraj Muḥammad b. Aḥmad al-Waʾwāʾ (d. 385/995)	I	1:289
al-Sarī al-Raffāʾ (d. 366/976)	I	2:117, 119
Kushājim (360/970)	I	2:118
al-Khālidiyyān (d. 380/990), (d. 371/981)	I	2:118
Tāj al-Dawla Abū l-Ḥusayn Aḥmad b. ʿAḍud al-Dawla	II	2:220
Abū l-Qāsim ʿAlī b. Muḥammad b. Dāwūd b. Fahm al-Qāḍī al-Tanūkhī (d. ca 352)	II	2:346
Abū Naṣr ʿAbd al-ʿAzīz b. Muḥammad b. Nubāta al-Saʿdī (d. 405/1014)	II	2:380
Abū l-Ḥasan Muḥammad b. ʿAbdallāh b. Muḥammad b. Sukkara al-Hāshimī (d. 385/995)	II	3:3
Abū ʿAbdallāh al-Ḥusayn b. Aḥmad b. al-Ḥajjāj (d. 391/1001)	II	3:31
Abū Muḥammad ʿAbdallāh b. Aḥmad al-Khāzin al-Iṣbahānī (d. ca. 383/993)	III	3:330
Abū l-Ḥasan al-Ghuwayrī (d. ca. 385/995)	III	3:340
Abū l-Qāsim ʿAbd al-Ṣamad b. Bābak (d. 410/1020)	III	3:379
Abū l-Ḥasan ʿAlī b. al-Ḥasan al-Laḥḥām (d. ca. 363/973)	IV	4:102
Abū Ṭālib ʿAbd al-Salām b. al-Ḥusayn al-Maʾmūnī (d. 383/993)	IV	4:172
Abū l-Fatḥ Aḥmad b. Muḥammad b. Yūsuf al-Kātib	IV	4:439
Abū ʿAbdallāh al-Ghawwāṣ	IV	4:442

TABLE 2.2 *Books*

Title	Region	Reference
al-Tājī fī akhbār Āl Buwayh by Abū Isḥāq Ibrāhīm b. Hilāl al-Ṣābī (d. 384/994)[1]	I, II, III	1:117 2:226–7 3:121–2 3:159
al-Fasr (*Sharḥ Dīwān al-Mutanabbī*) by Abū l-Fatḥ ʿUthmān Ibn Jinnī (d. 392/1002)	I	1:133 (Ibn Jinnī [IJ], *al-Fasr*, 2:784), 1:134 (IJ 3:402), 1:134 (IJ 3:385–6), 1:134 (IJ 3:710), 1:135 (IJ 3:763), 1:135 (IJ 3:711), 1:145 (IJ 3:329), 1:153 (IJ 1:538), 1:166 (IJ 3:196), 1:188 (IJ 3:597), 1:197 (IJ 3:504), 1:198 (IJ 2:655), 1:201 (IJ 1:812), 1:213 (IJ 3:380), 1:219 (IJ 2:804), 1:224 (IJ 3:570), 1:237 (IJ 3:701), 2:120 (IJ 329)
al-Wasāṭa bayna l-Mutanabbī wa-khuṣūmihi by ʿAlī b. ʿAbd al-ʿAzīz al-Jurjānī (d. 392/1002)	I, III	1:134 (Jurjānī [J], al-*Wasāṭa bayna l-Mutanabbī wa-khuṣūmih*, 337–8), 1:167 (J, 180), 1:173 (J, 468), 1:178 (J, 181), 1:179 (J, 95), 1:189 (J, 189), 1:197 (J, 383), 2:119–20 (J, 39), 4:4–7 (J, 1–4)
al-Kashf ʿan masāwiʾ shiʿr al-Mutanabbī by Ṣāḥib b. ʿAbbād (d. 385/995)	I	1:162 (Ṣāḥib b. ʿAbbād [Ṣ], *al-Khashf ʿan masāwiʾ shiʿr al-Mutanabbī*, 40), 1:162–3 (Ṣ, 62–3), 1:172 (Ṣ, 60), 1:175 (Ṣ, 63), 1:175 (Ṣ, 49), 1:175 (Ṣ, 54), 1:177 (Ṣ, 50), 1:177 (Ṣ, 58), 1:177 (Ṣ, 64), 1:177 (Ṣ, 66), 1:178 (Ṣ, 49), 1:181 (Ṣ, 48), 1:181 (Ṣ, 52), 1:183 (Ṣ, 58–9), 1:184 (Ṣ, 45–6), 1:187 (Ṣ, 45)
al-Rūznāmja by Ṣāḥib b. ʿAbbād (d. 385/995)[2]	I, III	2:227–9, 229–30, 230, 231, 3:120–21, 121

1 The work is considered lost except for a part that survives in a unique manuscript (Maktabat Jāmiʿat al-Duwal al-ʿArabiyya 145) under the title *al-Muntazaʿ min Kitāb al-Tājī*; it was edited by Muḥammad Ḥusayn al-Zubaydī (Baghdad: Dār al-Ḥurriyya, 1977).

2 The work is lost, but excerpts from it survive in various *adab* works. Muḥammad Ḥ. Āl Yāsīn collected several of these (among other texts by Ṣāḥib) and published them as *al-Amthāl al-sāʾira min shiʿr al-Mutanabbī wa-l-Rūznāmjah*, ed. M. Ḥ. Āl Yāsīn (Baghdad: Maktabat al-Nahḍa, 1965). The work, based on surviving texts, is al-Ṣāḥib's memoirs sent to Ibn al-ʿAmīd from his visit to Baghdad and his stay at the court of Muhallabī.

Title	Region	Reference
al-Muwāzana bayna shiʿr Abī Tammām wa-l-Buḥturī by al-Ḥasan b. Bishr al-Āmidī (d. 370/981 or 982)	I	1:120
Rawāʾiʿ al-tawjīhāt fī badāʾiʿ al-tashbīhāt by Abū Saʿd Naṣr b, Yaʿqūb al-Dīnawarī (d. before 429/1037)[3]	I	1:249
al-Tuḥaf wa-l-ẓuraf by Ibn Labīb (*ghulām* Abū l-Faraj al-Babbaghāʾ)[4]	I	1:305
Ashʿār al-nudamāʾ by Abū l-Ḥasan Muḥammad b. Aḥmad al-Ifrīqī al-Mutayyam[5]	I	1:306
Ḥāṭib layl by Abū l-Ḥusayn ʿAlī b. Aḥmad b. ʿAbdān[6]	I, II	1:250, 2:365
Siḥr al-balāgha by al-Thaʿālibī	II	2:235
al-Faraj baʿda l-shidda by al-Qāḍī al-Tanūkhī (d. 384/994)	II	2:347
Ḥadīqat al-ḥadaq by Hārūn b. Aḥmad al-Ṣaymarī[7]	II	2:219
A work by Ṣāḥib b. ʿAbbād (d. 385/995)	II	2:216

3 The work is lost. It is mentioned, in addition to the *Yatīma*, in Ṣafadī, *al-Wāfī bi-l-wafayāt*, ed. Aḥmad al-Arnāʾūṭ and Turkī Muṣṭafā (Beirut: Dār Iḥyāʾ al-Turāth al-ʿArabī, 2000), 27:57. Thaʿālibī adds in the *Yatīma* that Abū Saʿd sent a copy of it to Ṣāḥib b. ʿAbbād together with another book and a poem (*qaṣīda*), and was well received; see *Y* 4:389.

4 Little is known about this work or its author. Another work by a certain Muḥammad b. Aḥmad b. ʿAbd al-Mughīth al-Tamīmī (d. 378/988 or 989) that carries the same title survives but seems to be different, as it does not include Thaʿālibī's quotations in *al-Yatīma*; see Tamīmī, *al-Tuḥaf wa-l-ẓuraf*, ed. ʿInād Ismāʿīl (Baghdad: al-Jāmiʿa al-Mustanṣiriyya, 1991).

5 One of Thaʿālibī's oral sources, a physician and astrologer whom Thaʿālibī met in Bukhārā; see *Y* 4:157. His *Ashʿār al-Nudamāʾ* is lost.

6 The work is lost. The title, however, is a famous proverb that, as Thaʿālibī explains in *Thimār al-qulūb*, refers to a person who collects anything he finds (e.g., *ḥāṭib al-layl*, the nighttime wood gatherer); see *Thimār al-qulūb fī-l-muḍāf wa-l-mansūb*, ed. Muḥammad Abū l-Faḍl Ibrāhīm (Cairo: Dār Nahḍat Miṣr, 1965), 639–40, see also al-ʿAskarī, *Jamharat al-amthāl*, ed. M. A. Ibrāhīm (Cairo: al-Muʾassasa al-ʿArabiyya al-Ḥadītha, 1964), 1:441.

7 Little is known about this work other than what is mentioned in the *Yatīma*. One other quotation analyzing a line by Aʿshā survives in a later work: Zayn al-Dīn al-Bayyāḍī (d. 877/1472), *al-Ṣirāṭ al-mustaqīm ilā mustaḥiqqī al-taqdīm*, ed. M. B. al-Bahbūdī (Tehran: Al-Maktaba al-Murtaḍawiyya, 1964), 3:48. Ṣaymarī could be related to Abū Jaʿfar Muḥammad b. Aḥmad al-Ṣaymarī (d. 339/950), *wazīr* Muʿizz al-Dawla, or the *qāḍī* Aḥmad b. Sayyār al-Ṣaymarī (d. 368/978), who was appointed in Baghdad, then Khurāsān. We know that Hārūn b. Aḥmad al-Ṣaymarī came to Nīshāpūr, where he met Thaʿālibī and Abū l-Faḍl al-Mīkālī. Another Hārūn b. Jaʿfar al-Ṣaymarī appears as an oral source of Thaʿālibī and has a connection to Mīkālī; the two could be the same person. See *Y* 3:414.

TABLE 2.2 *Books (cont.)*

Title	Region	Reference
Tahdhīb al-taʾrīkh by ʿAlī b. ʿAbd al-ʿAzīz al-Jurjānī (d. 392/1002)[8]	III	4:7–9
Risāla fī l-ṭibb by Ṣāḥib b. ʿAbbād (d. 385/995)	III	3:204–6
Mulaḥ al-khawāṭir wa-subaḥ al-Jawāhir by Abū l-Faḍl al-Mīkālī (d. 436/1044–5)[9]	III	3:243
Kitāb Iṣbahān by Abū ʿAbdallāh Ḥamza b. al-Ḥusayn al-Iṣbahānī (d. 360/970 or 971)[10]	III	3:299
Safīna by Abū Muḥammad ʿAbdallāh b. Ismāʿīl al-Mīkālī (?)[11]	III	3:421
A work by Abū ʿAlī al-Salāmī	IV	4:95

8 This work unfortunately is lost. What Thaʿālibī quotes in the *Yatīma* seems to be the only surviving excerpt from it.

9 The work is lost, and the quotation in *Yatīmat al-dahr* is probably the only surviving excerpt of it. The title in *al-Wāfī bi-l-wafayāt* is *Mulaḥ al-khawāṭir wa-munaḥ al-jawāhir*; see Ṣafadī, *al-Wāfī bi-l-wafayāt*, 19:232.

10 The work is lost, but many excerpts from it survive in Rāfiʿī, *Kitāb al-tadwīn fī akhbār Qazwīn*, ed. ʿAzīz Allāh al-ʿUṭāridī (Beirut: Dār al-Kutub al-ʿIlmiyya, 1987), 1:47, 51, 69, 2:168, 482, 4:45; Abū Nuʿaym al-Iṣbahānī, *Dhikr akhbār Iṣbahān*, ed. Sven Dedering (Leiden: Brill, 1931–4), 1:14, 7:331; Ḥamawī, *Muʿjam al-udabāʾ: Irshād al-arīb ilā maʿrifat al-adīb*, ed. Iḥsān ʿAbbās (Beirut: Dār al-Gharb al-Islāmī, 1993), 59, 128–9, 163, 227, 263–4, 274, 293, 407–8, 432, 540, 621, 758, 766, 873–6, 1260, 1307, 1579, 1753, 1976, 1981, 2229, 2230, 2247, 2311, 2314, 2436–8; Ṣafadī, *al-Wāfī bi-l-wafayāt*, 1:764, 27:264, 29:12.

11 The caliph al-Muqtadir put him in charge of the *dīwān*; for information on him, see *Y* 4:418–19; Bākharzī, *Dumyat al-qaṣr wa ʿuṣrat ahl al-ʿaṣr*, ed. Muḥammad al-Ṭūnjī (Beirut: Dār al-Jīl, 1993), 2:953; Ibn al-ʿImād, *Shadharāt al-dhahab* (Cairo: Maktabat al-Qudsī, 1931–2), 3:41.

Oral/Aural Sources

TABLE 2.4 *Direct transmission*

Literary Figure	Region	Rf.
Abū l-Qāsim al-Muẓaffar b. ʿAlī al-Ṭabasī	I	1:240
Abū Bakr al-Khwārizmī	III	2:265
	III	3:217
Abū l-Ḥasan Aḥmad b. al-Muʾammal	IV	4:148, 158
Abū Ṭālib ʿAbd al-Salām b. al-Ḥusayn al-Maʾmūnī	IV	4:172
Abū al-Ghaṭārīf ʿImlāq b. Ghaydāq	IV	4:412
Abū l-Qāsim al-Ulaymānī	IV	4:144
Abū l-Ḥasan Muḥammad b. Aḥmad al-Mutayyam al-Ifrīqī	IV	4:157
Abū l-ʿAbbās al-ʿAlawī al-Hamadānī	IV	4:292
Abū Manṣūr Aḥmad b. Muḥammad	IV	4:408
Abū ʿAlī Muḥammad b. ʿUmar al-Zāhir	IV	4:415
Abū l-Qāsim Yaḥyā b. ʿAlī al-Bukhārī	IV	4:415
Abū l-Ḥusayn Muḥammad b. al-Ḥusayn al-Fārisī	IV	4:386
al-Qāḍī Abū Bakr ʿAbdallāh b. Muḥammad al-Bustī	IV	4:424
Abū Naṣr Aḥmad b. ʿAlī al-Zawzanī	IV	4:448
Abū l-Muʿallā Mājid b. al-Ṣalt (Nāqid al-Kalām al-Yamānī)	IV	4:412

TABLE 2.5 *Indirect transmission*

Guarantors and Transmitters	Material	Region	Rf.
ʿAbd al-Ṣamad b. Wahb al-Miṣrī	Poetry by Abū Naṣr b. Abī l-Fatḥ Kushājim	I	1:305
	Poetry by *al-qāḍī* Abū l-Ḥasan ʿAlī b. al-Nuʿmān	I	1:400–401
	Poetry by Abū Isḥāq b. Aḥmad al-Mārdīnī	I	1:401
	Poetry by Abū ʿUbaydallāh Muḥammad b. al-Nuʿmān	I	1:401
	Poetry by Ṣāliḥ b. Muʾnis	I	1:403
	Poetry by Abū Hurayra Aḥmad b. ʿAbdallāh b. Abī ʿIṣām	I	1:419
	Poetry by Abū l-Ḥasan al-Laṭīm	I	1:424
	Poetry by Abū Sulaymān b. Ḥassān al-Nuṣaybī	I	1:425
	Poetry by Abū l-Qāsim Aḥmad b. Muḥammad b. Ṭabāṭabā al-Ḥusaynī al-Rassī	I	1:428
	Poetry by Abū l-ʿAbbās Aḥmad b. Marwān b. Ḥammād al-Naḥwī	I	1:451
Abū ʿAlī Muḥammad b. ʿUmar al-Balkhī al-Zāhir	Poetry by *al-qāḍī* Abū l-Faraj Salāma b. Baḥr	I	1:116
	Poetry by Abū Muḥammad ʿAbdallāh b. ʿUmar b. Muḥammad al-Fayyāḍ	I	1:119
	Poetry by Tallaʿfarī	I	1:300
	Poetry by ʿAlī b. Muḥammad al-Shāshī	I	1:301
	Poetry by Abū Naṣr b. Abī l-Fatḥ b. Kushājim	I	1:301, 303
	Poetry by al-Mamshūq al-Shāmī	I	1:306
	Poetry by al-Ḥasan b. ʿAbd al-Raḥīm al-Zalāzilī (d. 374/984)	I	1:307

Guarantors and Transmitters	Material	Region	Rf.
	Poetry by Abū l-Ḥasan ʿAlī b. Muḥammad al-Anṭākī	I	1:307
	Poetry by Abū Ṣāliḥ b. Rashdīn al-Kātib	I	1:415
	Poetry by Aḥmad b. Muḥammad al-ʿAwfī	I	1:417
	Poetry by Abū l-Qāsim ʿAlī b. Bishr al-Kātib	I	1:420
	Ḥasan b. Khallād	I	1:423
	Abū ʿAbdallāh al-Ḥusayn b. Ibrāhim b. Aḥmad	I	1:431
	Abū l-Ḥasan al-ʿAqīlī	I	1:431
	Poetry by Aḥmad b. Muḥammad al-Kaḥḥāl	I	1:434
	Poetry by Muḥammad b. ʿĀṣīm al-Mawqifī	I	1:442
	Poetry by Abū l-Fatḥ al-Bustī	I	1:445
	Akhbār about Abū l-Qāsim ʿAlī b. Bishr	I	1:422
Abū Bakr al-Khwārizmī	Poetry by Sayf al-Dawla al-Ḥamdānī	I	1:45
	Poetry by a Ḥamdānid	I	1:105
	Poetry by Abū l-Fatḥ al-Baktimurī b. al-Kātib	I	1:120
	Poetry by Abū l-Faraj al-ʿIjlī	I	1:122
	Poetry by Nāshiʾ al-Aṣghar	I	1:248
	Akhbār and poetry by Khalīʿ al-Shāmī	I	1:287
	Akhbār about Waʾwāʾ	I	1:288
	Khabar and poetry by Waʾwāʾ al-Dimashqī	I	1:296
	Akhbār about Abū Ṭālib al-Raqqī	I	1:298
	Poetry by Tallaʿfarī	I	1:300

TABLE 2.5 *Indirect transmission* (*cont.*)

Guarantors and Transmitters	Material	Region	Rf.
	Poetry by ʿAbd al-Raḥmān b. Jaʿfar al-Naḥwī al-Raqqī	I	1:305
Abū Bakr al-Khwārizmī ← *baʿḍuhum*	Poetry by Abū l-Fatḥ al-Baktimurī b. al-Kātib	I	1:121
Abū Ḥafṣ ʿUmar b. ʿAlī al-Muṭṭawwiʿī	Poetry by Nizār b. Maʿadd b. Tamīm	I	1:309
Abū l-Faḍl ʿUbaydallāh b. Aḥmad al-Mīkālī	Poetry by a Ḥamdānid	I	1:106
	Akhbār by Abū l-Faraj al-Babbaghāʾ	I	1:252
Abū l-Ḥasan ʿAlī b. Maʾmūn al-Maṣṣīṣī (d. before 429/1037)	*Akhbār* and poetry by Waʾwāʾ al-Dimashqī	I	1:288
	Poetry by Abū l-ʿAmīd Hāshim b. Muḥammad al-Mutayyam al-Aṭrābulsī	I	1:305
	Poetry by *al-amīr* Tamīm b. Maʿadd	I	1:308, 309, 452–3, 457
	Poetry by Marwānī	I	1:309
Abū l-Ḥasan ʿAlī b. Maʾmūn al-Maṣṣīṣī ← *al-shaykh al-imām* Abū l-Ṭayyib	A *khabar* about Marwānī	I	1:310
Abū l-Ḥasan ʿAlī b. Muḥammad al-ʿAlawī al-Ḥusaynī al-Hamadānī al-Waṣī	*Akhbār* about Sayf al-Dawla al-Ḥamdānī	I	1:32
	Poetry by Sayf al-Dawla al-Ḥamdānī	I	1:44
Abū l-Ḥasan Muḥammad b. Abī Mūsā al-Karkhī ← *al-qāḍī* Abū l-Qāsim ʿAlī b. al-Muḥsin al-Tanūkhī	Poetry by Abū l-Muṭāʿ b. Nāḍir al-Dawla al-Ḥamdānī	I	1:106, 107

Guarantors and Transmitters	Material	Region	Rf.
Abū l-Ḥasan Muḥammad b. Abī Mūsā al-Karkhī	Poetry by al-Ḥusayn b. Nāṣir al-Dawla	I	1:107
Abū l-Ḥasan Muḥammad b. Aḥmad al-Ifrīqī al-Mutayyam	Poetry by Sayf al-Dawla al-Ḥamdānī	I	1:43
Abū Naṣr Sahl b. al-Marzubān	Poetry by Abū l-Qāsim al-Zāhī	I	1:249
	Poetry by Maʿadd b. Tamīm	I	1:308
Abū Saʿīd ʿAbd al-Raḥmān b. Muḥammad b. Dūst ← al-Walīd b. Bakr al-Faqīh	Poetry by Muḥammad b. Abī Marwān	I	1:310
	al-Wazīr al-Mustanṣir Abū l-Ḥasan Jaʿfar b. ʿUthmān al-Muṣḥafī	I	1:310
	ʿĪsā b. Waṭīs (*kātib* al-Mustanṣir)	I	1:311
	Ḥabīb b. Aḥmad al-Andalusī	I	1:311
	Poetry by *al-wazīr* Abū ʿĀmir Aḥmad b. ʿAbd al-Malik b. Shuhayd	I	1:36, 2:49
	Khabar and poetry by Ibn al-Qūṭiyya	I	2:74
	Poetry by Aḥmad b. Muḥammad b. ʿAbd Rabbihi	I	2:75
Khwārizmī and Maṣṣīṣī	Poetry by Waʾwāʾ al-Dimashqī	I	1:289
Abū ʿAbdallāh Muḥammad b. Ḥāmid al-Khwārizmī ← Ṣāḥib b. ʿAbbād	Poetry by Ibn Lankak	II	2:353
Abū ʿAlī Muḥammad b. ʿUmar al-Balkhī al-Zāhir	Poetry by Abū l-Ḥusayn al-Ṭāhir al-Baṣrī	II	2:370
Abū ʿAlī Muḥammad b. ʿUmar al-Balkhī al-Zāhir ← Abū l-Qāsim ʿAbd al-ʿAzīz b. Yūsuf	Poetry by ʿAḍud al-Dawla	II	2:217
Abū Bakr al-Khwārizmī	*Akhbār* about ʿAḍud al-Dawla	II	2:217

TABLE 2.5 *Indirect transmission (cont.)*

Guarantors and Transmitters	Material	Region	Rf.
Abū Bakr al-Khwārizmī ← Laḥḥām	Poetry by Mufajja' al-Baṣrī	II	2:363
Abū Bakr al-Khwārizmī, Abū Naṣr Sahl b. al-Marzubān, and Abū l-Ḥasan al-Maṣṣīṣī	*Akhbār* about Muhallabī	II	2:224
Abū Ḥafṣ 'Umar b. 'Alī al-Muṭṭawwi'ī ← Abū 'Alī al-Kindī	Poetry by Abū Muḥammad 'Abdallāh b. Muḥammad al-Nāmī al-Khwārizmī	II	2:128
Abū Ḥafṣ 'Umar b. 'Alī al-Muṭṭawwi'ī ← Abū Ya'lā al-Wāsiṭī	Poetry by Abū Muḥammad 'Abdallāh b. Muḥammad al-Nāmī al-Khwārizmī	II	2:128
Abū Ḥafṣ 'Umar b. 'Alī Muṭṭawwi'ī	Poetry by Khubza'aruzzī	II	2:369
Abū l-Ḥasan 'Alī b. Ma'mūn al-Maṣṣīṣī	*Akhbār* and poetry by 'Ubaydallāh b. Aḥmad al-Baladī	II	2:214
	Poetry by al-Aḥnaf al-'Ukbarī (Abū l-Ḥasan 'Aqīl b. Muḥammad)	II	3:123
Abū l-Ḥasan Muḥammad b. Abī Mūsā al-Karkhī ← Abū l-Qāsim 'Alī b. al-Ḥusayn al-Qāḍī	Poetry by Abū Muḥammad 'Abdallāh b. Muḥammad al-Nāmī al-Khwārizmī	II	3:127
Abū l-Ḥasan Muḥammad b. Abī Mūsā al-Karkhī ← Abū Muḥammad al-Ḥāmidī	Two lines by Abū Muḥammad 'Abdallāh b. Muḥammad al-Nāmī al-Khwārizmī	II	3:128
Abū l-Qāsim al-Ḥusayn b. Muḥammad b. Ḥabīb ← 'Abd al-Samī' b. Muḥammad al-Hāshimī	Poetry by Khubza'aruzzī [d. ca. 327/939]	II	2:368
Abū l-Qāsim 'Alī b. Muḥammad al-Karkhī	Prose by Ṣāḥib b. 'Abbād	II	2:246

Guarantors and Transmitters	Material	Region	Rf.
Abū Manṣūr Saʿīd b. Aḥmad al-Barīdī	*Akhbār* about Abū Isḥāq al-Ṣābī (d. 384/994)	II	2:243
Abū Manṣūr Saʿīd b. Aḥmad al-Barīdī and Abū Ṭāhir Muḥammad b. ʿAbd al-Ṣamad al-Kātib	*Akhbār* ʿAḍud al-Dawla and Abū Isḥāq al-Ṣābī	II	2:245
Abū Nāṣr al-Rūdhbārī al-Ṭūsī	Poetry by Mufajjaʿ al-Baṣrī	II	2:364
Abū Naṣr Sahl b. al-Marzubān	*Akhbār* about Abū Isḥāq al-Ṣābī	II	2:243
	Poetry by al-Qāḍī al-Tanūkhī	II	2:346
	Poetry by Abū Ṭāhir Saydūk al-Wāsiṭī	II	2:372
	Poetry by Abū Muḥammad b. Zurayq al-Kūfī	II	2:378
Abū Naṣr Sahl b. al-Marzubān ← Abū Sulaymān al-Manṭiqī	Poetry by Abū Muḥammad b. Zurayq al-Kūfī	II	2:377
Abū Saʿd Naṣr b. Yaʿqūb (d. before 429/1037)	Poetry by ʿAḍud al-Dawla	II	2:218
	Poetry by Abū ʿĀṣim al-Baṣrī	II	2:369
Abū Saʿīd ʿAbd al-Raḥmān b. Muḥammad b. Dūst	Poetry by Ṣāḥib b. ʿAbbād	II	2:201
Abū Saʿīd ʿAbd al-Raḥmān b. Muḥammad b. Dūst ← Abū Jaʿfar al-Ṭabarī	Poetry by ʿIzz al-Dawla Bakhtiyār b. Muʿizz al-Dawla	II	2:219

TABLE 2.5 *Indirect transmission (cont.)*

Guarantors and Transmitters	Material	Region	Rf.
Abū Saʿīd ʿAbd al-Raḥmān b. Muḥammad b. Dūst ← Abū l-Ḥasan b. Muḥammad b. al-Muẓaffar al-ʿAlawī al-Nīshāpūrī ← Abū l-ʿAbbās al-Milḥī	Poetry by Tāj al-Dawla	II	2:220
Abū Ṭāhir Maymūn b. Sahl al-Wāsiṭī, Abū l-Ḥasan al-Maṣṣīṣī, and Muḥammad b. ʿUmar al-Zāhir	Poetry by Abū l-Ṭāhir Saydūk al-Wāsiṭī	II	2:372
Hārūn b. Aḥmad al-Ṣaymarī	Poetry by ʿIzz al-Dawla Bakhtiyār b. Muʿizz al-Dawla	II	2:219
Badīʿ al-Zamān al-Hamadhānī	Poetry by Tāj al-Dawla Abū l-Ḥusayn Aḥmad b. ʿAḍud al-Dawla	II	2:220
Maymūn b. Sahl al-Wāsiṭī	Poetry by Abū Ṭāhir Saydūk al-Wāsiṭī	II	2:372
	Khabar and poetry by Abū ʿAbdallāh al-Ḥāmidī	II	2:373–4
Abū ʿAbdallāh Muḥammad b. Ḥāmid al-Khwārizmī	*Khabar* about Abū Muḥammad al-Khāzin and Ṣāḥib	III	3:195–7
Abū ʿAlī Muḥammad b. ʿUmar al-Balkhī al-Zāhir	Poetry by Abū Dulaf	III	3:358
Abū Bakr al-Khwārizmī	*Akhbār* about Ṣāḥib b. ʿAbbād	III	3:194
	Part of a *risāla* by Ṣāḥib b. ʿAbbād	III	3:256
	Poetry by Ṣāḥib b. ʿAbbād	III	3:260, 265
	Sariqa of Ṣāḥib b. ʿAbbād	III	3:279
	Poetry by ʿAbdān al-Iṣbahānī	III	3:302
	Poetry by Abū Saʿīd al-Rustamī	III	3:323
	Poetry by Abū Muḥammad al-Khāzin	III	3:329

Guarantors and Transmitters	Material	Region	Rf.
	Poetry by Abū l-ʿAlāʾ al-Asadī	III	3:340
	Khabar about Abū l-Ḥusayn ʿAlī b. Muḥammad al-Badīhī	III	3:343
	Poetry by Zaʿfarānī	III	3:356
Abū Ḥafṣ ʿUmar b. ʿAlī al-Muṭṭawwiʿī	Poetry by Abū l-Faraj b. Hindū	III	3:397, 398
	Poetry by Abū Saʿd ʿAlī b. Muḥammad b. Khalaf al-Hamadhānī	III	3:412
	Poetry by Abū ʿAlī al-Ḥusayn b. Abī l-Qāsim al-Qāshānī	III	3:414
Abū Ḥanīfa al-Dihishtānī	*Khabar* and Poetry by Ṣāḥib b. ʿAbbād	III	3:203
Abū l-Ḥusayn Muḥammad b. al-Ḥusayn al-Fārisī al-Naḥwī	*Akhbār* by Abū l-Fatḥ b. al-ʿAmīd	III	3:186
Abū Jaʿfar al-Kātib	*Akhbār* about Abū l-Fatḥ b. al-ʿAmīd	III	3:185, 191
	Khabar about Ṣāḥib b. ʿAbbād	III	3:196
Abū l-Faḍl ʿUbaydallāh b. Aḥmad al-Mīkālī	*Akhbār* about Ṣāḥib b. ʿAbbād	III	3:200
	Sariqa and poetry by Ṣāḥib b. ʿAbbād	III	3:275–6
	Poetry by Abū l-Qāsim Ghānim b. Abī l-ʿAlāʾ al-Iṣbahānī	III	3:325
	Poetry by Abū l-Qāsim ʿUmar b. ʿAbdallāh al-Harandī	III	3:414
Abū l-Faḍl ʿUbaydallāh b. Aḥmad al-Mīkālī ← *baʿḍ nudamāʾ* al-Ṣāḥib	*Khabar* about Ṣāḥib b. ʿAbbād	III	3:198
Abū l-Faḍl (Badīʿ al-Zamān) al-Hamadhānī	Poetry by Abū Dulaf al-Khazrajī	III	3:356
Abū l-Fatḥ ʿAlī b. Muḥammad al-Bustī	Poetry and a critical opinion by Ṣāḥib b. ʿAbbād	III	3:268
	Poetry by Abū ʿĪsā al-Munajjim	III	3:393

TABLE 2.5 *Indirect transmission (cont.)*

Guarantors and Transmitters	Material	Region	Rf.
Abū l-Ḥasan ʿAlī b. Maʾmūn al-Maṣṣīṣī	*Sariqa* of Ṣāḥib b.ʿAbbād	III	3:200
Abū l-Ḥasan ʿAlī b. Muḥammad al-ʿAlawī al-Ḥusaynī al-Hamadānī	*Akhbār* about Ṣāḥib b. ʿAbbād	III	3:203
Abū l-Ḥasan ʿAlī b. Muḥammad al-Ḥimyarī	*Akhbār* about Ṣāḥib b. ʿAbbād	III	3:200
Abū l-Ḥasan al-Ghuwayrī	Poetry by Abū Saʿīd al-Rustamī	III	3:323
Abū l-Ḥusayn al-Shahrazūrī al-Ḥanẓalī	Poetry by Mufajjaʿ al-Baṣrī	III	3:363
Abū l-Ḥusayn Muḥammad b. al-Ḥusayn al-Fārisī al-Naḥwī	*Akhbār* about Ṣāḥib b. ʿAbbād	III	3:201, 204
	Khabar about Abū ʿAbdallāh al-Mughallisī al-Marāghī	III	3:416
Abū l-Ḥusayn Muḥammad b. al-Ḥusayn al-Fārisī al-Naḥwī	*Khabar* and poetry by Abū l-Ḥasan b. Ghassān	III	3:428
Abū l-Naṣr Muḥammad b. ʿAbd al-Jabbār al-ʿUtbī	*Akhbār* about Ṣāḥib b. ʿAbbād	III	3:199
	Poetry by Abū l-Qāsim Ghānim b. Abī l-ʿAlāʾ al-Iṣbahānī	III	3:325
	Poetry by Muḥammad al-Bajalī al-Astarābādhī	III	4:50
Abū l-Naṣr Muḥammad b. ʿAbd al-Jabbār al-ʿUtbī ← Abū Jaʿfar Dihqān b. Dhū l-Qarnayn	*Khabar* about Ṣāḥib b. ʿAbbād	III	3:202
Abū l-Qāsim ʿAlī b. Muḥammad al-Karkhī	*Akhbār* about Ṣāḥib b. ʿAbbād	III	3:204

Guarantors and Transmitters	Material	Region	Rf.
	Poetry by Abū l-Qāsim Ghānim b. Abī l-ʿAlāʾ al-Iṣbahānī	III	3:325
Abū Manṣūr al-Bīʿ (al-Bayyīʿ?)	*Khabar* about Ṣāḥib b. ʿAbbād	III	3:198
Abū Manṣūr al-Lujaymī al-Dīnawarī	Poetry by Abū ʿAlī al-Ḥusayn b. Abī l-Qāsim al-Qāshānī	III	3:413
Abū Manṣūr al-Lujāymī	*Akhbār* about Ṣāḥib b. ʿAbbād	III	3:198
Abū Manṣūr Saʿīd b. Aḥmad al-Barīdī	*Khabar* about Abū l-Fatḥ b. al-ʿAmīd	III	3:190
Abū Naṣr al-Namarī	*Akhbār* about Ṣāḥib b. ʿAbbād	III	3:202
Abū Naṣr Sahl b. al-Marzubān	An anecdote and poetry by Ṣāḥib b. ʿAbbād	III	3:200
	An anecdote and poetry by Abū l-Munbasiṭ al-Shīrāzī	III	3:422
Abū Saʿd Naṣr b. Yaʿqūb	*Akhbār* Ṣāḥib b. ʿAbbād	III	3:200
Abū Saʿīd ʿAbd al-Raḥmān b. Muḥammad b. Dūst ← Abū ʿAlī al-ʿIrāqī al-ʿAwwāmī al-Rāzī	Poetry by Ṣāḥib b. ʿAbbād	III	3:206
Al-Qāḍī al-Imām al-Iṣbahānī	Poetry by Abū l-Qāsim Ghānim b. Abī l-ʿAlāʾ al-Iṣbahānī	III	3:324
ʿAwn b. al-Ḥusayn al-Hamadānī al-Tamīmī	*Khabar* about Ṣāḥib b. ʿAbbād	III	3:194
	Qiṭʿa by Ṣāḥib b. ʿAbbād	III	3:206
	Poetry by Abū Dulaf al-Khazrajī	III	3:357
	Poetry by Abū l-Ḥasan ʿAlī b. Muḥammad b. Maʾmūn al-Abharī	III	3:408
ʿAwn b. al-Ḥusayn al-Hamadānī al-Tamīmī ← Abū ʿĪsā b. al-Munajjim	A *khabār* about Ṣāḥib b. ʿAbbād	III	3:203
Badīʿ al-Zamān al-Hamadhānī	Poetry by Abū Dulaf al-Khazrajī	III	3:358

TABLE 2.5 *Indirect transmission (cont.)*

Guarantors and Transmitters	Material	Region	Rf.
	Poetry by Barākawayh al-Zanjānī	III	3:407
	Akhbār about Ṣāḥib b. ʿAbbād	III	3:197, 202
Hārūn b. Jaʿfar al-Ṣaymarī	Poetry by Abū l-Qāsim ʿUmar b. ʿAbdallāh al-Harandī	III	3:414
Abū ʿAbdallāh b. al-Sarī al-Rāmī	Poetry by Abū ʿAlī Muḥammad b. ʿĪsā al-Dāmghānī	IV	4:143
Abū ʿAbdallāh Muḥammad b. Ḥāmid al-Khwārizmī	Poetry by Aḥmad b. Shabīb al-Shabībī	IV	4:242
Abū Bakr al-Khwārizmī	*Khabar* about Khwārizmī's censure of Abū l-Ḥasan al-Laḥḥām	IV	4:102
	Poetry by Abū l-Ḥasan Aḥmad b. al-Mu'ammal	IV	4:150
	Khabar and poetry by Aḥmad b. Shabīb al-Shabībī	IV	4:242
Abū Ibrāhīm b. Abī ʿAlī al-Naḥwī	Poetry by ʿAlī b. Abī ʿAlī al-Naḥwī	IV	4:419
Abū l-Ḥusayn Muḥammad b. al-Ḥusayn al-Fārisī al-Naḥwī	*Khabar* and poetry by Abū l-Qāsim al-Iskāfī	IV	4:99
Abū Jaʿfar Muḥammad b. Mūsā al-Mūsawī	*Khabar* about Mūsawī's father (Abū l-Ḥasan)	IV	4:101
	Akhbār about Ibn Muṭrān al-Shāshī	IV	4:115
	Poetry by Ibn Abī al-Thiyāb (al-Thayyāb?)	IV	4:126
	Poetry by Abū l-Naṣr Al-Huzaymī (Muʿāfā b. Huzaym)	IV	4:131
Abū Jaʿfar	*Akhbār* about Abū Naṣr al-Ẓarīfī al-Abīwardī	IV	4:134
	Poetry by Abū Manṣūr Aḥmad b. Muḥammad al-Baghawī	IV	4:143

Guarantors and Transmitters	Material	Region	Rf.
Abū Jaʿfar Muḥammad b. Mūsā al-Mūsawī	Poetry by Abū ʿAlī Muḥammad b. ʿIsā al-Dāmghānī	IV	4:143–4
	Poetry by Abū ʿAbdallāh Muḥammad b. Abī Bakr al-Jurjānī	IV	4:154
Abū l-Faḍl ʿUbaydallāh b. Aḥmad al-Mīkālī	Poetry by Muḥammad ʿAbdallāh b. al-ʿAbdalakānī	IV	4:449
Abū l-Faraj Yaʿqūb b. Ibrāhīm	Poetry by Abū Jaʿfar b. al-ʿAbbās	IV	4:125
Abū l-Fatḥ ʿAlī b. Muḥammad al-Bustī	Poetry by Abū Sulaymān al-Khaṭṭābī	IV	4:335
	Poetry by Abū Muḥammad Shuʿba b. ʿAbd al-Malik al-Bustī	IV	4:337
Abū l-Ḥasan al-Fārisī al-Māwardī	Poetry by Abū Sahl Muḥammad b. Sulaymān al-Ṣuʿlūkī	IV	4:419
Abū l-Ḥasan ʿAlī b. Aḥmad b. ʿAbdān	Poetry by Abū ʿAlī al-Zawzanī	IV	4:145
Abū l-Ḥasan ʿAlī b. Aḥmad b. ʿAbdān	Poetry Abū l-Ḥusayn Muḥammad b. Aḥmad al-Ifrīqī al-Mutayyam	IV	4:158
	Poetry by Abū l-Ḥasan Aḥmad b. Muḥammad b. Thābit al-Baghdādī	IV	4:178
Abū l-Naṣr Muḥammad b. ʿAbd al-Jabbār al-ʿUtbī	Poetry by Abū Manṣūr al-Būshanjī	IV	4:160
	Akhbār about Abū l-Fatḥ al-Bustī	IV	4:303
Abū Naṣr Sahl b. al-Marzubān	*Khabar* and poetry by Abū Naṣr Aḥmad b. ʿAlī al-Zawzanī	IV	4:447
Abū l-Qāsim Aḥmad b. ʿAlī al-Muẓaffarī	Poetry by Abū Naṣr al-Huzaymī (al-Muʿāfā b. Huzaym)	IV	4:133
Abū l-Qāsim al-Ulaymānī	Poetry by Abū l-Ḥasan al-Laḥḥām (d. ca. 363/973)	IV	4:109–10
	Poetry by Abū Jaʿfar b. Abī l-ʿAbbās	IV	4:125
	Khabar and poetry by Abū l-Naṣr al-Huzaymī (Muʿāfā b. Huzaym)	IV	4:129
Abū l-Ṭayyib Sahl b. Muḥammad b. Sulaymān al-Ṣuʿlūkī	Poetry by Abū Sahl Muḥammad b. Sulaymān al-Ṣuʿlūkī	IV	4:419

TABLE 2.5 *Indirect transmission* (*cont.*)

Guarantors and Transmitters	Material	Region	Rf.
Abū Saʿd Naṣr b. Yaʿqūb	Poetry by Abū Muḥammad b. Abī al-Thiyāb (al-Thayyāb?)	IV	4:127
	Poetry by Rajāʾ b. al-Walīd al-Iṣbahānī	IV	4:136
	Poetry by Abū ʿAbdallāh Muḥammad b. Abī Bakr al-Jurjānī	IV	4:154
	Poetry by Abū Muḥammad ʿAbdallāh b. Muḥammad al-Harawī al-Faqīh	IV	4:345
Abū Saʿīd b. Dūst ← *baʿḍ mashāyikh al-ḥaḍra*	*Khabar* and poetry by Abū Manṣūr al-ʿAbdūnī	IV	4:78
Abū Saʿīd b. Dūst and Ismāʿīl b. Muḥammad	Poetry by Abū Naṣr Ismāʿīl b. Ḥammād al-Jawharī	IV	4:407
Abū Saʿīd Muḥammad b. Manṣūr	*Akhbār* about Abū ʿAbdallāh Muḥammad b. Ḥāmid	IV	4:249
	Poetry by Abū l-Ḥasan al-Nāhī	IV	4:383
Abū Zakariyyā Yaḥyā b. Ismāʿīl al-Ḥarbī	*Akhbār* about Abū l-Ṭayyib al-Ṭāhirī	IV	4:69
	A *qaṣīda* by Abū Manṣūr al-Khazrajī	IV	4:81
Badīʿ al-Zamān al-Hamadānī	Poetry by Abū Muḥammad b. Abī al-Thiyāb (al-Thayyāb?)	IV	4:127
	Ṭarāʾif by Ṣāḥib b. ʿAbbād	IV	4:197
Ḥāḍir b. Muḥammad al-Ṭūsī	Poetry by Abū Muḥammad b. Abī al-Thiyāb (al-Thayyāb?)	IV	4:126
	Poetry by Abū ʿAlī al-Zawzanī	IV	4:145
	Poetry by Abū Isḥāq Ibrāhīm b. ʿAlī al-Fārisī	IV	4:150
Manṣūr b. ʿAbdallāh b. ʿAbdallāh b. ʿAbd al-Raḥmān al-Dīnawarī	*Khabar* about his father ʿAbdallāh b. ʿAbd al-Raḥmān al-Dīnawarī	IV	4:138
Yaḥyā b. ʿAlī al-Bukhārī	Poetry by Abū l-Qāsim al-Dāwūdī	IV	4:345

APPENDIX 3

Sources of *Tatimmat al-Yatīma*

Written Sources

TABLE 3.1 *Dīwāns*

Poets with Dīwān	Region	Reference
al-Amīr Abū l-Muṭāʿ Dhū l-Qarnayn b. Nāṣir al-Dawla	I	9
Abū l-Faraj ʿAlī b. al-Ḥusayn b. Hindū (d. 410/1019 or 420/1029)	I	44
Abū Muḥammad ʿAbd al-Muḥsin b. Muḥammad b. Ṭālib al-Ṣūrī	I	46
Abū Saʿīd Muḥammad b. Muḥammad b. al-Ḥasan al-Rustamī	II	102
Abū l-Khaṭṭāb Muḥammad b. ʿAlī al-Jabalī	II	106
Abū ʿAdī al-Shahrazūrī	V	289
Abū Ṣāliḥ Sahl b. Aḥmad al-Nīshāpūrī al-Mustawfī	V	309

TABLE 3.2 *Books*

Title	Region	Reference
Al-Tashbīhāt by Abū Saʿīd b. Abī l-Faraj	I	21
Rasāʾil Abī Isḥāq al-Ṣābī	I	54
Safīnat Abī ʿAbdallāh al-Ḥāmidī	I, II	37, 54, 87
Al-Muḥibb wa-l-maḥbūb wa-l-mashmūm wa-l-mashrūb by al-Sarī al-Raffāʾ	I	60
Al-Wasāṭa bayna l-zunāt wa-l-lāṭa by Abū l-Faraj ʿAlī b. al-Ḥusayn b. Hindū (d. 410/1019 or 420/1029)	III	155

TABLE 3.3 *Other written material*

Material for …	Source	Region	Rf.	Comments
Abū l-Maḥāsin Saʿd b. Muḥammad b. Manṣūr	Abū l-Maḥāsin	III	165	Abū l-Maḥāsin sent Thaʿālibī his own verse.
Abū l-Maḥāsin Saʿd b. Muḥammad b. Manṣūr	Abū l-Maḥāsin (?)	III	166	A letter sent by Abū l-Maḥāsin to an unnamed personality in the service of Shams al-Kufāt.
Abū l-Maḥāsin Saʿd b. Muḥammad b. Manṣūr	Abū l-Maḥāsin (?)	III	167	Thaʿālibī copies some early poetry in Abū l-Maḥāsin's own handwriting.
Abū ʿAlī b. Miskawayhi	Abū l-Qāsim ʿAbd al-Ṣamad b. ʿAlī al-Ṭabarī	III	115	A *qaṣīda* from a letter to Abū l-ʿAlāʾ b. Ḥasūl (d. 450/1058).
Abū Ghānim Maʿrūf b. Muḥammad al-Qaṣrī	Abū Ghānim Maʿrūf b. Muḥammad al-Qaṣrī	III	150	He heard of Thaʿālibī while passing through Nīshāpūr, then copied and sent to him a few *kutub*, including his own poetry.
Abū l-Qāsim ʿAbd al-Ṣamad b. ʿAlī al-Ṭabarī	—	IV	189	A letter from Ṭabarī to Abū l-Ḥusayn al-Marwarrūzī.
Al-qāḍī Abū Aḥmad Manṣūr b. Muḥammad al-Azdī al-Harawī	Thaʿālibī	IV	232	A letter from Azdī to Thaʿālibī.
al-shaykh al-ʿAmīd Abū Sahl Muḥammad b. al-Ḥasan	Thaʿālibī	IV	254	A quotation describing Mīkālī from a letter addressed to Thaʿālibī.

Oral/Aural Sources

TABLE 3.4 *Direct transmission*

Source	Region	Reference
Abū l-Faḍl Muḥammad b. ʿAbd al-Wāḥid al-Tamīmī (d. 454/1062)	II	79
Abū Yaʿlā Muḥammad b. al-Ḥasan al-Baṣrī	II	108
Abū l-ʿAlāʾ b. al-Ḥasūl (al-Ḥassūl?) (d. 450/1058)	III	114
Abū l-Qāsim ʿAbd al-Wāḥid b. Muḥammad b. ʿAlī b. al-Ḥarīsh (al-Ḥirrīsh?) (d. 424/1032)	III	132
Abū l-Fatḥ Muḥammad b. Aḥmad al-Dabāwandī	III	153
Abū l-Muẓaffar b. al-Qāḍī Abī Bishr al-Jurjānī	III	170–71
Abū l-Faḍl Aḥmad b. Muḥammad al-ʿArūḍī	IV	205
Abū Jaʿfar Muḥammad b. ʿAbdallāh al-Iskāfī	IV	231
Abū l-Qāsim Ṭāhir b. Aḥmad al-Harawī	IV	241
Abū Masʿūd ʿIṣām b. Yaḥyā al-Harawī	IV	242
Al-shaykh al-ʿamīd Abū Sahl Muḥammad b. al-Ḥasan	IV	254
al-qāḍī Abū l-Ḥasan al-Muʾammal b. Khalīl b. Aḥmad al-Bustī	IV	267
al-qāḍī Abū l-Qāsim ʿĀlī b. ʿAlī b. ʿAbdallāh al-Shīrāzī	IV	268
al-qāḍī Abū l-Faḍl Aḥmad b. Muḥammad al-Rashīdī al-Lawkarī	IV	269
Abū l-Ḥasan ʿAlī b. Muḥammad al-Arbāʿī	IV	270–71
Abū l-Fatḥ al-Muẓaffar b. al-Ḥasan al-Dulayghānī	IV	278–9
Abū Manṣūr ʿAlī b. Aḥmad al-Ḥallāb	V	287
Abū Ṭālib Muḥammad b. ʿAlī b. ʿAbdallāh [al-Baghdadī al-Mustawfī]	V	288–9
Abū l-Qāsim ʿAlī b. ʿAbdallāh al-Mīkālī	V	305

TABLE 3.5 *Transmission through a guarantor*

Transmitter	Guarantor	Region	Rf.
Abū ʿAbdallāh b. Hirmizdān al-Fārisī	← *shaykh mina l-Furs* ← Abū Saʿīd al-ʿAfīrī		36
Abū ʿAbdallāh al-Ḥāmidī	← Abū Muḥammad al-Khāzin ← *Safīnat al-Ṣāḥib* (Poetry by Abū l-Ḍiyāʾ [al-Ḥimṣī])	I	37
Abū Bakr al-Quhistānī	← Abū l-ʿAbbās Aḥmad b. Jaʿfar al-Badīʿī	I	41
	← Abū Naṣr al-Ḥimṣī	I	36
	← Abū Yaʿlā Saʿīd b. Aḥmad al-Shurūṭī ← Ibn Wakīʿ al-Tinnīsī	I	40
	← Ibn al-Zamakdam al-Mawṣilī	I	62
Abū Ghānim Maʿrūf b. Muḥammad al-Qaṣrī	← Abū Muḥammad Ṭāhir b. al-Ḥusayn b. Yaḥyā al-Makhzūmī	I	30
Abū l-Faḍl Muḥammad b. ʿAbd al-Wāḥid al-Tamīmī	← Abū l-Ḥasan Muḥammad b. ʿAbd al-Wāḥid al-Qaṣṣār	I	66
Abū l-Ḥasan ʿAlī b. Fāris al-Qazwīnī (*wa-ghayruhu*)	← Abū ʿAlī al-Ḥusayn b. Bishr al-Ramlī	I	44
	← *al-wazīr* Abū l-Fatḥ b. Dardān al-Yahūdī	I	56
	← Ibn Ḥashīsha al-Maqdisī (*al-qāḍī* Abū ʿAbdallāh Muḥammad b. ʿAlī)	I	33
Abū l-Ḥasan ʿAlī b. Maʾmūn al-Maṣṣīṣī	← Abū l-ʿAlāʾ al-Maʿarrī	I	16
	← Abū l-Fatḥ al-Mawāzīnī al-Ḥalabī	I	21
	← Abū l-Hasan ʿAlī (Ibn Kūbrāt al-Ramlī)	I	82
	← Abū l-Qāsim al-Muḥsin (al-Muḥassin?) b. ʿAmr al-Muʿallā	I	17
	← al-Ḥasan al-Daqqāq	I	53
Abū l-Ḥasan Muḥammad b. al-Ḥasan al-Barmakī *al-faqīh*	← *al-wazīr* Abū l-Fatḥ b. Dardān	I	56

Transmitter		Guarantor	Region	Rf.
Abū l-Ḥasan Muḥammad b. al-Ḥusayn al-Fārisī	←	Abū ʿAbdallāh al-Ḥusayn b. Aḥmad al-Muʿallā	I	24
Abū l-Ḥasan Musāfir b. al-Ḥasan (d. after 429/1037) (*T* 258)	←	Abū l-Ḥasan Muḥammad b. al-Ḥusayn al-ʿUthmānī ← Abū l-Qāsim al-Ḥusayn Ibn al-Maghribī al-Wazīr	I	34, 35
Abū l-Ḥasan Musāfir b. al-Ḥasan	←	Abū l-Ḥasan Muḥammad b. al-Ḥusayn al-ʿUthmānī ← *al-qāḍī* Ibn al-Bassāṭ al-Baghdadī ← Ibn Wakīʿ al-Tinnīsī	I	40
Abū Muḥammad Khalaf b. Muḥammad b. Yaʿqūb al-Shirmiqānī	←	Abū l-Muṭāʿ Dhū l-Qarnayn	I	9
	←	Jawharī ← Abū l-Muṭāʿ Dhū l-Qarnayn	I	9, 10
Abū Naṣr Sahl b. al-Marzubān	←	Jurayj al-Muqill	I	58
Abū l-Qāsim Yaḥyā b. ʿAlāʾ al-Bukhārī al-Faqīh	←	Ibn Ḥammād al-Baṣrī	I	21
Abū Ṭālib al-Shahrazūrī	←	Muḥammad b. ʿUbaydallāh al-Baladī	I	66
Abū Ṭālib Maḥmūd b. al-Ḥasan al-Ṭabarī	←	Abū l-Qāsim al-Ḥusayn b. ʿAlī al-Wazīr al-Maghribī	I	35
Abū Ṭālib Muḥmmad b. ʿAlī b. ʿAbdallāh (al-Baghdadī)	←	Abū Manṣūr al-Ṣūrī	I	38
Abū Yaʿlā Muḥammad b. al-Ḥasan al-Ṣūfī al-Baṣrī	←	Abū l-Ḥasayn Aḥmad b. Muḥammad al-Maʿarrī (al-Qanūʿ)	I	13
	←	Abū l-Ḥusayn al-Mustahām al-Ḥalabī	I	18
	←	Abū l-Muṭāʿ Dhū l-Qarnayn	I	11
	←	Abū l-Qāsim ʿAlī b. Muḥammad al-Bahdalī	I	27
	←	Abū l-Qāsim al-Muḥsin (al-Muḥassin) b. ʿAmr b. al-Muʿallā	I	17

TABLE 3.5 *Transmission through a guarantor (cont.)*

Transmitter		Guarantor	Region	Rf.
	←	Ibn Ḥashīsha al-Maqdisī	I	33
Al-Dihqān Abū ʿAlī al-Qūmasī	←	Abū l-Makārim al-Muṭahhar b. Muḥammad al-Baṣrī	I	26
Abū ʿAbdallāh al-Ḥāmidī	←	*Safīnat al-Ṣāḥib* (Poetry by Abū l-Thurayyā al-Shimshāṭī)	II	87
Abū l-Faḍl Muḥammad b. ʿAbd al-Wāḥid al-Tamīmī	←	Abū Bakr al-ʿAnbarī	II	77
	←	Abū l-Ḥasan ʿAlī b. al-Rayyān al-Jurhumī	II	76
	←	Ibn al-Muṭarriz	II	73
Abū Ghānim Maʿrūf b. Muḥammad al-Qaṣrī	←	Abū l-ʿAbbās Khusraw -Fīrūz b. Rukn al-Dawla	II	113
Abū l-Ḥasan ʿAlī b. Fāris al-Qazwīnī	←	Abū al-Simṭ al-Rasʿanī	II	86
	←	Abū Ḥamza al-Dhuhalī	II	102
Abū l-Ḥasan ʿAlī b. Ma'mūn al-Maṣṣīṣī (and Abū Yaʿlā Muḥammad b. al-Ḥasan al-Baṣrī)	←	ʿAbd al-Munʿim b. ʿAbd al-Ḥasan al-Ṣūrī	II	83
	←	Abū al-Ghawth b. Niḥrīr al-Manbijī	II	90
	←	Abū l-Fahm ʿAbd al-Salām al-Naṣībī	II	85
	←	Abū l-Thurayyā al-Shimshāṭī	II	86, 87
Abū l-Ḥasan Muḥammad b. al-Ḥasan al-Barmakī *al-faqīh*	←	Abū l-Ḥasan al-Hāshimī al-Ma'mūnī	II	78
	←	Sharīf al-Murtaḍā	II	69
Abū l-Ḥusayn Muḥammad b. al-Ḥusayn al-Fasawī al-Naḥwī	←	Abū l-Ḥasan ʿAlī b. Ghassān al-Baṣrī	II	109
Abū l-Qāsim ʿAbd al-Ṣamad b. ʿAlī al-Ṭabarī	←	Makkī b. Muḥammad al-Baghdādī ← Abū l-Ḥasan al-Nuʿaymī	II	78

Transmitter		Guarantor	Region	Rf.
Abū Yaʿlā Muḥammad b. al-Ḥasan al-Ṣūfī al-Baṣrī (and al-Maṣṣīṣī)	←	ʿAbd al-Munʿim b. ʿAbd al-Muḥsin al-Ṣūrī	II	83
	←	Abū l-Ḥasan ʿAlī (Ibn Kūbrāt al-Ramlī)	II	82
	←	Ibn al-Muṭarriz	II	73
Abū Bakr al-Marjī	←	Abū l-Qāsim Ghānim b. Muḥammad b. Abī l-ʿAlāʾ al-Iṣbahānī	III	139
Abū Jaʿfar Muḥammad b. Abī ʿAlī al-Ṭabarī	←	Abū l-Faraj Muḥammad b. Abī Saʿd b. Khalaf al-Hamadānī	III	150
Abū l-Fatḥ Masʿūd b. Muḥammad b. al-Layth	←	Abū l-Qāsim Ghānim b. Muḥammad Abū l-ʿAlāʾ al-Iṣbahānī	III	138
Abū l-Fatḥ Muḥammad b. Aḥmad al-Dabāwandī	←	Abū l-ʿAlāʾ Muḥammad b. ʿAlī b. al-Ḥusayn Ṣafiyy al-Ḥaḍratayn	III	126
	←	Abū l-Ḥasan Muḥammad b. Aḥmad b. Rāmīn	III	145
	←	Abū Muḥammad al-Naẓẓām al-Khazrajī	III	146
	←	Abū Saʿd Manṣūr b. al-Ḥusayn al-Ābī	III	126
	←	*al-qāḍī* Abū Bakr al-Askī (al-Āsī?)	III	113
	←	Ṣāʿid b. Muḥammad al-Jurjānī	III	171
Abū l-Ḥasan ʿAbd al-Raḥmān b. Abī ʿUbayd al-Shīrāzī	←	Abū ʿAlī Muḥammad b. Ḥamd b. Fūrja al-Barūjirdī	III	143
	←	Abū l-Faḍl Yūsuf b. Muḥammad b. Aḥmad al-Jallūdī al-Rāzī	III	140–41
Abū l-Yaqẓān ʿAmmār b. al-Ḥasan	←	Abū Saʿd ʿAlī b. Muḥammad b. Khalaf al-Hamadānī	III	146–7
Abū ʿAlī al-Ḥusayn b. Muḥammad al-Kātib al-Nasafī	←	Al-Maʿrūf b. Abī l-Faḍl al-Dabbāgh al-Harawī	IV	242
Abū Jaʿfar Muḥammad b. Isḥāq al-Baḥḥāthī	←	Abū Manṣūr b. Mishkān	IV	254
Abū l-Ḥasan ʿAlī b. Abī l-Ṭayyib	←	Abū l-ʿAbbās al-Bākharzī	IV	219

TABLE 3.5 *Transmission through a guarantor (cont.)*

Transmitter		Guarantor	Region	Rf.
Abū l-Qāsim ʿAbd al-Ṣamad b. ʿAlī al-Ṭabarī	←	*al-shaykh al-ʿamīd* Abū Manṣūr b. Mishkān	IV	253
Abū l-Qāsim ʿAlī b. al-Faḍl al-Qāʾinī	←	Abū l-ʿAbbās al-Bākharzī	IV	218
Abū l-Qāsim b. Abī Manṣūr	←	Abū ʿAlī b. Abī Bakr b. Ḥashbawayhi al-Zawzanī	IV	216
(*aktabanī*) Abū Bakr [al-Quhistānī]	←	Abū l-Faraj Aḥmad b. ʿAlī al-Hamadānī	V	292
Abū Bakr al-Quhistānī	←	Abū Dirham al-Bandanījī	V	299
	←	*al-qāḍī* Abū Manṣūr ʿAbd al-Raḥmān b. Saʿīd al-Qāʾinī	V	306
	←	Ibn Abī ʿIllān (ʿAlāʾ ?) al-Ahwāzī	V	298
	←	Abū l-Ḥusayn al-Taghlibī		
Abū l-Faḍl Muḥammad b. ʿAbd al-Wāḥid al-Tamīmī	←	Abū Muḥammad Yaḥyā b. ʿAbdallāh al-Arzanī	V	300
Abū l-Ḥasan ʿAlī b. Muḥammad al-Ḥājibī	←	Abū Manṣūr Muḥammad b. ʿAlī al-Muhallabī	V	290
Abū l-Ḥasan Musāfir b. al-Ḥasan	←	Abū Manṣūr Naṣr b. Aḥmad b. Saʿd al-Saʿdī	V	291
Abū Jaʿfar Muḥammad b. Isḥāq al-Baḥḥāthī	←	Abū Sahl al-Junbudhī	V	288
Abū Saʿīd ʿAbd al-Raḥmān b. Dūst	←	*al-qāḍī* Abū ʿAlī ʿAbd al-Wahhāb b. Muḥammad	V	302

APPENDIX 4

Comparisons between Poets

Litterateurs	Comparison	Reason and/or comment	Volume and page
Ibn Sukkara and Ibn al-Ḥajjāj	Jarīr and Farazdaq	Ibn Sukkara and Ibn al-Ḥajjāj were like Jarīr and Farazdaq in their times.	*Y* 3:3
Ibn al-ʿAmīd	Jāḥiẓ	Ibn al-ʿAmīd was given the title *al-Jāḥiẓ al-akhīr* (the last Jāḥiẓ).	3:158
Abū l-Ḥasan al-Ghuwayrī	Abū l-ʿAlāʾ al-Asadī	Both poets restricted themselves to the service of Ṣāḥib b. ʿAbbād.	3:340
Abū l-Ḥasan ʿAlī b. Muḥammad al-Badīhī	ʿAmr al-Quṣāfī	Ṣāḥib made the analogy after finding only one good line for both poets; Thaʿālibī disagrees with this judgment.	3:343
Abū l-Ḥusayn Aḥmad b. Fāris	Ibn Lankak, Ibn Khālawayhi, Ibn ʿAllāf, Abū Bakr al-Khwārizmī	Ibn Fāris combines the precision of the scholars with the elegance of prose writers (*kuttāb*) and poets. Thaʿālibī compares him with these littérateurs.	3:400
Abū ʿUmar Aḥmad b. Muḥammad b. Darrāj al-Qasṭallī	Mutanabbī	He is the equal of Mutanabbī in al-Andalus.	2:104
Ibn Lankak	Abū l-Ḥusayn Aḥmad b. Fāris, Manṣūr al-Faqīh	He compares to Ibn Fāris in restricting his poems to two or three lines, and to Manṣūr al-Faqīh in achieving his aim in three lines.	2:348
Mufajjaʿ al-Baṣrī	Ibn Durayd	He compares to Ibn Durayd (*qāʾim maqāmahu*) in Baṣra in compiling books (*taʾlīf*) and dictating and teaching (*imlāʾ*).	2:424

Litterateurs	Comparison	Reason and/or comment	Volume and page
Abū l-Ḥasan ʿAlī b. ʿAbd al-ʿAzīz	Ibn Muqla, Buḥturī	His handwriting compares to the handwriting (*khaṭṭ*) of Ibn Muqla and the natural composition (*naẓm*) of Buḥturī.	4:3
Abū Aḥmad b. Abī Bakr al-Kātib	Ibn Bassām (?)	He follows Ibn Bassām's steps in composing poetry on the subject of jokes (*ʿabath al-lisān*), complaints about time (*shakwā l-zamān*), requesting more from a patron (*istizādat al-sulṭān*), and lashing out at leaders (*sāda*) and brethren (*ikhwān*).	4:64
Muḥammad b. Mūsā al-Ḥaddādī al-Balkhī	Abū l-Qāsim al-Balkhī, Abū Zayd al-Balkhī, Sahl b. al-Ḥasan	Thaʿālibī quotes a statement claiming that the city of Balkh contributed four distinguished personalities: Abū l-Qāsim al-Kaʿbī in speculative theology (*ʿilm al-kalām*), Abū Zayd al-Balkhī in rhetoric and *adab* compilations (*al-balāgha wa-l-ta'līf*), Sahl b. al-Ḥasan in Persian poetry, and Muḥammad b. Mūsā in Arabic poetry.	4:85
Abū ʿAlī al-Salāmī	Abū Bakr b. Muḥtāj, Ṣūlī	Salāmī and Ṣūlī write poetry similar to the poetry by compilers of books (*ashʿār mu'allifī l-kutub*)	4:95
Abū l-Qāsim ʿAlī b. Muḥammad al-Iskāfī al-Nīshāpūrī	Jāḥiẓ	He compares to al-Jāḥiẓ in that his prose is superior to his poetry.	4:95
Abū Muḥammad al-Muṭrānī (al-Ḥasan b. ʿAlī b. Muṭrān)	Abū ʿĀmir Ismāʿīl b. Aḥmad [al-Shajarī]	Thaʿālibī claims that no litterateur was the like of al-Muṭrānī in Shāsh and all Transoxania, except for Shajarī, who succeeded him.	4:132

Litterateurs	Comparison	Reason and/or comment	Volume and page
Abū Muḥammad ʿAbdallāh b. Ibrāhīm al-Raqāshī	Kushājim	He was, like Kushājim, a scribe, poet, and astrologer (*munajjim*).	4:245
Abū Sulaymān al-Khaṭṭābī	Abū ʿUbayd al-Qāsim b. Sallām	He is the like of Ibn Sallām in terms of knowledge (*ʿilm*), culture (*adab*), asceticism (*zuhd*), and fear of God (*waraʿ*). Thaʿālibī adds that Khaṭṭābī's poetry is of good quality (*ḥasan*), but Abū ʿUbayd was breathtaking (*mufḥim*).	4:334
Abū l-Faḍl al-Mīkālī	Ibn al-ʿAmīd, Ṣāḥib b. ʿAbbād, Abū Isḥāq al-Ṣābī, Ibn al-Muʿtazz, ʿUbaydallāh b. ʿAbdallāh b. Ṭāhir, Abū Firās al-Ḥamdānī	Mīkālī is the substitute of Ibn al-ʿAmīd, Ṣāḥib, and Abū Isḥāq in prose, and of Ibn al-Muʿtazz, ʿUbaydallāh b. ʿAbdallāh b. Ṭāhir, and Abū Firās al-Ḥamdānī in poetry.	4:354
ʿAbd al-Qādir b. Ṭāhir al-Tamīmī	Manṣūr al-Faqīh	His poetry is similar in style to that of Manṣūr al-Faqīh, especially since both poets are jurists.	4:414
Abū Firās al-Ḥamdānī	Ibn al-Muʿtazz	Both poets combine the comeliness of talent (*ruwāʾ al-ṭabʿ*), elegance (*simat al-ẓarf*), and the glory of royalty (*ʿizzat al-mulk*).	1:48
Abū Ḥāmid Aḥmad b. Muḥammad al-Anṭākī (Abū al-Raqaʿmaq)	Ibn Ḥajjāj	In Syria he is the equal of Ibn Ḥajjāj in Iraq.	1:326

Litterateurs	Comparison	Reason and/or comment	Volume and page
Abū l-Qāsim al-Ḥusayn b. al-Ḥasan b. Wāsāna (al-Wāsānī)	Ibn al-Rūmī	He is the equal of Ibn al-Rūmī in his times.	1:408
Abū Bakr al-Muwaswas	Abū l-ʿAynāʾ	Muwaswas reminds Thaʿālibī of Abū l-ʿAynāʾ in his improvisation (*ḥuḍūr al-jawāb*), clarity of discourse (*bayān al-khiṭāb*), well-formedness (*ḥusn al-ʿibāra*), and broad knowledge (*kathrat al-dirāya*).	1:449
Abū l-Ḥasan Muḥammad b. ʿAbd al-Wāḥid al-Qaṣṣār	Ibn al-Ḥajjāj	Al-Qaṣṣār followed the example of Ibn al-Ḥajjār, but, according to Thaʿālibī, fell behind.	*T* 22
Abū Muḥammad Ṭāhir b. al-Ḥusayn al-Makhzūmī	Ibn Nubāta, Ibn Bābak, Rustumī, Abū Muḥammad al-Khāzin	He was the like of Ibn Nubāta and Ibn Bābak of Iraq, and Rustumī and Khāzin of al-Jabal.	29
Abū l-Qāsim al-Ḥusayn b. ʿAlī al-Wazīr	Ibn al-Muʿtazz	He followed the style of Ibn al-Muʿtazz in prose and poetry.	35
Muḥammad b. Ayman al-Rahāwī	Abū l-ʿAtāhiya	Rahāwī attempted to emulate (*yuʿāriḍ*) Abū l-ʿAtāhiya and generally followed his method (*yajrī fī ṭarīqihi*).	39
Abū l-Dardāʾ al-Mawṣilī	al-Sarī al-Raffāʾ	Mawṣilī used to follow the example of Sarī.	65

Litterateurs	Comparison	Reason and/or comment	Volume and page
Abū Yūsuf Yaʿqūb b. Aḥmad b. Muḥammad	Ḥajjāj b. Yūsuf, ʿAbd al-Ḥamīd b. Yaḥyā, Abū ʿUbaydallāh al-Ashʿarī, Abū Zayd al-Balkhī, Abū Saʿīd al-Shabībī, Abū l-Fatḥ al-Bustī	He is among the teachers (*muʾaddibīn*) who achieved success after obscurity (*khumūl*).	201
Abū Muḥammad ʿAbdallāh b. Muḥammad al-Dūghābādī	al-Sarī al-Raffāʾ, al-Khālidiyyān, al-Babbaghāʾ, al-Sulāmī	He had the talent to match (*yuʿāriḍ*) these poets.	274
Abū l-Ḥusayn al-Ḥasanī al-Hamadānī	Yaḥyā b. ʿUmar al-ʿAlawī, Raḍī, and Murtaḍā	He was the equal of Yaḥyā b. ʿUmar al-ʿAlawī in terms of honor, prestige, and wealth (*al-sharaf wa-l-jāh wa-l-yasār*), and his poetry and *adab* matched that of al-Sharīf al-Raḍī and al-Sharīf al-Murtaḍā.	296

Bibliography

Primary Sources

ʿAbbāsī, ʿAbd al-Raḥīm b. Aḥmad. *Maʿāhid al-tanṣīṣ*. Ed. Muḥammad Muḥyī al-Dīn ʿAbd al-Ḥamīd. 4 vols. Beirut: ʿĀlam al-Kutub, 1947.

ʿAbdalakānī al-Zawzanī. *Ḥamāsat al-ẓurafāʾ min ashʿār al-muḥdathīn wa-l-qudamāʾ*. Ed. Muḥammad Jabbār al-Muʿaybid. 2 vols. Baghdad: Manshūrāt Wizārat al-Iʿlām, 1973.

Ābī, Abū Saʿd. *al-Uns wa-l-ʿurs*. Ed. Īflīn Farīd Yārd. Damascus: Dār al-Numayr, 1999.

Āmidī, al-Ḥasan b. Bishr. *al-Muwāzana bayna shiʿr Abī Tammām wa-l-Buḥturī*. Ed. Muḥammad Muḥyī l-Dīn ʿAbd al-Ḥamīd. Beirut: Dār al-Masīra, 1980.

ʿAskarī, Abū Hilāl. *Dīwān al-maʿānī*. Ed. Aḥmad Salīm Ghānim. 2 vols. Beirut: Dār al-Gharb al-Islāmī, 2003.

———. *Jamharat al-amthāl*. Ed. Muḥammad Abū l-Faḍl Ibrāhīm. 2 vols. Cairo: al-Muʾassasa al-ʿArabiyya al-Ḥadītha, 1964.

Asṭurlābī. *Durrat al-tāj min shiʿr Ibn al-Ḥajjāj*. Ed. ʿAlī Jawād al-Ṭāhir. Baghdad; Berlin: Manshūrāt al-Jamal, 2009.

Azdī, Ibn Ẓāfir ʿAlī. *Badāʾiʿ al-badāʾih*. Ed. Muḥammad Abū l-Faḍl Ibrāhīm. Cairo: Maktabat al-Anjlū al-Miṣriyya, 1970.

Bābānī, Ismāʿīl Bāshā. *Hadiyyat al-ʿārifīn: Asmāʾ al-muʾallifīn wa-āthār al-muṣannifīn*. 2 vols. Baghdad: Maktabat al-Muthannā, 1972.

Bākharzī, ʿAlī b. al-Ḥasan. *Dumyat al-qaṣr*. Ed. Muḥammad al-Ṭūnjī. 3 vols. Beirut: Dār al-Jīl, 1993.

Bayhaqī, Abū l-Faḍl. *Taʾrīkh-i Bayhaqī*. Ed. Manūchihr Dānish Pazhūh. 2 vols. Tehran: Hirmand, 1380 [2002].

Bayhaqī, ʿAlī b. Zayd. *Tatimmat Ṣiwān al-ḥikma*. Ed. Rafīq al-ʿAjam. Beirut: Dār al-Fikr al-Lubnānī, 1994.

Bayyāḍī, Zayn al-Dīn. *al-Ṣirāṭ al-mustaqīm ilā mustaḥiqqī al-taqdīm*. Ed. M. B. al-Bahbūdī. 3 vols. Tehran: Al-Maktaba al-Murtaḍawiyya, 1964.

Damīrī, Muḥammad b. Mūsā. *Ḥayāt al-ḥayawān al-kubrā*. Damascus: Dār Ṭalās, 1989.

Dhahabī, Muḥammad b. Aḥmad. *Taʾrīkh al-Islām wa-wafayāt al-mashāhīr wa-l-aʿlām*. Ed. ʿUmar ʿAbd al-Salām Tadmurī. 50 vols. Beirut: Dār al-Kitāb al-ʿArabī, 1993.

———. *al-ʿIbar fī khabar man ghabar*. 5 vols. Kuwayt: Dār al-Maṭbūʿāt wa-l-Nashr, 1960–86.

———. *Siyar aʿlām al-nubalāʾ*. Ed. Shuʿayb al-Arnaʾūṭ. 25 vols. Beirut: Muʾassasat al-Risāla, 1990–92.

 | DOI 10.1163/9789004317352_009

Ḥājjī Khalīfa. *Kashf al-ẓunūn ʿan asāmī al-kutub wa-l-funūn*. 2 vols. Baghdad: Maṭbaʿat al-Muthannā, 1972.

Hamadhānī, Badīʿ al-Zamān. *The Maqāmāt*. Trans. W. J. Pendergast. London: Luzac, 1915.

———. *Maqāmāt Badīʿ al-Zamān al-Hamadhānī*. Ed. Muḥammad ʿAbduh. Beirut: Dār al-Mashriq, 2000.

Ḥamawī, Yāqūt. *Muʿjam al-buldān*. 5 vols. Beirut: Dār al-Fikr, 1399 [1978].

———. *Muʿjam al-udabāʾ: Irshād al-arīb ilā maʿrifat al-adīb*. Ed. Iḥsān ʿAbbās. 7 vols. Beirut: Dār al-Gharb al-Islāmī, 1993.

Hidāyat, R. Q. Kh. *Majmaʿ al-Fuṣaḥāʾ*. Tehran: Kharkhānah-i Āghā Mīr Muḥammad Bāqir, 1295 [1878].

Ḥumaydī. *Jadhwat al-muqtabis fī dhikr wulāt al-Andalus*. Cairo: al-Dār al-Miṣriyya li-l-Taʾlīf wa-l-Tarjama, 1966.

al-Ḥuṣrī al-Qayrawānī. *Zahr al-ādāb wa-thimār al-albāb*. Ed. ʿA. M. al-Bajāwī. 2 vols. Cairo: al-Bābī al-Ḥalabī, 1970.

Ibn ʿAbd Rabbihi. *al-ʿIqd al-farīd*. Ed. Mufīd Muḥammad Qumayḥa. 7 vols. Beirut: Dār al-Kutub al-ʿIlmiyya, 1983.

Ibn Abī Ḥajala. *Dīwān al-ṣabāba*. Ed. Muḥammad Zaghlūl Sallām. Alexandria: Munshaʾāt al-Maʿārif, 1987.

Ibn al-Anbārī. *Nuzhat al-alibbāʾ fī ṭabaqāt al-udabāʾ*. Ed. Muḥammad Abū l-Faḍl Ibrāhīm. Cairo: Dār Nahḍat Miṣr, 1967.

Ibn al-Athīr, Ḍiyāʾ al-Dīn Naṣr Allāh b. Muḥammad. *al-Mathal al-sāʾir fī adab al-kātib wa-l-shāʿir*. Ed. Aḥmad al-Ḥūfī and Badawī Ṭabāna. 4 vols. Cairo: Dār Nahḍat Miṣr, 1973.

Ibn al-Athīr, Muḥammad b. Muḥammad. *al-Kāmil fī l-tārīkh*. Ed. Abū l-Fidāʾ ʿAbdallāh al-Qāḍī. 10 vols. Beirut: Dār al-Kutub al-ʿIlmiyya, 1995.

Ibn al-Bakkāʾ al-Balkhī. *Ghawānī al-ashwāq fī maʿānī al-ʿushshāq*. Ed. George Kanazi. Wiesbaden: Harrassiwitz, 2008.

Ibn Ḥamdūn. *al-Tadhkira al-Ḥamdūniyya*. Ed. Iḥsān ʿAbbās and Bakr ʿAbbās. 9 vols. Beirut: Dār Ṣādir, 1996.

Ibn al-Jawzī. *al-Adhkiyāʾ*. Ed. A. ʿA. Al-Rifāʿī. Damascus: Maktabat al-Ghazzālī, 1971, 195.

———. *Akhbār al-ḥamqā wa-l-mughaffalīn*. Ed. M. A. Farshūkh. Beirut: Dār al-Fikr al-ʿArabī, 1990.

Ibn Jinnī, Abū l-Fatḥ ʿUthmān. *al-Fasr* (*Sharḥ Ibn Jinnī al-kabīr ʿalā Dīwān al-Mutanabbī*). Ed. Riḍā Rajab. 5 vols. Damascus: Dār al-Yanābīʿ, 2004.

———. *al-Khaṣāʾiṣ*. Ed. Muḥammad ʿAlī al-Najjār. 3 vols. Cairo: Maṭbaʿat Dār al-Kutub al-Miṣriyya, 1952–6.

Ibn Khallikān. *Wafayāt al-aʿyān wa-anbāʾ abnāʾ al-zamān*. 8 vols. Ed. Iḥsān ʿAbbās. Beirut: Dār Ṣādir, 1968.

Ibn al-Nadīm. *al-Fihrist*. Ed. Riḍā Tajaddud. Beirut: Dār al-Masīra, 1988.

Ibn Qutayba, ʿAbdallāh b. Muslim. *Al-Shiʿr wa-l-shuʿarāʾ*. 2 vols. Beirut: Dār al-Thaqāfa, 1964.

———. *ʿUyūn al-akhbār*. 4 vols. Cairo: al-Muʾassasa al-Miṣriyya al-ʿĀmma li-l-Taʾlīf wa-l-Tarjama, 1964.

Ibn al-Ṣayrafī. *K. Natāʾij al-mudhākara*. Ed. Ibrāhīm Ṣāliḥ. Beirut: Dār al-Bashāʾir, 1999.

Ibn Shuhayd. *Risālat al-tawābiʿ wa-l-zawābiʿ*. Ed. Buṭrus al-Bustānī. Beirut: Dār Ṣādir, 1967.

———. *Risālat al-tawābiʿ wa-l-zawābiʿ* (*The Treatise of Familiar Spirits and Demons*). Trans. James T. Monroe. Berkeley: University of California Press, 1971.

Ibn al-Zubyr [attributed]. *K. al-Dhakhāʾir wa-l-tuḥaf*. Ed. Muḥammad Ḥamīdullāh. Kuwayt: Dāʾirat al-Maṭbūʿat wa-l-Nashr, 1959.

———. *Book of Gifts and Rarities*. Trans. Ghāda al-Ḥijjāwī al-Qaddūmī. Cambridge: Harvard Center for Middle Eastern Studies, 1996.

Iṣbahānī, Abū Nuʿaym. *Dhikr akhbār Iṣbahān*. Ed. Sven Dedering. 2 vols. Leiden: Brill, 1931–4.

Iṣfahānī, ʿImād al-Dīn. *Kharīdat al-qaṣr qism shuʿarāʾ Miṣr*. Ed. Aḥmad Amīn, Shawqī Ḍayf, and Iḥsān ʿAbbās. Cairo: Lajnat al-Taʾlīf wa-l-Tarjama wa-l-Nashr, 1951.

Iṣfahānī, al-Rāghib. *Muḥāḍarāt al-udabāʾ*. Ed. Riyāḍ ʿAbd al-Ḥamīd Murād. 5 vols. Beirut: Dār Ṣādir, 2006.

Jumaḥī, Ibn Sallām. *Ṭabaqāt fuḥūl al-shuʿarāʾ*. Ed. Maḥmūd Muḥammad Shākir. 2 vols. Cairo: Maṭbaʿat al-Madanī, 1974.

Jurāwī, Aḥmad b. ʿAbd al-Salām. *Al-Ḥamāsa al-maghribiyya: Mukhtaṣar Ṣafwat al-adab wa-nukhbat dīwān al-ʿArab*. Beirut: Dār al-Fikr al-Muʿāṣir, 1991.

Jurjānī, ʿAlī b. ʿAbd al-ʿAzīz. *al-Wasāṭa bayna l-Mutanabbī wa khuṣūmih*. Ed. Muḥammad Abū l-Faḍl Ibrāhīm and ʿAlī Muḥammad al-Bajāwī. Saida: al-Maktaba al-ʿAṣriyya, 1986.

Jurjānī, ʿAlī b. Muḥammad. *K. al-Taʿrīfāt*. Beirut: Maktabat Lubnān, 1969.

Kalāʿī, Muḥammad b. ʿAbd al-Ghafūr. *Iḥkām ṣanʿat al-kalām*. Ed. Muḥammad Riḍwān al-Dāya. Beirut: ʿĀlam al-Kutub, 1985.

Khafājī, ʿAbdallāh b. Muḥammad. *Sirr al-faṣāḥa*. Ed. ʿAbd al-Mutaʿāl al-Ṣaʿīdī. Cairo: Maktabat Ṣubayḥ, 1953.

Khāndamīr, Ghiyāth al-Dīn. *Dustūr al-wuzarāʾ*. Trans. Amīn Sulaymān. Cairo: al-Hayʾa al-Miṣriyya al-ʿĀmma li-l-Kitāb, 1980.

Khaṭīb al-Baghdādī. *Taʾrīkh Baghdād*. 14 vols. Beirut: Dār al-Kitāb al-ʿArabī, 1966.

Kirmānī, Nāṣir al-Dīn Munshī. *Nasāʾim al-asḥār min laṭāʾim al-akhbār dar tārīkh-i vuzarāʾ*. Ed. Jalāl al-Dīn Ḥusaynī Urmavī. Tehran: Dānishgāh-i Tehrān, 1959.

Kutubī, Ibn Shākir. *Fawāt al-wafayāt*. Ed. Iḥsān ʿAbbās. 5 vols. Beirut: Dār Ṣādir, 1973.

Majmūʿat al-maʿānī. Ed. ʿAbd al-Muʿīn al-Mallūḥī. Damascus: Dār Ṭalās, 1988.

Maqqarī, Aḥmad b. Muḥammad. *Nafḥ al-ṭīb min ghuṣn al-Andalus al-raṭīb*. Ed. Iḥsān ʿAbbās. 8 vols. Beirut: Dār Ṣādir, 1968.

Maymunī, ʿAbd al-ʿAzīz. *al-Ṭarāʾif al-adabiyya*. Cairo: Maṭbaʿat Lajnat al-Taʾlīf wa-l-Tarjama wa-l-Nashr, 1937.

Mīkālī, Abū l-Faḍl. *al-Muntakhal*. Ed. Yaḥyā Wahīb al-Jubūrī. 2 vols. Beirut: Dār al-Gharb al-Islāmī, 2000.

Mufaḍḍal al-Ḍabbī. *al-Mufaḍḍaliyyāt*. Ed. Aḥmad Muḥammad Shākir and ʿAbd al-Salām Hārūn. Cairo: Dār al-Maʿārif, 1942.

———. *The Mufaḍḍaliyyāt: An Anthology of Ancient Arabian Odes*. Ed. Charles James Lyall. Oxford: Clarendon Press, 1918.

Muṭṭawwiʿī, ʿUmar b. ʿAlī. *Darj al-ghurar wa-durj al-durar*. Ed. Jalīl al-ʿAṭiyya. Beirut: ʿĀlam al-Kutub, 1986.

Naḥḥās, Aḥmad b. Muḥammad. *Sharḥ al-qaṣāʾid al-tisʿ al-mashhūrāt*. Ed. Aḥmad Khaṭṭāb. 2 vols. Baghdad: Wizārat al-Iʿlām, 1973.

Niẓāmī, ʿArūḍī. *The Chahār Maqāla (The Four Discourses)*. Trans. E. G. Browne. Hertford: S. Austin and Sons, 1899.

Qalqashandī, Aḥmad b. ʿAlī. *Ṣubḥ al-aʿshā*. 14 vols. Cairo: *Dār al-Kutub al-Miṣriyya*, 1922.

Raffāʾ, al-Sarī b. Aḥmad. *al-Muḥibb wa-l-maḥbūb wa l-mashmūm wa-l-mashrūb*. Ed. Miṣbāḥ al-Ghalāwinjī. 4 vols. Damascus: Majmaʿ al-Lugha al-ʿArabiyya, 1986–7.

Rāfiʿī. *Kitāb al-tadwīn fī akhbār Qazwīn*. Ed. ʿAzīz Allāh al-ʿUṭāridī. 4 vols. Beirut: Dār al-Kutub al-ʿIlmiyya, 1987.

Rawḥ al-rūḥ. Ed. Ibrāhīm Ṣāliḥ. 2 vols. Abu Dhabi: Hayʾat Abū Ẓabī li-l-Thaqāfa wa-l-Turāth, 2009.

Ṣābī, Ibrāhīm b. Hilāl (Abū Isḥāq). *Al-Mukhtār min rasāʾil Abī Isḥāq Ibrāhīm b. Hilāl b. Zahrūn al-Ṣābī*. Ed. Shakīb Arslān. Beirut: Dār al-Nahḍa al-Ḥadītha, 1966.

———. *Al-Muntazaʿ min Kitāb al-Tājī*. Ed. Muḥammad Ḥusayn al-Zubaydī. Baghdad: Dār al-Ḥurriyya, 1977.

Ṣafadī, Khalīl b. Aybak. *al-Wāfī bi-l-wafayāt*. 29 vols. Ed. Aḥmad al-Arnāʾūṭ and Turkī Muṣṭafā. Beirut: Dār Iḥyāʾ al-Turāth al-ʿArabī, 2000.

Ṣāḥib b. ʿAbbād. *al-Amthāl al-sāʾira min shiʿr al-Mutanabbī wa-l-Rūznāmjah*. Ed. M. Ḥ. Āl Yāsīn. Baghdad: Maktabat al-Nahḍa, 1965.

———. *al-Khashf ʿan masāwiʾ shiʿr al-Mutanabbī*. Ed. Muḥammad Ḥasan Āl Yāsīn. Baghdad: Maktabat al-Nahḍa, 1965.

———. *al-Rūznāmja*. Ed. Muḥammad Ḥasan Āl Yāsīn. Baghdad: Maktabat al-Nahḍa, 1965.

Samʿānī. *K. al-Ansāb*. Ed. ʿA. al-Bārūdī. 5 vols. Beirut: Dār al-Jinān li-l-Ṭibāʿa wa-l-Nashr, 1988.

Shantarīnī, Ibn Bassām. *al-Dhakhīra fī maḥāsin ahl al-Jazīra*. Ed. Iḥsān ʿAbbās. 8 vols. Beirut: Dār Ṣādir, 1998.

Subkī, Tāj al-Dīn Abū Naṣr. *Ṭabaqāt al-shāfiʿiyya*. Ed. ʿAbd al-Fattāḥ al-Ḥulw and Maḥmūd Muḥammad al-Ṭanāḥī. 11 vols. Cairo: Dār Iḥyāʾ al-Kutub al-ʿArabiyya, 1992.

Ṣūlī, Muḥammad b. Yaḥyā. *Akhbār Abī Tammām*. Ed. Kh. M. ʿAsākir et al. Beirut: al-Maktab al-Tijārī, n.d.

Ṣūrī, ʿAbd al-Muḥsin b. Muḥammad. *Dīwān al-Ṣūrī*. Ed. Makkī al-Sayyid Jāsim and Shākir Hādī Shukr. 2 vols. Baghdad: Manshūrāt Wizārat al-Thaqāfa wa-l-Iʿlām, 1981.

Suyūṭī, Jalāl al-Dīn. *Bughyat al-wuʿāt fī ṭabaqāt al-lughawiyyīn wa-l-nuḥāt*. Ed. Abū l-Faḍl Ibrāhīm. 2 vols. Cairo: al-Bābī al-Ḥalabī, 1964–5.

———. *al-Muzhir fī ʿulūm al-lugha wa-anwāʿihā*. Ed. Muḥammad Abū l-Faḍl Ibrāhīm et al. 2 vols. Cairo: al-Bābī al-Ḥalabī, 1958.

Tamīmī, Muḥammad b. Aḥmad. *al-Tuḥaf wa-l-ẓuraf*. Ed. ʿInād Ismāʿīl. Baghdād: al-Jāmiʿa al-Mustanṣiriyya, 1991.

Tanūkhī, Abū ʿAlī al-Muḥassin. *Nishwār al-muḥāḍara*. Ed. ʿAbbūd al-Shāljī. 5 vols. Beirut: Dār Ṣādir, 1971–3.

Tawḥīdī, Abū Ḥayyān. *Akhlāq al-wazīrayn*. Ed. Muḥammad b. Tāwīt al-Ṭūnjī. Beirut: Dār Ṣādir, 1992.

———. *al-Baṣāʾir wa-l-dhakhāʾir*. Ed. Wadād al-Qāḍī. 10 vols. Beirut: Dār Ṣādir, 1988.

Tibrīzī, Yaḥyā b. ʿAlī. *Sharḥ Dīwān al-Ḥamāsa*. 4 vols. Ed. M. M. ʿAbd al-Ḥamīd. Cairo: al-Maktaba al-Tijāriyya, 1938.

Thaʿālibī. *Ādāb al-mulūk*. Ed. Jalīl ʿAṭiyya. Beirut: Dār al-Gharb al-Islāmī, 1990.

———. *Aḥsan mā samiʿtu*. Ed. A. ʿA. Tammām and S. ʿĀṣim. Beirut: Muʾassasat al-Kutub al-Thaqāfiyya, 1989.

———. *Ajnās al-tajnīs*. Ed. M. ʿA. al-Jādir. Beirut: ʿĀlam al-Kutub, 1997.

———. *al-Anīs fī ghurar al-tajnīs*. Ed. Hilāl Nājī. Beirut: ʿĀlam al-Kutub, 1996.

———. *Dīwān al-Thaʿālibī*. Ed Māḥmūd al-Jādir. Beirut: ʿĀlam al-Kutub, 1988.

———. *Fiqh al-lugha wa-sirr al-ʿarabiyya*. Ed. Yāsīn al-Ayyūbī. Beirut: al-Maktaba al-ʿAṣriyya, 2000.

———. *al-Iʿjāz wa-l-ījāz*. Ed. Ibrāhīm Ṣāliḥ. Damascus: Dār al-Bashāʾir, 2004.

———. *al-Iqtibās min al-Qurʾān*. Ed. I. al-Ṣaffār and M. M. Bahjat. 2 vols. Al-Manṣūra: Dār al-Wafāʾ, 1992.

———. *Khāṣṣ al-khāṣṣ*. Ed. Ṣādiq al-Naqwī. Hyderabad: Maṭbūʿāt Majlis Dāʾirat al-Maʿārif al-ʿUthmāniyya, 1984.

———. *K. al-Kināya wa-l-taʿrīd aw al-Nihāya fī fann al-kināya*. Ed. Faraj al-Ḥawwār. Baghdad: Manshūrāt al-Jamal, 2006.

———. *Laṭāʾif al-maʿārif*. Ed. I. al-Abyārī and Ḥ. K. al-Ṣayrafī. Cairo: Dār Iḥyāʾ al-Kutub al-ʿArabiyya, 1960.

———. *Laṭāʾif al-ẓurafāʾ*. Ed. Q. al-Samarrai. Leiden: Brill, 1978.

———. *Lubāb al-ādāb*. Ed. Ṣ. Q. Rashīd. Baghdad: Dār al-Shuʾūn al-Thaqāfiyya, 1988.

———. *Man Ghāba ʿanhu l-muṭrib*. Ed. Yūnus Aḥmad al-Sāmarrāʾī. Beirut: ʿĀlam al-Kutub, 1987.

———. *Mirʾāt al-murūʾāt*. Ed. Yūnus ʿAlī al-Madgharī. Beirut: Dār Lubnān, 2003.

———. *al-Mubhij*. Ed. Ibrāhīm Ṣāliḥ. Damascus: Dār al-Bashāʾir, 1999.

———. *al-Muntaḥal*. Ed. Aḥmad Abū ʿAlī. Alexandria: al-Maṭbaʿa al-Tijāriyya, 1901.

———.[falsely attributed]. *al-Muntakhab fī maḥāsin ashʿār al-ʿArab*. Ed. ʿA. S. Jamāl. 2 vols. Cairo: Maktabat al-Khānjī, 1993–4.

———.[falsely attributed]. *al-Shakwā wa-l-ʿitāb wa-mā waqaʿa li-l-khillān wa-l-aṣḥāb*. Ed. I. ʿA al-Muftī. Kuwayt: al-Majlis al-Waṭanī li-l-Thaqāfa, 2000.

———. *Nathr al-naẓm wa-ḥall al-ʿaqd*. Ed. Aḥmad ʿAbd al-Fattāḥ Tammām. Beirut: Muʾassasat al-Kutub al-Thaqāfiyya, 1990.

———. *Sajʿ al-manthūr*. Ed. Usāma al-Buḥayrī. Riyāḍ: Kitāb al-Majalla al-ʿArabiyya, 2013.

———. *Siḥr al-balāgha wa-sirr al-barāʿa*. Ed. ʿA. al-Ḥūfī. Beirut: Dār al-Kutub al-ʿIlmiyya, 1984.

———. *Siḥr al-balāgha wa-sirr al-barāʿa*. Ed. A. ʿUbayd. Damascus: al-Maktaba al-ʿArabiyya, 1931.

———. *Taḥsīn al-qabīḥ wa-taqbīḥ al-ḥasan*. Ed. Shākir al-ʿĀshū. Baghdad: Wizārat al-Awqāf, 1981.

———. *al-Tamthīl wa-l-muḥāḍara*. Ed. ʿA. al-Ḥulw. Cairo: Dār Iḥyāʾ al-Kutub al-ʿArabiyya, 1961.

———. *Tatimmat al-Yatīma*. Ed. M. M. Qumayḥa. Beirut: Dār al-Kutub al-ʿIlmiyya, 1983.

———. *al-Tawfīq li-l-talfīq*. Ed. Ibrāhīm Ṣāliḥ. Beirut: Dār al-Fikr al-Muʿāṣir, 1990.

———. *Thimār al-qulūb fī-l-muḍāf wa-l-mansūb*. Ed. Muḥammad Abū l-Faḍl Ibrāhīm. Cairo: Dār Nahḍat Miṣr, 1965.

———. *K. al-Tuḥaf wa-l-anwār min al-balāghāt wa-l-ashʿār*. Ed. Yaḥyā al-Jubūrī. Ammān: Dār Majdalāwī, 2008.

———. *Tuḥfat al-wuzarāʾ*. Ed. Ḥ. ʿA. al-Rāwī and I. M. al-Ṣaffār. Baghdad: Wizārat al-Awqāf, 1977.

———. *Yatīmat al-dahr fī maḥāsin ahl al-ʿaṣr* (*Yatīma*). Ed. Muḥyī al-Dīn ʿAbd al-Ḥamīd. 4 vols. Cairo: al-Maktaba al-Tijāriyya, 1956.

———. *Zād safar al-mulūk*. Ed. Ramzi Baalbaki and Bilal Orfali. Beirut: Bibliotheca Islamica 2011.

———. *al-Ẓarāʾif wa-l-laṭāʾif wa-l-Yawāqīt fī baʿḍ al-mawāqīt*. Ed. Nāṣir Muḥammadī Muḥammad Jād. Cairo: Dār al-Kutub wa-l-Wathāʾiq, 2006.

Tibrīzī, Yaḥyā b. ʿAlī. *Sharḥ Dīwān al-Ḥamāsa*. Ed. M. M. ʿAbd al-Ḥamīd. 4 vols. Cairo: al-Maktaba al-Tijāriyya, 1938.

ʿUtbī, Muḥammad b. ʿAbd al-Jabbār. *al-Yamīnī fī sharḥ akhbār al-sulṭān yamīn al-dawla wa-amīn al-milla Maḥmūd al-Ghaznawī*. Ed. Iḥsān Dh. al-Thāmirī. Beirut: Dār al-Ṭalīʿa, 2004.

Wāḥidī, ʿAlī b. Aḥmad. *al-Daʿawāt wa-l-fuṣūl*. Ed. ʿĀ. al-Furayjāt. Damascus: ʿA. al-Furayjāt, 2005.

Washshāʾ. *al-Muwashshā*. Beirut: Dār Sādir, 1965.

Yāfiʿī, ʿAbdallah b. Asʿad. *Mirʾāt al-jinān*. 4 vols. Beirut: Muʾassasat al-Aʿlamī, 1970.

Yamanī, Muḥammad b. Ḥusayn b. ʿUmar. *Muḍāhāt amthāl Kitāb Kalīla wa-Dimna*. Ed. Muḥammad Yūsuf Najm. Beirut: Dār al-Thaqāfa, 1961.

Secondary Sources

ʿAbbās, Iḥsān. *Tārīkh al-naqd al-adabī ʿinda l-ʿarab*. Beirut: Dār Ṣādir, 1971.

ʿAbdullahi, ʿAlī. "Ghurar al-siyar, barrasī dar bāriy-i nām-i aṣlī wa-muʾallif-i ān." *Tārīkh va-tamaddun-i īslāmī* 100 (1393), 105–12.

Abu Deeb, Kamal. "Literary Criticism," in *ʿAbbasid Belles-Lettres*. Ed. Julia Ashtiany et al. Cambridge: Cambridge University Press, 1990, 339-87.

Ahlwardt. *Sammlungen alter arabischer Dichter*. Berlin: Reeuther and Reichard, 1902–3.

Aḥmad, Ḥasan. *Abʿād al-naṣṣ al-naqdī ʿinda al-Thaʿālibī*. Damascus: al-Hayʾa al-ʿĀmma al-Sūriyya li-l-Kitāb, 2007.

Ahmad, M. *Muslim Education and the Scholars' Social Status up to the 5th Century Muslim Era in the Light of Taʾrīkh Baghdād*. Zürich: Verlag "Der Islam," 1968.

Ali, Samer. *Arabic Literary Salons in the Islamic Middle Ages*. Notre Dame: University of Notre Dame Press, 2010.

Alwan, M. B. "Is Ḥammād the Collector of the Muʿallaqāt?" *Islamic Culture* 45 (1971), 263–5.

Antoon, Sinan. *The Poetics of the Obscene in Premodern Arabic Poetry: Ibn al-Ḥajjāj and* Sukhf. New York: Palgrave Macmillan, 2014.

Arafat, Walid. "Landmarks of Literary Criticism in the 3rd Century A.H.," *Islamic Quarterly* 13 (1969), 70–78.

Arazi, A. "*al-ḥanīn ilā al-awṭān* entre la Ǧāhiliyya et l'Islam: Le Bédouin et le citadin réconciliés." *Zeitschrift der deutschen morgenländischen Gesellschaft* 143 (1993), 287–327.

———. "Risāla," *EI2*, VII:532–44.

Asad, Nāṣir al-Dīn. *Maṣādir al-shiʿr al-jāhilī*. Cairo: Dār al-Maʿārif, 1978.

Auchterlonie, Paul. *Arabic Biographical Dictionaries: A Summary Guide and Bibliography*. Durham: Middle East Libraries Committee, 1987.

Bauer, Thomas. "Fremdheit in der klassischen arabischen Kultur und Sprache," in *Fremdes in fremden Sprachen*. Ed. Brigitte Jostes and Jürgen Trabant. Munich: W. Fink, 2001, 85–105.

———. "Literarische Anthologien der Mamlūkenzeit," in *Die Mamluken. Studien zu ihrer Geschichte und Kultur*. Ed. S. Conermann and A. Pistor-Hatam. Hamburg: EB-Verlag, 2003, 71–122.

———. "Mamluk Literature: Misunderstandings and New Approaches." *Mamlūk Studies Review* 9 (2005), 105–32.

Blachere, R. "al-Hamadhānī,"*EI2*, III:106a.

Blochet, E. *Catalogue de la collection des manuscrits orientaux, arabes, persans et turcs*. Ed. Charles Shefer. Paris: Leroux, 1900.

Bonebakker, S. A. "*Adab* and the Concept of Belles-Lettres," in *The Cambridge History of Arabic Literature: Abbasid Belles-Lettres*. Ed. Julia Ashtiany et al. Cambridge: Cambridge University Press, 1990, 16–30.

———. *Ḥātimī and His Encounter with Mutanabbī, A Biographical Sketch*. Amsterdam; New York: North-Holland Pub. Co., 1984.

Bosworth. C. E. "Ḳābūs b. Wushmgīr," *EI2*, IV:357b–358b.

———. "Khwārazm-shāhs," *EI2*, IV:1068b–1069b.

———. "Maḥmūd b. Sebüktigin," *EI2*, VI:64b.

———. "Manuscripts of Tha'ālibī's "Yatīmat ad-dahr" in the Süleymaniye Library, Istanbul." *Journal of Semitic Studies*, 16 (1971), 41–9.

———. "Mīkālīs." *EI2*, VII:25b–26b.

———. "Nūḥ b. Manṣūr b. Nūḥ." *EI2*, VIII 110a.

———. "al-Rukhkhadj." *EI2*, VIII:595a–595b.

———. "Sebüktigin." *EI2*, IX:121a–121b.

———. *The Ghaznavids: Their Empire in Afghanistan and Eastern Iran, 994:1040*. Edinburgh: University Press, 1963.

———. *The Islamic Dynasties*. Edinburgh: University Press, 1967.

———. trans. *The Laṭā'if al-Ma'ārif of Tha'ālibī* [*The Book of Curious and Entertaining Information*]. Edinburgh: Edinburgh University Press 1968.

———. *The Mediaeval Islamic Underworld: The Banū Sāsān in Arabic Society and Literature*. Leiden: Brill, 1976.

Brockelmann, C. "Das Dichterbuch des Muḥammad ibn Sallām al-Ǧumaḥī," in *Orientalische Studien Theodor Nöldeke gewidmet* I. Gieszen: Alfrad Töpelmann, 1906, 109–26.

———. *Geschichte der arabischen Litteratur* (*GAL*). Leiden: Brill, 1943–9.

———. *Geschichte der arabischen Litteratur*, supplement (*GALS*). Leiden: Brill, 1937–42.

———. "al-T͟haʿālibī, Abū Manṣūr al-Ḥusayn b. Muḥammad al-Maraghānī." *EI1*, VIII:732b.

Browne, Edward G. *A Literary History of Persia*. Cambridge University Press, [1928].

Burrell, R. M. "al-Mubarrad." *EI2*, VII:279–82.

Busse, H. *Chalif und Grosskönig; die Buyiden im Iraq (945–1055)*. Beirut: In Kommission bei F. Steiner, 1969.

Chiabotti, Francesco. "The Spiritual and Physical Progeny of ʿAbd al-Karīm al-Qushayrī: A Preliminary Study in Abū Naṣr al-Qushayrī's (d. 514/1120) *Kitāb al-Shawāhid wa-l-Amthāl*." *Journal of Sufi Studies* 2/1 (2013), 46–77.

Cheikh-Moussa, Abdallah. "L'historien et la littérature arabe médiévale." *Arabica* 43 (1996), 152–88.

Chejne, A. J. "The Boon Companion in Early ʿAbbāsid Times." *Journal of the American Oriental Society* 85 (1965), 327–35.

Coulson, N. J. "European Criticism of *Ḥadīth* Literature," in *Arabic Literature to the End of the Umayyad Period*. Cambridge: Cambridge University Press, 1983, 317–21.

Crone, Patricia. *Slaves on Horses: The Evolution of the Islamic Polity*. Cambridge: Cambridge University Press, 1980.

Dānishpažūh. *Fihrist-i Microfilmhā*. Tehran: Kitābkhāna-i-Markazī-i Dānishgāh, 1348 A.H.

Dickie, J. "Ibn Shuhayd: A Biographical and Critical Study." *al-Andalus* 29 (1964), 243–310.

Dyck, Edward van. *Iktifāʾ al-qanūʿ bi-mā huwa maṭbūʿ*. Tehran: Maṭbaʿat Behman, 1988.

Encyclopaedia of Islam [*EI1*]. Leiden: Brill, 1908–38.

Encyclopaedia of Islam [*EI2*]. Leiden: Brill, 1960–2002.

Encyclopaedia of Islam [*EI3*]. Leiden: Brill, 2008–.

El Cheikh, Nadia Maria. "In Search for the Ideal Spouse." *Journal of the Economic and Social History of the Orient* 45 (2002), 179–96.

———. "Women's History: A Study of al-Tanūkhī," in *Writing the Feminine: Women in Arab Sources*. Ed. Randi Deguilhem and Manuela Marín. London: I. B. Tauris, 2002, 129–52.

Fähndrich, H. "Der Begriff 'Adab' und sein literarischer Niederschlag," in *Orientalisches Mittelalter*. Ed. Wolfhart Heinrichs. Wiesbaden: AULA-Verlag, 1990, 326–45.

———. "al-Tanūk͟hī." *EI2*, X:192b–193b.

Fāris, Bishr. *Mabāḥith ʿarabiyya*. Cairo: Maṭbaʿat al-Maʿārif, 1939.

Fayṣal, Shukrī. *Manāhij al-dirāsa al-adabiyya*. Cairo: Maṭbaʿat Dār al-Hanāʾ, 1953.

Fleischhammer, Manfred. *Die Quellen des Kitāb al-Aġānī*. Wiesbaden: Harrassowitz, 2004.

Fück, J. W. "al-Bustī, Abu' l-Fatḥ b. Muḥammad." *EI2*, I:1348b.

Fück, Johann. "Die Rolle des Traditionalismus im Islam." *Zeitschrift der Deutschen Morgenländischen Gesellschaft* 93 (1939), 1–32.

Gabrieli, F. "Adab." *EI2*, I:175–6.

Gamal, Adel Sulayman. "The Basis of Selection in the *Ḥamāsa* Collections." *Journal of Arabic Literature* 7 (1976), 28–44.

———. "The Organizational Principles in Ibn Sallām's *Ṭabaqāt Fuḥūl al-Shuʿarāʾ*: A Reconsideration," in *Tradition and Modernity in Arabic Language and Literature*. Ed. J. R. Smart. New York: Routledge, 1996, 186–210.

Gelder, G. J. H. van. "Against Women, and Other Pleasantries: The Last Chapter of Abū Tammām's *Ḥamāsa*." *Journal of Arabic Literature* 16 (1985), 61–7.

———. "Beautifying the Ugly and Uglifying the Beautiful: The Paradox in Classical Arabic Literature." *Journal of Semitic Studies* 48.2 (2003), 321–51.

———. "Complete Men, Women and Books: On Medieval Arabic Encyclopaedism," in *Pre-Modern Encyclopaedic Texts*. Ed. Peter Binkley. Leiden: Brill, 1997, 251–9.

———. "Mirbad," in *Encyclopedia of Arabic Literature*. Ed. Julie Scott Meisami and Paul Starkey. New York: Routledge, 1998, 2:527.

———. "Mixtures of Jest and Earnest in Classical Arabic Literature," I: *Journal of Arabic Literature* 23 (1992), 83–108; II: *Journal of Arabic Literature* 23 (1993), 169–90.

———. "Muḥdathūn." *EI2* Suppl., 637–40.

Geries, Ibrāhīm. "On Jaakko Hämeen-Antilla, *Maqama: A History of a Genre*." *Middle Eastern Literatures* 8 (2005), 187–95.

Giffen, Lois Arita. *Theory of Profane Love among the Arabs: The Development of the Genre*. New York: New York University Press, 1971.

Gruendler, Beatrice. *Medieval Arabic Praise Poetry*. London: RoutledgeCurzon, 2003.

———. "Meeting the Patron: An *Akhbār* Type and Its Implication for *Muḥdath* Poetry," in *Ideas, Images, and Methods of Portrayal*. Ed. Sebastian Günther. Leiden: Brill, 2005, 59–88.

———. "Motif vs. Genre: Reflections on the *Dīwān al-Maʿānī* of Abū Hilāl al-ʿAskarī," in *Ghazal as World Literature I: Transformations of a Literary Genre*. Ed. Thomas Bauer and Angelika Neuwirth. Beirut: Orient-Institut; Würzburg: Ergon 2005, 57–85.

———. "Originality in Imitation: Two *Muʿāraḍas* by Ibn Darrāj al-Qasṭallī." *al-Qantara* 29.2 (2008), 437–65.

———. "*Tawqīʿ*," in *The Weaving of Words: Approaches to Classical Arabic Prose*. Ed. Lale Behzadi and Vahid Behmardi. Beirut: Orient Institut, 2009, 101–29.

Grunebaum, G. E. von. "The Concept of Plagiarism in Arabic Theory." *Journal of Near Eastern Studies* 3 (1944), 234–53.

———. *Medieval Islam: A Study in Cultural Orientation*. Chicago: University of Chicago Press, 1953.

———. "The Response to Nature in Arabic Poetry." *Journal of Near Eastern Studies* 4 (1945), 137–51.

Günther, Sebastian. "Assessing the Sources of Classical Arabic Compilations: The Issue of Categories and Methodologies." *British Journal of Middle Eastern Studies* 32 (2005), 75–98.

———. "» . . . nor have I learned it from any book of theirs« Abū l-Faraj al-Iṣfahānī: A Medieval Arabic Author at Work," in *Islamstudien ohne Ende: Festschrift Für Werner Ende Zum 65. Geburtstag*. Ed. R. Brunner et al. [Heidelberg]: Deutsche Morgenländische Gesellschaft, 2000, 139–54.

Gutas, Dimitri. "Classical Arabic Wisdom Literature: Nature and Scope." *Journal of the American Oriental Society* 101 (1981), 49–86.

———. "Ethische Schriften im Islam," in *Orientalisches Mittelalter*. Ed. W. Heinrichs. Wiesbaden: AULA-Verlag, 1990, 346–65.

———. *Greek Wisdom Literature in Arabic Translation: A Study of the Graeco-Arabic Gnomologia*. New Haven: American Oriental Society, 1975.

Guzman, Roberto Marín. "La literatura árabe como fuente para la historia social: El caso del Kitab al-Bukhala' de el-Jahiz." *Estudios de Asia y Africa* 28 (1993), 32–83.

Hafsi, I. "Recherches sur le genre 'Ṭabaqāt' dans la littérature arabe." Arabica 24 (1977), 150–186.

Hämeen-Anttila. "*Adab*, Arabic, Early Developments." *EI3*.

Hamori, Andras. "The Silken Horsecloths Shed Their Tears." *Arabic and Middle Eastern Literatures* 2 (1999), 43–59.

Hamori, A. and T. Bauer. "Anthologies." *EI3*.

Heath, Peter. "Al-Jāḥiẓ, *Adab*, and the Art of the Essay." In *Al-Jāḥiẓ: A Muslim Humanist for Our Time*. Ed. A. Heinemann et al. Beiruter Texte und Studien 119. Würzburg: Ergon-Verlag, 2009, 133–72.

Heinrichs, W. "An Evaluation of *Sariqa*." In *Quaderni di studi arabi* 5–6 (1987–8), 357–68.

———. "Manierismus in der arabischen Literatur," in *Islamwissenschaftliche Abhandlungen Fritz Meier zum sechzigsten Geburtstag*. Ed. R. Gramlich. Wiesbaden: Franz Steiner, 1974, 118–28.

———. "Poetik, Rhetoric, Literaturkritik, Metric und Reimlehre," in *Grundriss der arabischen Philologie II: Literaturwissenschaft*. Ed. Helmut Gätje. Wiesbaden: Reichert, 1987, 177–207.

———. "Review of *Cambridge History of Arabic Literature: 'Abbasid Belles-Lettres*." *al-'Arabiyya* 26 (1993), 129–37.

———. "Sariqa." *EI2*, supplement, 707–10.

———. "The Classification of the Sciences and the Consolidation of Philology in Classical Islam." In *Centres of Learning: Learning and Location in Pre-Modern Europe and the Near East*. Ed. J. W. Drijvers and A. A. MacDonald. Leiden: Brill, 1995, 119–39.

Hell, Joseph. *Die Klassen der Dichter des Muḥ. B. Sallām al-Ǧumaḥī*. Leiden: Brill, 1916.

Hodgson, Marshall. *The Venture of Islam: The Classical Age of Islam*. Chicago: University of Chicago Press, 1974.

Holmberg, Bo. "*Adab* and Arabic Literature." In *Literary History: Towards a Global Perspective*. Berlin: W. de Gruyter, 2006, 180–205.

Ḥuwwar, Muḥammad Ibrāhīm. *al-Ḥanīn ilā l-waṭan fī l-adab al-ʿarabī ḥattā nihāyat al-ʿaṣr al-umawī*. Cairo: Dār Nahḍat Miṣr, 1973.

Ibrāhīm, Ṭāhā. *Taʾrīkh al-naqd al-adabī ʿinda l-ʿarab min al-ʿaṣr al-jāhilī ilā l-qarn al-rābiʿ al-hijrī*. Beirut: Dār al-Ḥikma, n.d.

Jackson, A. V. Williams. *Early Persian Poetry, from the Beginnings Down to the Time of Firdausi*. New York: Macmillan, 1920.

Jacobi, Renate. "qaṣīda." *EAL*, 2:630.

———. "al-Mufaḍḍaliyyāt." *EI2*, VII: 306.

Jādir, Muḥmūd ʿAbdallāh. "Dirāsa tawthīqiyya li-muʾallafāt al-Thaʿālibī." *Majallat Maʿhad al-Buḥūth wa-l-Dirāsāt al-ʿArabiyya* 12 (1403/1983). Reprinted in *Dirāsāt tawthīqiyya wa-taḥqīqiyya fī maṣādir al-turāth*. Baghdad: Jāmiʿat Baghdād, 1990, 382–454.

———. *al-Thaʿālibī nāqidan wa-adīban*. Beirut: Dār al-Niḍāl, 1991.

Jubūrī, Yaḥyā. *al-Ḥanīn wa-l-ghurba fī l-shiʿr al-ʿarabī*. ʿAmmān: Majdalāwī li-l-Nashr wa-l-Tawzīʿ, 2008.

Kadi, Wadad. "Biographical Dictionaries as the Scholars' Alternative History of the Muslim Community," in *Organizing Knowledge*. Ed. G. Endress. Leiden: Brill 2006, 23–75.

———. "Biographical Dictionaries: Inner Structure and Cultural Significance," in *The Book in the Islamic World*. Ed. George Atiyeh. Albany: State University of New York Press, 1995, 93–122.

———. "Dislocation and Nostalgia: *al-ḥanīn ilā l-awṭān*: Expressions of Alienation in Early Arabic Literature," in *Myths, Historical Archetypes and Symbolic Figures in Arabic Literature*. Ed. Angelika Neuwirth et al. Beirut: Franz Steiner Verlag Stuttgart, 1999, 3–31.

Kanazi, George. *Studies in the Kitāb Aṣ-ṣināʿatayn of Abū Hilāl al-ʿAskarī*. Leiden: Brill, 1989.

Khalidi, Tarif. *Arabic Historical Thought in the Classical Period*. Cambridge: Cambridge University Press, 1996.

Khaṭīb, Ḥāmid Ibrāhim. *al-Thaʿālibī nāqidan fī Yatīmat al-dahr*. Cairo: Maṭbaʿat al-Amāna, 1988.

Kilito, Abdelfattah. *The Author and His Doubles*. Trans. Michael Cooperson. Syracuse: Syracuse University Press, 2001.

Kilpatrick, Hilary. "Abū l-Farağ's Profiles of Poets: A 4th/10th Century Essay at the History and Sociology of Arabic Literature." *Arabica* 44 (1997), 94–128.

———. "adab," in *Encyclopedia of Arabic Literature*. Ed. Julie Scott Meisami and Paul Starkey. New York: Routledge, 1998, 1:56.

———. "A Genre in Classical Arabic: The *Adab* Encyclopedia," in *Union Européenne des Arabisants et Islamisants, 10th Congress, Edinburgh, September 1980, Proceedings*. Ed. Robert Hillenbrand. Edinburgh: Edinburgh University Press, 1982, 34–42.

———. "Anthologies, Medieval," in *Encyclopedia of Arabic Literature*. Ed. Julie Scott Meisami and Paul Starkey. New York: Routledge, 1998, 1:94–6.

———. "Context and the Enhancement of the Meaning of *aḫbār* in The *Kitāb al-Aġānī*." *Arabica* 38 (1991), 351–68.

———. "Cosmic Correspondences: Songs as a Starting Point for an Encyclopaedic Portrayal of Culture," in *Pre-Modern Encyclopaedic Texts*. Ed. Peter Binkley. Leiden: Brill, 1997, 137–46.

———. "Criteria of Classification in the *Ṭabaqāt fuḥūl al-shuʿarāʾ* of Muḥammad b. Sallām al-Jumaḥī (d. 232/846)," in *Proceedings of the Ninth Congress of the Union Européenne des Arabisants et Islamisants*. Ed. Rudolph Peters. Leiden: Brill, 1981, 141–52.

———. *Making the Great Book of Songs: Compilation and the Author's Craft in Abū l-Faraj al-Iṣbahānī's Kitāb al-Aghānī*. London: RoutledgeCurzon, 2003.

———. "On the Difficulty of Knowing Mediaeval Arab Authors: The Case of Abū l-Faraj and Pseudo-Iṣfahānī," in *Islamic Reflections, Arabic Musings: Studies in Honour of Professor Alan Jones*. Ed. Robert G. Hoyland and Philip F. Kennedy. Cambridge: Gibb Memorial Trust, 2004, 230–42.

———. "The "Genuine" Ashʿab: The Relativity of Fact and Fiction in Early *Adab* Texts," in *Story-telling in the Framework of Non-fictional Arabic Literature*. Ed. Stefen Leder. Wiesbaden: Harrassowitz, 1998, 94–117.

Kister, M. J. "The Seven Odes: Some Notes on the Compilation of the *Muʿallaqāt*." *Revista degli studi orientali* 44 (1968), 27–36.

Klein-Franke, F. *Die Hamasa des Abu Tammam*. Cologne: Phil. F., Diss, 1963.

———. "The *Ḥamāsa* of Abū Tammām." *Journal of Arabic Literature* 2 (1971), 13–55; 3 (1972), 142–78.

Kraemer, Joel L. *Humanism in the Renaissance of Islam*. Leiden: Brill, 1986.

Larkin, Margaret. "Abu Tammam (circa 805–845)," in *Arabic Literary Culture*. Ed. Michael Cooperson and Shawkat M. Toorawa. *Dictionary of Literary Biography, Vol. 311*. Detroit: Gale, 2005, 33–52.

Lazarus-Yafeh, H., et al., eds. *The Majlis: Interreligious Encounters in Medieval Islam.* Wiesbaden: Harrassowitz, 1999.

Lecomte, G. "al-Muʿallaḳāt." *EI2*, VII: 254–5.

Leder, Stefan. "Authorship and Transmission in Unauthored Literature: The Akhbār of al-Haytham ibn ʿAdī." *Oriens* 31 (1988), 61–81.

———. "Conventions of Fictional Narration in Learned Literature," in *Story-telling in the Framework of Non-fictional Arabic Literature.* Ed. Stefan Leder. Wiesbaden: Harrassowitz, 1998, 34–60.

———. *Ibn al-Ǧauzī und seine Kompilation wider die Leidenschaft: Der Traditionalist in gelehrter Überlieferung und originärer Lehre.* Beirut: Orient-Institut der Deutschen Morgenländischen Gesellschaft, 1984.

———. "al-Madā'inī's Version of Qiṣṣat al-Shūrā," in *Myths, Historical Archetypes and Symbolic Figures in Arabic Literature.* Ed. Angelika Neuwirth et al. Beirut: Franz Steiner Verlag Stuttgart, 1999, 379–98.

———. "Prosa-Dichtung in der aḫbār Überlieferung Narrative Analyse einer Satire." *Der Islam* 64, 1987, 6–41.

———. "Riwāya." *EI2*, VIII:546.

———. "The Literary Use of the *Khabar*, a Basic Form of Historical Writing," in *The Byzantine and Early Islamic Near East I: Problems in the Literary Source Material.* Ed. A. Conrad and L. Conrad. Princeton: Darwin Press, 1992, 277–315.

Leder, S., and H. Kilpatrick. "Classical Arabic Prose Literature: A Researchers' Sketch Map." *Journal of Arabic Literature* 23 (1992), 2–25.

Le Strange, G. *The Lands of the Eastern Caliphate: Mesopotamia, Persia, and Central Asia from the Moslem Conquest to the Time of Timur.* Cambridge: Cambridge University Press, 1930.

Levi della Vida, G. "Sulle Ṭabaqāt aš-šuʿarā' di Muḥammad b. Sallām." *Revista degli studi orientali* 8 (1919), 611–36.

Lyall, *The Mufaḍḍaliyyāt.* Oxford: Clarendon Press, 1918.

Lyons, M. C. "Notes on Abū Tammām's Concept of Poetry." *Journal of Arabic Literature* 9 (1978), 57–64.

Madelung, W. "Madjlis." *EI2*, V:1031ff.

Maghribī, M. ʿA. *Majālis al-adab wa-l-ghinā' fī l-ʿaṣr al-umawī.* Cairo: Dār al-Hudā li-l-Ṭibāʿa, 1985.

Malti-Douglas, Fedwa. *Structures of Avarice: The Bukhalā' in Medieval Arabic Literature.* Leiden: Brill, 1985.

Mandūr, Muḥammad. *al-Naqd al-manhajī ʿinda l-ʿArab.* Cairo: Dār Nahḍat Miṣr, n.d.

Marlow, Louise. "The Way of Viziers and the Lamp of Commanders (*Minhāj al-wuzarā' wa-sirāj al-umarā'*) of Aḥmad al-Iṣfahbadhī and the Literary and Political Culture of Early Fourteenth-Century Iran," in *Writers and Rulers: Perspectives on Their*

Relationship from Abbasid to Safavid Times. Ed. B. Gruendler and L. Marlow. Wiesbaden: Reichert, 2004, 169–93.

Mehiri, Abdelkader. *Les théories grammaticales d'Ibn Ginnī*. Tunis: Université de Tunis, 1973.

Motzki, Harald. *Origins of Islamic Jurisprudence*. Trans. Marion H. Katz. Leiden: Brill, 2002.

Mubārak, Zakī. *al-Nathr al-fannī fī l-qarn al-rābiʿ*. Cairo: al-Maktaba al-Tijāriyya al-Kubrā, [1957].

Muhanna, Elias. *Encyclopaedism in the Mamluk Period: The Composition of Shihāb al-Dīn al-Nuwayrī's (d. 1333) Nihāyat al-Arab fī Funūn al-Adab*. PhD diss., Harvard University.

Müller, K. "*al-Ḥanīn ilā l-awṭān* in Early *Adab* Literature," in *Myths, Historical Archetypes and Symbolic Figures in Arabic Literature*. Ed. Angelika Neuwirth et al. Beirut: Franz Steiner Verlag Stuttgart, 1999, 33–58.

Naaman, Erez. *Literature and Literary People at the Court of al-Ṣāḥib Ibn ʿAbbād*. PhD diss., Harvard University, 2009.

———. "Women Who Cough and Men Who Hunt: Taboo and Euphemism (*kināya*) in Medieval Islamic World. *Journal of the American Oriental Society* 133 (2013), 467–93.

Naficy, Said. "Bayhaḳī." *EI2*, I:1130b–1132a.

Nājī, Hilāl. "Ḥawl kitāb Tuḥfat al-wuzarāʾ al-mansūb li-l-Thaʿālibī," in *Buḥūth fī l-naqd al-turāthī*. Beirut: Dār al-Gharb al-Islāmī, 1994, 211–17.

———. *Muḥāḍarāt fī taḥqīq al-nuṣūṣ*. Beirut: Dār al-Gharb al-Islāmī, 1994.

———. "al-Mustadrak ʿalā ṣunnāʿ al-dawāwīn." *al-Mawrid* 15 (1986), 199–210.

Najjār, Ibrāhīm. *Shuʿarāʾ ʿabbāsiyyūn mansiyyūn*. Beirut: Dār al-Gharb al-Islāmī, 1997.

Nöldeke, Th. *Geschichte des Qorans* 2. Hildesheim: Olms, 1961.

Omidsalar, Mahmoud. "Thaʿālibī Nīshāpūrī yā Thaʿālibī Marghānī?" *Nama-yi Baharistan* 8–9 (1386), 131–44.

Orfali, Bilal. "Abū Saʿd Naṣr b. Yaʿqūb al-Dīnawarī." *EI3*.

———. "An Addendum to the *Dīwān* of Abū Manṣūr al-Taʿālibī." *Arabica* 56 (2009), 440–49.

———. *The Art of Anthology: Al-Thaʿālibī and His Yatīmat al-dahr*. PhD diss., Yale University, 2009.

———. "The Art of the *Muqaddima* in the Works of Abū Manṣūr al-Thaʿālibī (d. 429/1039)." In *The Weaving of Words: Approaches to Classical Arabic Prose*. Ed. Lale Behzadi and Vahid Behmardi, Beirut-Wiesbaden: Ergon, 2009, 181–202.

———. "The Sources of al-Thaʿālibī in *Yatīmat al-Dahr* and *Tatimmat al-Yatīma*." *Middle Eastern Literatures* 16 (2013), 1–47.

———. "The Works of Abū Manṣūr al-Thaʿālibī." *Journal of Arabic Literature* 40 (2009), 273–318.

Orfali, Bilal, and Maurice Pomerantz. "'I See a Distant Fire': Al-Thaʿālibī's *Kitāb al-Iqtibās min al-Qurʾān al-Karīm*," in *Qur'an and Adab*. Ed. Omar Ali-de-Unzaga and Nuha Shaar. Oxford: Oxford University Press, forthcoming.

Orfali, Bilal and Ramzi Baalbaki. *The Book of Noble Character*. Leiden: Brill, 2015.

Ouyang, W. *Literary Criticism in Medieval Arabic-Islamic Culture: The Making of a Tradition*. Edinburgh: Edinburgh University Press, 1997.

Peled, M. "On the Concept of Literary Influence in Classical Arabic Criticism." *Israel Oriental Studies* 11 (1991), 37–46.

Pellat, Ch. "Ibn Lankak." *EI2*, III:854a.

———. "Ibn Shuhayd." *EI2*, III:938b–940a.

———. "al-Khʷārizmī, Abū Bakr Muḥammad b. al-ʿAbbās." *EI2*, IV:1069b.

———. "Variations sur le thème de l'adab." *Correspondance d'Orient: Études* 5–6 (1964), 19–37.

Pertsch, Wilhelm. *Die arabischen Handschriften der herzoglicher Bibliothek zu Gotha*. Frankfurt am Main: Institute für Geschichte der Arabisch-Islamischen Wissenschaften an der Johann Wolfgang Goethe-Universität, 1987.

Qāḍī, Muḥammad. *al-Khabar fī l-adab al-ʿarabī: dirāsa fī l-sardiyya al-ʿarabiyya*. Beirut: Dār al-Gharb al-Islāmī, 1998.

Radwan, Ahmad Shawqi A.F. *Thaʿālibī's "Tatimmat al-Yatīmah": A Critical Edition and a Study of the Author as Anthologist and Literary Critic*. PhD diss., University of Manchester, 1972.

Rescher, O. *Alfabetischer Index zur Jetīma ed-Dahr des Taʿālibī*. Constantinople: n.p. 1914.

Rosenbaum, G. "A Certain Laugh: Serious Humor and Creativity in the Adab of Ibn al-Ǧawzī," in *Israel Oriental Studies XIX: Compilation and Creation in Adab and Luġa in Memory of Naphtali Kinberg (1948–1997)*. Ed. Albert Arazi, Joseph Sadan, and David J. Wasserstein. Winona Lake: Eisenbrauns, 1999, 97–130.

Rosenthal, Franz. "Fiction and Reality: Sources for the Role of Sex in Medieval Muslim Society," in *Society and the Sexes in Medieval Islam*. Ed. Afaf Lutfi al-Sayyid-Marsot. Malibu: UNDENA Publications, 1979, 2–22.

———. "From Arabic Books and Manuscripts: III. The Author of the *Ġurar as-siyar*." *Journal of the American Oriental Society* 70 [1950], 181–2.

———. *Knowledge Triumphant: The Concept of Knowledge in Medieval Islam*. Leiden: Brill, 1970.

———. "The Stranger in Medieval Islam." *Arabica* 44 (1997), 35–75.

Rowson, Everett. "Religion and Politics in the Career of Badīʿ al-Zamān al-Hamadhānī." *Journal of the American Oriental Society* 107 (1987), 653–73.

———. "al-Thaʿālibī, Abū Manṣūr ʿAbd al-Malik b. Muḥammad b. Ismāʿīl." *EI2*, X:426a–427b.

Rowson, Everett, and Seeger A. Bonebakker. *A Computerized Listing of Biographical Data from the* Yatīmat al-Dahr *by al-Thaʿālibī*. Malibu: UNDENA Publications, 1980.

Sadan, Joseph. "An Admirable and Ridiculous Hero: Some Notes on the Bedouin in Medieval Arabic Belles-Lettres, on a Chapter of *Adab* by al-Rāghib al-Iṣfahānī, and on a Literary Model in which Admiration and Mockery Coexist." *Poetics Today* 10 (1989), 471–92.

———. "Hārūn al-Rashīd and the Brewer: Preliminary Remarks on the *Adab* of the Elite versus *Ḥikāyāt*," in *Studies in Canonical and Popular Arabic Literature*. Ed. Shimon Ballas and Reuven Snir. Toronto: York Press, 1998, 1–22.

———. "Vine, Women and Seas: Some Images of the Ruler in Medieval Arabic Literature." *Journal of Semitic Studies* 34 (1989), 133–52.

Saʿdū, Zahiyya. *al-Tamaththul wa-l-muḥāḍara li-Abī Manṣūr al-Thaʿālibī: Dirāsa wa-taḥqīq*. PhD diss., Jāmiʿat al-Jazāʾir, 2005–6.

Sallām, Muḥammad Zaghlūl. *Taʾrīkh al-naqd al-adabī min al-qarn al-khāmis ilā-l-ʿāshir al-hijrī*. Cairo: Dār al-Maʿārif, n.d.

al-Samarrai, Q. "Some Biographical Notes on al-Thaʿālibī." *Bibliotheca Orientalis* 32 (1975), 175–86.

Sanni, Amidu. "On *Taḍmīn* (Enjambment) and Structural Coherence in Classical Arabic Poetry." *Bulletin of the School of Oriental and African Studies* 52 (1989), 463–6.

Savant, Sarah. *The New Muslims of Post-Conquest Iran*. Cambridge: Cambridge University Press, 2013.

Sayyid, Fuʾād. Fihrist al-Makhṭūṭat al-Muṣawwara. Cairo: Dār al-Riyāḍ li-l-Ṭabʿ wa-l-Nashr, 1954–63.

Schacht, Joseph. *The Origins of Muhammadan Jurisprudence*. Oxford: Clarendon, 1950.

Schippers, A. "Muʿāraḍa." *EI2*, VII:261.

Schoeler, Gregor. "Die Frage der schriftlichen oder mündlichen Überlieferung der Wissenschaften im frühen Islam." *Der Islam* 62 (1985), 201–30.

———. *The Genesis of Literature in Islam*. Trans. and in collaboration with Shawkat M. Toorawa. Edinburgh: Edinburgh University Press, 2009.

———. "W. Werkmeister: *Quellenuntersuchungen zum Kitāb al-ʿIqd al-farīd des Andalusiers Ibn ʿAbdrabbih (246/860–328/940)*." *Zeitschrift der Deutschen Morgenländischen Gesellschaft* 136 (1986), 118–28.

Sezgin, Fuat. *Geschichte des arabischen Schrifttums* (*GAS*). Leiden: Brill, 1967–2000.

———. "*Maṣādir kitāb al-aghānī li-Abī l-Faraj al-Iṣfahānī*," in *Vortäge zur Geschichte der Arabisch-Islamischen Wissenschaften*. Frankfūrt: Maʿhad Tārīkh al-ʿUlūm al-ʿArabiyya wa-l-Islāmiyya fī iṭār Jāmiʿat Frankfūrt, 1984, 147–58.

Shahsavari, Mojtaba. "Abū Naṣr al-Qushayrī and His *Kitāb al-Shawāhid wa-l-amthāl.*" *Ishraq* 3 (2012), 279–300.

Shak'a, Muṣṭafā. *Manāhij al-ta'līf, qism al-adab.* Beirut: Dār al-'Ilm li-l-Malāyīn, 1974.

Shalaby, A. *History of Muslim Education.* Beirut: Dār al-Kashshāf, 1954.

Shanṭī, Muḥammad. *Fihris al-Makhṭūṭat al-Muṣawwara al-adab.* Cairo: Ma'had al-Makhṭūṭāt al-'Arabiyya, 1995.

Sharlet, Jocelyn. *Patronage and Poetry in the Islamic World.* London: I. B. Tauris, 2011.

———. "Tokens of Resentment: Medieval Arabic Narratives about Gift Exchange and Social Conflict." *Journal of Arabic and Islamic Studies* 11 (2011), 62–100.

Shayzarī, 'Abd al-Raḥmān b. Naṣr. *Rawḍat al-qulūb wa-nuzhat al-muḥibb wa-l-maḥbūb.* Ed. David Semah and George Kanazi. Wiesbaden: Harrassowitz, 2003.

Shuraydi, Hasan. *The Raven and the Falcon.* Leiden: Brill, 2014.

Sperl, S. *Mannerism in Arabic Poetry.* Cambridge: Cambridge University Press, 1989.

Spitaler, A. "Ibn Khālawayh." *EI2*, III:824a–825a.

Stetkevych, Suzanne Pinckney. *Abū Tammām and the Poetics of the 'Abbāsid Age.* Leiden: Brill, 1991.

Stewart, Devin. "Professional Literary Mendicancy in the Letters and *Maqāmāt* of Badī' al-Zamān al-Hamadhānī," in *Writers and Rulers.* Ed. Beatrice Gruendler and Louise Marlow. Wiesbaden: Reichert, 2004, 39–48.

Ṭabāna, Badawī. *al-Sariqāt al-adabiyya: dirāsa fī ibtikār al-a'māl al-adabiyya wa-taqlīdihā.* Beirut: Dār al-Thaqāfa, 1986.

Talib, Adam. *Out of Many, One: Epigram Anthologies in Pre-modern Arabic Literature.* PhD diss., University of Oxford, 2013.

———. "Pseudo-Ṯa'ālibī's *Book of Youths.*" *Arabica* 59 (2012), 599–649.

Toelle, Heidi, and Katia Zakharia. "Pour une relecture des textes littéraires arabes: Éléments de réflexion." *Arabica* 46 (1999), 523–40.

Toorawa, Shawkat. "Defining Adab by (Re)defining the Adīb," in *On Fiction and Adab in Medieval Arabic Literature.* Ed. Philip F. Kennedy. Wiesbaden: Harrassowitz Verlag, 2005, 287–304.

———. *Ibn Abī Ṭāhir Ṭayfūr and Arabic Writerly Culture: A Ninth-Century Bookman in Baghdad.* London: RoutledgeCurzon, 2005.

———. "Proximity, Resemblance, Sidebars and Clusters: Ibn al-Nadīm's Organizational Principles in *Fihrist 3.3.*" *Oriens* 38 (2010), 217–47.

Topozoglu, Tevfik Rüştü. "Further Istanbul Manuscripts of Tha'ālibī's *Yatīmat al-dahr.*" *Islamic Quarterly*, 15 (1971), 62–5.

———. "Istanbul Manuscripts of Works (Other Than *Yatīmat al-Dahr*) by Tha'ālibī." *Islamic Quarterly* 17 (1973), 64–74.

Trabulsi, A. *La critique poétique des arabes.* Damas: Institut français de Damas, 1955.

Ullmann, M. *Wörterbuch der klassischen arabischen Sprache, Lām.* Wiesbaden: Harrassowitz, 1989.

Vadet, Jean-Claude. "Les grands thèmes de l'adab dans le Rabīʿ d'al-Zamakhsharī." *Revue des études islamiques* 58 (1990), 189–205.

Vajda, G. "Une anthologie sur l'amitié attribuée à al-Ṯaʿālibī." *Arabica* 18 (1971), 211–13.

Weipert, Reinhard. *Classical Arabic Philology and Poetry: A Bibliographical Handbook of Important Editions from 1960–2000.* Boston: Brill, 2002.

Werkmeister, Walter. *Quellenuntersuchungen zum Kitāb al-ʿiqd al-farīd des Andalusiers (240/860-328/940).* Berlin: Klaus Schwarz Verlag, 1983.

Zaydān, Jurjī. *Taʾrīkh ādāb al-lugha al-ʿarabiyya.* Beirut: Maktabat al-Ḥayāt, 1967.

Ziriklī, Khayr al-Dīn. *al-Aʿlām.* Beirut: Dār al-ʿIlm li-l-Malāyīn, 1992.

Index

ʿAbbās, Iḥsān 28n, 40n, 105n
ʿAbbāsid 11, 14, 15, 93, 175, 190, 191
ʿAbd al-Ḥamīd, M. M. 37n
ʿAbd al-Ṣamad al-Miṣrī 115, 150, 212
ʿAbdalakānī, Abū l-Ḥasan 122, 223
ʿAbdalkānī al-Zawzanī 15n
ʿAbdallāh b. al-ʿAbbās b. ʿAbd al-Muṭṭalib 168n
ʿAbdānī, Abū Bakr Muḥammad 167
ʿAbdūnī, Abū Manṣūr 169, 224
Ābī, Abū Saʿd 144
Abīwardī, Abū l-Naṣr al-Muʿāfā al-Huzaymī 119, 143n, 222, 223
al-Abniya fī l-naḥw 143n
Abū l-ʿAbbās Aḥmad b. al-Muqtadir b. al-Muʿtaḍid 153n
Abū l-ʿAbbās Khusraw-Fayrūz b. Rukn al-Dawla 111, 121, 132-133, 164n, 230
Abū ʿAbdallāh Muḥammad b. al-Nuʿmān 115
Abū ʿAbdallāh Muḥammad b. Ḥāmid 35, 46, 71, 103, 133n, 134, 142, 215, 218, 222, 224, 225, 228, 229
Abū Aḥmad b. Abī Bakr al-Kātib 164, 168, 172, 175, 176n, 234
Abū Aḥmad b. Manṣūr 176
Abū l-ʿAlāʾ b. al-Ḥasūl 148, 226, 227
Abū ʿAlī ʿAbd al-Wahhāb b. Muḥammad 165, 232
Abū ʿAlī al-Hāʾim 93
Abū ʿAlī b. Sīmjūrī 61, 123n
Abū l-ʿAtāhiya 19n, 236
Abū Bakr Muḥammad b. Khalaf b. al-Marzubān 23
Abū l-Barakāt ʿAlī b. al-Ḥasan al-ʿAlawī 107, 122
Abū Bishr al-Faḍl b. Muḥammad 148n, 180n
Abu Deeb, Kamal 189, 190
Abū Firās al-Ḥamdānī 99, 122, 164n, 168, 186, 235
Abū Ḥafṣ ʿUmar (or ʿAmr) b. al-Muṭṭawwiʿī 33, 110, 122, 165, 214, 216, 219
Abū l-Ḥasan ʿAlī b. Hārūn al-Munajjim 120, 121, 167
Abū l-Ḥasan ʿAlī b. al-Nuʿmān 115, 212
Abū l-Ḥasan b. Sīmjūr 181
Abū l-Ḥusayn Muḥammad b. Kathīr 61, 123n
Abū Ibrāhīm b. Abī ʿAlī 174, 222
Abū Jaʿfar Muḥammad b. al-ʿAbbās b. al-Ḥasan 132
Abū l-Maḥāsin Saʿd b. Muḥammad b. Manṣūr 38, 162n, 226
Abū Manṣūr b. al-Marzubān 23, 25, 74, 77, 90
Abū Manṣūr Kuthayyir b. Aḥmad 181
Abū Manṣūr Yaḥyā b. Yaḥyā al-Kātib 179
Abū l-Muẓaffar Naṣr b. Nāṣir al-Dīn Sebüktegin 35, 47, 50, 53, 61, 68
Abū Naṣr Aḥmad b. Muḥammad b. Abī Zayd 36
Abū Naṣr b. Abī Zayd 152
Abū Naṣr Manṣūr b. Mushkān 173
Abū Naṣr Sahl b. al-Marzubān 37, 108, 128, 134, 141, 142, 144n, 145, 148, 150, 153, 170, 210, 215, 216, 217, 221, 223, 229
Abū Nuwās 24, 191
Abū l-Qāsim ʿAbd al-ʿAzīz b. Yūsuf 99, 181, 198, 215
Abū l-Qāsim ʿAlī b. Jalabāt 124, 131
Abū l-Qāsim ʿAlī b. Munjib b. Sulaymān 76, 91
Abū l-Qāsim al-Ḥusayn al-ʿĀmirī 108n, 114
Abū Saʿd Muḥammad b. Manṣūr 124, 162n
Abū l-Qāsim Maḥmūd b. Sebüktegin 52
Abū l-Qāsim al-Muḥassin b. ʿAmr b. al-Muʿallā 130
Abū Saʿd Naṣr b. Yaʿqūb 134, 143n, 150, 153, 217, 221, 224
Abū Saʿīd al-Ḥasan b. Ṣahl 62
Abū Saʿīd b. Dūst 145, 207, 224
Abū Taghlib b. Nāṣir al-Dawla 162n
Abū Ṭālib b. Ayyūb 155
Abū Tammām 14, 15, 16, 20, 26, 33, 191, 192
Abū l-Ṭayyib al-Mutanabbī mā lahu wa-mā ʿalayhi 44
Abū l-Ṭayyib al-Mutanabbī wa-akhbāruhu 44
Abū l-Ṭayyib Ṭāhir b. ʿAbdallāh 155
Abū Zayd ʿAbd al-Raḥmān al-Thaʿālibī 83

 | DOI 10.1163/9789004317352_010

Abyāt al-maʿānī 18
adab 1, 2, 3, 4, 5, 7, 9, 10, 13, 14, 29, 35, 36, 37, 41, 52, 65, 78, 82, 85, 88, 98, 106, 110, 111, 113, 123, 128, 139, 141n, 153, 156, 160, 167, 168, 173n, 178, 184, 194, 204n, 234, 235, 237
al-Ādāb 72
al-Ādāb fī-l-ṭaʿām wa-l-sharāb 37n, 144n, 153
Adab al-ghurabāʾ 25
Adab al-kātib 143n
al-Adab mimmā li-l-nās fīhi arab 94
Ādāb al-mulūk 46, 71, 72, 81, 94n
Adab al-nadīm 24n
al-Aʿdād 48
al-ʿAdad al-Maʿdūd 48, 77
al-Adhkiyāʾ 152
al-Adʿiya 143n, 153
ʿAḍud al-Dawla 102, 110, 151, 179, 180, 181, 182, 184, 203, 208, 215, 217, 218
ʿAdwī al-Shimshāṭī 24
al-aḍyāf wa-l-madīḥ 14
al-Afʿāl 143n
al-Afḍaliyyāt 91
Afrād al-maʿānī 94
al-ʿAfw wa-l-iʿtizār 23
Āghā, Aḥmad Effendi 72
Aghājī, Abū l-Ḥasan 132, 174
al-Aghānī 5, 6, 13n, 32, 112, 140, 143, 160, 161
aghrāḍ 40, 193
Aḥāsin al-maḥāsin 47, 54, 73, 79, 92
al-Aḥāsin min badāʾiʿ al-bulaghāʾ 94
Aḥāsin kalim al-nabī 72
ahl al-ʿaṣr 132, 190
Aḥmad b. ʿAbd al-Ṣamad 54
Aḥmad b. Fāris 16n, 100, 120, 154, 169, 172n, 191, 192, 209, 233
Aḥmad b. Ismāʿīl 164, 175
Aḥmad ʿUbayd 89
Aḥsan mā samiʿtu 46, 47, 71, 79, 91, 144
Ahwāzī, Abū l-Ḥusayn 66, 73, 74, 94n, 143n
al-ʿAjāʾib wa-l-ṭuraf 25
Ajnās al-tajnīs 32, 47, 94, 144, 188
Akhbār al-ḥamqā wa-l-mughaffalīn 93
Akhbār Ibn al-Rūmī 37n, 143n, 153
Akhbār Jaḥẓa al-Barmakī 37n, 143, 153
Akhfash al-Aṣghar 19
Akhlāq al-wazīrayn 180
Aʿlam al-Shantamarī 16, 33n
ʿAlawī, Abū l-Ḥasan Muḥammad 165, 166, 182, 220
ʿAlawī, Aḥmad b. Abī ʿAlī 133n
ʿAlī b. al-Bishrī 12
Ali, S. 3
ʿAlids 111
Aleppo (Ḥalab) 67, 103, 150, 151, 187
Alf ghulām 92, 93
alghāz 18
Āl Yāsīn, Muḥammad Ḥ. 55, 81, 204n
amālī 3, 7, 21
ʿĀmirī, Abū l-Qāsim al-Ḥusayn 108n
ʿĀmirī, Abū Naṣr Ṭāhir 114
al-Amthāl 55, 58, 73, 80, 81
al-Amthāl al-sāʾira 66
al-Amthāl wa-l-istishhādāt 27, 80, 91
al-Amthāl wa-l-tashbīhāt 80
ʿAnbarī, Abū Bakr 166, 230
al-Anīs fī ghurar al-tajnīs 32, 44n, 47
al-Ansāb wa-l-ashrāf 161
al-Anwār al-bahiyya 82
al-Anwār fī āyāt al-nabī 83
al-Anwār wa-maḥāsin al-ashʿār 24
Arghandāb River 154n
al-Ashbāh wa-l-naẓāʾir 16n, 22, 65
ʿāriḍ 48n, 51
ʿĀriḍ, Abū l-Ḥasan Musāfir 51
Aristotle 85
Arzanī, Abū Muḥammad Yaḥyā 178, 232
Asadī, Abū l-ʿAlāʾ 135n, 173, 191n, 219, 233
Aʿshā 205
Ashʿār al-nisāʾ 26
Ashʿar al-nudamāʾ 143, 205
Ashʿarite 165
Ashraf b. Fakhr al-Mulk 111
al-Asjāʿ 143n
ʿAskarī, Abū Hilāl 8n, 15, 16n, 17, 38n
Askī (al-Āsī?), Abū Bakr ʿAbdallāh 121, 231
Asmāʾ al-aḍdād 81
Aṣmaʿī 11, 146
al-Aṣmaʿiyyāt 11, 14n
ʿaṣriyyūn 20, 191n
Asṭurlābī, Hibatullāh Badīʿ al-Zamān 33
Aswānī al-Miṣrī, Aḥmad b. ʿAlī al-Zubayr 30n
ʿAṭf al-alif al-maʾlūf ʿalā l-lām al-maʿṭuf 22
ʿAttābī 19n
awqāf 167

Aws b. Ḥajar 191
awṣāf 16, 17, 21, 32, 159
al-ʿAyn 143
ʿAynī 16
ayyam al-ʿArab 24
Azdī al-Harawī, Manṣūr b. Muḥammad 35, 50, 94n, 122, 226
Azdī, ʿAlī b. Ẓāfir 26, 32, 38

Bābānī 82, 85, 95n
Babbaghāʾ, Abū l-Faraj 99, 162, 197, 205, 207, 214, 237
Badāʾiʿ al-badāʾih 26, 38
al-Badīʿ fī waṣf al-rabīʿ 24
badīha 26
Badīhī 174, 191n, 219, 233
Baghawī, Aḥmad b. Muḥammad 135, 143n, 144, 222
Baghdad 5, 10, 13n, 30n, 33, 103, 104, 120, 134, 137n, 139, 141, 150, 153, 155, 162n, 165, 176, 187, 198, 204n, 205n, 207
Baghdādī, Abū l-Ḥusayn Aḥmad 170
Bahdilī 123
Baḥḥāthī 37, 231, 232
Bahjat al-majālis 13
Bahjat al-mushtāq (*al-ʿushshāq*?) 94
Baḥrayn 28
Bākharzī 30, 35, 37n, 39n, 92, 142, 154, 172, 231
Bakr b. Naṭṭāḥ 19n
Baktamarī, Abū l-Fatḥ 170
Balādhurī 161
Baladī, Muḥammad b. ʿUbaydallāh 123, 216, 229
balāgha 21, 27, 144, 171, 173n, 188, 234
Balāghāt al-nisāʾ 19
Balʿāmī, Abū l-Faḍl 175, 176
Balkh 150, 173n, 234
Balkhī, Abū Zayd 39n, 173n, 234, 237
Banū Makhzūm 168n
Banū Murra 29
Banū Sāsān 109
Banū Tamīm 115n
Banū Warqāʾ 106
al-Barāʿa fī-l-takallum wa-l-ṣināʿa 94
barāʿat al-istihlāl 77
Bard al-akbād fī-l-aʿdād 27, 48
Bāriʿ al-Baghdādī 19
al-Bāriʿ fī akhbār wilāyat Khurāsān 29n, 143n
Bāriʿ al-Zawzanī 78
barīd 167
al-Barq al-wamīḍ 73
Barūjirdī, Abū Muḥammad al-Ḥasan 170
Baṣāʾir wa-l-dhakhāʾir 7, 13n
Bashshār b. Burd 29n, 33
Baṣra 108, 171, 198, 233
Baṣrī, Abū Yaʿlā 115n, 150, 156, 162n, 166, 227, 229, 230
Baṭshān, Ibrāhīm b. Muḥammad 77
al-Bayāḍ wa-l-sawād 27
Bayhaqī, Abū l-Faḍl 38
Bayhaqī, Abū l-Ḥasan b. Zayd 30
Bayhaqī, Ibrāhīm b. Muḥammad 26
Bayyāḍī, Zayn al-Dīn 205n
Bayyāsī 16n
Bedouins 5n, 108n, 166, 169n
Bibliothèque Nationale of Paris 68
Birdhawniyyāt 102
Bīrūnī 153
Bonebakker, S. 1n, 68n, 110n, 115n, 117, 124, 125, 126, 127, 129n, 131, 137, 138
Bosworth, C. E. 48n, 52, 68, 158n
British Museum 12, 46
Brockelmann, C. 43, 62, 68, 75, 78, 85, 90
Buḥturī 15, 26, 33, 191, 205, 234
Bukhāra 35, 100, 103, 104, 106, 152, 162n, 165, 171, 179, 187, 200, 205n, 210, 211
Bukhārī, Abū l-Qāsim Yaḥyā 133, 165, 171, 211, 229
Būshanj 171
Būshanjī, Abū Aḥmad 132, 171
Bustī, Abū Bakr ʿAbdallāh 133, 145, 162, 211
Bustī, Abū l-Fatḥ 37, 46, 47, 95, 100, 213, 219, 223, 237
Bustī, Abū Ḥātim 26
Byzantine 85

Cheikho, Louis 66, 74

al-Daʿawāt wa-l-fuṣūl 19, 38, 78
Dabāwandī, Abū l-Fatḥ 148, 150, 155, 227, 231
Ḍabbī, Abū l-ʿAbbās 99, 117, 181, 199
Dāghistānī, ʿUmar b. ʿAbd al-Salām 30n
Dahhān, Abū Muḥammad Ismāʿīl 111, 121
Dallāl al-Kutub 32
Dāmād Ibrāhīm Pāshā 68

Damascus 111n, 124, 126
Damghānī, Abū ʿAlī Muḥammad 132, 222, 223
Dāmghānī, Abū l-Fatḥ al-Muẓaffar 126
dār al-ḍarb 186
Dār al-ṭirāz 12
Darj al-ghurar wa-durj al-durar 33, 144n
Daʿwat al-Najjār 143
Daylamī, Abū l-Ḥasan 23
al-Dhakhāʾir wa-l-tuḥaf 24
al-Dhakhīra fī maḥāsin ahl al-Jazīra 31, 34n, 113n
Dhamm al-hawā 23
Dhayl Yatīmat al-dahr 32n
Dhikr al-aḥwāl fī Shaʿbān wa-shahr Ramaḍān wa-Shawwāl 37n, 143n, 153
Dhū l-Qarnayn b. al-Ḥasan b. ʿAbdallāh 111n
Dhū l-Qarnayn, Abū Muṭāʿ b. Nāṣir al-Dawla 135, 225, 229
Diʿbil al-Khuzāʿī 19n, 191
Dīnawar 126
Dīnawarī, Abū l-Qāsim 135n, 168n, 171
Dīnawarī, Abū Manṣūr 134, 135n, 221
Dīnawarī, Abū Saʿd Naṣr b. Yaʿqūb 134, 150, 153, 205
Diogenes 85
Dīwān Abī l-Ḥasan al-Laḥḥām 92
Dīwān al-Ḥamāsa 14n, 15, 192
dīwān al-kharāj 167
Dīwān al-maʿānī 8n, 15, 17
dīwān al-maẓālim 167
dīwān al-rasāʾil 164, 167, 178, 185
Dīwān al-Thaʿālibī 92
al-Diyārāt 102, 143
Dumyat al-qaṣr 30, 37n, 142n, 154
Durar al-ḥikam 73
al-Durra al-khaṭīra min shuʿarāʾ al-Jazīra 31
Durrat al-tāj min shiʿr Ibn al-Ḥajjāj 33
Durrat al-wishāḥ 30n

Egypt (Miṣr) 29, 81, 85, 98, 106, 115, 117, 131n, 137, 142, 150, 152, 157, 197
El Cheikh, N. 5

al-Fāḍil fī ṣifat al-adab al-kāmil 27
Faḍl al-kilāb ʿalā kathīr mimman labisa l-thiyāb 23
Faḍl man ismuhu l-Faḍl 94, 144n
Fahmī, Khālid 55
al-Fajrī (al-Fakhrī?), Aḥmad b. Sulaymān 117
Fakhr al-Dawla 121
Fakhr al-Dīn al-Rāzī 72
faqīh (jurist) 100, 103, 111, 133, 153, 161, 165, 167, 171, 172, 183, 188, 235
al-Farāʾid wa-l-qalāʾid 66, 73, 74, 80, 94
al-Faraj baʿda l-shidda 134, 141, 143, 187n, 205
Fārisī, Abū l-Ḥusayn Muḥammad 184, 208, 211, 219, 220, 222
Fārs 29, 98, 103, 145, 157, 172n, 198, 199
faṣāḥa 169, 170, 188
al-Fasr 142, 143, 204
Fatḥ b. Khāqān 31
Fāṭimid 25, 76, 110, 111n
al-Fawāʾid wa-l-amthāl 54
faylasūf 167
Fayrūzābād 140
Fī gharīb al-ḥadīth 143n, 144
Fī l-Jawāhir wa-l-ashbāh 153
Fihrī al-Būnisī, Abū Isḥāq Ibrāhīm 31
al-Fihrist 113n
Fīliyyāt 102, 135
Fiqh al-lugha wa-sirr al-ʿarabiyya 36n, 40, 49, 53, 55, 65, 68n, 81, 93, 140
Fleischhammer, M. 6, 139, 140, 156
Furayjāt, ʿĀdil 78
al-Fuṣūl al-fārisiyya 94
al-Fuṣūl fī l-fuḍūl 95
Fuṣūl al-tamāthīl fī tabāshīr al-surūr 23

Galen 85
Gelder, G. J. van 5
gharābat al-lafẓ 19n
Gharāʾib al-tanbīhāt ʿalā ʿajāʾib al-tashbīhāt 32
Gharchistān 151
Gharnāṭī, Ibn Saʿīd 33
Ghawwāṣ, Abū ʿAbdallāh 174, 203
ghazal 92, 108, 109, 141n, 158, 159
Ghazna 35, 36, 48n, 50, 51, 52, 54, 58, 61, 62, 137n, 154, 155
Ghaznavid 35, 36, 47, 48, 51n, 52, 58, 59, 61, 123n, 124, 149, 155, 186, 200
Ghaznawī, Abū l-Ḥasan ʿAlī 131
Ghazūlī 24
al-Ghilmān 73, 92
Ghurar akhbār mulūk al-Furs wa-siyarihim 67

Ghurar al-balāgha fī-l-naẓm wa-l-nathr 49, 50, 81
Ghurar al-balāgha wa-ṭuraf al-barā'a 49
al-Ghurar fī siyar al-mulūk wa-akhbārihim 67
Ghurar al-maḍāḥik 94
Ghurar al-nawādir 93
Ghurar mulūk al-Furs 67
Ghurar wa-siyar 67
ghurba 25, 62
Ghuwayrī 108, 203, 220, 233
Greek 3, 85
Gruendler, Beatrice 17, 181, 182n
Grunebaum, Gustave von 17
Günther, Sebastian 6, 140, 156

Ḥaddādī, Muḥammad b. Mūsā 170, 173n, 234
al-Ḥadīqa fī shu'arā' al-Andalus 31n
Hadiyyat al-'ārifīn 95n
Hadm 162n
Hadrusi, S. M. H. 77
ḥājib 103
Ḥajjī Khalīfa 30, 31n, 43, 68,
Ḥākim, Abū al-Ṣalt Umayya 31n
ḥalaqāt 6, 139, 175
ḥalāwa 188
Ḥalbat al-Kumayt 24n
Ḥall al-'aqd 39, 56
Hamadhān 103, 148n, 187, 202
Hamadhānī, Badī' al-Zamān 38n, 39n, 57, 86, 99, 118, 143n, 150, 154, 158n, 159, 162, 174, 176, 180, 183, 199, 218, 219, 221
ḥamāsa 1, 8, 14, 15, 16, 17
al-Ḥamāsa, see *Dīwān al-Ḥamāsa*
al-Ḥamāsa al-Baṣriyya 16
al-Ḥamāsa al-Maghribiyya 15
al-Ḥamāsa al-muḥdatha 16n, 192
Ḥamāsat al-muḥdathīn 16n
al-Ḥamāsa al-sa'diyya 16n
al-Ḥamāsa al-Shajariyya 15
al-Ḥamāsa al-ṣughrā 15
Ḥamāsat al-ẓurafā' 15
Ḥamd man ismuhu Aḥmad 144
Ḥamdūnī/al-Ḥamdawī, Abū Sahl 35, 48, 51n, 53, 54, 58
al-Ḥamd wa al-dhamm 74
Hämeen-Anttila, J. 2
Ḥāmidī, Muḥammad b. Ḥāmid 103, 134, 218, 225, 228, 229
Ḥammād al-Rāwiya 11n
Hamori, A. 8, 10n, 102n
Ḥamza al-Iṣbahānī 80, 206
Ḥanafī 165
Ḥanīn al-ibil ilā l-awṭān 26n
al-Ḥanīn ilā l-awṭān 25, 26n, 62
Harawī al-Azdī 94n
Harawī, Abū Sa'd Aḥmad 170, 173
Harawī, Manṣūr b. al-Ḥākim 132
al-Harawī, Manṣūr b. Muḥammad, see Azdī al-Harawī
Ḥarbī, Abū Muḥammad al-Ḥasan 165, 166
Ḥarīrī 77
Hārūn al-Rashīd 168
Hārūn b. 'Alī al-Munajjim al-Baghdādī 29n
al-Ḥasan b. 'Alī b. Muṭrān 170, 171, 172n, 234
ḥashw 93
Ḥashw al-lawzīnaj 93
Ḥāṭib layl 143, 205
Ḥātimī, Abū 'Alī Muḥammad 114, 115n, 133n
Ḥaẓīrī 30n, 32, 33
Heinrichs, W. 1, 2, 18, 190
Herat 35, 122n, 154
Hermetic 85
Hibatallāh b. al-Shajarī 12, 15
hijā' (invective poetry) 14, 22, 158, 159, 160, 164, 169, 173, 176, 191n
Ḥilyat al-muḥāḍara 58, 83
Ḥimṣī, Dīk al-Jinn 191
Ḥimyarī, Abū al-Walīd 24
Ḥimyarī, Abū l-Ḥasan 'Alī 132, 220
Ḥubb al-awṭān 26n
Ḥujjat al-'aql 94
Ḥulw, 'Abd al-Fattāḥ 43, 59, 92
Ḥuqqat al-jawāhir fī l-mafākhir 153
al-Ḥusayn b. Muḥammad al-'Amīd 132
Ḥusaynī, 'Alī b. Muḥammad b. al-Riḍā 93
ḥusn al-maqṭa' 189
ḥusn al-ta'rīḍ 189
ḥusn al-taṣarruf 169
ḥusn takhalluṣ 189
al-Ḥuṣrī al-Qayrawānī 13n, 23, 29n, 34n, 48n, 144, 151
Ḥuṭay'a 12
Huzaymī, Abū Naṣr 119, 143n, 222, 223

Ibn 'Abd al-Barr 13

Ibn ʿAbd Rabbihi 5, 6, 7, 8, 13, 139, 141n, 156
Ibn Abī ʿAwn 32
Ibn Abī Ṭāhir Ṭayfūr 19, 26n, 113, 156
Ibn al-Abbār 131
Ibn al-ʿAllāf 172n
Ibn al-ʿAmīd, Abū l-Faḍl 39n, 100, 102, 114, 119, 120, 167, 172, 184, 198, 204n, 208, 233, 235
Ibn al-ʿAmīd, Abū l-Fatḥ 100, 102, 122, 131, 167
Ibn al-Ḥajjāj 33, 100, 107, 109, 168, 169, 172, 173, 184, 233, 236
Ibn al-Jarrāḥ 113n
Ibn al-Jawzī 23, 76, 93, 152
Ibn al-Kattānī 32
Ibn al-Khuḍayrī 183
Ibn Lankak 108, 109, 119, 133n, 171, 172n, 173, 183, 215, 233
Ibn al-Marzubān 16, 37, 108, 128, 134, 141, 142, 144n, 145, 148, 150, 153, 170, 210, 215, 216, 217, 221, 223, 229
Ibn al-Munajjim, Abū ʿĪsā 12, 219, 221
Ibn al-Munajjim, Abū Muḥammad 131n
Ibn al-Muʿtazz 23, 24, 33, 113n, 191, 235, 236
Ibn al-Nadīm 11, 16n, 17n, 113
Ibn al-Qaṭṭāʿ 31
Ibn al-Qūṭiyya 143n, 215
Ibn al-Rūmī 26, 37n, 143n, 153, 191, 236
Ibn al-Sarrāj 23
Ibn al-Ṣayrafī 76, 91
Ibn al-Shajarī 15
Ibn al-Zubayr 24
Ibn Bābak 236
Ibn Bassām 31, 92, 113n, 234
Ibn Darrāj al-Qasṭallī al-Andalusī 127, 169, 172n
Ibn Dāwūd al-Iṣfahānī 22
Ibn Diḥya al-Kalbī 31
Ibn Fāris 16n, 100, 120, 169, 191, 192, 209, 233
Ibn Ḥamdūn 18n, 70
Ibn Hindū, Abū l-Faraj 141n
Ibn Jinnī 142, 166n, 204
Ibn Khālawayhi 172n, 233
Ibn Khallikān 8n, 16n, 30n, 34, 55n, 88, 92, 120n, 131
Ibn Maʿrūf 187
Ibn Miskawayhi, Abū ʿAlī 78n, 122, 226
Ibn Muqla 167, 234
Ibn Nubāta al-Saʿdī 169, 236
Ibn Qāḍī Shuhba 43, 92, 95n
Ibn Qurayʿa 187
Ibn Qutayba 5, 13, 18, 143n, 161
Ibn Saʿīd 31n
Ibn Sanāʾ al-Mulk 12
Ibn Shams al-Khilāfa 72
Ibn Shuhayd 126, 127
Ibn Sukkara 100, 168, 169, 173, 233
Ibn Wahab al-Miṣrī 115
Ibrāhīm Abū Isḥāq 133n
Ifrīqī al-Mutayyam 143n, 178, 205, 215, 223
iftikhār (*fakhr*) 22, 193
Ifyarī, Abū Saʿīd 164
al-Ihdāʾ wa-l-istihdāʾ 94
Iḥsān ẓurafāʾ al-shuʿarāʾ 143
al-Iʿjāz wa-l-ījāz 27, 49, 66, 72, 81, 94n
Ikhtiṣār Kitāb al-ʿAyn 143n
Ikhtiyār 1, 7, 8
al-Ikhtiyārāt 10n, 11
Ikhtiyār al-muqaṭṭaʿāt 15n
Ikhtiyār ashʿar al-shuʿarāʾ 19n
Ikhtiyār mujarrad min ashʿār al-muḥdathīn 15n
Ikhtiyār shuʿarāʾ al-fuḥūl 15n
ikhwāniyyāt 20, 55, 117, 145, 151, 158, 173, 175
ʿImād al-Iṣfahānī 48n
Imruʾ al-Qays 19n
Injāz al-maʿrūf wa-ʿumdat al-malhūf 83, 85
al-Intiṣār li-l-Mutanabbī 143n
Iqbāl, ʿA. 60, 124
al-ʿIqd al-farīd 5, 6, 7, 13, 139, 141n
al-ʿIqd al-nafīs wa-nuzhat al-jalīs 73
iqtibās 39, 50, 65, 125, 186, 189, 190n, 193
al-Iqtibās min al-Qurʾān 39, 50, 125, 144n
Iraq 29, 32, 98, 104, 105, 110, 149, 150, 157, 170, 171, 172n, 198, 199, 207, 235, 236
Irshād al-arīb 113n
Iṣbahān 102, 105, 153, 187, 199, 202
Iṣbahānī, ʿAbdān 191n, 218
Iṣbahānī, Abū l-Faraj 6, 13n, 25, 32, 112, 140, 143, 156, 160
Iṣbahānī, Abū l-Qāsim Ghānim 122
Iṣfahānī, ʿImād al-Dīn al-Kātib 30, 48n
Isfarāʾīn 35, 208
Isfarāʾīnī, Abū l-ʿAbbās al-Faḍl b. ʿAlī 35, 133n
Isfarāʾīnī, Abū l-ʿAbbās al-Faḍl b. Aḥmad 124

al-ʿIshra al-mukhtāra 84
Iskāfī, Abū Jaʿfar Muḥammad 125, 227
Iskāfī al-Nīshāpūrī, Abū l-Qāsim ʿAlī 119, 164, 170, 173, 184, 185, 222, 234
islāmiyyūn 191n
Ismāʿīlī al-Juwaynī 133n
Ismāʿīlī, Abū Maʿmar 168
isnād 6, 31, 36, 38, 68, 76, 113, 115, 123, 126, 127, 140, 141, 146, 147, 148, 150, 151, 152, 154, 155, 156, 157, 209
istiʿṭāf 193
Iʿtilāl al-qulūb 22

Jabahānī 175
Jabal 29, 98, 103, 104, 145, 155, 157, 199, 202, 236
Jādir, M. ʿA. 35, 38, 39, 44, 46, 48, 50, 52, 53, 54, 55, 57, 58, 60, 61, 65, 66, 68, 72, 73, 76, 78, 80, 81, 82, 84, 85, 86, 88, 91, 92, 95n, 123n
jāhilī 11, 16n, 20, 22, 28, 29
jāhiliyyūn 191n
Jāḥiẓ 3, 25, 26n, 38n, 39, 233, 234
Jamāl, ʿĀdil Sulaymān 12n
al-Jamhara 144n
Jamharat ashʿār al-ʿArab 11
Jāmiʿat al-Duwal al-ʿArabiyya 91, 204n
al-Jāmiʿ al-kabīr fī l-taʿbīr 143n, 153
Jawāhir al-ḥikam 84, 85
al-Jawāhir al-ḥisān fī ṭafsīr al-Qurʾān 74
Jawāmiʿ al-kalim 94
Jawharī, Abū l-Ḥasan ʿAlī b. Aḥmad 162n, 171, 176, 179, 181
Jawharī, Abū Naṣr Ismāʿīl b. Ḥammād 111n, 121, 144, 154, 178, 224
Jaysh al-tawshīḥ 12n
jazāla 170, 188
Jibāl 51n, 198
jidd-hazl 5
Jinān al-janān 30n
jinās 32, 33, 47
Jubūrī, Yaḥyā 26n, 55
Jumaḥī, Abū Dihbil 191
Jumaḥī, Ibn Sallām 28, 161
Jurāwī, Aḥmad b. ʿAbd al-Salām 15
Jurayj al-Muqill 135, 229
Jurjān 29, 35, 54, 58, 61, 98, 103, 124, 145, 151, 154, 157, 162n, 171, 186, 198, 199, 202
Jurjānī, ʿAbd al-Qāhir 33
Jurjānī, Abū ʿAbdallāh Muḥammad 119, 223, 224
Jurjānī, Abū ʿĀmir 154
Jurjānī, Abū l-Muẓaffar 148
Jurjānī, ʿAlī b. ʿAbd al-ʿAzīz 18n, 19n, 141, 142, 171, 178, 179, 204, 206, 209
Jurjāniyya 35, 46, 61
Juwaynī, Abū Manṣūr Muḥammad 133n

K. Iṣbahān 143
Kaʿbī, Abū l-Qāsim 173n, 234
Kalabādhī 27
Kalāʿī 34n, 43, 57, 73, 94n
Kalīla wa-dimna 22, 85
al-Kāmil fī l-adab 19
Kanazi, George 17n, 23n
Kanz al-kuttāb 20, 31, 55
Karābīsī 172
Karajī, Abū l-Ḥasan Muḥammad b. ʿĪsā 35, 58, 59, 60
Karkhī, Abū al-Ḥasan ʿAlī b. Mūsā 135, 214, 215, 216, 220
al-Kashf ʿan masāwiʾ shiʿr al-Mutanabbī 142, 143, 204
Kashf al-ẓunūn 30, 31n, 43
kātib (secretary) 23, 69, 71, 78, 103, 117, 119, 132, 134, 135, 141, 153, 155, 164, 167, 173, 174, 175, 178, 181
Khabbāz al-Baladī 165, 166, 167
Khafājī, Ibn Sinān 91, 188
Khafājī, Shihāb al-Dīn Aḥmad 30n
Khalīʿ al-Shāmī 99, 169, 197, 213
Khāliʿ, Abū ʿAlī al-Ḥasan b. ʿAlī 119
Khālidiyyān 16n, 22, 24, 33, 117, 128, 129, 159, 175, 203, 237
Khalīl b. Aḥmad al-Farāhīdī 143
khamriyya (wine poetry) 17, 158, 159
Kharāʾiṭī 22
Khargūshī 27
Kharīdat al-qaṣr wa-jarīdat al-ʿaṣr 30
Kharjīk 185
al-Khaṣāʾiṣ 166n
Khaṣāʾiṣ al-buldān 94
Khaṣāʾiṣ al-faḍāʾil 94
Khaṣāʾiṣ al-lugha 55
Khāṣṣ al-khāṣṣ 21, 51, 60, 66, 93
Khāṣṣ al-khāṣṣ fī al-amthāl 80

Khaṭṭābī, Abū Sulaymān 143n, 144, 165, 223, 235
khawārij 161
khāzin kutub 103, 167
khāzin māl (treasurer) 103, 167
Khāzin, Abū Muḥammad 184, 203, 208, 209, 218, 228, 236
Khazraj 12
Khazrajī, Abū Dulaf 93, 109, 181n, 219, 221
khiffa 169, 176, 188
Khizānat al-adab 15n
Khubza'aruzzī 108, 109, 167, 216
Khurāsān 29, 35, 36, 39n, 47n, 48n, 51n, 52n, 68, 98, 99, 103, 106, 135, 143, 145, 148, 150, 154, 155, 157, 166, 167, 170, 171, 172, 173n, 179, 183, 199, 200, 202, 205n
Khusraw-Fayrūz b. Rukn al-Dawla 111, 121, 132, 164n
Khwārizmī, Abū ʿAbdallāh Muḥammad 142, 218, 222
Khwārizmī, Abū Bakr 36, 57, 68, 81, 86, 100, 103, 119, 130n, 133n, 145, 147, 148, 150, 151, 154, 155, 162, 173n, 179, 180, 181, 199, 207, 208, 209, 210, 211, 213, 214, 215, 216, 218, 222, 233
Khwārizmī, Abū Muḥammad ʿAbdallāh 35, 165
al-Khwārazmiyyāt 94
Khwārizmshāh Ma'mūn b. Ma'mūn 35, 46, 51, 53, 56, 71, 81, 124
Kilpatrick, H. 2, 5, 7, 9, 10, 13, 28n, 111, 112, 160, 161
Kināya 32, 51, 188n
al-Kināya wa-l-taʿrīḍ 32, 51, 188
Kindī, Abū Yūsuf b. Isḥāq 153
Kisrawī 25
kudya (mendicant poetry) 158, 171, 173
al-Kunā 51
Kurdī, Abū ʿImrān Mūsā 57
Kushājim 24, 128, 191n, 203, 212, 235
Kuthayyir ʿAzza 191
Kutubī, Ibn Shākir 43, 55n, 92, 95n

al-La'ālī wa-l-durar 46, 47
Labīd 191
lafẓ 19n, 188, 189, 190, 194
Laḥḥām, Abū l-Ḥasan 92, 125, 142, 160, 164, 169, 173, 176, 203, 216, 222, 223
Laṭā'if al-kuttāb 144n
Laṭā'if al-luṭf 52, 53
Laṭā'if al-maʿārif 43, 52, 79
Laṭā'if al-ṣaḥāba wa-l-tābiʿīn 52
al-Laṭā'if wa-l-ẓarā'if 62, 65
Laṭā'if al-ẓurafā' min ṭabaqāt al-fuḍalā' 52, 53, 152n
al-Laṭīf fī l-ṭīb 94, 122n
Laṭīm, Abū l-Ḥasan 115n, 212
Leder, S. 4n, 7, 10
Lisān al-Dīn al-Khaṭīb 12n
Lubāb al-ādāb 33, 53, 66, 191n
Lubāb al-aḥāsin 94
al-Lumaʿ 27
al-Lumaʿ al-ghaḍḍa 93
Lumaḥ al-mulaḥ 32
al-Luṭf wa-l-laṭā'if 53

Mā jarā bayna l-Mutanabbī wa-Sayf al-Dawla 53
maʿānī 15, 17, 18, 94, 169, 189, 190
al-Maʿānī al-kabīr 18
Maʿānī al-shiʿr 18
Madanī, Ibn Maʿṣūm 30n
al-Madīḥ 94
Madgharī, Yūnus ʿAlī 44, 47, 73
madḥ, madīḥ (panegyric, praise) 14, 16, 22, 158, 159, 193
Madḥ al-shay' wa-dhammuh 61, 94
Madīna 28
Maghrib 29, 31, 98, 106, 117, 127, 137, 142, 150, 157, 197
Maghribī, Abū l-Ḥasan ʿAlī 115
Maʿhad al-Makhṭūṭat al-ʿArabiyya 72, 84, 85, 88
Maḥāsin al-shiʿr 143n
maḥāsin-masāwi' 5
al-Maḥāsin wa-l-aḍdād 58, 65, 83
al-Maḥāsin wa-l-masāwi' 7, 26
Mahdī (caliph) 11
Maḥmūd al-Ghaznawī 60, 152n, 153, 182n
majālis 3, 6, 7, 17, 20, 139, 175, 186, 187
majmūʿ 1, 72, 142
Majmūʿat al-maʿānī 17
Makārim al-akhlāq 21, 32, 65, 66, 67, 73, 74
Makhzūmī, Abū ʿAlī Ṣāliḥ 117n
Makkī (*al-munshid*) 186
al-Maktaba al-Aḥmadiyya 67, 80
malāḥa 170, 188

Mālikī 165
Malti-Douglas, F. 4
Mamlūk 9n, 10n, 13n, 17, 73, 93
Ma'mūnī, Abū l-ʿAbbās 46, 48, 53, 56, 171
Ma'mūnī, Abū Ṭālib 100, 104, 152n, 162, 175, 181, 184, 199, 200, 203, 211, 230
al-Manāhil wa-l-aʿṭān wa-l-ḥanīn ilā l-awṭān 26n
Man aʿwazahu l-muṭrib 54, 95n
al-Manāzil wa-l-diyār 25
al-Māniʿ, ʿAbd al-ʿAzīz 91
Man ghāba ʿanhu l-mu'nis 95
Man ghāba ʿanhu l-muṭrib 21, 54, 66, 69, 79, 95n, 132
Man ghāba ʿanhu l-nadīm 144
maʿnā 17, 18, 188n, 189, 190, 192, 193, 194
Manṣūr (caliph) 11
al-Manẓūm wa-l-manthūr 19
maqāmāt 3, 39n, 143n, 154, 159
al-Maqāmāt 3, 38n, 39n, 143n
al-Maqāṣid al-naḥwiyya 16n
Maqātil al-ṭālibiyyīn 6, 140
Maqdisī, Abū Naṣr 62, 65, 74
maqṭūʿāt 134
Marāghī, Abū Yaḥyā Zakariyyā 48, 89
marāthī 12, 14, 28, 173
al-Marāthī 21
Mārdīnī 115, 212
Mārdīnī, Isḥāq b. Ahmad 115, 212
Marghanī, Ḥusayn b. Muḥammad 68
Maʿrifat al-rutab fī-mā warada min kalām al-ʿArab 49
Marjānī, Hārūn b. Bahā' al-Dīn 73
Maʿrūfī 174, 191n
Marwarrūzī 172, 226
Marzubānī, Abū ʿUbaydallāh 26
Maṣāriʿ al-ʿushshāq 23
al-Maṣāyid wa-l-maṭārid 24
Maṣṣīṣī, Abū l-Ḥasan ʿAlī 93, 115n, 130, 148, 150, 152, 156, 214, 215, 216, 218, 220, 228, 230
Masʿūd al-Ghaznavī 51n
Masʿūdī 113
al-Maṣūn fī sirr al-hawā l-maknūn 23
Maṭmaḥ al-anfus wa masraḥ al-ta'annus 31
Mawāsim al-ʿumr 75, 76
Mawlawī, Muḥammad Saʿīd 78
Mawṣil 29, 98, 103, 157, 197
Mawṣilī, Abū l-Ghanā'im b. Ḥamdān 122
Maymandī, Abū l-Qāsim Aḥmad 52, 54n
Mayyāfāriqīn 150
Mecca 28, 66
Miftāḥ al-faṣāḥa 95
Mīkālī, Abū ʿAbbās 173
Mīkālī, Abū Ibrāhīm Naṣr 111, 174
Mīkālī, Abū l-Faḍl 8n, 20, 33, 35, 36, 37n, 48, 49, 53, 55, 57, 60, 94n, 99, 102, 110, 127, 140, 143, 145, 151, 152, 173n, 179, 200, 205n, 206, 208, 214, 219, 223, 226, 235
Mīkālī, Abū Muḥammad 166n, 173, 210
Minhāj al-wuzarā' wa-sirāj al-umarā' 46n
Mir'āt al-murū'āt 44, 54, 60, 95n
Mirbad 108
al-Miṣbāḥ 143n
Miskawayhi 78n, 122, 226
Monroe, J. 126n
mu'addib 167, 171, 237
Muʿallaqāt 10, 11n, 12
al-Muʿammarūn 26
mu'ānasa 3
muʿāraḍa 98, 189, 190n
Mubarrad 19, 23
al-Mubhij 54, 55, 62, 80, 81, 125
Muḍāhāt amthāl Kitāb Kalīla wa-Dimna 22
al-Muḍāf wa-l-mansūb 60
mudarris 167
Mufaḍḍal al-Ḍabbī 11, 14n
al-Mufaḍḍaliyyāt 11, 14n
Muftī, Ilhām 77
Mughallisī al-Marāghī, Abū ʿAbdallah 120, 220
muḥāḍara 2, 169, 171
Muḥāḍarāt al-udabā 3, 5, 13, 76
al-Muhadhdhab min ikhtiyār Dīwan Abī l-Ṭayyib 85
Muhallabī 100, 102, 110, 118, 121, 125, 159, 166, 179, 180, 183, 187, 198, 204n, 216, 232
Muḥammad b. ʿAbd al-Malik b. ʿAbd al-Raḥmān al-Nāṣir 131
Muḥammad b. ʿAbd al-Malik b. Ṣāliḥ 29n
Muḥammad b. al-ʿAbbās al-Yazīdī 21
Muḥammad b. al-Mubārak b. Maymūn 12
Muḥammad b. ʿImrān al-ʿAbdī 23
Muḥammad b. Kathīr 61, 123n
Muḥammad b. Maḥmūd b. Sebüktigin 155

Muḥammad b. Mūsā b. ʿImrān 189
Muḥammad b. Saʿīd al-Kātib 191, 209
Muḥammad b. ʿUmar b. Aḥmad 80
Muhandis 167
muḥdath/muḥdathūn 15, 16, 19n, 20, 29n, 46, 92, 120, 180n, 188n, 190, 191n, 209
Muḥibbī 30n
al-Muḥibb wa-l-maḥbūb 22, 23, 122, 143, 225
Muʿizz al-Dawlā 205, 217, 218
mujālasāt 3
al-mujamharāt 12
Muʿjam al-udabāʾ 78
Mujarrad al-Aghānī 143
Mujmal al-lugha 144n
mujūn (obscene poetry) 109, 158, 165, 172, 173
Mukātabāt 21, 57, 120, 159, 210
Mukhtārāt shuʿarāʾ al-ʿArab 12
al-Mukhtār fī l-naẓm wa-l-nathr 31n
Muktafī 132n
mulaḥ 14, 173
al-Mulaḥ al-ʿaṣriyya 31n
Mulaḥ al-khawāṭir wa-subaḥ al-jawāhir 152, 206
al-Mulaḥ al-nawādir 93, 95
al-Mulaḥ wa-l-ṭuraf 95
al-Mulūkī 46, 69, 70, 71, 95
Munādamat al-mulūk 95
Munajjim, Abū l-Ḥusayn (or al-Ḥasan) ʿAlī b. Hārūn 120, 167
Munajjim, Abū Muḥammad 131
Muʾnis al-waḥīd 76, 88
al-Muntaḥal 8, 20, 36n, 55, 191n
Muntahā l-ṭalab min ashʿār al-ʿArab 12
al-Muntakhab fī maḥāsin ashʿār al-ʿArab 12, 76
al-Muntakhab al-Mīkālī 55
al-Muntakhab min sunan al-ʿArab 49
Muntakhab al-Thaʿālibī 55
al-Muntakhal 8n, 20, 36n, 55, 76
al-Muntazaʿ min Kitāb al-Tājī 204n
muqillūn 11
al-muqīmūn 178
Muqtadir 132n, 206
Murādī, Abū l-Ḥusayn 164, 171
Murtaḍā 26, 111, 123, 230, 237
murūʾa 54
Murūj al-dhahab 113n
Muṣʿabī, Abū l-Ṭayyib 164n, 170, 174, 178
Mūsawī, Abū l-Ḥasan 152
al-Mushriq (*al-mashūq*?) 95
Muslim b. al-Walīd 19n, 33
Mustanṣir Billāh 131
Mutanabbī 19n, 33, 44, 45, 53, 85, 99, 100, 114n, 115n, 119, 121, 142, 143, 147, 162, 164n, 165, 172n, 179, 180, 188n, 189, 197, 204, 233
al-Mutashābih 47, 188n, 193n
al-Mutashābih lafẓan wa-khaṭṭan 47
Muʿtazila 164, 175, 184
Muṭrānī, al-Ḥasan b. ʿAlī 170, 234
al-Muṭrib min ashʿār ahl al-Maghrib 31
Muwallad 16n, 20, 191n, 192
muwashshaḥ 12
al-Muwāzana 143, 205
Muzanī, Abū l-Ḥasan (or al-Ḥusayn?) 133
Muzdawija 153

Nabateans 105
nadīm 24n, 103, 167
Nafḥat al-rayḥāna wa-rashḥat ṭilāʾ al-ḥāna 30n
Naḥḥās 11
naḥwī (grammarian) 111, 121, 153, 154, 167, 186
Nājī, Hilāl 44, 47, 48, 57, 67, 70, 71, 72, 78, 79, 83, 84, 88, 89, 90, 92, 94n
Nājim 151
Najjār, Ibrāhīm 7
Najm, Muḥammad Yūsuf 22n
Namarī 19n, 154, 207, 221
Nāmī al-Būshanjī, Abū Aḥmad 132
Nāmī, Abū l-ʿAbbās 99, 151, 169, 179, 197, 203
naqīb al-Ṭālibiyyīn 162
Naṣabī, Sulaymān b. Ḥassān 115n
Nāshiʾ al-Aṣghar 99, 131n, 213
Nasīb 14, 16, 159
Naṣībī, Sulaymān b. Ḥassān 131n
Naṣībīn 150
naṣīḥat al-mulūk 3
nāsikh 167
Nasīm al-Saḥar 55, 56
Nasīm al-uns 95
Nāṣir al-Dawla 86, 111, 120, 121, 135, 162n, 168
Nāṣir al-Dīn Abū Manṣūr 152
Nāṣir Muḥammadī Muḥammad Jād 62

Naṣr b. Nāṣir al-Dīn Sebüktegin 35, 53
Natāʾij al-mudhākara 76
nathr 57
Nathr al-durr 144n
Nathr al-naẓm wa-ḥall al-ʿaqd 35, 39, 56, 57
al-Nawādir wa-l-bawādir 95
Nawājī, Muḥammad b. Ḥasan 24n
Nūqātī, Abū l-Ḥasan al-Sijzī 181, 184
Naẓm al-nathr wa-ḥall al-ʿaqd 56
Naẓm Fiqh al-lugha 49
al-Nihāya fī fann al-kināya 51
al-Nihāya fī l-kināya 51
Nihāyat al-arab fī funūn al-adab 13n, 113n
Nīlī, Abū ʿAbd al-Raḥmān 115
Nīlī, Abū Sahl 115, 119
Nīshāpūr 35, 36, 37, 38, 39, 46n, 48n, 50, 51, 55, 61, 98, 99, 102, 103, 104, 111, 126, 128, 134, 137n, 145, 147, 148, 149, 151, 153, 154, 155, 156, 157, 162, 166, 173n, 200, 201, 202, 205n, 226
Nīshāpūrī, Abū ʿAlī al-Ḥasan 30n
Nīshāpūrī, Abū Bakr Muḥammad b. ʿUthmān 130, 210
Nīshāpūrī, Abū Muḥammad al-Ḥusayn 38
Nīshāpūrī, Abū Muḥammad Ismāʿīl 38
Nūḥ b. Manṣūr 152n, 180
al-Nuhya fī-l-ṭard wa-l-ghunya 66
Nūr al-qabas 113n
Nutaf al-ẓarf 143n
Nuwayrī 13n, 113
Nuzhat al-albāb wa-ʿumdat al-kuttāb 86
al-Nuzūʿ ilā l-awṭān 26n

paideia 3
Persian 38, 39n, 43, 46, 52, 54, 58, 60, 68, 105, 109n, 124n, 137, 153, 173n, 174, 191n, 234
Plato 8n, 85
Post-Mongol 10n
Proverbs 18, 20, 27, 46, 51, 57, 58, 66, 78n, 80, 137, 158, 159, 168, 170, 174, 205n
Ptolemy 85
Pythagoras 85

Qābūs b. Wushmgīr 35, 54, 58, 100, 124, 125, 199
qāḍī (judge) 24, 30n, 35, 37, 46, 49, 103, 114, 115n, 120, 121, 122, 133, 134, 161, 165, 167, 168, 171, 172, 178, 179, 180n, 187, 188, 197, 198, 205n, 207n, 209, 211, 212, 214, 226, 227, 228, 229, 231, 232
Qāḍī al-Ḥalabī, Abū l-Faraj 122
qadīm 188n, 190
Qādir Billāh 115n, 153, 155
al-Qādirī fī l-taʿbīr 153
Qaḥṭān Rashīd Ṣāliḥ 53
Qāʾinī, Abū Manṣūr Qāsim b. Ibrāhim 174
Qalāʾid al-ʿiqyān fī maḥāsin al-aʿyān 31
al-Qalāʾid wa-l-farāʾid 143n
Qālī al-Baghdādī 11
Qandahār 154n
Qāshānī, Abū l-Qāsim ʿAlī 99, 198
qaṣīda 7, 10, 11, 12, 17, 76, 78, 102, 107, 110, 115n, 126, 131n, 137, 152n, 156, 182, 187, 189, 193, 194, 205n, 209, 224, 226
Qaṣīda al-Sāsāniyya 109
Qayrawān 31, 137, 144, 155
Qāzān 73
Qazwīnī, Abū l-Ḥasan ʿAlī 150, 155, 228, 230
al-Qiyān 143
qubḥ al-maṭlaʿ 189
Quhistānī, Abū Bakr 142, 150, 154, 155, 228, 231
Qurāḍat al-dhahab 57
Qurʾān 7, 32, 39, 49, 50, 51, 65, 74, 77, 80, 84, 86, 125, 144n, 182, 186, 189
Qurashī, Abū Zayd Muḥammad 11, 12
Qushayrī, Abū l-Qāsim 27
Qushayrī, Abū Naṣr 27
Quss b. Sāʿida 85
Quṭb al-surūr fī awṣāf al-khumūr 24

Rabīʿ al-abrār 13, 77
Rabīʿa al-Baṣrī 26n
Radwan, Ahmad Shawqi 59
Rāfiʿī al-Qazwīnī 93
al-Rāghib al-Iṣfahānī 5, 13, 76, 135n
rajaz 12, 19n, 29n
Rāmahurmuzī, Ibn Khallād 120
Ramlī, Abū l-Ḥusayn (or al-Ḥasan) 141, 228, 230
Raqīq al-Qayrawānī 24
Raqqām al-Baṣrī 23
Raqqī, Abū Ṭālib 99, 197, 213
Rasāʾil al-Ṣābī 143
rashāqa 188
Rashīdī, Abū l-Faḍl Aḥmad 168, 227
Rassī, Abū l-Qāsim Aḥmad 115n, 212

Rassī, Abū Muḥammad al-Qāsim 115n
Rawāʾiʿ al-tawjīhāt 143, 153, 205
Rawḍat al-faṣāḥa 76
Rawḍat al-qulūb 23
al-Rawḍ al-naḍir 31n
Rawḥ al-rūḥ 8n, 20, 67, 69, 92
Rāwī, Ḥabīb ʿAlī 70
Rāyāt al-mubarrizīn 31n
Rayḥānat al-alibbāʾ 30n, 32n
Rayy 51n, 104, 148n, 151, 154, 155, 175, 180n, 187, 202
Rescher, O. 47
riqqa 188
Risāla fī l-ṭibb 143, 206
al-Risāla al-Ḥātimiyya 114n
Risālat Sajʿiyyāt al-Thaʿālibī 21, 57
Rosenbaum, Gabriel 4n
Rosenthal, F. 2, 5, 68
Rowson, Everett 44, 68n, 78n, 110n, 117, 124, 125, 126, 127, 129n, 131, 137, 138, 180n
Rukhkhaj 154
Rukhkhajī, Abū l-Ḥusayn 144n
Rūm 32n
ruqʿa 145, 157, 208, 209
Rusūm al-balāgha 90
al-Rūznāmja 102, 121, 141, 142, 143, 204

Ṣābī, Abū Isḥāq 99, 110, 118, 125, 142, 143, 162, 164, 171, 180 198, 204, 207, 208, 217, 225, 235
Ṣābiʾite 164
Sābūr b. Ardashīr 100, 101, 119, 125, 198
Sadan, J. 3, 5, 10n, 62
al-Ṣadāqa wa-l-ṣadīq 23
Ṣadr al-Dīn ʿAlī b. Abī l-Faraj al-Baṣrī 16
Saʿdū, Zahiyya 58
Ṣafadī 31n, 43, 55n, 92, 94, 95n, 115n, 117n, 121n
Ṣaffār, Ibtisām Marhūn 70
Ṣafī l-Ḥaḍratayn, Muḥammad 148n
Safīnat al-Ḥāmidī 143
Safīnat al-Mīkālī 143
Ṣafwat al-adab wa-nukhbat dīwān al-ʿArab 15
Ṣāghānī, Abū ʿAlī 185
Saghāniyyān 185
Ṣāḥib, Abū l-Qāsim 52
Ṣāḥib b. ʿAbbād 20n, 52, 53, 54, 60, 69, 71, 78n, 86, 93, 100, 102, 103, 104, 107, 109, 117, 118, 119, 120, 121, 135, 141, 142, 145, 150, 151, 153, 154, 160, 164, 171, 174n, 175, 176, 179, 180, 181, 182, 183, 184, 186, 199, 204, 205, 206, 207, 208, 209, 215, 216, 217, 218, 219, 220, 221, 224, 228, 229, 233, 235
Sahl b. al-Ḥasan 173n, 234
sajʿ 8n, 21, 32, 33, 57, 59, 188n
Sajʿ al-manthūr 8n, 21, 57, 59, 188n
Salāmī, Abū ʿAlī 143, 172n, 206
Salāmī, Abū l-Ḥasan 162, 168, 171, 181, 184
salāsa 188
Ṣāliḥ b. Rashdīn 115n, 117
Ṣāliḥ b. Yūnus 115
Ṣāliḥ, Ibrāhīm 60, 67, 76
Saljūq 35, 155, 186
Salwat al-ʿārifīn 27
samāʿ 27
Sāmānī, Abū l-Qāsim Nūḥ 119, 152n, 180
Samʿānī, Abū Saʿd 26n
Sāmānid 35, 47, 68, 100, 106, 119, 149, 164, 175, 179, 180, 186, 200
Samarrai, Qasim 44, 46, 48, 52, 53, 54, 55, 62, 65, 66, 72, 81, 124
Ṣanʿat al-shiʿr wa-l-nathr 95
Ṣanawbarī 191n
Saragossa 127
Sarawī, Abū l-ʿAlāʾ 120
al-Sarī al-Raffāʾ 17n, 22, 36n, 117, 122, 128, 159, 169, 175, 203, 207, 225, 236, 237
sariqa/sariqāt 3, 22, 158, 159, 188n, 189, 190, 191, 192, 193, 218, 219, 220
Sarkhasī (or Sarakhsī) 38
Sarrāj 27
Sasanian 85
Satan 68n, 135
Ṣāwī, Abū l-Faraj 107n, 178
Ṣaymarī, Abū Jaʿfar Muḥammad 205n
Ṣaymarī, Abū l-Fatḥ al-Ḥasan 36, 55
Ṣaymarī, Aḥmad b. Sayyār 205n
Ṣaymarī, Hārūn b. Aḥmad 205, 218
Ṣaymarī, Hārūn b. Jaʿfar 205n, 222
Sezgin, F. 6, 15n, 18n, 43, 140, 156
Shabībī, Abū Saʿīd Aḥmad 134, 222, 237
Shāfiʿite 165
shāhid 27
Shahwājī, al-Ḥasan b. Muḥammad 117
Shajarī al-ʿUqaylī 166n

Shajarī, Abū l-Qāsim Ismāʿīl 131
al-Shajar wa-l-ṣuwar fī-l-ḥikam wa-l-mawʿiẓa 87, 88
al-Shakwā wa-l-ʿitāb wa-mā li-l-khillān wa-l-aṣḥāb 77
al-Shams 49, 95
Shams al-adab 49, 95n
Shantarīnī, Ibn Bassām 31, 113
Sharīf al-Jurjānī 77n
Sharīf al-Murtaḍā 26, 111, 230, 237
Sharīf al-Raḍī 99, 123, 125, 152, 162, 170, 171, 173, 198, 237
Sharlet, Jocelyn 25n, 109n, 161n
Shāsh 171, 185, 234
Shāshī, Abū ʿĀmir 131n
Shāshī, Abū Ibrāhīm 131n
Shāṭibī 16n
al-shawāhid wa-l-amthāl 27
al-Shawq ilā l-awṭān 26n
Shayzarī, Ibn al-Faraj 23
al-Shihāb fī l-shayb wa-l-shabāb 26
shiʿr fuqahāʾ 188
shiʿr kitābī 188
Shīrāz 151, 181, 187
Shīrāzī, Abū Aḥmad 99, 198, 199
al-Shiʿr wa-l-shuʿarāʾ 161
shuʿarāʾ al-qurā 28
Sicily 31n
al-Ṣiḥāḥ fī l-lugha 144
Siḥr al-balāgha 39, 53, 57, 73, 86, 89, 125, 143, 205
Sijistānī, Abū Ḥātim 26
Sijistānī, Khalaf b. Aḥmad 153
Sijzī, Abū l-Qāsim Muḥammad 108n
Sijzī, Khalīl b. Aḥmad 165
Sīmjūrī 61, 123n, 181n
Simonides 85
Ṣiqillī, Abū l-Qāsim ʿAlī b. Jaʿfar 31n
Ṣiqillī, Ibn Bishrūn 31n
Sirāj al-mulūk 46
Sīrjānī 27
Sirr al-adab fī majārī kalām al-ʿArab 49, 53
Sirr al-balāgha 89
Sirr al-bayān 95
Sirr al-ḥaqīqa 89, 90
Sirr al-ṣināʿa 95
Sirr al-wizāra 95
al-Siyāsa 94
Socrates 85
Solomon 85
Ṣūfī, Abū Suwayd 166
Sufi/Sufism 27, 88, 91, 150, 156, 166, 229, 230
Suhaylī 124
sukhf 173
Sukkarī al-Marwazī, Abū l-Faḍl 137, 171
Sulāfat al-ʿaṣr 30n
Sulamī, Abū ʿAbd al-Raḥmān 27, 91
Ṣūlī, Abū Bakr 26, 172n, 234
Sulṭān Maḥmūd of Ghazna 35, 47, 48n, 54, 58n, 60
Sulṭān Masʿūd of Ghazna 36, 48n, 51, 52n, 54
sulṭāniyyāt 20, 55, 173, 175n
Ṣūrī, ʿAbd al-Muḥsin 117, 131, 225
Ṣūrī, Abū Manṣūr 123, 229
Ṣūrī, Abū ʿUmāra 123
Suyūṭī 16, 18n, 49n
Syria 29, 98, 105, 106, 110, 117, 137, 142, 147, 150, 152, 157, 172n, 197, 202, 235

al-Taʿarruf li-madhhab ahl al-taṣawwuf 27
al-Taʿāzī 23
Ṭabaqāt al-mulūk 67, 68, 70
Ṭabaqāt al-naḥwiyyīn wa-l-lughawiyyīn 143n
Ṭabaqāt al-shuʿarāʾ 113n
Ṭabaqāt fuḥūl al-shuʿarāʾ 27, 28n, 29n, 161
Ṭabarī, Abū Khalaf 27
Ṭabarī, Abū l-Fayyāḍ 169
Ṭabaristān 29, 98, 103, 120n, 134, 145, 157, 198, 199, 202
Ṭabasī, Abū l-Qāsim 211
ṭabīb (physician) 46, 115, 119, 167, 205n
al-Tadallī fī-l-tasallī 91
al-Tadhkira al-ḥamdūniyya 18n, 70, 71
al-Tadhkira al-Saʿdiyya 16
taḍmīn 189n, 190n
al-Tadwīn fī akhbār Qazwīn 93, 206n
Tafaḍḍul al-muqtadirīn wa-tanaṣṣul al-muʿtadhirīn 95
Tafṣīl al-siʿr fī tafḍīl al-shiʿr 47
Tafsīr al-Thaʿālibī 74
al-Taghazzul bi-miʾatay ghulām 92, 125
al-Tahānī wa-l-taʿāzī 23, 77, 90
Tahdhīb al-asrār 27
Tahdhīb al-lugha 144n
Tahdhīb al-taʾrīkh 143, 206

Ṭāhirī, Abū l-Ṭayyib 179, 224
Taḥsīn al-qabīḥ wa-taqbīḥ al-ḥasan 26, 58, 60
al-Taḥsīn wa-l-taqbīḥ 58
Ṭā'if 28
tajnīs, jinās 32, 33, 47, 94, 144n, 188n, 189n, 193n
Talʿafrī 130n
talfīq 32, 60, 66, 92
Ṭāliʿ 151
Talib, Adam 17n, 73, 74, 93
Ṭālibid/Ṭālibiyyīn 6, 162, 171
talmīḥ 189
al-Tamaththul wa-l-muḥāḍara 58, 65, 69, 80, 81, 83, 113n, 135n, 191n
Tamīm b. al-Muʿizz 138
Tamīmī, ʿAbd al-Qādir b. Ṭāhir 103, 165, 235
Tamīmī, Abū l-Faḍl Muḥammad 132, 136, 148, 150, 155, 227, 228, 230, 232
Tamīmī, Muḥammad b. Aḥmad b. ʿAbd al-Mughīth 205n
al-Tamthīl wa-l-muḥāḍara 58, 65, 69, 80, 81, 83, 113n, 135n, 191n
Tanbīh al-nā'im al-ghamr ʿalā mawāsim al-ʿumr 76
Tanūkhī, Abū ʿAlī al-Muḥassin 114, 120, 134, 135, 141, 169, 187n, 205
Tanūkhī, Abū l-Qāsim ʿAlī 114, 120, 187, 203, 214, 217
Ṭarā'if al-ṭuraf 19, 78
al-Ṭarā'if wa-l-laṭā'if 65
Tarājim al-Shuʿarā' 91
al-Tarbīʿ wa-l-tadwīr 3
al-Ta'rīkh 144
Ta'rīkh ghurar al-siyar 39n, 67, 95n
ṭāri'ūn 104, 178
Tarjamat al-kātib fī ādāb al-ṣāḥib 23, 69, 71
Ṭarṭūshī, ʿAbd al-Karīm 48
tashbīh 18, 21, 32, 65, 66, 80, 121
al-Tashbīhāt 32, 143, 225
al-Taslīm wa-l-ziyāra 26n
Tatimmat Yatīmat al-dahr 6, 9, 29n, 30, 36, 40, 43, 59, 68n, 92, 95n, 97, 98, 99, 100, 104-182, 185, 188, 191, 193n, 194, 195, 197, 202, 225
al-Taṭfīl wa-ḥikāyāt al-ṭufayliyyīn 113n
tawaḥḥush al-kalām 19n
al-Tawfīq li-l-talfīq 32, 60, 92
Tawḥīdī, Abū Ḥayyān 17, 13n, 23, 26n, 135n, 180
taʿwīṣ al-lafẓ 189
Ṭawlaqī, Abū l-Ḥusayn 154
tawqīʿ/tawqīʿāt 46, 145, 178, 185, 186, 208
Ṭayf al-Khayāl 26
Thaʿālibī, al-Jazā'irī 74
Thaʿālibī, Marghanī 68
al-Thalj wa-l-maṭar 95
Thayyāb, Abū Muḥammad 131n, 210, 224
Thimār al-qulūb 40, 48, 60, 65, 93, 94n, 132, 152n, 159n, 160n, 176n, 205n
Thimār al-uns fī tashbīhāt al-furs 143n, 153
Tibrīzī 14n
Toledo 155
Toorawa, Sh. 5, 36n, 113, 139, 156
Topuzoglu, T. R. 57, 58, 60, 74, 77, 90
Transoxania 29, 98, 143, 145, 148, 157, 172, 185n, 200, 234
al-Tuffāḥa 95
al-Tuḥaf wa-l-anwār 61
al-Tuḥaf wa-l-hadāyā 24
al-Tuḥaf wa-l-ẓuraf 143, 205
Tuḥfat al-arwāḥ 95
Tuḥfat al-dahr 30n
Tuḥfat al-wuzarā' 69, 71, 152n
Tuḥfat al-ẓurafā' 78
Tujībid 127
al-Ṭuraf min shiʿr al-Bustī 94
Ṭūsī, Abū Jaʿfar Muḥammad 152

ʿUbaydallāh b. ʿAbdallāh b. Ṭāhir 132, 235
ʿUbaydallāh b. Aḥmad b. Maʿrūf 187n
ʿUbaydī 16n
ʿUddat al-jalīs 12
ʿudhūba 170, 188
ʿUkbara 109n
ʿUkbarī, Abū l-Ḥasan 109, 171, 173
Ulaymānī, Abū al-Qāsim ʿAlī b. al-Ḥusayn 104, 211, 223
ʿUmarī, ʿIṣām al-Dīn ʿUthmān b. ʿAlī 31n
ʿUmdat al-Kuttāb 86
ʿUmrawī, Alī b. Ḥafṣ 135
al-Unmūdhaj fī shuʿarā' al-Qayrawān 31n
Uns al-farīd 78n
Uns al-musāfir 95
Uns al-waḥīd 20n, 78, 88
al-Uns wa-l-ʿurs 20, 78

ʿUnwān al-maʿārif 95
ʿUnwān al-murqiṣāt wa-l-muṭribāt 33
urjūza 12n, 76
Usāma al-Buḥayrī 21n
Usāma b. Munqidh 25, 31n
Ushnāndānī 18
al-Uṣūl fī l-fuṣūl 95
ʿUtbī, Abū Naṣr Muḥammad 144n, 220, 223
Uṭrūsh, Abū Saʿīd (Saʿd?) 153, 154
ʿUyūn al-ādāb 95
ʿUyūn al-akhbār 5, 13
ʿUyūn al-nawādir 93, 96

al-Wadāʿ wa-l-firāq 26n
Wāḥidī, ʿAlī b. Aḥmad 19, 38, 78
al-Waḥshiyyāt 15
Walīd b. Bakr al-Faqīh al-Andalusī 126, 215
Walīd Qaṣṣāb 91
al-Waraqa 113n
al-Ward 96
Wāsānī, Abū l-Qāsim 173, 236
al-Wasāṭa bayna l-zunāt wa-l-lāṭa 143, 225
waṣf 17, 21, 24, 159,
Washshāʾ 26n, 27
Waṣī al-Hamadhānī, Abū l-Ḥasan 182
Wāthiq bi-Allāh 168
Wāthiqī, Abū Muḥammad ʿAbdallāh 100, 104, 165, 167, 200, 210
Waʾwāʾ al-Dimashqī 99, 197, 213, 214, 215
Werkmeister, W. 6, 139, 156
Wishāḥ al-Dumya 30n
Wright, William 19

Yaghmūrī 113n
Yaḥyā b. Mundhir 127
Yaman 85
Yamanī, Abū ʿAbdallāh 22
Yaʿqūb b. Aḥmad b. Muḥammad al-Nīshāpūrī 37, 154, 237
Yāqūt al-Ḥamawī 30n, 31n, 37, 78, 113n, 154, 155, 165n
Yāqūt al-Mustaʿṣī (al-Mustaʿṣimī?) 73
Yārid, Īflīn Farīd 20, 78
Yatīmat al-dahr 6, 9, 13n, 29, 30, 31, 34n, 36-44, 46, 47, 58, 59, 61, 66, 68n, 69, 85, 92, 97, 98, 100-199, 201, 203, 205, 206n, 207, 208, 209, 211, 213, 215, 217, 219, 221, 223
al-Yawāqīt fī baʿḍ al-mawāqīt 26, 61, 62, 65, 85
Yawāqīt al-mawāqīt 61
Yūsuf Aḥmad Jamal al-Dīn 48n

Zād safar al-mulūk 25, 62, 64, 92
Zaʿfarānī, Abū l-Qāsim ʿUmar 171, 180n, 209, 219
Zāhī, Abū l-Qāsim 99, 122, 151, 197, 215
Zāhir al-Balkhī, Abū ʿAlī 131, 133, 150, 211, 212, 215, 218
Zahr al-ādāb 13n, 29n,
al-Zahra 22
Zallālī, al-Ḥasan b. ʿAbd al-Raḥīm 143
Zamakhsharī 13, 39n, 77,
Zāmilat al-nutaf 143, 144
al-Ẓarāʾif wa-l-laṭāʾif 26, 63, 65, 74, 95n
ẓarf/ẓarīf/ẓurafāʾ 3, 15, 52, 53, 78, 143, 167, 169, 171, 173, 176, 205, 235
Zawzanī, Abū ʿAlī 176, 178
Zawzanī, Abū l-Qāsim ʿAlī 165, 166
Zawzanī, Abū Naṣr 164n, 176n, 211, 223, 224, 231
Zaydān, Jurjī 43, 79, 92
Zaynahum, Muḥammad 47, 72
Zīnat al-dahr 30n
Ziyārid 54
Zotenberg 68, 69
Zubaydī, Abū Bakr 143n, 169
zuhd (ascetic poetry) 16, 88, 165, 235